Public Assembly Facility Law

Public Assembly Facility Law

A Guide for Managers of Arenas, Auditoriums, Convention Centers, Performing Arts Centers, Race Tracks and Stadiums

First Edition

Turner D. Madden

Whitney S. Hoffman
Jonathan D. Shaffer
Allen G. Siegel
Richard F. Smith

International Association of Assembly Managers

ISBN 0-9665670-0-5
Library of Congress Catalog Card Number: 98-86562

Published by
International Association of Assembly Managers
4425 W. Airport Freeway, Suite 590
Irving, TX 75062-5835

About the Contributors

Turner D. Madden, the managing partner in the Washington, D.C. office of the law firm of Madden & Patton, L.L.P., has practiced facility and corporate law for over fourteen years. Mr. Madden is a member of the District of Columbia, Maryland and Pennsylvania Bar Associations. Mr. Madden is the Lobbyist and Legislative Counsel for the International Association of Assembly Managers, Inc. in Washington, D.C. Mr. Madden is an Editorial Advisory Board Member for *Facilities Magazine* and a long time member of the American Society of Association Executives Legal Section Council. He is the former General Counsel at the Washington Convention Center Authority in Washington, D.C., a position which he held for eight years. Mr. Madden was the first Chairman of the International Association of Assembly Managers Senior Executive Program and the past Chairman of the IAAM Government Affairs Committee.

Richard F. Smith has practiced in the construction and public contracts areas for over 25 years. After receiving his law degree from the University of Virginia in 1970, Mr. Smith entered the United States Air Force Judge Advocate General Corps, reviewing base procurement contracts. In 1971, he began serving as legal assistant to the Chairman of the Armed Services Board of Contract Appeals, working on a broad array of government contracts including those for the Department of Defense. In 1973, he obtained a Masters of Laws with highest honors from the National Law Center of the George Washington University with a specialization in Government Procurement Law. In 1972, Mr. Smith entered private practice with Lewis, Mitchell & Moore and has been with construction and government contracts firms since that date. He has specialized in representing owners of U.S. and foreign companies in construction and government contract matters before various courts including alternative dispute resolution forums. He is currently a partner with Smith, Pachter, McWhorter & D'Ambrosio, P.L.C.

Mr. Smith serves as a lecturer in government procurement at Marshall-Wythe School of Law, College of William & Mary, and has served as adjunct professor of law at the T.C. Williams School of Law, University of Richmond. He has lectured throughout the country on subjects dealing with construction law, public contract law and project scheduling. He has spoken at the Annual Meeting of the ABA Forum on the Construction Industry in 1994 and 1996 and is scheduled to speak at the meeting in 1998. Mr. Smith is a member of the American Bar Association, Public Contract Law section, Litigation Section and Forum on the Construction Industry, where he serves as Chairman of Division I –

Disputes Avoidance and Resolution. He is a member of the Bar Association of the District of Columbia and Virginia State Bar, and has served as past chairman of the Construction Law Section of the Virginia State Bar. He is also a member of the American College of Construction Lawyers.

Jonathan D. Shaffer is a partner with Smith, Patcher, McWhorter and D'Ambrosio, P.L.C. in Vienna, Virginia where he practices primarily in the areas of public contracts, construction law and commercial litigation. Mr. Smith earned a Bachelor of Arts Degree from the University of Pennsylvania and a Juris Doctor degree, Magna Cum Laude from the American University, Washington College of Law. He is a member of the Bars of the District of Columbia, and Commonwealth of Virginia as is a member of the American Bar Association. He served as Vice-chair of the ABA's Public Contract Law section Bid Protest Committee from 1991 to 1995.

     Mr. Shaffer has co-authored many publications on construction and public contract law, and is a frequent lecturer on public contracts, construction law and alternative dispute resolution. He has spoken at the National Contract Management Association World Congress and the Board of Contract Appeals Judges Association Annual Seminar. He has also lectured on contract claims for the George Washington University National Law Center, Government Contracts Program.

Claire E. Kreese is an associate with Smith, Pachter, McWhorter & D'Ambrosio, P.L.C. in Vienna, Virginia where she practices primarily in the areas of construction law, government contracts and commercial litigation. Ms. Kreese earned a Bachelor of Arts degree from Georgetown University and a Juris Doctor degree from Duke University School of Law. Ms. Kreese is a member of the Bar of the Commonwealth of Virginia, the American Bar Association, Public Contracts Law Section and Litigation section, and the American Federal Inn of Court.

     Ms. Kreese co-authored a chapter on construction, lien and bond law for the District of Columbia for *Construction and Design Law*, a fifty state survey to be published in 1998 by the American Bar Association.

Whitney S. Hoffman is an associate with Madden & Patton, L.L.P. in Washington, D.C. where she practices primarily in the area of public facility law. Ms. Hoffman earned a Bachelor of Arts degree from the University of Pennsylvania and a Juris Doctor degree from the Dickinson School of Law, now of Penn State University. Ms. Hoffman is a member of the Pennsylvania Bar Association and American Bar Association. She also serves as Treasurer and member of the Executive Board of the Junior Board of Christiana Care, Inc., a non-profit corporation dedicated to hospital service and fund raising for Christiana Care, the lead health care provider in Delaware.

Allen G. Siegel received his law degree from Duke University School of Law in 1960, and began practice with a major firm in Jacksonville, Florida. Thereafter, he was appointed as a field attorney for the National Labor Relations Board where he served until 1964 when he became associated with Arent Fox. The firm did not initially have a significant labor practice, but now enjoys the largest local labor practice in the Washington area, with an expanding number of clients throughout the United States. Mr. Siegel is a member of the District of Columbia and Florida bars, and serves as a professor at Duke University Law School, where he regularly teaches a course in collective bargaining, holding the rank of Senior Lecturing Fellow-in-Law.

Mr. Siegel practices primarily in the areas of collective bargaining and labor law related to the Taft-Hartley Act and also has extensive experience in matters arising under the Fair Labor Standards Act, various civil rights laws and the critical area of "unjust termination". Mr. Siegel also engages in numerous charitable and community projects including serving as General Counsel to the local affiliate of the United Cerebral Palsy Association of America, General Counsel of the Jewish Social Services Agency, and member of the Board of Regents at the Catholic University of America. Mr. Siegel has been instrumental in establishing scholarships for students at the Duke University Law School and The Catholic University of America, as well as the Jeanette Siegel memorial Scholarship administered by the Jewish Social Service Agency. He has also established the Rabbi Seymour Siegel Memorial Moot Court Competition coordinated and administered by the Duke University Law School, open to law students from all major law schools, centered in the area of medical-legal ethics.

Table of Chapters

Table of Contents

Chapter 1

Organization of Arenas, Auditoriums, Convention Centers, Performing Arts Centers, Race Tracks and Stadiums

By Turner D. Madden

1.00 Introduction

A little planning goes a long way when a state or municipality creates an entity to operate, maintain and possibly to construct a public assembly facility. Planners of a facility should not only consider the purpose and operational matters of the facility or facility complex but also the legal nuances of the entity. A privately owned facility may draft the articles of incorporation and by-laws to permit the entity to perform any legal function. It is quite different for a facility that is part of a state or local government. For example: Does the planning body desire a tax-exempt organization? Will the facility be financially independent? Does the planning body desire the tenants or users of the facility to be exempt from certain local taxes? Will the facility be *sui juris*, meaning will it be a separate legal entity that can sue and be sued independently of the municipality that created the facility? This chapter will assist the entity planners in identifying most of these issues.

1.01 Facilities Created by Legislative Bodies

A state or subdivision of a state such as a city or county creates a majority of all auditoriums, arenas, stadiums, convention centers, amphitheaters, and other public assembly facilities. Because a government body creates most of these facilities, they have certain operating restrictions. A state's general assembly, city council or city manager, whichever is applicable, may have issued special rules and regulations on the general operation of the facility, employment, and procurement of goods and services. Therefore, prior to forming a legislative entity, the originator of the legislation should consider all legal aspects and possibilities. A properly drafted facility enabling statute may have all the items listed in the below section.

1) Independent Authorities

One of the most flexible forms for a governmental entity is the independent authority. It can provide services that are comparable to the private sector and still function with appropriated funds. An independent authority may be structured so that community business leaders and high-level government officials serve on the board of directors. The statute may even state by position description who sits on the board of directors and the length of their term. For example, arena or stadium officials may desire the Director of the local Athletic or Sports Commission to be a designated member of the board by statute. For a convention center, it may desire the Executive Director of the local visitors bureau or visitors association. For a performing arts center, it may be appropriate to include the Chairperson of the local arts commission. You may also designate these "statutory board members" as voting members or non-voting, ex-officio members. The highest-ranking political official such as the governor or mayor usually appoints the board members. In order to provide consistent policy decisions, the board members must have staggered terms. The staggered board terms provide the board with several seasoned board members that have the institutional history of the policy decisions.

When drafting a bill to create an authority to operate a public assembly facility, one should consider the following items:

a) Declaration of Policy - General economic and public interest goals should be included in this section of the bill. If a feasibility study was completed, a summary of that information may communicate the economic objectives of the facility.

b) Establishment Clause - This section actually creates the entity. The purpose of the facility should be stated in the "Establishment Clause" section. For example, this section may state " The general purpose of the facility is to acquire, construct, equip, maintain, and operate the XYZ Convention Center. The Authority may engage in other activities as it deems appropriate to promote and book tradeshows and conventions."

c) General Powers - The general powers clause is one of the most important parts of the statute. It provides the Authority with the specific powers listed in the section. If the power is not listed in this section, or you cannot logically conclude from the other enumerated powers that you have the authority to perform the function, then most likely the Authority may not perform the function. This clause should include powers such as the power to sue and be sued, to make and alter bylaws, rules and regulations; to acquire, by gift, purchase, lease or otherwise hold, improve, use and sell, convey, exchange, transfer, dispose of, lease and sublease real and personal property of every kind and character, to borrow money, accept grants and loans; and to enter into contracts with private corporations, the state and the federal government. The Authority shall have the power to elect and appoint officers, hire employees or other agents, including fiscal agents, attorneys and other professional experts. A catchall statement should also be included in this section. For example, the clause may state: "The Authority may exercise any power usually possessed by public enterprises or private corporations performing similar functions."

d) Establishment of the Board of Directors - As the title indicates, this clause establishes the board of directors for the authority. This clause should include how the board members are appointed, the number of voting board members, what constitutes a quorum, the specific term or terms they are permitted to serve on the board, how member vacancies are addressed, any special skills or experience needed as a board member, compensation for

procurement and financial rules and regulations. Because of jurisdictional concerns, it is harder to resolve disputes between agencies.

In *Mile High Enterprises Inc., v. Dee,*[2] the question was presented as to which city agency had the authority to enter into long term concession contracts for Denver Mile High Stadium. In 1968, the city bought the former Bears Stadium, and the responsibility for the stadium maintenance, operations and concessions was placed under the Manager of the Department of Parks and Recreation.[3] In 1974, voters approved an expansion for the stadium that was still in process when the case was decided, which would have involved the destruction of existing concession facilities, in favor of remodeled and additional concession facilities. As a result, the city, through the Manager of the Department of Parks and Recreation, modified the existing contract with Mile High Enterprises, in existence since 1968, to extend the term of the contract for an additional 18 years, and obligated Mile High to spend between $750,000 and $850,000 to purchase equipment and construct concession facilities at the Stadium. The title of all equipment purchased was to vest in the city, and the receipt formula under which the city was paid by Mile High was modified.

This third agreement was approved by the Mayor's cabinet by executive order, but the Auditor refused to sign, based on his judgment that the authority for managing the stadium should be under the Department of General Services and not the Department of Parks and Recreation. In review, the Supreme Court of Colorado held that the delegation of stadium management and contracts regarding the Stadium could be properly delegated to the Department of Parks and Recreation[4] and then ordered the Auditor to countersign the agreement, that was held to be valid.

3) Sovereign Immunity

Sovereign immunity is derived from the Eleventh Amendment of the United States Constitution. In 1793, a lawsuit against the State of Georgia by a non-resident provoked the U.S. Congress to amend the Constitution by including a prohibition that a citizen of one state cannot sue another state without its

---

[2] 558 P.2d 568 (Colo. 1977).
[3] Id. at 569.
[4] Id. at 572.

permission. In addition, the concept of immunity from suit relates to the federal government. One cannot sue the Federal government without its permission or waiver of the immunity. Over the past two hundred years, there are numerous exceptions to sovereign (state or federal) immunity. This legal concept governs lawsuits between state citizens and state owned and operated facilities.

In *Diamond v. Springfield Metropolitan Exposition Auditorium Authority,*[5] a woman sued the Exposition authority (SMEAA) following a fall at the Prairie Capital Convention Center located in Springfield, Illinois. The woman had tripped in the doorway of an underground tunnel leading to the convention center on her way to attend a career-related conference.[6] The woman alleged she had broken bones and sustained other serious injuries because of her fall. SMEAA claimed it was immune from suit under the Tort Immunity Act which provided that a local public entity or public employee was immune from liability for an injury based on a condition on public property permitted for public use for recreational purposes, not limited to parks, playgrounds, and the like, and that the Convention Center was used for "recreational purposes" under the meaning of the act. [7] It was noted that many of the uses of the convention center were recreational in purpose, including city basketball tournaments, karate tournaments, boxing and wrestling, and the like. The woman felt that her purpose in going to the center was not recreational, but career oriented, and thus the Tort Immunity Act should not apply.

The Trial Court entered judgment for SMEAA, holding that it was immune from suit under the Tort Immunity Act, and the woman appealed. The Court of Appeals held that the facility's overall character needed to be determined in order to be able to decide whether the facility was entitled to immunity under the Tort Immunity Act. The Court then upheld the Trial Court's determination that the facility was recreational in purpose and thus was entitled to immunity from negligence-type lawsuits under the Tort Immunity Act, barring the Plaintiff's claim.[8]

---

[5] 44 F.3d 599 (7th Cir. 1995).
[6] Id. at 601.
[7] Id.
[8] Id. at 604.

maintained so as to lead to the accident that occurred, making the State Fair ineligible for immunity under the Tort Claims Act.

In *Federal Sign v. Texas Southern University*,[13] Federal Sign sought to sue Texas Southern University (TSU) for breach of contract regarding a basketball scoreboard to be installed in the University's Health and physical education facility.

In 1988, TSU began to accept bids for a scoreboard for its new gym facilities. In 1989, it accepted Federal Sign's bid, and Federal Sign secured PepsiCo as a sponsor for the scoreboard. Federal Sign began to construct the scoreboard, but in September of 1989 before anything had been delivered to the University, TSU notified Federal Sign that its bid was unacceptable. TSU stated that they would pursue other avenues to obtain a scoreboard. TSU eventually obtained a scoreboard from Spectrum Scoreboards and Coca-Cola. Federal Sign then sued TSU in 1990, alleging breach of contract, violation in competitive bidding procedures and open meeting law requirements and for damages of $67,000 in lost profits and $22,000 in expenses incurred. TSU alleged immunity, and the court put the case on hold while Federal Sign was to pursue legislative permission to sue. Instead, Federal Sign asked for rehearing in the matter. The Court granted Federal Sign's motion and the matter was tried before a jury, rendering judgment for Federal Sign. TSU appealed on the sovereign immunity issue, and the Court of Appeals agreed with TSU and reversed the trial court's decision. Federal Sign then appealed the case to the Texas Supreme Court.

The Texas Supreme Court held that when a private person seeks to hold the state liable on breach of contract claims and seeks money damages, legislative consent for the suit must be obtained. Federal Sign's contention that the State waived its immunity when it entered a contract with a private citizen. The Court analyzed sovereign immunity based on immunity from liability in comparison to the process of immunity from suit. The State did not create or admit liability when it consents to be sued, When the State does contract, it is liable on contracts made for its benefit as if it were a private person. A state, when it becomes a litigant in its own courts, must have its rights determined by the same principles applicable to every other person. The Court held that when the state contracted with individuals, it waived only its immunity from liability,

---

[13] No. 94-1317, 1997 Tex. LEXIS 58 (June 20, 1997), 951 S.W.2d 401 (Tex. 1997).

however a private litigant must obtain legislative consent to sue the state on a breach of contract claim. The very act of contracting for the scoreboard did not waive the state's immunity from suit, as claimed by Federal Sign. Therefore, until Federal Sign obtained consent from the legislature to sue TSU, the suit was precluded by sovereign immunity and could not go forward.

4) Local Taxes and the Private Use of Public Facilities

Because public facilities are tax-exempt, the private short-term or intermittent use of public lands and facilities raises local tax questions. State and municipal tax authorities are always seeking additional entities or ways to tax. However sometimes their shortsightedness to increase tax revenues for that specific year conflicts with legislative goals to increase the tourism and convention business within the region. As in all state and municipal governments, not everybody understands the value of a convention center, arena, or stadium to a region. In creating an entity to operate a convention center or other similar facility, it may be beneficial to include a general provision that excludes the application of certain taxes on short-term users of your facility.

In *Denver Center for the Performing Arts v. Briggs*,[14] Denver Center for the Performing Arts (DCPA) appealed the decision of the Denver Manager of Revenue, assessing a Facilities Development Admission tax on events held at the Denver Center Theatre and Denver Center Cinema. The DCPA contended that the collection of the tax violated state and federal equal protection laws. The District Court held not only that DCPA did not have standing to bring the suit, but also ruled against it on the merits. DCPA appealed. In 1973, Denver and DCPA entered into an agreement where DCPA was to raise $5 million towards building a performing arts center. Denver would build the hall, and lease it to DCPA for nominal rent. DCPA was to construct other theaters and facilities on the land purchased by Denver for the performing arts center, also to be leased to DCPA for nominal rent. Legal title to all land and buildings was to remain in the city's name. DCPA could retain all revenues from the center and facilities and would be responsible for the maintenance thereof. In 1974, Denver passed a facilities development admission tax, imposing a 10% tax on admissions to all events at

---

[14] 696 P.2d 299 (Colo. 1985).

city-owned facilities, including the new performing arts center. The tax was to be separate from the admissions price, and the center was prohibited from absorbing the tax. In 1977, DCPA leased from Denver land for the Denver Center Theatre and Denver Center Cinema. Later in 1977, the city and DCPA entered into a lease for the Boettcher Concert Hall, under construction by the city. The lease stated that all the revenues were to be retained by DCPA except for the Facilities Development Admissions tax, specifically requiring DCPA to collect tax on all admissions to the concert hall.

DCPA opened the Denver Center Theatre and Denver Center Cinema in late 1979/early 1980. In 1981, the Department of Revenue audited the ticket sales and assessed DCPA for $98,972.91 including tax, penalty, and interests on admissions from the opening of the center through December, 1980. DCPA filed a petition for review, and the Manager of Revenue continued to assess tax on ticket sales during the early months of 1981. DCPA did not challenge the amount of the assessment, but whether it should be subject to tax at all for events at the theatre and cinema. At hearing, the Manager of Revenue sustained his assessments, finding the facilities were city-owned and admission taxes should be collected on all tickets sold. The Manager also found that DCPA did collect the taxes. On appeal to the district court, the court found that the lease did not exempt DCPA from collecting the tax, and that passage of the tax did not modify or impair contracts or in any other way violate DCPA's constitutional rights. DCPA appealed, alleging that the facility was not owned by the city, or that the 1973 lease did not require DCPA to collect the tax. The Supreme Court of Colorado held that DCPA did have standing to bring the claim, but that the tax was constitutional, and that the tax exemption for the property as a whole did not prohibit the city from imposing an admissions tax on patrons of the facilities. The "retain all revenues" provision did not exempt DCPA from collecting the tax from its patrons, and that in fact, the city did own the Cinema and Theatre under the terms of the lease agreement and thus affirmed the decision of the District Court.

The City of Cleveland v. Carney Aud., et al.,[15] the State of Ohio assessed a municipal auditorium and exhibit hall owned by the City of Cleveland with state property taxes. The city requested an exemption and the State Board of Tax Appeals denied the request. The question for the Supreme Court of Ohio was whether the Cleveland auditorium and exhibition hall is "public property used exclusively for a public purpose" under the Constitution of Ohio. The Supreme Court of Ohio reviewed numerous cases on federal housing, public transportation, libraries, airports, parking lots, stadiums and sports arena cases and could not fit an exhibition facility into the pattern of the other cases which would determine whether the State could tax the property. The Court ruled against applying the tax to short-term users of the facilities by stating:

> "In each of the stadium and sports arena cases, the property was leased to a single tenant, which tenant was responsible for the operation. The record here indicates that employees of the City of Cleveland actually operate the auditorium and exhibit hall. Moreover, the record is equally clear that private organizations come into the auditorium and exhibit hall not as users or operators, as in the cases of stadium and sports arena, but as concessionaires. The nature of this right is a permit of short duration, which the elements of service necessary to the exercise of the permit are provided directly by the city.
>
> "Undoubtedly, trade shows and conventions, although not open to the public generally, nevertheless provide a benefit to the city as a whole. Hotels, restaurants, department stores, nightclubs and other businesses profit directly and others connected therewith as employees profit indirectly from the presence of such events in a city. Were not such affairs of general benefit to a community there would not be the competition which exists among cities in the inducing of organizations to bring their conventions and trade shows to one city or another. Such a benefit is a public benefit because it affects all the community directly and indirectly.

---

[15] 174 N.E.2d 254 (1961).

intermission times, and selection of the provider of novelties, concessions, and programs. However, the Court held that the restrictions were not so severe as to make users of the facility agents of the city, and thus they did not enjoy the city's tax-exempt status. As to exclusivity, it did not imply continuous access to the premises, as the city suggested, but right to physical possession and use of the property together with the ability to exclude from occupancy others who interfere with that enjoyment. In conclusion, the California Court of Appeals affirmed the judgment of the trial court, allowing the Assessor to impose tax on groups who used the facility on any sort of regular basis.

  In *Pier 30 Associates v. The School District of Philadelphia*, [22] the school district had imposed a local use and occupancy tax on tennis courts operated and constructed by Pier 30 on property owned by the city, leased by the Philadelphia Port Commission and sublet to Pier 30 Associates.[23] While Pier 30 Associates agreed that the property was public in nature, the dispute centered on whether the use by Pier 30 was for a "public purpose," thereby exempting it from the tax. The Commonwealth Court noted that the courts were open to the public, used for recreation of the public and were located on public property, but this in and of itself was not enough to establish a public purpose for tax exemption.[24] Membership fees were required in order to use the courts, and non-members could "rent" the courts through an hourly fee. While the courts were a permanent improvement to the property, the tennis courts did not further the purposes of the governmental agency from which the property was leased, and thus was not serving a public purpose.[25] Pier 30 Associates was therefore responsible for the local use and occupancy tax, despite having opened its courts for public access.

———————————————

5) Local Bond Issues to Fund the Facility

Municipal bonds fund many different projects for a municipality, some of which are public assembly facilities. However, state referendum laws may complicate and delay financing for the facility.

In *Poe v. Hillsborough County*,[26] a taxpayer and resident of the Tampa Bay area accused the county, city and Tampa Stadium Authority (TSA) of using the tax power and of pledging public credit to build a new Tampa Stadium, which was felt to be a violation of the Florida constitution.[27] The county had placed a referendum on the ballot to institute a one-half cent local government infrastructure tax for thirty years to support financing of jails, police, sheriff's equipment, fire stations, emergency vehicles, libraries, parks, trials, storm water improvements and public facilities, which passed by 53% of the vote.[28] An interlocal agreement distributed the proceeds of the tax as follows: 25% to the school district, $318 million for construction of a new stadium, and any remaining proceeds to be distributed to the localities as provided by Florida statutes. An agreement was then entered into with the Tampa Bay Buccaneers ("Bucs") for the construction of a new 65,000-seat stadium to serve as the Bucs home field and to build a $12 million dollar training facility for the Bucs. The Bucs were to lease the facility for 30 years with an annual fee paid to the TSA of $3.5 million, $2 million for the stadium, $1 million for the training facility and $500,000 to retain development right to surrounding property. The TSA was also to receive almost $2 million annually from a surcharge on Bucs tickets and tickets for other events.

The constitutional provision in question prohibited the state, county, school district or municipality from becoming joint owners or stockholders of a corporation, association or partnership; nor could it lend or use its taxing and credit to aid such a group. Shortly after Mr. Poe filed his complaint, the TSA, county and city filed a complaint seeking to

---

. May 22, 1997).

[27] Id. at *5.
[28] Id. at *4.

validate a series of bond issues for constructing and equipping the sta-dium.[29] The two complaints were consolidated for trial.

The Circuit Court failed to validate the bond issues. The Court held that the purpose of the bonds would be valid, except for one clause that allowed the Bucs the first $2 million in revenues generated from non-Buc events. The Court concluded due to this clause, the bond issue served a largely private rather than public purpose, and that if the parties chose to revise this provision, it would validate the bond issue. On appeal, the Florida Supreme Court ruled that the bonds were valid and complied with the Florida Constitution because the construction of the facility created an attraction of tourists and generated publicity for the area across the nation resulting in quantifiable benefits to the Tampa Bay area. The Court declined to invalidate the bonds just because the Bucs got "too sweet" a deal and chastised the lower court for trying to micro-manage the contractual negotiations of the parties.[30] The Court finally stated that the taxpayer's relief was at the ballot box if he, the plaintiff, believed his city officials had not served him well.[31]

In *Peterson v. City of San Diego, et. al.*,[32] a voter challenged the city's ordinance allowing election by mail ballot as violating the constitu-tional right to ballot secrecy.[33] The City Council had approved a lease between the city and the redevelopment agency for construction of the San Diego Convention Center, and the council wanted to submit approv-al of the lease to voters, by mail ballot only. The voter alleged that such a mail ballot allowed many opportunities for fraud and coercion, and violated constitutional provisions requiring that "voting shall be secret." The Court reviewed the case law and held that while absentee ballots are valid as protecting the voter's right of access to voting at all, mail ballot-ing for a "general election" or referendum was different. The City alleged that this was more cost effective than polling places, more convenient and potentially assured a greater response rate than poll voting by mail balloting.

---

[29] Id. at *7.
[30] Id. at *22.
[31] Id. at *23.
[32] 134 Cal. App. 3d 31 (4th Dist. 1982); decision subsequently vacated as improper grant of summary judgment.
[33] Id.

The Court ruled that the convenience of mail balloting did not outweigh the voter's right to privacy in the voting booth and secrecy, and the city had no compelling reason to utilize this procedure.[34]

In *Rider v. City of San Diego*, [35] San Diego and the Port District entered into an agreement under which the San Diego Convention Center would be expanded on Port District property and that this would be financed by a leaseback arrangement.[36] A Joint Powers Agency (JPA) was formed for this purpose, and the Convention Authority was separate from both the City of San Diego and the San Diego Port District, and was administered by a board that included the Port Director, City Manager, City Mayor, and a member of the Board of Port Commissioners. The Convention Authority was to issue bonds not to exceed 205 Million to finance the expansion of the Convention Center and the bonds were to be paid by revenues generated from renting of the center to the City of San Diego under a sublease and 'support payments' from the Port District. This arrangement is referred to as the leaseback arrangement. Several residents challenged the validity of the leaseback arrangement, alleging voter approval was necessary as the city was attempting to incur indebtedness that would have required a vote under the constitution of California. The Court held that this type of arrangement had been previously upheld by the court involving the partial renovation of Jack Murphy Stadium (now referred to as Qualcomm Stadium). Additionally, because the JPA and not the city issued bonds, the city did not violate the city charter that prohibited it from issuing bonds without voter approval. Prior to a decision by the Supreme Court of California, the case was settled by the parties.

In *Leventhal v. Philadelphia*, [37] the General Assembly of Pennsylvania enacted the Convention Center Authority Act, creating the Pennsylvania Convention Center Authority to oversee construction and operation of the Convention Center in Philadelphia. The State of Pennsylvania Act authorized Philadelphia to impose an excise tax on hotel rooms.

---

[34] Id.
[35] 1996 Cal. App. LEXIS 1208 (December 27, 1996).
[36] Id. at *3.
[37] No. 1849, 16 Phila. 605, 1987 Phila. Cty. Rptr. LEXIS 56 (December 15, 1987).

the Commission's contract with its ticket-purchaser of last resort, General Mills, throughout the term of the agreement. General Mills' counsel sent a letter to the Commission prior to the repeal stating it doubted their agreement would be valid upon repeal of the statute, and later sent a letter implying that the repeal nullified their contract. In February of 1985, the Commission notified General Mills that the contract was still in effect, and General Mills responded, two and one-half years later, in November of 1987, that there had been no anticipatory breach of the agreement notwithstanding the repeal of the statute.[44] After the repeal, General Mills continued to receive the free advertising and shuttle bus access through the 1988-1989 seasons, but prior to the 1988 season, General Mills was not called upon to purchase tickets because all home games had been sold out at least 72 hours prior to the game. Prior to the first regular season game in 1988, the Commission realized 90 percent of the tickets had been sold within 120 hours before the game, but that some tickets would remain unsold prior to the 72-hour cutoff. Red Lobster, a wholly owned General Mills subsidiary, purchased the remaining tickets and the game was telecast locally. General Mills stated it voluntarily purchased the tickets, not doing so under the agreement.[45] After the purchase, General Mills made changes in the one-minute advertising seen during the game. The issue of unsold tickets did not arise again until the 1989-1990 season when the same unsold ticket situation occurred. The trial court found that General Mills may have helped to purchase those tickets. The situation arose again during the season, at which time, General Mills said it would not buy the remaining tickets and the Commission then sued to enforce the obligations under the agreement.

General Mills alleged that the Vikings were unable to comply with the repealed statute, which was a condition precedent to its obligation to purchase tickets, and that the repeal of the section meant that the condition precedent could not exist, thus the obligation to purchase the tickets under the contract could not arise.[46] However, the initial agreement

---

[44] Id. at 628.

[45] Id.

[46] Id. A condition precedent is an event or action that must occur before another party becomes obligated to perform its duties under a contractual agreement. For example, someone must first obtain a mortgage commitment under most real estate contracts before the party selling the property becomes obligated to sell or relinquish that property to you. The mortgage commitment is a *condition precedent*

clearly contemplated the possibility the statute could be repealed, and that in such event, the contract was to remain binding. General Mills argued that the legislature could not conditionally repeal a statute. The Court of Appeals, affirming the trial court's decision, held that both General Mills and the Commission were sophisticated parties and had clearly defined and limited terms of the repeal of the statute as to terminate the agreement. Further, despite voicing objections in 1985 to the continuation of the agreement, General Mills continued to accept benefits under the agreement in the form of free advertising, bus service, preferred tickets, etc. through 1989. Further, General Mills stated in 1987 that it was not anticipatory breaching the agreement. Thus, because all parties including General Mills acted as if the agreement was still in effect and made specific provisions for the agreement to remain effective despite the repeal, General Mills remained obligated under the agreement for the full 20-year term.[47]

1.02   Facilities Created by Non-Profit Corporations

In order to create a non-profit corporation the organizers of the facility must review the local and state non-profit corporation statutes for the proper structure of the organization, the tax benefits and the tax restrictions. The articles of incorporation and the by-laws must be drafted so that the facility has the authority and operational flexibility to perform its intended functions.

If public dollars are to be distributed to the non-profit corporation, provisions in the bylaws and the tax statute of the donating governmental entity must reflect the long-term commitment to the non-profit entity. If the facility will operate from charitable donations, it is essential to make sure that the donations will be tax deductible to the donors. A key part of any non-profit charitable organization is to have the entity "approved" by the Internal Revenue Service ("IRS") through an Opinion Letter. Most state tax departments only recognize organizations properly registered with the IRS.

Generally, non-profit corporations that own and manage their own facilities (regional theater groups, symphony orchestras, and others) qualify for exemption from federal income tax as charitable organizations under Section 501(c)(3) of the Internal Revenue Code of 1986 (the "Code").[48] The advantages to be derived from such qualification are that:

    (a) the organization's income, other than income classified as unrelated business income ("UBIT"), is not subject to income tax;

    (b) most states and municipalities exempt charitable organizations from income, property, sales and use taxes;

    (c) individuals and corporations making contributions to such organizations may deduct the amount of contributions, subject to certain limitations, from income tax; and

    (d) federal estate and gift tax deductions are available for testamentary or lifetime gifts to charities.[49]

As you can see from the above, the tax benefits may be substantial. However, there are some important disadvantages

to qualifying as Section 501(c)(3) organization. The most important of these are:

    (i)   Strict operating requirements that must be complied with to maintain the exemption. Foremost among these is the prohibition against private inurement by control-

---

A Section 501 (c)(3) organization is a corporation, community chest, fund or foundation which is both organized and operated exclusively for religious, charitable, scientific, literary, or educational purposes. The section requires that (i) the organization be both organized and operated exclusively to further a qualified exempt purpose; (ii) no part of the net earnings of the organization inure to the benefit of any private shareholder or individual; (iii) no substantial part of the organization's activities consist of carrying on propaganda or otherwise attempting to influence legislation and the organization does not participate or intervene in any political campaign on behalf of or in opposition to any candidate for public office; and (iv) it operates as a common-law charity.

[49] Section 170 (c) of the Code allows individuals and corporations to deduct contributions to qualified organizations described in Section 501(c)(3) (other than organizations engaged in testing for public safety or foreign organizations) and Sections 2055 and 2522 generally permit a federal estate tax deduction and a federal gift tax deduction, respectively for contributions to similar organizations.

ling persons. Therefore, any self-dealing or unreasonable compensation for services will be closely examined and penalties imposed in cases of violations.

(ii)   Section 501 (c)(3) organizations that are not publicly supported are generally treated as private foundations whose managers and founders may be subject to substantial excise taxes where private inurement is found.

(iii)   Section 501 (c)(3) organizations are absolutely prohibited from engaging in partisan political campaigns and their lobbying activities are severely restricted.[50]

1) Income Exempt from Tax

The exemption from income tax of a Section 501(c)(3) organization is determined by examining gross receipts of the organization to see whether any portion of these receipts are being treated as "unrelated trade or business taxable income" ("UBIT"). UBIT is defined in Section 512(a) of the Code as a gross income derived by the exempt organization from an unrelated trade or business that is "regularly carried on" less the deductions directly connected with the trade or business, computed with the modifications described in Section 512(b).

Thus, in order to generate UBIT, the organization must engage in an "unrelated" trade or business. The mere fact that an organization engages in a commercial, profit-making activity is not sufficient in itself to give rise to UBIT. For example, an exempt charitable theater group would not realize UBIT from the proceeds from ticket sales. Secondly, the trade or business must be regularly carried on. Consequently, it has been held that advertising in programs for an annual sporting event, although giving rise to income from an unrelated trade or business, was not subject to tax because it was not being regularly carried on.[51]

---

[50] Organizations that wish to lobby may qualify for exemption from tax under Section 501(c)(4) of the Code which exempts nonprofit civic organizations which are operated exclusively for public welfare. Under Treasury regulations, an organization is operated exclusively for the promotion of social welfare if it is primarily engaged in promoting the common good and general welfare of the people of the community. Regs. § 1.501(c)(4) – 1(a)(2)(I). However, contributions to Section 501(c)(4) organizations do not qualify as deductible charitable contributions.

[51] See *National Collegiate Athletic Assoc. v. Commissioner,*

The modifications under Section 512(b) are certain items of income and any deductions directly connected with them that are excluded from the calculation of UBIT. These items are generally referred to as "passive" income that are presumed not to arise from the active conduct of a trade or business. Accordingly, Section 512(b)(I) of the Code excludes all dividends, interest, payments with regard to securities, loans, amounts received for agreeing to make loans and annuities from UBIT.

Royalty income is also excluded from UBIT. In order to be a nontaxable royalty, the payment must relate to the use of a valuable right, such as the use of a name, trademark, or copyright. Whether an item of income is a royalty is determined from all the facts and circumstances and has been the subject of an on-going controversy between exempt organizations and the Internal Revenue Service (IRS).

The position of the IRS is that where an organization actively promotes the use of its name, trademark, or copyright among its members and the public, income from such promotion is not derived from a royalty. Consequently, the IRS held in Rev. Rule. 81-178, 1981-2 C.B, 135 that payment for the use of a professional athlete's name received by an organization of professional athletes under a license agreement is a royalty, and hence it is not taxable. However, a payment for endorsement of products and services by personal appearance was compensation for services and was not a royalty because the income did not arise from a passive source.

This issue has been most recently litigated in two cases of *Sierra Club, Inc. v. Commissioner.*[52] In Sierra I, the Club had entered into an agreement with a banking services corporation to promote an affinity card to club members. The bank services company marketed and also promoted the card. From this activity, the Club received a "royalty" based on the percentage of sales charged on the cards and from travel services provided through the card.

In Sierra II, the case involved the sale by the Club of members and donors mailing lists in exchange for appropriate fees which the Club claimed were royalties. The Tax Court held in favor of the Club in both cases. It determined that the term "royalty" in the statute applied to a "payment for the use of valuable, intangible property rights" regardless of whether it was derived from passive or active promotion of these rights. On appeal, the Ninth Circuit rejected the Tax Court's holding that all payments for use of intangible personal property qualify for the royalty exclusion. It agreed with the IRS that a royalty is, by definition "passive" and thus cannot extend to income derived from actively promoting the intangible property. Accordingly, the Court of Appeals affirmed the tax court decision in regards to sale of the mailing lists because the Club provided no ancillary services with respect to the sale. The Court then reversed and remanded the case in regards to the affinity card program, because there was evidence that the Club was actively promoting the program.

In light of the Sierra Club decisions, where exempt organizations adopt affinity cards or similar programs where they license the use of the organization's name and logo, care must be taken to draft any royalty agreements in such a manner that would not call into question the passive nature of the royalty income derived from such a license.

Under Section 512(b)(3) of the Code, rental income from real property is excluded from UBIT. If personal property is leased in conjunction with the real estate, income from that lease is not taxable if it is incidental, meaning no more than 10% of the total rental received.[53] As in the case of royalty income, if the exempt organization provides services in connection with the rental of real property, the rents may not be exempt from tax. Therefore, if any exempt organization leases a part of its facility, it must be careful not to provide anything more than what would be normally provided to a tenant by way of services, such as maintenance, adjacent parking, and similar amenities.[54]

Finally, capital gains are excluded from UBIT, including gains or losses on the lapse or termination of securities or real estate options.[55]

2) Partnerships With Non-exempt Entities

Section 512(c)(1) of the Code provides that if an exempt organization is a partner in a partnership which carries on a trade or business which is an unrelated trade or business with respect to the organization, then the organization must treat a proportionate share of its partnership income and deductions as being from an unrelated source, and hence, taxable.

At one time, the IRS took the position that where an exempt organization participated in a limited partnership as a general partner, then it would lose its exemption because its active role in the business negated an exempt purpose.[56] However, that position was modified following the Tax Court's decision in *Plumstead Theater Society, Inc. v. Commissioner.*[57]

In the *Plumstead* case, a 501(c)(3) organization that cultivated and promoted public interest in theater, dance and other forms of classical entertainment, acted as a general partner in a partnership with two individuals and a non-tax-exempt organization to present professional theater productions and operate a workshop for new American playwrights. Under the limited partnership arrangement, only the limited partners provided the capital. The IRS contended that this enterprise operated by a charity would provide a private benefit to the non-exempt partners. The Tax Court disagreed. The Court found that there was no danger of private inurement since the organization was under no obligation to return the limited partners' capital contributions. Furthermore, the Court noted that there was a significant difference between a tax exempt theater organization which usually uses amateur actors, performs works by unknown playwrights and subsidizes unprofitable productions as opposed to the commercial theater which exists to make a profit and employs professional actors.[58]

Following the *Plumstead* decision, the IRS Chief Counsel's office revised its position and adopted a two-part test for determining whether a charitable organization's participation in a limited partnership with non-exempt partners as a general partner would give rise to revocation of its exempt status. The IRS would first determine whether the organization is serving a charitable purpose by its participation in the partnership and assuming it does, whether the charity's role as a general partner inhibits its charitable purposes. Under this

---

GCM 36293 (May 30, 1975).

[57] 74 T.C. 97 (1980), aff'd per curiam, 675 F.2d 244 (9th Cir. 1982).

[58] See also *Broadway Theater League of Lynchburg, VA v. United States*, 293 F.Supp. 346 (W.D.Va. 1968), where a charitable foundation entered into contacts with for-profit organizations to bring professional theater to Lynchburg was held to be exempt from tax on income from ticket sales and was not held to be engaged in a commercial venture, thereby jeopardizing its exempt purpose.

latter test, the IRS will examine whether the limited partners receive an express economic benefit from the partnership and how excessive are the charity's day-to-day commercial activities as general partner.[59]

Charitable organizations that enter into partnerships with for-profit persons for the purpose of raising capital to promote theatrical productions must be careful to avoid the aura of commercial risk-taking in such arrangements. According to the IRS, among the factors that would indicate a charitable purpose are:

1. Limited contractual liability of the charity;
2. A limited rate of return on the invested capital of the non-exempt limited partners that is reasonable under the circumstances;
3. The charity's right of first refusal upon sale of assets;
4. The presence of additional general partners who are obligated to protect the interests of the limited partners so that the charity would not become liable for the acts of its partners; and
5. The absence of an obligation to return the limited partners' capital from the charity's finds.

Factors indicating a non-exempt purpose would include:
1. Disproportionate allocations of profits or losses;
2. Commercially unreasonable loans by the charity to the partnership;
3. Inadequate compensation for services to be rendered by the charity; and control of the exempt organization by the limited partners.[60]

---

[59] GCM 39005 (June 28, 1983).
[60] GCM 39862 (November 21, 1991).

In *Connecticut Performing Arts Foundation v. Brown,*[61] the Connecticut Performing Arts Foundation (CPAF) had applied for tax exempt status under the Internal Revenue Code, Section 501(c)(3). The IRS in review, denied exempt status in 1962.[62] In 1971, the CPAF applied for state tax exemption in Connecticut, alleging it was "of a similar nature" to exempt organizations, although it itself was not exempt, due to the fact that the Oakdale Musical Theater Company, who controlled CPAF's operations, did so for their own financial advantage.[63]

The state initially granted the tax-exempt status, but later, in 1973 notified CPAF that it would revoke its status unless they obtained federal tax-exempt status. CPAF contested the commissioner's ruling, and it was held that the tax-exempt status was properly revoked due to the failure of CPAF to qualify for federal tax exemption.[64] CPAF appealed the ruling and the case was removed to the Bankruptcy Court, where CPAF was seeking a refund for taxes it had paid. The Bankruptcy Court held that the Commissioner had overstepped his authority when granting tax exempt status to CPAF, and that his acts were reversed as soon as he became aware of his error in granting tax exempt status.[65] While the CPAF urged a reading of the statute that would allow its tax exempt status because it functioned similarly to a tax exempt organization, the IRS had specifically ruled that the organization was not exempt, and the language "similar to an exempt organization" had been meant to cover small organizations too small to apply for federal exempt status, like PTAs.[66] Additionally, the court held that since the tax on admission tickets collected was a transactional tax, the only party due a refund was the customers of CPAF, and they were not before the court, thus the CPAF could not obtain a refund of taxes paid to the state.[67]

In *Broadway Theater League of Lynchburg, VA v. United States,*[68] the Theater League sought to recover income taxes and penal-

---

[61] 47 Bankr. 911 (Conn. 1985).
[62] Id. at 913.
[63] Id. at 913, 914.
[64] Id. at 914.
[65] Id. at 917.
[66] Id. at 918.
[67] Id. at 918, 919.
[68] 293 F.Supp.346 (W.D. Va. 1968).

ties paid, alleging that the IRS had wrongfully refused to grant it tax-exempt status under 501(3)(c) of the IRS Code. The League was organized 1962 to promote theater, professional theatrical performances, build and maintain a permanent theater audience and encourage the appreciation and study of drama. The Theater League is a non-stock, non-profit corporation with no members. The Directors volunteered their services and were not compensated. Workers, soliciting memberships and selling seasonal tickets were also not compensated for their time and effort. Students used as ushers were allowed to see plays free, but were not otherwise compensated in any way.

The League did engage services from various persons and organizations, including legal services, secretarial and clerical services, rental services of a high school auditorium, newspaper advertisement, and the services of a booking agent. In its first year of operation, the League contracted with United Performing Arts, Inc., a booking agent, with a term of one year and renewable by plaintiff at their option.

The contract between United and the League required the League to have at least a week's membership drive to sell season tickets to at least four attractions; price of the tickets was to be determined by United and the League; United was to provide campaign and promotional materials for the drive. United was to provide at least four high-quality attractions during the season, and the League was to deal exclusively with United for the term of the contract. No single admission tickets were to be sold to the general public. Programs were to be prepared by United but all advertising revenues were to belong only to the League. The League executed the contract on April 9, 1962, signed by both the League and a representative from United.

The IRS contended that the League did not qualify for tax exempt status due to the overly broad nature of its purpose in the articles of incorporation, and that it existed to benefit a for-profit corporation, United. The League subsequently amended its articles to conform with the IRS regulations and was granted tax-exempt status thereafter. The District Court, in review, held that the purpose of the League had always been for a non-profit charitable purpose and that its arrangement with United was not one for the benefit of United, but that selling of season tickets only was done to assure financial security of the undertaking. United only received 15% of the aggregate membership dues, and the

Court found that this contingency fee was reasonable under the circumstances. The Court held that the League was indeed eligible for tax exempt status during its initial year of existence, and the subsequent taxes,
interest and penalties assessed and paid were inappropriate and were to
be refunded to the corporation.

In *Metropolitan Tickets Inc., v. City of St. Louis,*[69] a regional
ticket seller sought to enjoin the City of St. Louis and its ticket seller,
Tickets Now, from selling ticketing services to Riverport Performing
Arts Center and other private entities.

The trial court ruled that Tickets Now could not sell tickets to Illinois riverboat casino operations, but held that it could sell its services to
private venues in St. Louis and Illinois. Tickets Now was a ticket service
purchased in 1986 by a Mr. Shanahan, who transferred the agency to
Community Facilities Corp. (CFC), a non-profit corporation set up to
operate the agency and to operate The Arena, leased from the city
through the Land Clearance for Redevelopment Authority (LCRA).[70]
Tickets Now was, and is, a for profit business. When first acquired, it
solely provided tickets for The Arena, but subsequently took over ticketing for Kiel Auditorium, previously serviced by Ticketmaster. Ticketmaster challenged Tickets Now acquisition of the auditorium contract,
but a federal judge ruled that the City, CFC and Tickets Now were
exempt from damages for antitrust violations because their actions were
directed by city officials. Ticketmaster left the St. Louis market, but Fox
Associates, managing the Fox Theater, began Metrotix, directly competing with Tickets Now. In 1991, the Riverport Amphitheater opened in St.
Louis County, and Tickets Now agreed to provide ticketing for it.

Metrotix sued, seeking to enjoin Tickets Now from contracting with any
private entities.[71] The Trial Court had concluded that Tickets Now and
CFC were municipal entities, in part due to the fact that the mayor of St.
Louis appoints most of the board of directors of CFC and the officers of
Tickets Now. The St. Louis City Convention Center and Tourism Board
is also responsible to make up any annual shortfall in operating revenue
of Tickets Now through the hotel and restaurant tax, but this agreement
came about as the Tourism Board sought assurances that it could use the

---

[69] 849 S.W.2d 52 (Mo. App. Ct. 1993).
[70] Id.
[71] Id. at 53.

arena in consideration for such a payment, although CFC and Tickets Now were never parties to that agreement.[72]

The Court of Appeals held that in fact, CFC and Tickets Now were not municipal entities under the Missouri Constitution, despite their close governmental ties. The Court held that they were both private entities properly organized under the incorporation laws, and that neither corporation was supported by tax money, neither had the power to govern, regulate, or administer the local nor internal affairs of the community, nor could it levy, collect or receive taxes. Because Tickets Now was private and not public in nature, it did not have to comply with regulations prohibiting public agencies from participating in riverboat gambling, illegal in Missouri, and thus was released from the injunction preventing it from selling riverboat gambling tickets.[73]

In *John Marshall Law School et. al. v. United States*,[74] John Marshall Law School and John Marshall University sought to overturn a determination by the Tax Court that both institutions were not entitled to tax exempt status. The Tax Court alleged that part of the net earnings of the schools inured to the benefit of private individuals. The law school received its first tax exempt determination in 1947, and the University in 1965. In 1977, a notice of final determination was sent, revoking their tax-exempt status retroactive to 1966, alleging that net earnings had inured to Theo Fenster, Martin Fenster and their respective families during that period. The Tax Court alleged that the Fensters had received payments for automobiles, education, travel expenses, insurance policies,

basketball and hockey tickets, membership in a private eating establishment, membership in a health spa, interest-free loans, home repairs, household furnishings, and golf equipment between 1967 and 1973 from the law school. On appeal, the question arose as to whether the payments made to or for the benefit of the Fensters were ordinary and necessary expenses incurred in the course of the operations of the school. S.B. Fenster had established the law school in 1933 as a non-profit corporation. The University was a two-year junior college established in 1941, with classes discontinued in the early 1970s. JMU was essentially a subsidiary of the law school; separate books of account were never kept,

---

[72] Id. at 55.

[73] Id.

[74] 228 Ct. Cl. 902 (1981).

and the schools were housed in the same building in Atlanta. Theo Fenster, son of the founder, became Dean in 1958 and held that position in all times relevant to the case. Martin Fenster, his brother, served as secretary of both institutions until his death in 1972, when Theo Fenster's wife took over his duties. No other officers of the school existed. Martin and Theo Fenster were also employed as instructors at the schools, with few other full time faculty being employed. A board, controlled by members of the Fenster family, ran both schools, set Theo Fenster's salary, and he, in turn set the salaries for all other employees.

Mr. Fenster also received several interest-free loans from the school with no set payback schedule, nor required any security. Similar loans were not available to the Fensters in the community, and thus the Tax Court properly treated them as the inurement of a benefit to the Fensters. The Plaintiffs tried to contend that the loans to purchase a home for the dean was an ordinary business expense, since many other institutions provide housing for their faculty and deans. The Court of Claims stated that when housing was provided at other institutions, it did not amount to the purchasing of an asset by a private individual, as it did in this case, and did not directly benefit the institution as required, and even if used for business entertainment purposes, it still did not justify the interest-free loan to Fenster.

The numerous other purchases made for the benefit of the Fenster family could only be partially justified as relating to law school business or recruiting. The majority of the expenses directly benefited the family, such as the inclusion of children and payment of their expenses on trips around the country and overseas and scholarships to the children of the two Fenster brothers. The college then attempted to claim that such

expenditures were fringe benefits of the job, and thus should be countable as salary to the individuals receiving them, rather than to the school, but they were not so treated in the records of the corporation. The Court concluded that Theo Fenster used corporate funds whenever and however he chose to do so, in violation of the corporation's tax-exempt status. Point by point, they discuss the inappropriate use of college funds for the personal benefit of the Fenster family, and the Court of Claims ruled that such expenditures provided ample reason for the revocation of the tax exempt status of the institution.

In *Birmingham Business College, Inc. v. Commissioner of Internal Revenue*,[75] Birmingham Business College sought tax exempt status, which was denied by the Tax Court, and Birmingham appealed. The Tax Court had held that Birmingham had failed to meet the requirements for tax exempt status, stating that it was not organized and operated exclusively for educational purposes, and that part of the net earnings benefited an individual or shareholder, making it ineligible for tax exempt status.

On appeal, the Court considered the history of the school and the fact that it had been incorporated by a public school teacher with a part-time law practice and his two siblings to be run as a non-profit educational institution, and that salaries were to be determined in proportion to the stock owned in the Corporation. In 1946, the corporation received tax exempt status, despite the fact that much of the information contained in their application was erroneous. Following a revenue agent's examination in 1952, the Commissioner revoked the tax-exempt status which led to this lawsuit.

The agent's examination revealed that Birmingham had few records or books, and those that were kept were error ridden. After extensive review and reconstruction of records, it was shown that the school had substantial earnings and income that had been distributed in one form or another to the stockholders, with the exception of capital investments. There had been extensive commingling of funds of the corporation and the stockholders. While it was shown that this pooling of resources was done more to keep the institution alive rather than for fraud or personal gain, the relationship between the corporation and its shareholders worked more like that of a for-profit corporation than that of a

not-for-profit institution. For example, approximately $17,000 was used to help finance the home of one of the shareholders. The Commissioner originally treated this as a dividend, but the Circuit Court held it was more like a loan. However, the most disturbing aspect of this practice was that the shareholders felt entitled to use the money of the corporation as might be needed, and that the check given to the shareholder, signed by the president, indicated it was an "advance payment against her interest" in the corporation.

---

[75] 276 F.2d 476 (5th Cir. 1960).

Because returns were never filed, the Court held the deficiency went back to tax years prior to 1946, and that it could retroactively revoke the tax-exempt status of the corporation. The Tax Court had been generous in determining the taxable income for the Corporation, noting that the numerous errors that occurred were done for the sake of the institution, rather than for fraudulent purposes. The Court upheld the determinations of the tax court, including the imposition of 25% penalties on the corporation for failing to file returns, and that a negligence penalty as to the individual taxpayers/shareholders was also warranted under the circumstances, and the case was remanded to the Tax Court for exact computation of tax penalties to be assessed.

This case is a classic example of "piercing the corporate veil." When a corporation is formed in part to shield individual stockholders from liability, that veil may be lifted when the individuals treat the corporation as their personal business or checking account, and do not follow delineated
business practices.

1.03   Specific Limitations on Liability

In *Bell Atlantic-Maryland, Inc. v. Maryland Stadium Authority*,[76] the Stadium Authority ("MSA") was in charge of expansions made to the Baltimore City Convention Center. During this expansion,

Bell Atlantic was forced to relocate and reroute underground cables and conduits and then sought reimbursement for the costs from MSA by sending them a bill for $110,000. [77] MSA refused to pay the bill and Bell Atlantic sued MSA for the costs associated with this relocation.[78] The trial court dismissed Bell Atlantic's complaint based on a prior court decision which had held that Bell Atlantic was to pay all of its own costs

---

[76] 688 A.2d 545 (Md. 1997).

[77] Id. at 548.

[78] Id. at 547.

associated with relocating cables when such areas were closed due to an exercise of municipal function. The trial court held the expansion of the convention center under the MSA was a municipal function and that Bell needed to bear its own expenses; Bell appealed, claiming that because the expansion of the convention center was state action rather than local municipal action, it should be reimbursed for its costs. The Court of Appeals upheld the lower court's dismissal of the case, stating that no contract existed between MSA and Bell regarding reimbursement for relocation costs, that the expansion was a municipal, not State act, and that Bell would need to bear its own costs.

In *Crouch v. National Association for Stock Car Auto Racing, Inc.,*[79] Crouch was initially awarded first place in an auto race sponsored by the National Association for Stock Car Auto Racing, Inc. (NASCAR), but the decision was overturned upon review by national NASCAR officials, declaring Randy LaJoie the winner of the race. Crouch sued, alleging the national NASCAR officials had no authority to overturn the local track official's determination that Crouch had won the race.

NASCAR is a for-profit corporation which promotes stock car racing. In order to participate in a NASCAR event, one must be a member of NASCAR and agree to comply with its rules.

In the race in question, two events occurred that affected the outcome. A restart of the race took place because of an accident involving the LaJoie car. During the restart, the LaJoie car remained in the Pit area behind the start/finish line, and then entered the track with the rest of the cars. The official scorer of the race determined LaJoie could not receive credit for any laps completed until he had crossed the start/finish line on the track, rather than in the pits. LaJoie maintained that the scorer's decision was incorrect and counter to the national rules and that his car was scored with one less lap than others throughout the race because of this ruling.[80] Then between laps 68 and 71, a yellow caution flag was displayed due to an accident, during which time racers are not to pass other drivers, holding their positions. The local NASCAR official, Curley, stated that LaJoie improperly passed several cars after the yellow flag was displayed, in violation of the rules. LaJoie believed he had the right to pass these cars due to the initial first lap scoring error.

Curley stated a black flag was displayed to the LaJoie car for four laps, although the pit crew stated they saw it only once. With a black

---

[79] 845 F.2d 397 (2d Cir. 1988).
[80] Id. at 398.

official's decision by NASCAR headquarters.[87] The Court of Appeals held that the District Court had improperly conducted its own analysis of the NASCAR rules and should have deferred to NASCAR's interpretation of its own rules in absence of an allegation of bad faith, and thus granted LaJoie and NASCAR summary judgment, dismissing Crouch's complaint.[88]

1.04 Appropriation Law – Basic Concepts

Appropriation laws are drafted and enacted by legislative bodies such as state legislators, city councils, town councils and the United States Congress. Because appropriations control where, when and how much money is spent by governmental entities, it is beneficial for the manager of a government-owned facility to understand some basic concepts of appropriation law. After reading this section, you may want to review your own locality's statutory basis for receiving and spending funds. Using the federal system as a guide, appropriations are classified in different ways for different purposes. The term appropriation means "an amount of money which is available for obligation. Usually, only the legislative body may designate how much money is provided in specific budgets. The general rule is that when a legislative body makes an appropriation, the appropriation must be expressly stated. An appropriation cannot be inferred or made by implication.[89] While the statutory

authority must be expressly stated in the statute, it is not necessary that the statute use the word "appropriation." The statute may contain a direction "to pay" out of specific funds. In this case, where there is a direction to pay, there must also be a designation of the source of the funds.[90]

In *City of Phoenix v. Phoenix Civic Auditorium & Convention Center Association, Inc.*,[91] the city and the association entered into an agreement in December of 1963 whereby the association would fund construction of a civic center and related facilities to be leased to the city.

The Association later refused to perform under the agreement, alleging the city did not have the authority to enter into the agreement, and the city sought a declaratory judgment regarding the validity of the agreement.

Under the agreement, the city would purchase and condemn land within the City of Phoenix and call for competitive bids; the successful bidder would lease the land for 40 years and build an auditorium thereon. The city and the association would then enter into a city lease where the lessee of the land would lease the land back to the city for 35 years, with the five intervening years to ensure the construction of the auditorium would be completed before the lease-back arrangement began.

The association was also to operate the auditorium on the city's behalf, not withstanding that the association might not be the successful bidder. In the ground lease, the lessee was to pay the city back for all costs associated with the land condemnation and purchase, and bear all construction risks and insurance coverage. The lessee was to receive monthly rental payments from the city under the leaseback arrangement once the Auditorium was completed. No particular source of city revenue was pledged to pay the rental amount of approximately $250,000 per year for the 35-year period.

The trial court determined that the agreement could not be enforced, and the City appealed. The Supreme Court of Arizona first considered the condemnation action of land to be used for the civic center and auditorium. The Court held that the municipal corporation had the right to expend public funds to construct the auditorium under Arizona law and that the civic center and auditorium were intended for public use, for which the eminent domain power could be exercised. The Court then addressed whether the leaseback arrangement was in violation

of the constitutional limitation prohibiting municipal corporations from carrying indebtedness in excess of 4% of the taxable property. Because the city could only incur approximately $4 million additional indebtedness without violating the four-% rule, and the value of the lease over time was estimated to be $8,750,000, this would violate the constitutional debt limitation and statutory budget limitation. The Court then considered other cases, and determined that the so-called rental payments were in fact purchase payments for the facility to be constructed. Because the rental payments were to be made from the general fund rather than from a specific revenue source, the amount to be paid must be added to the general debt limitation amount. As such, such an agreement would violate the constitutional debt ceiling, because the tax revenues of the city were the funds securing payment, not merely civic center and auditorium profits similar separate fund assurances. The Court cited references stating that annual rental payments were indistinguishable from annual debt service on bonds, and that in essence, the agreement was a purchase agreement for the facility, not a mere periodic rental.

While the Court agreed that the facilities proposed were most likely in the best interests of the citizens, it could not violate the constitutional debt ceilings put in place by the legislature for reasons of the economy of the state, and to act as a safeguard for the population. The Court held that the agreements proposed would violate both the constitutional debt ceiling limitation and statutory budget limitations, and thus could not be enforced by the city.

In *City of Fairbanks v. Fairbanks Convention Center and Visitors Bureau*,[92] the city had enacted a motel and hotel tax that supported the Fairbanks Convention Center and Visitors Bureau (FCVB) with approximately 85% of its operating budget from 70% of the tax revenues received.[93] The city sought to place on the ballot a voter initiative to reallocate the tax revenues, and FCVB sought and was awarded an injunction prohibiting the initiative from appearing on the ballot. The city was empowered to change the allocation of the tax on its own, but the question remained whether such a change in allocation could be accomplished by a voter initiative and whether such an initiative was valid under the Alaska constitution. The Supreme Court concluded that the initiative was not repealing nor making an appropriation, but just broadening what the City Council could do with the revenue generated from the bed tax,[94] and was therefore constitutional and should be placed on the ballot.[95]

---

818 P.2d 1153 (AK 1991).
[93] Id. at 1154.
[94] Id. at 1156.
[95] Id. at 1158.

Organization of Facilities

Also reserves the right to designate where the holder of this ticket shall be seated," and that this allowed the manager to act as he did. The Court held that the small print on the ticket was not sufficient to provide Mr. Vogel with notice that his admission could be refused, and that to allow such small print to be binding on all patrons would allow theaters to potentially discharge all their obligations to attendees without their knowledge and consent. The Court also held that under the circumstances, Vogel had been humiliated in front of his wife and numerous female employees, and that he was entitled to recover the $250.00 he sought for such embarrassment.

This case took place in 1945, 45 years before the enactment of the ADA, and gives us some perspective on the view of the disabled in our society. The minor disability suffered by the plaintiff made him a "cripple" in the eyes of theater employees and its manager, even though his condition did not affect his day-to-day activities. The Supreme Court of Louisiana took a very progressive approach in this case, and awarded the Plaintiff damages for humiliation and embarrassment that normally would not have been available in a contract dispute. The refusal to seat Mr. Vogel and his wife seems ludicrous today, especially following the enactment of the ADA, but it also shows us that our standards of what constitutes a disability and an accommodation for the disabled are vastly different now than they were

The Americans with Disabilities Act of 1990[2] (the "Act" or the "ADA") prohibits discrimination against individuals with disabilities with regard to employment and public accommodations. In passing the ADA, Congress recognized that 43,000,00 Americans are affected by a physical or mental disability. Congress found that because of these disabilities, discrimination exists in the areas of employment, recreation, education, housing, transportation, voting, public accommodations, health services and access to public services.[3] Because of these barriers, Congress intended the ADA to provide full integration into society to people with disabilities. The Act is divided into five titles:

- Title I Employment and Accommodation (This Title was effective 7/26/92)

---

[2] Public Law 101-336, 42 U.S.C. §12101 et. seq. (1990).
[3] 42 U.S.C. §12101, §§ 2 (a).

- Title II Government Services and Public Transportation (Effective 1/26/92)
- Title III Public Accommodations and Commercial Facilities (Effective 1/26/92)
- Title IV Telecommunications (Effective 7/26/93)
- Title V Miscellaneous Provisions

This Chapter discusses the public access provisions required under Titles II and III.[4] First, we will review the general rule for Title II. If a facility is owned and operated by the state or local government, Title II of the ADA will apply to the entity. Title II of the ADA prohibits discrimination in public services and provides in relevant part:

> "No qualified individual with a disability shall, by reason of such disability, be excluded from participation in or be denied the benefits of services, programs or activities of a public entity, or be subjected to discrimination by such entity.[5] A 'public entity' includes 'any department, agency, special purpose district, or other instrumentality of a State or States or local government' "[6]

The U.S. Department of Justice allows states to pass their own ADA laws. As of the date of this book's publication, four state ADA programs (Florida, Maine, Texas and Washington) were approved by the U.S. Department of Justice.

In *Bechtel v. East Penn School District of Lehigh County,*[7] a child confined to a wheelchair by spina bifida sought access to Emmaus High School stadium to attend band performances by his sister and to enroll within the next year as a student at the school. In recent renovations to the school, the school was advised of existing law requiring access for disabled individuals and that such access would not be financially

---

[4] Title I, Employment, will be discussed in Chapter 6.
[5] 42 U.S.C. at 12132
[6] Id. at § 12132.
[7] 1994 U.S. Dist. LEXIS 1327 (January 4, 1994).

which relief could be granted, and the Plaintiffs appealed. The Plaintiffs alleged the blackout rule discriminated against hearing-impaired people unfairly, because they had no other means by which to access the game via telecommunications technology, denying them equal access to the game. The defendants contended that the NFL's blackout rule was non-discriminatory because it applied to hearing and hearing-impaired persons equally. They also alleged that even though people without hearing disabilities could listen to a blacked out game on the radio, this was irrelevant because the blackout rule did not apply to radio, just TV. Recently developed technology also allowed radio broadcasts to be accessible to the hearing impaired, giving hearing and hearing-impaired equal footing in this venue of access.[18]

The Trial Court had reviewed the ADA which prohibits discrimination against the physically challenged in the full and equal enjoyment of goods, facilities, privileges, advantages or accommodations at any place of public accommodation by those who operate the accommodation. The Trial Court held that television broadcast of football games did not qualify as a public accommodation. The Court of Appeals agreed, stating that none of the Defendants were places of public accommodation, and although the game was played at a place of public accommodation, this did not imply that TV broadcast of the game was also a public accommodation. The Court also held that the Communications Act, covering "common carriers" did not apply to TV stations, nor did the Television Decoder Circuitry Act, which applied only to manufacturers of televisions. The Court of Appeals affirmed the District Court's decision and likewise held that Stoutenborough failed to state a claim upon which relief could be granted and dismissed the suit.

In *Brown v. 1995 Tenet ParaAmerica Bicycle Challenge*,[19] a cyclist with paralyzed lower extremities registered in 1994 to participate in the ParaAmerica Bicycle Challenge, a cross-country bicycle tour for disabled and able-bodied riders.

---

[18] Id.

[19] 959 F.Supp. 496 (N.D. Ill. 1997).

The defendants prevented Brown from riding in the race due to his refusal to wear a bicycle helmet,[20] and Brown sued, alleging the defendants violated his rights under the ADA and the Rehabilitation Act, and Defendants moved to dismiss.[21] The Defendants argued that they did not qualify as a place of public accommodation under the ADA. The Court held that neither the Tenet organization nor the race itself fell under the public accommodation definition under the ADA. Further, the chance to participate in the event itself had no connection to any place of public accommodation, but merely an event where participants rode on public roads, and were not operated, owned or leased by a private entity. Therefore, the Court dismissed Brown's claims under the ADA.

Under the Rehabilitation Act, the Court found that Brown had alleged enough facts to allow the claim to go forward, in that he was a disabled person qualified to participate in the event, but was discriminated against due to his disability and use of his tricycle, and that the ParaAmerica Challenge may have received federal assistance. The Court did dismiss Brown's intentional infliction of emotional distress claim, but allowed his claim for breach of contract stemming from the advertisement for the race and Brown's acceptance of the offer presented in the advertisement were allowed to go forward.

A "public accommodation" will not be found in every case, however. In *Ellit v. USA Hockey,*[22] a hearing and speech impaired youngster sought to participate in a hockey club involving interleague play, but required several accommodations to be able to do so. The hockey club was a membership organization that had a "house program" and a "league program" that taught and played hockey in several age categories. Because of the child's numerous disabilities, his family sought to allow him to "play down" in a class with younger children and to allow a family member on the ice with him at all times in order to help focus his attention on the sport.[23] The hockey club and its parent organization sought to prevent this, as they felt the child's size could pose a danger to younger children and that an additional person on the ice could

---

[20] His ability to wear the helmet required was impaired by the design of his racing tricycle.
[21] Id. at 498.
[22] 922 F. Supp. 217 (E.D. Mo. 1996).
[23] Id. at 218.

Alonzo chose to sue only Mr. Gatti's and not Mr. Baker or his business organization, maintaining that the Corporate franchiser retained the right to direct and control many aspects of day-to-day business at the franchised stores, as well as the right to approve all plans and specifications for remodeling under the franchise agreement. Alonzo maintained this obliged Mr. Gatti's to make the necessary structural alterations to make the rest rooms accessible to disabled patrons in compliance with the ADA, based on the specific layout and structural designs for the restaurants specified in the franchise agreements.[40]

The corporate representatives alleged that the franchiser did not own or operate the individual restaurant in Corpus Christi, had no control, key or access to the business, and that in essence, the franchisee was not an employee of the corporate franchiser, and thus they were not responsible for any ADA violations on the premises. Alonzo argued that because a franchisee had to get corporate approval for any changes to be made before being permitted to do so under the agreement, this gave the franchiser operational control over the store, thus making it responsible for ADA compliance. The Court of Appeals upheld the Trial Court's ruling that the corporate franchiser, Mr. Gatti's, did not exercise control over the Corpus Christi's store operations, nor had it denied approval to the store to make it ADA-accessible, and thus it was entitled to summary judgment.

Alonzo also alleged that summary judgment was improper because franchisers are responsible for ADA violations and that to allow franchisors to avoid responsibility for ADA compliance would undermine the purpose of the ADA to try to make all places of public accommodation accessible to the disabled. The Court stated that a landlord and tenant relationship would make both of those parties responsible for ADA compliance, but Mr. Gatti's was neither a landlord nor tenant of the franchised store in Corpus Christi and thus had no responsibility under the ADA, affirming the Trial Court's conclusion to the same effect.[41]

---

[40] Id. at 296.
[41] Id. at 297, 298.

2.04   What is the Standard of Compliance For Existing Facilities?

For new construction, defined as a facility constructed after January 23, 1992, hopefully the architect considered the ADA and designed their facilities accordingly. Obviously, an auditorium facility built prior to 1990 does not fully comply with the ADA. Therefore, how does the federal government measure compliance for such a facility?

1)   Commercial Facilities

For commercial facilities or privately owned facilities, the standard of compliance is what is "readily achievable." The ADA provides that:

> "Readily achievable means easily accomplishable and able to be carried out without much difficulty or expense. In determining whether an action is readily achievable, factors to be considered include- a) the nature and cost of the action needed … b) the overall financial resources of the facility or facilities involved in the action; the number of persons employed at such facility; the effect on expenses and resources or the impact otherwise of such action upon the operation of the facility; c) the overall financial resources of the covered entity; the overall size of the business of a covered entity with respect to the number of employees; the number, type and location of the facilities; and d) the type of operation or operations of the covered entity, including the composition, structure, and functions of the workforce of such entity; the geographic separateness, administrative or fiscal relationship of the facility or facilities in question to the covered entity."[42]

In *First National Bank Association v. Federal Deposit Insurance Corporation,* [43] the Federal Deposit Insurance Corporation

---

[42] 42 U.S.C. §12181(9).
[43] 79 F.3d 362 (3rd Cir. 1996).

inaccessible to Tyler. The Commission offered to give Tyler accommodations on the first floor where he could watch the meeting on television and have a "runner" communicate his concerns to the Commission, but Tyler declined this accommodation. No effort was made to relocate the meeting to the first floor, where Tyler would have been able to attend.

Tyler filed suit against the City in February of 1993, alleging numerous ADA violations. Parks had disability accessible parking, but one could not enter the park in a wheelchair due to barricades in the pathway. Restrooms at public ballparks were inaccessible to people in wheelchairs. Parts of the Zoo operated by the City were inaccessible, and accessible restrooms in the municipal courthouse were locked and required locating a key from a court employee for their use by the public.

The District Court found that Mr. Tyler was a qualified individual with disabilities, and that the City was subject to ADA compliance under Title II. The Court held that the City had failed to make an adequate transition plan as required under federal regulations. Further, the Court held that the City Commission had excluded Tyler from participation by virtue of his disability, by refusing to relocate the meeting to an accessible room. The Court also found that Tyler had been discriminated against due to the City's failure to make its public parks accessible pursuant to Title II of the ADA. The City had embarked on a comprehensive project to remove these physical barriers, with a projected completion date of September, 1994. Tyler had also been denied equal access to restroom facilities in the City's Municipal Court building in violation of Title II.

The Court found that because monetary damages were not available under Title II, and thus injunctive relief against the City was necessary in order to prevent further irreparable harm from occurring. The Court urged the City to continue with its compliance program, and then ordered the City to adopt a schedule for installing curb ramps, to conduct an adequate self-evaluation consistent with federal regulations, and to relocate ball games from an inaccessible park to an accessible field.

This case is a very good example of how the ADA mandates accessibility to the disabled to a variety of municipal activities under Title II. Programs sponsored by the City, like public meetings, must be held in accessible meeting places. City-run recreational facilities and public buildings must be accessible, from the parking lot through the front door and into the office areas where services are available. Restrooms must be accessible in all of these places, so as not to exclude the disabled from participation. As applied to publicly run facilities, this also means that care must be taken to assure adequate disability parking, curb cuts to allow access to the sidewalks surrounding the facility, accessible doorways into the facility, and access to all floors, restrooms, concessions and ticket counters within the facility.

2.05   Accessible Routes – Barrier Removal

All primary entrances to a building, facility, an event, exhibit booth, shop or location must be accessible to people with disabilities. For new construction, facilities constructed after January 23, 1992, the maximum slope of a ramp should be 1:12. Barriers to access include such things as door lips, objects protruding aisles, a hinged swinging door less than 32" in width, and other impediments. The entrance for the disabled should be located at the front of the building, tent or temporary structure and should be the same entrance used by those people without disabilities.

1)   Passenger Loading Zones
Where passenger-loading zones are provided, at least one of these zones must be accessible. However, the requirements for a passenger-loading zone vary for each function that they serve. For example, a restaurant passenger-loading zone will be different from an airport passenger-loading zone.

For the mobility impaired, ramps are required for access to a building or other structure not at ground or street level. The least possible slope shall be used for a ramp. Where an accessible route that has a slope greater then 1:20, it is considered to be a ramp and must comply the specifications set forth in ADAAG Survey Forms, which are available from the Access Board.

2) Parking

There is a graduated scale for the number of accessible parking spaces required under the American with Disabilities Act Accessibility Guidelines ("ADAAG"). Generally, one disability parking space must be provided for the first 25 spaces and one disability space thereafter for every 50 parking spaces up to 500 spaces. From 501 to 1000, 2 percent of the total is required by the regulations. For 1001 parking spaces, you must have 20 accessible spaces plus 1 additional space for each 100 spaces provided over 1000 spaces.

Accessible parking spaces (disability parking) serving a particular building shall be located on the shortest accessible route of travel from the parking lot to the accessible entrance to the building. The Disability Parking spaces shall be designated as reserved by a sign showing the International Symbol of Accessibility. Parking spaces and access aisles shall be level with surface slopes not exceeding 2 percent in all directions. For more information on parking, see ADAAG Survey Form No. 1.

✓ Operational Pointer – The facility should have a written pamphlet or guide for people with disabilities. This guide should state that "Disability parking is available and a valid disability parking permit is required to park in the area."

3) Ramps

For the mobility impaired, ramps are required for access to a building or other structure not at ground or street level. The least possible slope shall be used for a ramp. Where an accessible route that has a slope greater then 1:20, it is considered to be a ramp and must comply the specifications set forth in ADAAG Survey Form No. 7

4) Entrances and Internal Hallways and Doors

For individuals with disabilities, accessible entrances and circulation within a public facility must be provided. This means that attention must be paid not only to the entrances and exits to the facility, but also the pathway from area to area within the building, including hall width, floor covering, obstacles, doors, or thresholds that might inhibit access. A "path of travel" includes a continuous, unobstructed way of pedestrian passage by means of which the altered area may be approached, entered and exited, and which connects the altered area with the exterior approach (including sidewalks, streets, and parking areas), an entrance to the facility and other parts of the facility.[47] The path of travel also includes the restrooms, telephones, and drinking fountains serving the area.

There should be at least one accessible path of travel from the entrance to the facility to all spaces within the facility.

In newer buildings, at least 50 percent of the entrances must be accessible. For buildings constructed prior to January 1992, at least one entrance must be accessible to those with disabilities. Entrances that are not accessible should provide signage to the nearest accessible entrance. This also means that there should be a clear path of travel over the threshold of the doorway, and that any existing thresholds ¾" high should have beveled edges on each side to allow a wheelchair to pass through them without difficulty. Doorways must be at least 36 inches wide to allow a wheelchair to pass through. Additionally, doors should not be so heavy that a wheelchair bound person could not operate them, or they should have an assistive opening system to allow access. All internal doorways, hallways and passageways should be at least 36 inches in width. Any protruding object, such as a telephone attached to the walls should not impede access, and thus these areas must exceed 36 inches in width. This means that to check the width of the hallway in such an area, one must measure from the edge of the protruding object to the opposite wall to ensure enough room for accessible passage.

Carpet or carpet tile on floors must be securely attached, have a firm cushion or pad or none at all, and a pile of no more than ½ inch. Exposed edges of the carpeting must be fastened to the floor and have trim along the entire length of any exposed edges. This means that any high pile, low-density carpet that would prevent a wheelchair from freely rolling should be replaced in the public areas.

Please refer to ADAAG Survey Forms 10, 11 and 12 for additional information, including information regarding door opening and closing specifications.

---

[47] 28 C.F.R. Sec. 36.403 (e)

5) Elevators

Elevators are essential to allow those with disabilities to access different floors of a facility. Thus, most of the guidelines and specifications for elevators are critical to those with disabilities, and are somewhat obvious in nature. Elevators must be located on an accessible route (see above for hallway guidelines). Elevators must have automatic operation with a self-leveling feature to bring the car within ½ inch of the main floor and have call buttons 42 inches above the floor, with visual signals showing that the "call" has been registered, and answered.

Buttons, inside and outside the car must be at least ¾ inch in the smallest dimension, and the up button shall be located on top. Buttons may be raised or flush with the wall.

Hall signs will indicate which car is answering the call, with audible signals indicating one sound for up and two sounds for down, or provide oral announcements of up or down. All elevators should have raised and braille indicators of the floor number on both doorjambs, 60 inches above the finished floor. There must be a minimum of five seconds between the signal that the car is answering a call, and the close of the elevator doors, with a minimum full and complete opening time of the doors of three seconds.

The floor area of the elevator must provide a space for wheelchair users to enter, and maneuver within reach of the controls, and exit the car. This means the entrance must be at least 36 inches wide, and the car itself must be at least 68 inches by 51 inches. Floor surfaces must comply with hallway floor regulations (see above). Illumination of a minimum of 5 foot-candles must be provided, and interior buttons must have raised or tactile indications, and must be no higher that 54 inches above the finished floor. In addition, internal indicators of car position, i.e. floor indicators must be present, indicating visually and by sound when floors are passed.

A good example of a case where elevators were required to be installed by a public facility is in the recent settlement between the Department of Justice and the occupiers of 3Com Park. The Department of Justice entered into a settlement agreement with the San Francisco Forty-Niners and the San Francisco Giants in September of 1996, after a disabled individual complained about the lack of accessibility to events at 3Com Park. In order to improve accessibility, the Giants, the

Forty-Niners and the City of San Francisco agreed to install an elevator for use by persons with disabilities; renovate restrooms to make them accessible; provide accessible drinking fountains; add additional accessible seating and companion seating; upgrade signage; remove protruding barriers; install an assistive listening system; TDD service was to be installed; and the teams were to provide employee training in non-discriminatory services to assist those with disabilities. Additionally, ticket windows and concession counters were agreed to be altered to allow access, and additional accessible parking would be provided.

A lift to the dugout, and accessibility to all skyboxes were to be completed as well. Please consult ADAAG Survey Form 13, which includes additional elevator specifications.

In *Coalition of Montanans Concerned with Disabilities, Inc. v. Gallatin Airport Authority*,[48] the Coalition of Montanans Concerned with Disabilities ("Coalition") sued the Airport Authority over whether the expansion of the Airport complied with the Americans with Disabilities Act ("ADA"). The Airport started a three-phase 8.7 million-dollar expansion of the terminal.

The project involved both remodeling the existing portions of the terminal and constructing additions onto the terminal. The added parts of the building would comprise about one-half to two-thirds of the finished building. During Phase I, the Airport Authority moved the restaurant and the bar from the ground floor to the mezzanine level, which is about three feet (and five or six steps) above the second floor level. The existing elevator went only to the second floor and not to the mezzanine level. This situation presented a problem of how the mobility impaired would have access to the restaurant and bar. In order to solve this problem, the Airport proposed installing a platform lift that would raise wheelchairs the three feet necessary for access. The Coalition was opposed with this solution. The members of the Coalition claimed that the use of a platform lift discriminates against the disabled by forcing them to use different facilities than the public. Testimony was presented to the Court that lifts are not always reliable and sometimes malfunction, stranding people on the lift and forcing people to call for help. During the planning of Phase I, the Coalition met with the Airport and expressed their concerns about the lift. Despite the objections, the Airport went

---

[48] 957 F. Supp 1166 (D. Mont. 1997).

In *Hodges v. BP Exploration and Oil, Inc.*, [52] BP had several retail facilities in California, and was sued by Hodges regarding the lack of accommodations for people with mobility disabilities at BP service stations, shops and foodmarts, under the ADA. The parties decided to settle the suit by entering into a consent decree to achieve improvements in access to the BP Stations and shops. The Court declined to make any findings regarding the alleged ADA violations, or of any other law or regulation, nor did the parties need to admit any guilt.

Tosco, the franchisee of the BP stations, was given two years in which to bring all stations constructed after January 26, 1993 into compliance with the ADA accessibility guidelines, and that all stations altered after January 26, 1992 will be made accessible to the extent feasible.

For stations constructed before 1993, and not altered after 1992, Tosco will remove all architectural barriers at each station, including provision of access ramps into the stores, accessible parking spaces in the parking areas, and doors and doorways allowing disability access. Counters will be changed to be accessible, and in the meantime, portable-writing surfaces will be provided to customers in wheelchairs or scooters. Aisles were to be widened to allow access, and ramps and necessary changes to make rest rooms accessible were to be made.[53] Pass-through doors, where used, will be within ADA reach requirements, gas pumps will comply with reach requirements, as will the credit card readers. Additionally, all pay phones would be required to come into compliance. Within 90 days from entry of the consent decree, station attendants would provide assistance in fueling to individuals with disabilities at self-serve prices, and assist with water and tire air needs as necessary. Sales assistance will be given, unless only one employee was on duty. Compliance with the decree would consist of semi-annual reports, and would provide $20,000 for Plaintiff's counsel to monitor compliance. Hodges also collected $8,000 and attorney's fees for her non-ADA claims under the decree. Hodges had to agree to dismiss her suit and agree never to commence another suit against them in the future. 149 stations were covered to various degrees.

---

[52] No. C95-02215 JLQ (BZ), 1997 U.S. Dist. LEXIS 15199 (N.D. Cal. July 9, 1997).
[53] Id. at *14.

✓ Operational Pointer – Please keep in mind that the ticket counters and refreshment counters are the services that "set-the-tone of accessibility" because they are usually the first services provided to the disabled. Also please do not set up a separate table for the disabled outside the ticket booths and have a person shuttle back and forth from the ticket booth to the table. First, when the booth gets busy, the ticket seller forgets about the disabled persons and second, it looks like a second-rate make-shift operation.

13) Restaurant Tables

Almost every public assembly facility today includes at least one restaurant. Concerning restaurant tables in your facility, at least 5 percent of the tables must be accessible. May I suggest that the tables have at least 32" to 34" between the bottom edge of the table and the floor. (See 4.32 of the ADAAG).

Many motorized wheelchairs cannot fit under a table that is 28" above the finished floor. Please note that these tables should be reserved for the disabled until the entire room is filled to capacity.

14) Dressing, Fitting and Locker Rooms

Under the Accessibility Guidelines, a wheelchair bound patron should be able to make a 180-degree turn in a dressing room without interference from any door. A bench must be provided, and where provided, full-length mirrors should be available allowing a seated or standing person a full view of the mirror.

15) First Aid Stations

First aid stations should be located on an accessible level of the facility and should comply with doorway and hallway accessibility guidelines, where provided. While the accessibility guidelines specifical-ly cover medical facilities where a person may stay longer than 24 hours, First aid Stations should be accessible to those with disabilities.

auxiliary aids will be improved, and advertising of the availability of the above services will be included in all Disney advertising.[56]

In *Naiman v. New York University*, [57] a deaf patient sued New York University Medical Center (NYUMC) under the ADA, alleging that the Center effectively excluded him from the facility by failing to provide sign language interpreters during his visits to the center.[58] NYUMC moved to dismiss the claim. The patient had sought treatment at the Center for a kidney stone attack, and requested, but was not provided with a sign language interpreter.

On a second visit, a person who was eventually presented could not understand the patient or communicate effectively in sign.[59] On third and fourth visits, no interpreter was provided. The patient claimed an interpreter was needed in order to effectively communicate with the NYUMC doctors and staff, and claims that he is effectively prohibited from communicating with the staff in the future unless an interpreter is available. NYU admitted it was a public accommodation under the ADA but claimed that the patient did not have a claim because he did receive effective medical care during his visits despite his inability to communicate with the staff.[60] NYU also admitted that it was subject to the Rehabilitation Act, which required that auxiliary aids be provided to allow people equal opportunity to benefit from the service in question. The Court held that the patient had stated a valid claim under the ADA and Rehabilitation Act and refused to dismiss the claim.[61]

In *Clarkson et. al. v. Coughlin*,[62] male and female deaf and hard-of-hearing inmates in New York's Department of Corrections (DOCS) sued for the failure of the Department to provide them with adequate accommodations for their disability, including the provision of interpreters, TDD telephone systems, closed-captioning systems and visual safety alarms. The Department was encouraged by state regulations to provide telephone and television services to inmates, yet closed

---

[56] DOJ settlement with Walt Disney World, <http://www.usdoj.gov/drt/ada/disney.htm>.
[57] No. 95 Civ. 6469 (LMM) 1997 U.S. Dist. LEXIS 6616 (S.D. N.Y. May 13, 1997).
[58] Id. at *1.
[59] Id. at *3.
[60] Id. at *6
[61] Id. at *16.
[62] 898 F.Supp. 1019 (S.D. N.Y. 1995).

captioning decoders which allow "subtitles" to be printed on the screen for spoken text on TV or film were not provided, and some inmates had to make phone calls using third party prison officials with amateur signing skills as intermediaries. The Court found that the Department had violated the ADA, Rehabilitation Act, and the Equal Protection clause of the Constitution by failing to provide adequate interpretive services for the deaf, just as if they had failed to provide a translator for a Spanish-only speaking inmate. Further, the inmates had been penalized by not being allowed access to telephone or television privileges by the inadequacies of the facilities provided by the Department in violation of the ADA.

While this case addresses inmates in a correctional facility, in any area of public accommodation, services provided to the able-bodied public are also to be provided to those with disabilities. This means that if televisions, monitors, audio announcements, or the like are made, closed captioning should be available on any monitors provided for those unable to hear the sound provided by the unit.

If feasible, any public service announcements should also be captioned on the monitors to provide notice of these announcements to the hard-of-hearing. These accommodations are essential to keep those with disabilities.

The lesson to facilities from this case is that failure to provide effective communication for those with disabilities, especially if the person will be a returning patron could be problematic in the end. This should not require facilities to provide interpreters at every event, but should particularly require interpreters to be available if safety or medical issues exist.

✓ Operational Pointer – Sign language interpreters will not always be available. Therefore, security personnel, guest services and ushers should carry small tablets and writing instruments to communicate when necessary with people who have hearing disabilities. These writing materials should also be available to assist the facility worker in completing standard incident reports.

3) Public Telephones

Accessible Telephones include amplification capability and TDD/TTY capability (keyboard). At least one telephone unit with both capabilities should be available on each level of your facility for use by any patron. This will allow the deaf or hard of hearing to have access to telephone services. These units are not prohibitively expensive and are required under the ADAAG, Section 4.1.3. Signage is also required for all the above under ADAAG Section 4.30.

4) Signage

Signage must also comply with the ADA, and letters on signs must be at least 3 inches tall. Where feasible, Braille signage should be made available, or a person should be available to assist those with visual difficulties. ADAAG Survey Form contains additional specifications regarding signage requirements.

✓ Operational Pointer – Please note that state, city and local laws also apply to signs in parking lots and numerous other places. Therefore, you must check the ADA, state, local municipal laws, and ordinances.

5) Written Information

Where applicable, large print and/or Braille menus should be made available for those with sight impairments. If written brochures and information sheets are available or handed out to the public, a few large print and/or Braille copies should also be made available. There are no current regulations regarding typeface, type size or the like regarding written materials (exclusive of signs), but your facility may desire to take a pro-active approach and make this information available to those with sight impairments.

6) Service Animals

Service animals are an integral part of mobility for many people with sight disabilities, and are even employed to help some people with mobility impairments. The Department of Justice has been clear that wherever feasible, service animals should be allowed and accommodated, including in restaurant facilities. There have been a large number of lawsuits where an owner of an establishment has had a policy forbidding animals and extended this to include service animals, relying on FDA regulations and the like. In each case, the Courts have ruled that under the ADA, the service animal must be allowed to accompany their master. Please make every attempt to accommodate those with service animals.

In *Johnson v. Gambrinus Company/Spoetzl Brewery*,[63] a blind person accompanied by a guide dog was denied entrance to a brewery tour at the Spoetzl Brewery in Texas. Mr. Johnson, his guide dog and two friends visited the brewery in order to take the tour. A tour guide saw the dog and called the brewmaster, who confirmed no animals were allowed on the tour. This policy was based on the brewery's interpretation of Food and Drug Administration regulations. The tour guide informed Johnson that he would not be allowed on the tour with his dog.

Johnson insisted that he had a legal right to take the tour with his guide dog, but the brewery refused to budge on its no animal policy.[64] Johnson then waited outside while his friends took the tour.

While Johnson could have waited in the hospitality room for his friends, the tour guide neglected to inform him of this, even though the blanket no animal policy also applied to the hospitality room.

Johnson subsequently filed suit under Title III of the ADA and Texas law. The trial court determined that the blanket no animals policy was not compelled by any law and violated the ADA, and ordered the Brewery to establish practices or procedures to assure that disabled guests with service animals had the broadest possible access to the public tour "consistent with the brewery's safe operation". The Brewery and its owners appealed, alleging primarily that it could not be held liable for a violation of state law when the federal FDA regulations mandated its actions.

The Court of Appeals affirmed the District Court's findings, stating that the brewery tour, a public accommodation under Title III of the ADA, was not compelled by FDA to prohibit all animals on the tour, and that allowing the animal would not fundamentally alter the nature of the public accommodation. The Court stressed the importance of service animals to their masters, that a person should never be involuntarily

---

[63] 116 F.3d 1052 (5th Cir. 1997).
[64] Id. at 1056.

separated from their animal, and that such animals were not equivalent to normal "pets" and thus could not be excluded under a "no pets" policy. Further, the Court noted that contamination of the brewing process was much more likely to occur from the 5,800 annual tourists than from the one request they had received to bring a guide dog on the tour, and that the overall risk of contamination from visitors or a guide dog was extremely small. Through a detailed analysis of both the brewing process and the tour, it was determined that a guide dog would pose no risk that would subject the Brewery to a citation from the Texas Board of Health or the FDA, after a subsequent placement of a glass partition between the pre-sealed bottles and the tourists.

Other accommodations are often requested by those with disabilities, besides the specific equipment or assistance needs mentioned above.

To a certain extent, personalized service and attention can help diffuse potentially contentious situations, turning them into win-win situations for all parties. If this middle ground is reached, the disabled patron is happy, the facility is happy, and the patron will have a positive feeling about his experience, resulting in positive public relations, the goal of any facility manager.

2.07   Assembly Seating – General

Seating is one the most important issues under the ADA for facility managers. The scoping requirements for seating directly affect the facility's revenue and "bottom line."

The applicable section of the ADAAG that applies to seating states:

"Wheelchair areas shall be an integral part of any fixed seating plan and shall be provided so as to provide people with physical disabilities a choice of admission prices and lines of sight comparable to those for members of the general public. At least one companion fixed seat shall be provided next to each wheelchair seating area. When seating capacity exceeds 300, wheelchair spaces shall be provided in more than one location."

In 1996, the Department of Justice entered into a settlement agreement under the ADA with the Atlanta Committee for the Olympic Games to ensure accessibility for the disabled. The facilities built for the games were to be used for major league baseball after the games had ended. The Atlanta Committee agreed through the facilities to install wheelchair-seating locations to meet the 1 percent of total seating requirement both in the "Olympic" configuration and baseball configuration. Companion seating was to be next to the disabled person, rather than in seats above or below the wheelchair seating space. Lines of sight were required to allow sight over standing spectators, and dispersal of seating locations throughout the stadium was also mandated. Restrooms were required to be accessible, as were portable toilets, shower stalls, dressing rooms, locker rooms, and storage facilities.

The dugout was required to be accessible, as were the camera platforms, and other employee work areas.

Perhaps the most interesting fact about this settlement is that one of the architectural firms involved with the construction of the facilities was Ellerbe Becket, which has had substantial problems with the accessibility to the facilities it has designed, including the Rose Garden in Portland, Oregon and the MIC Center in Washington, D.C., both subjects of recent court decisions regarding ADA violations.

The DOJ entered into a settlement agreement with the Mississippi Coliseum, in which the Mississippi Fair Commission and Department of Finance and Administration will, in its renovations of the facility, make 1 percent of the 10,000 seats accessible to those in wheelchairs, provide required companion seating, disperse this seating throughout the facility, and provide lines of sight for the disabled over standing spectators. The State is also to provide accessible restrooms, concession stands, and parking lots, institute new ticketing policies for accessible seating, and train staff on the ADA, including the appointment of ADA coordinators to assist those with disabilities.

1) Assembly Seating and "Comparable Lines of Sight"

A topic that has received a lot of attention recently has been the seating design in sports facilities that allow equal access to individuals with disabilities. General requirements state that seating in facilities with over 300 fixed seats should be dispersed throughout the seating area, and allow a line of sight comparable to that with non-disabled individuals. This has become a contested issue as to whether wheelchair seating must provide a line of sight over standing patrons because in many instances, people stand at their seats at concerts and sporting events blocking the view of wheelchair bound patrons, and as to whether adequate dispersal throughout the facility may actually pose a hazard to both the disabled person and the able-bodied public also attending the event.

In *Fiedler v. American Multi-Cinema Inc.,*[65] a quadriplegic patron sought to have an operator of cinemas in Union Station in Washington, D.C. provide a variety of seating for disabled persons in wheel chairs in its theaters, instead of locating all wheel chair accessible seating in the rear.[66] Despite AMC's assertions it was immune from suit as it was renting space from the Department of Transportation,[67] the Court held that the ADA did apply to this "place of public accommodation." The Court stated that:

> "By its terms, however, Title III of the ADA applies to a "place of public accommodation," which in turn is defined as "a facility, operated by a private entity, whose operations affect commerce and fall within at least one of the following categories . . . (3) a motion picture house, theater, concert hall, stadium or other place of exhibition or entertainment."[68]

The theater here was, without question, a motion picture house operated by a private entity, and by regulation, had been declared to affect commerce. The Court thus concluded that the AMC Theater

---

[65] 871 F. Supp. 35 (U.S. D.C. 1994).
[66] Id. at 36.
[67] Id. at 36, 37.
[68] 28 C.F.R. § 36.104, see also 42 U.S.C. §12181(7) (c).

was a "place of public accommodation" subject to Title III of the ADA and added:

> "Moreover, the ADA itself expressly contem-
> plates that entities to which it applies might be
> subject to two or more separate sets of obliga-
> tions with respect to their treatment of handi-
> capped patrons. . . . AMC maintained that the
> provisions of the ABA [Architectural Barriers
> Act] and the ADA may potentially conflict
> with one another, but have made no showing
> here that its compliance with the ADA in this
> case would be inconsistent with any obliga-
> tion it may also have inherited under the ABA
> as a lessee of a federal landlord."[69]

The Court held that notwithstanding the federal government's fee simple ownership of the leased property, the ADA was applicable to AMC.

AMC further asserted that providing several wheelchair access-ible seats throughout the theater could pose a safety hazard to able-bodied persons in the event of an emergency.[70] While the ADA does state in the regulations that to the extent it is readily achievable, wheel-chair seating spaces are to be dispersed throughout the seating area, provide lines of sight and choice of admission prices comparable to those for the general public, adjoin a route for egress in an emergency and to permit individuals in wheelchairs to sit with companions,[71] it also states that "individualized assessments" must be made of the facility. AMC admitted that dispersion of wheelchair seating at the theater was "readily achievable" but alleged it was exempted from doing so by the Technical Regulations of the ADAAG allowing the clustering of wheelchair seating where sight lines require slopes greater than 5 percent. This would mean that if the grade of the floor exceeds a one-inch rise in twenty inches of horizontal travel, a more difficult ascent for someone in

---

[69] 871 F. Supp at 38.
[70] Id.
[71] Id. at 37, quoting 42 U.S.C. §12186(b).

15 percent, and are intended to be used with lawn chairs and blankets. Caruso alleged that "comparable lines of sight" meant that enhanced lines of sight enabling wheelchair bound patrons to see over the heads of standing able-bodied patrons.[82] The Department of Justice's Technical Assistance Manual (TAM) regarding the ADA requirements was adopted after construction of the E-Centre had commenced, and there was no evidence that at the time of construction, anyone would have considered the TAM to require enhanced lines of sight.[83] However, The E-Centre did provide some wheelchair seating within the pavilion area that had sight lines over the heads of standing patrons, in greater numbers than actually required under the ADA.[84]

Additionally, the E-Centre contended that the lawn seating did not have to be made accessible to disabled patrons under the ADA because of the grade of the lawn, and because there was no fixed seating arrangement. The Court agreed, stating that the ADA did not require viewer capacity in the lawn area to be included in computing the number of wheelchair spaces and their placement. Caruso also complained that there was no accessible route to lawn seats for wheelchair users, however the E-Centre did provide higher quality seats in the pavilion at lawn-seating prices available to disabled patrons.[85] The Court held that the E-Centre had appropriately clustered the wheelchair seating in the pavilion area, and the regulations did not require enhanced lines of sight of wheel-chair users.[86]

In a recent case, *Independent Living Resources v. Oregon Arena Corp.*,[87] disabled individuals sued Oregon Arena Corp., the owners of the Rose Garden Arena in Portland, Oregon, which opened to the public in 1995. The Rose Garden serves as home for the Portland Trailblazers and the Winterhawks hockey team and hosts a variety of other events throughout the year. The disabled

---

[82] , 1997 U.S. Dist. LEXIS 9401 at *5.

[83] Id. at *16. In part, the TAM stated that "[I]n assembly areas where spectators can be expected to stand during the event or show being viewed, the wheelchair locations must provide lines of sight over spectators who stand." Id. at *6.

[84] Id. at *5, footnote 6.

[85] Id. at *25.

[86] Id. at *26

[87] No. 95-84-AS, 1997 U.S. Dist. LEXIS 18349 (D. Or. Nov. 12, 1997).

individuals maintained that the wheelchair accessible seating in the Rose Garden was limited to either "nosebleed" seats or "end-zone corner" seating, functionally limiting the accessible seating to the least desirable seats in the house, violating the requirements under Section 4.33.3 of the ADA that require adequate dispersal of accessible seating. The patrons further maintained that there were not enough disability seats available, and that many of the seats shown by the Rose Garden as accessible seats had been in-filled with seating for long-term non-disabled season ticket holders, making many of the accessible seats in the plans for the Rose Garden non-existent in reality. The patrons also alleged that existing accessible seats did not have adequate sight-lines over standing spectators, the luxury boxes or executive suites were not accessible to the disabled, and many other secondary issues. The Magistrate Judge, in an extremely detailed opinion, found that the architects for the arena, Ellerbe Becket, actively disregarded what it knew to be the Department of Justice's opinion that accessible seating must have sight lines above standing patrons. However, the Judge found that Standard 4.33.3 under the ADA did not currently require that wheelchair users be given sight lines over standing patrons, although such a regulation would be permissible under the ADA. The Access Board and the Department of Justice had not properly promulgated such a rule for sight lines, and it could not be inferred from the general non-discrimination provisions of the ADA, consistent with a prior ruling in *Caruso v. Blockbuster-Sony Entertainment Centre.*[88]

While the Judge held that the ADA had not been violated by failing to provide "enhanced lines of sight," he did hold that the Rose Garden had violated standard 4.33.3 by failing to adequately disburse and integrate accessible seating, both vertically and horizontally, into the permanent seating plan, but instead inappropriately clustered wheelchair seating into less desirable areas.

This problem had been further complicated by the Trailblazers selling long term season tickets for four and five year periods to ambulatory patrons and in-filling accessible seating areas with risers to accommodate ambulatory patrons, freezing disabled patrons out of blocks of accessible seating in desirable areas of the Arena, and instead having ticket agents steer disabled patrons into less desirable areas of the Arena.

---

[88] 968 F.Supp. 210 (D. NJ 1997).

The Judge reviewed the huge financial advantage this held for the Arena, replacing 33 accessible seats and their companion seating with 1,028 ambulatory seats, leading to an extra $2 million in ticket revenues over a basketball season alone. The Arena had maintained that they were allowed to in-fill once a particular class of tickets were sold out, where the Department of Justice maintained that the appropriate requirement regarding in-fill was that all tickets must be sold out before in-fill into wheelchair accessible seating is allowed. The Judge did not rule on the in-fill and ticket sale policy, but instead requested further information from both sides before rendering a decision on the issue.

The Judge did grant a partial summary judgment to the Oregon Arena Corporation, ruling that the high-quality Clarin folding chairs for companion seating were an adequate "equivalent facilitation" and were as comfortable as the regular fixed arena seats. The Judge also held that the luxury boxes were public accommodations subject to ADA regulations, not private clubs, and each suite must be made accessible and include a visual alarm in case of fire or emergency. Lastly, the camera positions in the Arena were also required to be accessible, the parking garages needed to comply with the standards governing protruding objects, and self-service food carts present in the Arena did not violate the standards regarding protruding objects.

It was clear from the Judge's opinion that the architectural firm had been aware of the Department of Justice's interpretation of the line of sight requirement but actively ignored this "warning" in its design and construction of the Rose Garden. While the Judge held the letter of the law did not currently require enhanced sight lines, it did not condone the design of the Rose Garden, especially since the Trailblazers actively encouraged patrons to stand by flashing messages on its scoreboard to that effect, thus taking an active role in potentially limiting the sight of disabled patrons at an event.

While the important issue of enhanced sight lines was decided in favor of the Arena, the Arena clearly failed to adequately disperse accessible seating and most likely further complicated the situation by its in-fill interpretation, further limiting the seats available to disabled patrons. The message to all facility owners is that it is required under the ADA to disperse accessible seating vertically (i.e. on all levels) and horizontally (i.e. in all sections as feasible) to give disabled patrons an adequate choice of seating with different prices and visual access to the event. Further, in-fill into "unused" accessible seating must be done very carefully, and that it is most likely improper to in-fill seating on a semi-permanent basis with long-term ambulatory season ticket holders. Finally, skyboxes or other luxury suite seating must also be accessible to the disabled on a permanent basis rather than by requiring advanced notification of a disabled patron's arrival.

This case, along with the MCI Center case above, shows that currently wheelchair seating with enhanced sight lines over standing patrons should be available, but it appears that not every wheelchair seat needs to have this sight line. Clearly, an attempt should be made by the facility to have the best sight line available to disabled patrons, while also distributing the seating throughout the facility and making accessible seating available at comparable prices to those paid by the general public. However, it appears that not every single seat must have superior sight lines under the current court cases.

In *Johanson v. Huizenga Holdings, Inc.,* [89] two disabled minors and a parent filed an ADA claim against Broward County and others involved in planning and constructing the Broward Arena, future home of the Florida Panthers, claiming that as planned, the arena will violate the ADA. The potential patrons were Panthers' fans and had purchased tickets in the past, and claimed that the released plans for the arena contained several ADA violations. The County alleged that the Plaintiffs did not have grounds to bring the complaint since the arena was not yet built, but the Court held that Title III of the ADA allowed the right to sue in anticipation of a violation, and the architect hired by the County had built arenas in the past which had violated the ADA. The Plaintiff's claims thus withstood the Motions to Dismiss filed by the Defendants.

It is important to note that facilities *even in the planning stages* can be sued under the ADA for failure to comply. Multiple cases have been presented regarding seating plans and the like, showing that it is very important to begin reviewing ADA requirements and perhaps seeking expert review of proposed facilities during the design phase of the project.

---

[89] 963 F.Supp. 1175 (S.D. Fla. 1997).

In *Arnold v. United Artists Theatre Circuit, Inc.*, [90] the Plaintiffs sought to file a class action suit against United Artists Theatres on behalf of disabled persons in wheelchairs or who walk with aides such as crutches, charging that the theaters did not offer equal access to disabled people in violation of both federal and state law.[91] United Artists operated more than 70 theaters in California and the Plaintiffs challenged the accessibility to these facilities under the Americans with Disabilities Act [92] and the California Disabled Persons Act.[93] Under the ADA, any facility constructed or last remodeled before January 26, 1993, the effective date of the ADA's requirements regarding new construction, owners are required to remove architectural barriers that are structural in nature, where such removal is readily achievable and where the barriers interfere with the disabled person's full and equal enjoyment of the facilities.[94] The Plaintiffs charged that the UA theaters built or remodeled before January 26, 1993 failed to make the changes necessary to achieve "full and equal enjoyment" of the facilities by disabled people by failing to create an adequate number of wheelchair accessible seats sufficiently integrated with the main seating area, and for theaters over 300 seats, the seating was not dispersed as required under the regulations; removable barriers to accessible paths of travel had not been done; and modifications of restroom facilities were necessary to ensure access. The Plaintiffs stated that in all the theaters, the wheelchair seating was only located in the back row. Under the California Code, seating for disabled individuals is required to be accessible from the main lobby, together with accessible bathroom facilities.

Similarly to the ADA, the California code also requires level seating and in theaters over 300 seats, disbursed seating is required. Each space must be 60 inches long and 30 inches wide, and it permitted readily removable seats to be placed in the handicapped spaces when not in use. Sufficient integration with non-disabled seating was required so that disabled persons could sit with their family and companions rather than being

---

[90] 158 F.R.D. 439 (N.D. Cal. 1994).
[91] Id. at 443.
[92] 42 U.S.C. §12101.
[93] California Civil Code § 54.1.
[94] 158 F.R.D. at 444.

relegated to a different section of the facility. Likewise, the Plaintiffs alleged that the UA theaters failed to comply with the seating requirements under the California Code.

Under the Federal Rules of Civil Procedure, in order to file a class action suit, there must be:

a. a class so numerous joining all parties is impractical;
b. common questions of law or fact common to the class;
c. the claims or defenses of parties are similar and typical to the class; and
d. the represented parties will fairly represent and adequately protect the interests of the class.

The party moving for class certification has the burden of showing the requirements that have been satisfied. The Plaintiffs showed that there were at least 175,000 wheelchair bound citizens in California, and an additional 700,000 semi-ambulatory people, whom the Court found met the numerous requirement. Likewise, the issues of discrimination in seating arrangements in the theaters under the ADA and California Code were significantly similar between all members of the class to meet the Commonality requirement. Further, the claims of the representative parties were typical of any member of the class and their interests were not in any way conflicting with other members of the class as to prohibit class certification. The Court did find that class certification was inappropriate for individual "deterrence" claims where the deterrence was based on the individuals actual visits to the theater, and were individually specific, meaning that the plaintiffs would need to pursue these claims individually, rather than as a class.

Most of the plaintiffs' claims were eligible for class certification based on the similarity of the claims of each individual, should they choose to sue UA individually. The court did exclude the relatives and companions of disabled persons from the class, since the ADA and California code provisions allowed damages to be awarded solely to the injured parties, and could not be extended to the people who accompany disabled people to theaters.

The plaintiffs also moved to bifurcate the trial, or split it as to issues of liability, with injunctive relief and damages to be litigated first, and if liability was found, then the issue of class damages was to be addressed. The Court also granted this motion.

2) Wheelchair Space Clusters

People with mobility difficulties are often sensitive to being clustered into one area of a theater or assembly area, feeling isolated from the group as a whole, or otherwise feeling apart from the main action or event. Regulations currently address clustering, and state that in any seating area over 300 seats, disability seating should be provided, as feasible, in a variety of locations, rather than clustered in one area. In *Independent Living Resources v. Oregon Arena Corp.,* [95] disabled individuals sued Oregon Arena Corp., the owners of the Rose Garden Arena in Portland, Oregon, which opened to the public in 1995. The disabled individuals maintained that the wheelchair accessible seating in the Rose Garden was limited to either "nosebleed" seats or "end-zone corner" seating, functionally limiting the accessible seating to the least desirable seats in the house, violating the requirements under Section 4.33.3 of the ADA that require adequate disbursal of accessible seating. While the Judge held that the ADA had not been violated by failing to provide "enhanced lines of sight," he did hold that the Rose Garden had violated standard 4.33.3 by failing to adequately disburse and integrate accessible seating, both vertically and horizontally, into the permanent seating plan, but instead inappropriately clustered wheelchair seating into less desirable areas.

3) Companion Seating

Currently, companion seating for those accompanying the disabled must be next to the wheelchair accessible seating, not in front of or behind the wheelchair seat. The purpose of this regulation is to keep friends and families together, rather than requiring them to be seated separately.

As you can imagine, it is important to those with disabilities to be treated like everyone else as nearly as possible, and thus side by side seating is very important to them.

Also in *Independent Living Resources v. Oregon Arena Corp.,* [96] cited above, the disabled patrons further maintained that there were not enough disability seats available, and that many of the seats shown by the Rose Garden as accessible seats had been in-filled with seating for long-term non-disabled season ticket holders, making many of the accessible

---

[95] No. 95-84-AS, 1997 U.S. Dist. LEXIS 18349 (D. Or. Nov. 12, 1997),
[96] No. 95-84-AS, 1997 U.S. Dist. LEXIS 18349 (D. Or. Nov. 12, 1997).

seats in the plans for the Rose Garden non-existent in reality. Originally, the architects had designed the companion seating to be in a separate row from the disability seating. The Court held that this method of accommodation was not acceptable and that side by side companion seating is required under the ADA.

On March 3, 1998, DOJ entered into a settlement agreement with SCOPE Arena in Norfolk, Virginia regarding accessibility under the ADA. SCOPE Arena is a venue for hockey, basketball, circus and concert events, and was found inaccessible under the ADA after a DOJ investigation following a complaint from a disabled patron. Norfolk is required under the agreement to provide accessible seating and companion seats around the seating bowl; provide fully accessible parking; modify floor surfaces, ticket counters, ramps, and stairs to be accessible; make all restrooms accessible; and provide accessible floor seating when floor seating is employed for an event. Norfolk must also advertise the availability of accessible seating and modify its ticket policy so that accessible seats and companion seats will not be sold to non-disabled patrons until all other seats are sold out, or until 5:00 pm the day prior to an event, and that seats in front of an accessible area will also not be sold until all other seats are sold out, in order to provide those with disabilities a line of sight over the head of standing spectators. All such changes are to be made by April 27, 1998.

4) In-fill Seating

Under the ADA, the in-filling of unsold wheelchair accessible seats and companion seats is permitted. In fact, the ADA Accessibility Guidelines ("ADAAG"), Section 4.33.3, "Placement of Wheelchair Locations" permits in-filling of ambulatory seats by stating "Readily removable seats may be installed in wheelchair spaces when the spaces are not required to accommodate wheelchair users." In several cases, the Department of Justice has taken the position that seats for disabled patrons should be held open up until 24 hours before the event if the event has not been sold out. In addition, in a letter to Mr. Paul Tagliabue, the Commissioner of the NFL, from Mr. Deval Patrick, the Assistant United States Attorney General, Mr. Patrick states in part, that "… The Standards recognize that not every wheelchair location will be sold for every game. Wheelchair locations may be filled in with temporary, readily removable seats if they are not needed for wheelchair users.

Before wheelchair locations can be replaced with other seating, however, all other seats in the stadium must first be sold...."

In addition, Mr. Patrick's October 1996 interpretation that all seating in the stadium must first be sold in order to convert the wheelchair seating to ambulatory seats has not been decided or confirmed by any federal court. The better ticketing policy which has been discussed in the Rose Garden Arena case is one in which once a stadium or arena section on a level is sold out, then the stadium may convert the wheelchair seats in that section to ambulatory seats. However, the law on this issue is not clear. In the Rose Garden Arena case, the Judge stated:

> "...it is understandable that an arena operator may seek to minimize the loss of seats and revenue by clustering several wheelchairs in a single wheelchair area–and in-filling the remaining wheelchair locations–instead of each wheelchair occupying a different wheelchair area (that is designed to hold five or six wheelchairs) which effectively precludes in-filling any of those wheelchair locations. This presents a classic public policy question: ... However, neither the statute (the ADA) nor the applicable regulation has delineated precisely where that line is drawn, ..."[97]

The issue as to proper in-fill procedure is not settled, and we ask that you err on the side of caution with any in-fill seating policy or procedure you choose to implement.

5) Suite Seats or Box Seats

Seats located in private suites or boxes are considered separate from the public seats in the stadium or arena. The disability box seats are not counted towards to the total disability seating and the non-disability seats are not counted towards the total seating capacity in the facility. However, several cases have held that luxury boxes or suites must be accessible to people in wheelchairs.

---

[97] 1997 U.S. Dist. LEXIS 18349, 71

6) Arena Floor Seating

With assembly floor seating, the largest concern is making sure that any accessible seating adjoins an accessible route for egress in case of an emergency. While the overall ADA seating requirements refer to fixed seating and not to mobile, temporary, floor seating arrangements, there will be times, such as during conventions, where assembly floor seating is the only seating utilized. In such cases, assuring accessibility for any disabled guests will be necessary, and attempts should be made to provide them with several seating options, rather than clustering the seating in any one area, or in the back of the hall. Attempts should be made to determine how many people with disabilities would need to be accommodated ahead of time, so that appropriate arrangements can be made in the seating plan.

7) Lawn and Open Air Seating

Lawn and open air seating arrangements have been the subject of recent litigation in the *Caruso v. Blockbuster-Sony Entertainment Centre* case, discussed more fully above. Currently, the interpretation favored by the Federal District Court in *Caruso* was that the lawn seating area was a) not fixed seating, so it did not clearly have to meet the 1 percent + 1 guidelines; b) the slope of the lawn area was so great as to preclude access and c) any attempt to make the lawn area accessible to wheelchair users would be extremely costly and ruin the sloped, auditorium style lawn seating arrangement for over 18,000 patrons currently available. Unfortunately, this seating arrangement has not been specifically addressed in the ADA regulations, and thus a definitive answer on accessibility cannot be given at this time.

2.08   Accessible Activities–Education and Sports

ADA accommodations may take the form of providing access to sports activities or an equivalent education. Therefore, here we distinguish between access to services provided as addressed below and access to activities where the disabled participate in the sports event or educational activity.

In *Casey Martin v. PGA Tour, Inc.*,[98] a golfer with disabilities sought to use a golf cart during professional golf tournaments sponsored by the PGA. The PGA alleged that it was a private club and exempt from complying with the Americans with Disabilities Act (ADA), and that use of the cart would provide Martin with an unfair competitive advantage. Martin sued, seeking to enjoin the PGA from prohibiting him from using a golf cart during its third stage qualifying school event and subsequent tournaments. The Court issued an initial preliminary injunction, allowing Martin to use a cart on the 3rd part of the qualifying school and on the first two tournaments of the Nike Tour.

The PGA, a non-profit association of professional golfers, sponsors three tours: a PGA tour consisting of 200 players; a senior PGA tour consisting of 100 players 50 years old and older; and the Nike tour, consisting of 170 players. In order to obtain tour privileges, a player must first pay $3,000 and submit two letters of reference. At the first stage, 72 holes are played and carts are allowed, and if the score is low enough, the player will advance to the second stage. At this point, 72 more holes are played, again allowing carts, and the top 168 qualifiers will advance to the third stage. The third stage, in which carts had not been allowed, consists of 108 holes, with the lowest 35 scores and ties receiving PGA tour privileges, and the next 70 lowest scoring players receiving Nike Tour privileges. Martin, through his court action, was allowed to use a cart on the third stage of the qualifying event, and had a score permitting him to play on the Nike Tour, but not high enough to play on the PGA Tour. Martin also subsequently won the first Nike Tour event, but did not do well in the second such event. Those on the Nike Tour may obtain PGA tour privileges if they win three Nike Tour events or finish within the top 15 places on the money list.

Martin's disability is a rare malformation of the veins in his leg, in which the valves that permit the blood pumped into one's leg to return, against gravity, to the heart, do not function properly. This causes pooling of blood in his extremity, atrophy and weakening on the affected leg, and bone deterioration that limit is ability to walk. Martin must wear a double set of support stockings at all times when upright, and endures

---

[98] No. 97-6309-TC, 1998 U.S. Dist. LEXIS 1503 (January 30, 1998) and 1998 U.S. Dist. LEXIS 1980 (February 19, 1998).

significant pain in his leg, even at rest. Martin argued that the PGA was a private entity operating a public accommodation, and thus was required to make that accommodation accessible to those with disabilities under Title III of the ADA, or, in the alternative, acted as an employer of golfers on the tour and was subject to the "reasonable accommodations" provisions of Title I of the ADA. The PGA agreed that Martin was a qualified individual with a disability as defined under the ADA, but maintained that it was exempt from the ADA as a "private club," and did not employ Martin, and thus was not subject to the reasonable accommodation requirements of Title I.

The Court held that while the PGA was not an employer of Martin under Title I, it did operate a public accommodation under Title III, citing the tour's dependence on public interest, attendance and concurrent revenue generation for the very existence of the events. The PGA did not fall within the "private club" exception to the ADA, because they clearly operated golf courses, named as a place of public accommodation in the ADA; were a commercial enterprise as part of the entertainment industry by offering competitive events to the public in turn generating sponsors, network fees, advertising and prize money; despite selectivity in membership, membership was limited only to talented golfers, and any talented golfer meeting the requirements could join- there was no voting involved in selection of new members. Thus, while the PGA was a non-profit organization, it existed for a commercial purpose, and could not allege that it was only "public" in certain aspects of its functioning but "private" in other areas.

The Court held that under the United States Golf Association's (USGA) rules of golf and those of the Royal and Ancient Golf Club of St. Andrews, Scotland, the game consists of playing a ball from the teeing ground into the hole by a stroke or successive strokes in accordance to the rules. However, nothing in the definition of the game requires or defines walking as part of the game.

Further, the USGA rules allowed the use of a cart unless prohibited by the local rules for a particular event. The PGA argued that it prohibited carts on the third leg of the qualifying school events and on the tour to inject fatigue as a factor into the events. Martin's physician testified regarding his disability, and that by walking even short distances, Martin endured severe pain. Attempts to provide him with orthopedic corrections either inhibited his ability to play golf, or failed to improve his situation. Further, Martin's condition continued to deteriorate, and has increased the amount of pain he endures in daily living, as well as playing golf. The physician testified that even using the cart, Martin was unable to complete a round when required to walk further than usual due to wet conditions on the course. The Court concluded that allowing Martin to use a golf cart did not put him at a competitive advantage over other players, nor did it fundamentally alter the nature of the PGA's game, and thus the requested accommodation was "eminently reasonable" in light of Martin's disability.

In *Slaby v. Berkshire*, [99] a disabled golfer sought to force the country club to which he belonged to remove rope barriers around the golf course, and to increase access to several areas of the clubhouse.[100] The Club had specifically contemplated the needs of the disabled in its golf course policy, and allowed official disabled carts only within the rope barriers, and had made accommodations to allow disabled persons access to clubhouse events and locker rooms.[101] While it was clear that the golfer had standing to bring his claim, the evidence showed that the golf course was very accessible to disabled golfers and the erected barriers were only a mild inconvenience, necessary to protect the growing turf. [102] Further, the accommodations for the disabled made in the clubhouse were sufficient to discharge the club's obligations under the ADA for adapting structures, and the elevator sought by the golfer for the two story structure was not required by the ADA.[103] The Club in this case did itself a favor by specifically addressing the needs of disabled members, and making the accommodations it could.

In *Bowers v. National Collegiate Athletic Association*,[104] a student at Temple University sued the NCAA regarding its eligibility requirements, alleging that it discriminated against him in violation of the ADA and Rehabilitation Act based on his learning disability. Bowers received special assistance in high school and many courses were

---

[99] 928 F. Supp. 613 (Md. 1996); aff'd. 110 F.3d 60 (4th Cir. 1997).
[100] Id. at 613, 614.
[101] Id. at 614.
[102] Id.
[103] Id.
[104] 974 F.Supp. 459 (D. N.J. 1997).

"special education" courses, due to his learning disability. Despite his academic problems, Bowers was a talented football player, and submitted a form to the NCAA Clearinghouse, seeking certification as a "qualifier" in order to participate in athletics and be eligible for athletic scholarships for college.

The NCAA bylaws require that all of its 1200 member institutions establish minimum academic eligibility standards for students wishing to participate in collegiate athletics and to be eligible for scholarships during their freshman year. These rules were instituted to ensure proper emphasis on educational objectives, prevent exploitation of student-athletes, and promote competitive equity among institutions. The NCAA thus requires any students wishing to participate in collegiate athletics apply to the NCAA Clearinghouse for certification that such a student is qualified to participate in sports under NCAA guidelines. Any such student must have graduated from high school, pass at least thirteen classes defined as "core courses" by the NCAA with a minimum grade point average. Exempted from the core course definition are courses taught below grade level, such as special education, remedial or compensatory courses, regardless of the actual course content. The bylaws do allow special education courses for the learning disabled to fulfill the core-curriculum requirements, if the principal of the school can certify that the contents of any such courses expect the same knowledge, both quantitatively and qualitatively, as required of students in other core courses. The learning disabled student may also obtain a waiver of normal course requirements from the NCAA after it has reviewed the student's individual education program, as well as the content of any non-core courses taken by the student.

The NCAA began to review Bowers application for "qualifier" status in April, 1996. In its review of Bower's courses, it noted several of the special education courses did not appear on the high school's NCAA registration forms, and thus requested more information from the high school as to content of these courses, to make a core-course determination. Despite receiving additional information from the school's guidance counselors, the Clearinghouse never received all the information it sought. By July, 1996, the Clearinghouse classified Bowers as a non-qualifier, due to remaining questions regarding the core-course equivalent of the courses he took during high school.

As a non-qualifier, Bowers was not eligible for athletic scholar-ships, nor could he participate in inter-collegiate athletics during his freshman year. None the less, Bowers enrolled as a freshman at Temple, an NCAA institution in January, 1997. In May of 1997, Bowers sued the NCAA, alleging that his classification as a non-qualifier violated the ADA, Rehabilitation Act and Sherman Act for illegal restraint of trade. The Court requested the NCAA to determine whether Bowers was entitled to a waiver of the core-course requirement, and its panel of experts ruled that he was not, based on the likelihood that he would perhaps not succeed academically while also participating in the de-mands of intercollegiate athletics during his freshman year.

The Court found that Bowers was seeking a complete waiver of the core-course requirement, rather than a mere modification or accom-modation required by the ADA. The NCAA had provided the necessary modification through its waiver procedure, for which it had found that Bowers was not qualified. The Court went on to state that "While the ADA requires 'even handed treatment' of individuals with disabilities, it does not require 'affirmative action.'"[105] The Court held that the NCAA requirements were essential to accomplish the purpose of the program, and that the criteria were essentially minimum requirements to assure that freshman athletes could handle college academic work along with the demands required of participants in intercollegiate athletics. The Court further held that only seven of Bowers' courses qualified as core courses, and that his failure to achieve "qualifier" status was not based on his learning disability, but upon the inability to meet the core course requirement. The Court then stated "The ADA is meant to provide a remedy for those who have been victimized by illegal disability-based discrimination—it is not meant to provide a remedy for every individual who has been screened out by eligibility criteria for whatever reason."[106] The Court denied Bowers' application for a preliminary injunction and disposed of the case, based on the inability of Bowers to sustain a viable ADA claim.

In *Rothman v. Emory University*, [107] a former law student sued Emory University for discrimination against him based on his

---

[105] Id. at 466.
[106] Id. at 467.
[107] 828 F.Supp. 537 (N.D. Ill. 1993).

epilepsy. During his first year, the dean of students urged him to get psychological counseling and to consider dropping out of school. During the second semester, the student requested accommodations of additional time to take exams due to his disability, and he provided documentation of the disability from his neurologist. Several other classmates complained regarding the student's special treatment, and the dean subsequently stated he would no longer receive accommodation without updated medical records. The student also complained of being glowered at in hallways by the dean, and generally encouraged to leave the school. This treatment led the student not to seek any additional accommodations during his second year. Despite his treatment, the student graduated from the law school, and sought admission to the Illinois Bar. The Dean of the law school sent a letter to the Illinois Board of Bar Examiners claiming the student was hostile to students and faculty and attributed all of his problems solely to his chronic epilepsy. This prompted an interview with the Board of Bar Examiners, and the committee noted nothing in the letter rendered him unfit for practice. After passing the bar examination, the student was admitted to practice in Illinois.

The student subsequently filed an action under the Americans with Disabilities Act. The law school is a place of accommodation under the ADA and they were required to make reasonable accommodations. However, the ADA became effective in January 1992, eighteen months after the student entered school and well after the initial allegedly illegal acts occurred. The only act that would possibly fall under ADA proscriptions was the letter written by the Dean of the school to the Board of Bar Examiners. The Court stated that despite the fact that the letter did not prevent the student from practicing law, all graduating law students expect such letters of recommendation and conditional or poor recommendations could potentially prevent a student from practicing law. The Court held that the student would need to show at trial that the poor letter of recommendation was based on the student's disability or retaliation for his complaints about the school's allegedly discriminatory policies, and thus dismissed Emory's motion for summary judgment as to the ADA claim concerning the recommendation, but granted as to those acts predating the ADA's enactment. The student's claims under the Rehabilitation Act were also allowed to stand, despite the dismissal of several other claims, including violation of constitutional rights.

Reasonable accommodations must be made for those with disabilities, and they must be treated like everyone else as to the rights and privileges available for members of the community. Retaliation for past behavior or any act that may be so construed must be avoided.

2.09   Construction

1)   What are the differences between ANSI and the ADA?

Accessibility standards have been part of the Building Code for several years. The most notable were ANSI A117.1- "Providing Accessibility and Usability for the Physically Handicapped People." Currently, both the ADA and the Building Code will be applicable on all construction and building renovations.

The Americans with Disabilities Act (ADA) has made many changes in building code requirements to ensure access for the disabled in public places. ANSI, in existence before the ADA, also has sections regarding accessibility for the physically disabled, and the differences between the two codes, both applicable and enforceable, is important. It is also important to note the more stringent requirement between the two codes will have to be met. In most cases, the newer ADA accessibility guidelines require much more accessibility than previously required under ANSI.

For example, ANSI regulations only apply to commercial facilities where known employment opportunities for the disabled exist. Some employers, in fact, write job descriptions that exclude the disabled. In contrast, under the ADA, facilities must be designed to allow the approach, enter and exit of virtually all work areas by the disabled. Under ANSI, elevators are not required in most cases, and only the ground floor of buildings are required to be accessible, where the ADA requires all buildings over 3,000 square feet and three or more stories high to be accessible and require a passenger elevator meeting ADA regulations.

Further, the ADA requires that if a toilet is provided, at least one type of each fixture must be accessible, including a stall 60 inches by 60 inches to allow wheelchair access. In contrast, ANSI specifies dimensions of stalls and types of fixtures, but does not require their use. Likewise, ANSI only requires raised, tactile letters on signs if an "authority having jurisdiction" so mandates, where the ADA requires room number signs to have raised letters and Braille, and additionally specifies the location and mounting height for the signs. Any overhead signs are required to have letters at least three inches high.

The last main difference between ANSI and ADA deals with accessible entrances. Where ANSI does not specify the number or location of accessible entrances, it does prohibit the sole use of service entrances as the only accessible entrance to the facility except where the service and main entrance are the same. The ADA, again, more stringent in its approach, requires the number of accessible entrances to be at least equal to the number of required exits under applicable building code.

As we can see, there are clearly differences between ANSI and the ADA, but both codes need to be followed, with the requirement for more access trumping the lesser requirement. All newly built or contemplated facilities will need to ensure that the ADA and ANSI are followed during the design process in order to prevent later problems in after-the-fact renovations and remediations to ensure greater access.

2) ADA Requirements In Designing Facilities

Facility managers and their organizations rely on architects as ADA experts to design facilities in compliance with the ADA. Serious concerns have arisen due to the numerous new facilities that have been sued under the ADA because of equal access design problems, including the Fleet Center, CoreStates Arena, Rose Garden Arena, MCI Center and Blockbuster-Sony Entertainment Centre, to name a few. Facility managers desire that their organizations be insulated or protected, either by contract or by statute or both, from being held liable for major structural changes due to non-compliance with equal access requirements.

Recently, in *United States of America v. Ellerbe Becket, Inc.,*[108] The United States Department of Justice filed an action against Ellerbe Becket, an architectural firm, for violations of the Americans with Disabilities Act (ADA), claiming that the architects had engaged in a pattern or practice of designing new sports arenas and stadiums across the country that failed to comply with Title III of the ADA.

---

[108] Civ. No. 4-96-995, 1997 U.S. Dist. LEXIS 15549 (D. Minn. Sept. 30, 1997); 976 F.Supp. 1262 (D.Minn. 1997).

The United States alleged that Ellerbe repeatedly designed stadiums and arenas with wheelchair seating locations that did not provide wheelchair users with lines of sight to the field or floor comparable to those available to other spectators. The United States sought civil penalties and an injunction against Ellerbe compelling them to comply with the ADA requirements in designing arenas and stadiums in the future. Ellerbe then sought to dismiss the Government's complaint, alleging architects were immune from liability under the ADA for their designs and numerous procedural points. The District Court found Ellerbe's arguments unpersuasive on all aspects of their motion to dismiss, and held that architects were not excluded from liability under the ADA as a matter of law.[109] While the Court was concerned about pending lawsuits regarding several of the stadiums, including the MCI Center in Washington, D.C., the Fleet Center in Boston, the Rose Garden Arena in Portland, Oregon, and the CoreStates Arena in Philadelphia, and the possibility of inconsistent rulings in the different cases, the Government was seeking prospective relief only, and any collateral estopple issues would arise in the future and could be addressed at that time if necessary. Further, the Court found that the Department of Justice's interpretation of the ADA regulations regarding sight lines more persuasive, and that Congress clearly intended that commercial facilities be subject to the accessibility standards for new construction.[110]

2.10 What Remedies are Available to Patrons under the ADA?

The primary relief available to patrons is injunctive relief, that would require a facility to make accommodations to disabled patrons. It is, of course, desirable to make these changes prior to any legal action being taken, and thus the importance of having an evaluation being done becomes obvious.

1) Injunctive Relief

Generally, injunctive relief is sought to prevent discriminatory practices, or to order a party to act in a certain way. In *Casey Martin v. PGA Tour, Inc.*, injunctive relief was used to force the PGA

---

[109] Id. at *19.
[110] Id. at *14.

to allow Martin to use a golf course pending the outcome of the litigation. The Court in its final decision ruled that Martin could use his cart on all tour events, essentially making the temporary injunction a permanent injunction. A court will only grant injunctive relief when other relief, such as monetary damages, is inappropriate to "solve" the problem at hand. Injunctive relief is often used in civil rights discrimination cases, because the problem at hand involves the unequal treatment of a segment of society, and the only way to effectively resolve this issue is through an injunction, rather than monetary damages. Any injunctive relief sought under the ADA shall include an order to alter the facility to make it readily accessible and usable by individuals with disabilities, including the provision of appropriate assistive devices.

2) Attorney's Fees

A private person-bringing suit under the ADA may seek to have their attorney's fees paid by the opposing party. This means that besides being forced to make alterations to a facility, compensate a victim of discrimination, and potentially face civil penalties, a violator will also be forced to pay their attorney and the attorney for the person who brought the suit, often a very expensive proposition in its own right.

In *Flores v. Villerose, Inc.,*[111] a person with muscular dystrophy sought to have her service dog accompany her to the restaurant operated by Villerose. The patron prevailed in a pretrial settlement in which the defendant agreed to allow service animals in the restaurant, and was awarded attorney's fees by the District Court in Pennsylvania since the settlement accomplished most of the Plaintiff's objectives, although the attorney's fees were adjusted downward due to less than complete success in the suit. This case is exemplary of a patron's right to collect their attorney's fees, which in prolonged litigation could be substantial, against the facility denying adequate access to the disabled. This is also further motivation for a complete audit of the facility to be done at the earliest possible time.

---

[111] 1996 U.S. Dist. LEXIS 11171 (July 29, 1996).

3) Punitive Damages if the U.S. Department of Justice is Involved

The Department of Justice is allowed to file lawsuits in federal court to enforce the ADA and may obtain court orders including compensatory damages and back pay to remedy past discrimination. Under Title III concerning access to public accommodations, the Department may also seek civil penalties of up to $50,000 for the first violation and $100,000 for any subsequent violation. These fines act as punitive damages, punishing the party violating the ADA with large civil fines. Punitive damages per se are not allowed under the ADA.

4) Settlement Agreements With the Department of Justice

The Department of Justice ("DOJ") entered into a settlement agreement with the Warner Theater, located in Washington D.C., regarding disability access under the ADA on April 1, 1997. In the settlement agreement, Warner agreed to provide sign language interpretation of performances for the deaf and hard-of-hearing individuals that communicate through sign language to allow them full enjoyment of the performances at the theater. A policy statement of interpretation will be formulated and available at the box office.

Comprehensive training will be given to employees for dealing with prospective patrons, including the handling of calls from the deaf and hard-of-hearing using relay services. Any ticketing services employed by the Theater will also be informed of the policy and asked to comply with it. Any request for interpretive services must be made at least ten days prior to the performance, and the ticket purchase must be made at least that far in advance. Patrons will be encouraged to provide as much advanced notice to the Theater as possible, due to the preparation required to assure high quality interpretation. If interpretation requests are received closer than ten days prior to a performance, efforts will be made to comply with the request.

DOJ entered into a settlement agreement with The Mississippi Coliseum, in which the Mississippi Fair Commission and Department of Finance and Administration will, in its renovations of the facility, make 1 percent of the 10,000 seats accessible to those in wheelchairs, provide required companion seating, disperse this seating throughout the facility, and provide lines of sight for the disabled over standing spectators. The State is also to provide accessible restrooms, concession stands, and parking lots, institute new ticketing policies for accessible seating, and train staff on the ADA, including the appointment of ADA coordinators to assist those with disabilities.

On March 3, 1998, DOJ entered into a settlement agreement with SCOPE Arena in Norfolk, Virginia regarding accessibility under the ADA. SCOPE Arena is a venue for hockey, basketball, circus and concert events, and was allegedly found inaccessible under the ADA after a DOJ investigation, which was prompted by a complaint from a disabled patron. Norfolk is required under the agreement to provide accessible seating and companion seats around the seating bowl; provide fully accessible parking; modify floor surfaces, ticket counters, ramps, and stairs to be accessible; make all restrooms accessible; and provide accessible floor seating when floor seating is employed for an event. Norfolk must also advertise the availability of accessible seating and modify its ticket policy so that accessible seats and companion seats will not be sold to non-disabled patrons until all other seats are sold out, or until 5:00 pm the day prior to an event, and that seats in front of an accessible area will also not be sold until all other seats are sold out, in order to provide those with disabilities a line of sight over the head of standing spectators. All such changes are to be made by April 27, 1998.

2.11 ADA Self-Evaluation and Transition Plan Requirements for Public Entities

The ADA requires that a public entity evaluate its current services, policies and practices, and the effects thereof." A self-evaluation is to be conducted within one year of the effective date of the regulations no later than July 26, 1992.[112] Public entities employing at least 50 persons must adopt a transition plan by July 26, 1992 if structural changes are needed to achieve program access.[113]

---

[112] 28 C.F.R. § 53.105 (a); see also 42 U.S.C. § 12134 (a).
[113] 28 C.F.R. § 35.150 (d) (1).

- Please have the necessary information to direct them to accessible facilities, restrooms, phones, etc. or to an information booth that may be able to assist the person;
- Request your employees and co-workers to be sensitive to the needs and feelings of those with disabilities;
- Please do not lean against or hang on someone's wheelchair. People with disabilities treat their wheelchairs as an extension of their bodies; and
- When admitting a disabled person into an event, please do not ask for proof of his or her disability.

2.13 The National Football League's Super Bowl Disability Access Program

With the enactment of the Americans with Disabilities Act of 1990 ("ADA"), the number of regulations affecting facilities has increased dramatically. Moreover, many facilities are currently facing lawsuits regarding their accessibility to the disabled, and many more lawsuits are sure to follow. The National Football League ("NFL") recently enacted a Disability Services Program to ensure that its events, including the Super Bowl, were accessible to the disabled. The author of this chapter, Turner D. Madden, created, coordinated and implemented the Program at Super Bowl XXXII for the NFL.

The NFL Disability Services Program included the following:
- Disability access policy and brochure, covering ticketing, location of accessible services and facilities in the stadium and the NFL Experience. The Brochure informed disabled patrons about how to obtain necessary services and accommodations;
- An NFL ADA Compliance Manual for Super Bowl contractors and subcontractors;
- An ADA audit of hotels and other facilities used by the NFL for the Super Bowl; and
- On-site disability services to personally assist people with disabilities that attended Super Bowl events. This highly trained team of forty (40) service personnel located needed

services, seating, concessions, and other services for patrons with disabilities. The team supplemented the security, first aid and medical units by assisting people with disabilities and by assisting the elderly and people with temporary disabilities by providing mobility assistance.

Chapter 3

Government Contracts and the Procurement Process

By Jonathan D. Shaffer, Richard Smith and Claire E. Kresse[*]

3.00   Introduction

General Overview - This chapter is written for managers of government owned or operated large facilities. Non-government managers may also find it useful. The purpose of this section is to provide the public assembly facility manager ("facility manager") with basic information and procedural guidelines for conducting an acquisition and for spending money under the restrictions of a government procurement system. Because of space limitations we do not discuss the procurement and appropriation law for every state and municipality. Instead, we focus on the Federal Acquisition Regulation ("FAR")[1], the American Bar Association's Model Procurement Code ("MPC")[2], which has been adopted by numerous state and local governments, and other procurement techniques that are common to most government entities. Many of the techniques discussed are also used by large commercial organizations. If your facility does not have its own regulations governing specific procurement issues, you should consider adopting relevant provisions from the FAR or MPC. Federal and MPC regulations are helpful models for

---

[*] Richard Smith, Jonathan D. Shaffer and Claire E. Kresse are with the law firm of Smith, Pachter, McWhorter & D'Ambrosio, P.L.C., at 8000 Towers Crescent Drive, Suite 800, Vienna, VA 22182.

[1] 48 C.F.R. §1.101, *et seq.*; FAR Part 15 (which covers negotiated procurements) and related sections of the FAR were substantially revised in late 1997. References are to the 1998 version of the FAR unless otherwise noted.

[2] *The Model Procurement Code for State and Local Governments, Recommended Regulations*, The American Bar Association, March 1997. Copies may be obtained by calling the ABA Service Center at 800-285-2221 [hereinafter MPC].

facility procurement managers because of the well-established administrative and judicial precedent interpreting such regulations.

Purchasing goods and services under a state, city or municipal procurement system may be complicated. When a governmental entity enters into a commercial relationship to purchase goods or services, various procurement rules and procedures apply for the purpose of promoting competition and other public policies. For the government, the applicable procurement statute preempts or takes the place of standard commercial law and practices during each step of the purchasing process. The procurement statute governs who has the authority to purchase goods and services and what clauses must be included in the contract. A statute or regulation may even prohibit certain contract clauses or provisions from being included in the government contract.[3] Statutes and regulations should be applied to reach the overall goal of purchasing the goods or services in an efficient, cost effective and timely manner.

In accordance with most government procurement rules, the selection procedure must be conducted in an impartial and equitable manner, that is subject to administrative or judicial review. Accordingly, it is essential that the public facility adopt written procurement policies and rules that clearly establish a reasonable procurement model. Equally important is that the facility's personnel receive adequate training in the requirements of the governing rules.

In adopting rules, the public facility first must be guided by the governing statutes or regulations already in existence. To the extent that the governing rules do not cover issues discussed in this chapter, the public facility should consult and consider adopting well-established procurement rules from other sources, such as the FAR or the Model Procurement Code. The benefit of using these well-established rules is that there will be a body of case law interpreting those rules. This body of case law will fill in the gaps to the extent that the rules adopted by the public facility do not address all factual situations. These rules provide a level of certainty for the facility and prospective contractors. Moreover,

---

[3] *Carrier Corp.* GSBCA No. 8516, 90 -1 BCA ¶ 22,409; *Charles Breseler, Co.,* ASBCA No. 22669, 78-2 BCA ¶ 13,483.

written procurement policies and rules help ensure that the procurement process is conducted impartially and on a rational basis, two tests often used by reviewing bodies in evaluating whether a particular procurement decision was appropriate and lawful.

3.01   Contracting Process

(1)   Source Selection Methods

Source selection is the process used by the facility owner ("facility") to identify one or more contractors for award using regimented procedures. There are numerous procedures that can be used to select the contract awardee, depending on, among other things, (1) the size and complexity of the procurement, (2) the type of goods or services being procured and (3) the available time. Discussed below are the most common procurement methods, including sealed bidding, negotiated procurements, best value procurements, two step procurements and simplified or low cost procurements.

In addition, some agencies may develop unique approaches. However, using unusual procurement methods runs a risk that a reviewing court or body will have no precedents to look to in evaluating whether conduct of the procurement was proper. A reviewing court could conclude that unusual procedures are not authorized by the governing statute or otherwise frustrate competition or other public policies. Moreover, unusual techniques are more likely to be found unreasonable; after all, the traditional approaches have been validated by the federal government through years of experience. Accordingly most facilities use the traditional methods such as sealed bidding and negotiated procurements that have been recognized by governments and courts as being fair and reasonable.

(i)   Sealed Bidding

Sealed bid procurements are procurements conducted solely on the basis of price and without discussions with offerors. Prospective bidders submit sealed bids on a specified common date and time. After that time has expired, the bids are publicly opened by the facility and award is made to the low responsive, responsible bidder. A responsive bid is one that conforms to all material requirements of the solicitation. A responsible bidder is a contractor that (a) has adequate financial resources to perform the contract, (b) is able to meet the required performance schedule, (c) has a satisfactory performance record and (d) the necessary experience applicable to the contract work.[4]

When award is based on "sealed bids," the federal government's procurement statute, the Competition in Contracting Act ("CICA") requires the agency solicitation to state (1) that bids will be evaluated without discussions and (2) the time and place where the bids will be opened.[5] As a matter of good practice, non federal public and private party facilities should use these CICA requirements as guidelines for drafting solicitations based on sealed bidding.

Most controversies regarding sealed bidding arise where a bidder bids on a basis different than that stated in the solicitation. These types of disputes have been the subject of lawsuits since at least the 1800's. For example, in *Holmes v. Common Council of City of Detroit*,[6] the City of Detroit ("City") sought bids from various contractors for the paving of streets with brick, specifying that all bids submitted must contain separate pricing for each of three named brick types the City found acceptable. The City received a bid from Holmes & Strachan which was the lowest bid for the work, but did not bid on the specified brick and instead used a brick similar in type, yet did not name the brick they would use.[7] The City accepted the bid of the next lowest bidder, McLaughlin, who complied with the bidding procedure exactly. Holmes sued seeking to prevent the Council from ratifying the contract with McLaughlin, stating Holmes was the lowest bidder and that the Council's requirement of specified brick obtainable from one source only did not allow real competition in the bidding process.[8] The Court stated that the City was free to specify what materials it deemed acceptable and superior

---

[4] FAR § 9.104-1.
[5] 41 U.S.C. § 253a(b)(2)(A) (1996); 10 U.S.C. § 2305(a)(2)(B)(i) (1997).
[6] 120 Mich. 226, 79 N.W. 200 (1899).
[7] *Id.* at 227.
[8] *Id.* at 228.

the additional cost . . . , even though, . . . cost may be weighted less heavily than technical and management factors."[20]

A protest is more likely to be sustained where the facility has not sufficiently documented the basis for its decision. Accordingly, facility procurement personnel should ensure that the best value determination is consistent with the evaluation criteria and documented in a formal memorandum or determination which sets forth exactly why the facility believes the award is justified under the stated criteria. For example, if the facility intends to award to a higher priced, higher rated offeror, the best value determination should explain in detail why the facility believes the higher rated technical approach is worth the price premium.

(iii) Other Techniques

Although sealed bidding and negotiated procurements constitute the vast majority of public procurements, there are other methods used by federal, state and local governments, as well as public and private facilities. Some of the most common are simplified acquisition techniques, sole source or non-competitive awards and two step procurements.

(a) Simplified Acquisition Techniques

Simplified acquisition techniques are often used for low cost acquisitions. For example, the federal government has authorized buyers to make purchases using a federal government credit card for purchases under $2,500.00.[21] Additionally, the federal government has authorized agencies to use simplified acquisition methods, such as, limiting the number of prospective offerors that receive the solicitation, and the use of blanket purchase agreements to provide supplies or services to one or more offices or projects for procurements under $100,000.00.[22]

---

[20] *TRW, Inc.*, B-260788.2, August 2, 1995, 96-1 CPD ¶ 11, at 3-4.

[21] 41 U.S.C. § 428 (1996); FAR Part 13.

[22] 41 U.S.C. § 252a (1996); 10 U.S.C. § 2302a (1997); FAR Part 13; *see also* MPC §§ 3-204 (Small Purchases) *et seq.* and 3-206 (1998). Usually, the determination to proceed without competition on the basis of an emergency must be supported by a written determination by a senior procurement executive.

(b)　Sole Source or Noncompetitive Awards

Additionally, most public entities have procedures allowing for sole source or non-competitive awards in the event of emergencies, other urgent and compelling circumstances or where the agency determines that there is only one source for the required supply, service or construction item.[23] Agency determinations to award sole source or use non-competitive approaches are usually subject to strict scrutiny by reviewing courts or administrative agencies.[24] Accordingly, facilities should ensure that any determination to award a contract sole source is consistent with the facilities governing statutes or regulations and that the appropriate procurement official has provided a detailed determination setting forth the factual and legal basis for the sole source or non-competitive award.

(c)　Two Step Procurements

Some public entities have determined to blend sealed bidding and negotiated procurements to take advantage of the benefits of both techniques. One problem with sealed bidding is that the facility will often receive a large number of bids from sources that may not be technically qualified. Accordingly, a facility may solicit technical and management proposals, without pricing, to determine which proposals are acceptable and should be included in the pool of qualified bidders or competitive range. Then, the facility requests those offerors in the competitive range to submit sealed bids based on relatively mature specifications and fixed prices.

---

[23] 41 U.S.C. § 253(c)(1) and (2) (1996); 10 U.S.C. § 2304(c) (1997); *see also* MPC §§ 3-205 and 3-206 (1998).

[24] *Mine Safety Appliances Co.*, B-233052, 89-1 CPD ¶ 127. However, the agency decision will usually be upheld if the agency can establish that its determination is reasonable under the terms of the governing procurement statute or regulation.

(2)   Preparation of Solicitation

The first step in source selection is preparing a solicitation that will be provided to selected prospective offerors or the public at large. Depending on the contracting arrangement that the facility has chosen, the facility may contract with one or several entities for the project work. This section discusses factors that public and private facilities need to address when preparing any such solicitation. Public facilities are often subject to state and local competition requirements similar to those imposed on federal agencies by CICA. CICA requires an agency preparing to procure property or services to "specify its needs and solicit bids or proposals in a manner designed to achieve full and open competition . . . [and] include specifications which — . . . permit full and open competition."[25] In addition to specifications, CICA requires agency solicitations, to include, at a minimum, "a statement of — (A) all significant factors and significant subfactors which the executive agency reasonably expects to consider in evaluating sealed bids (including price) or competitive proposals (including cost or price, cost-related or price-related factors and subfactors, and noncost-related or nonprice-related factors and subfactors); and (B) the relative importance assigned to each of those factors and subfactors."[26] Even if the governing rules do not require this type of disclosure, this information should be disclosed to prospective offerors so that they can provide their best possible offers in response to the facility's minimum needs.

With regard to the timing for issuance of the solicitation and receipt of offerors' proposals, federal procurement regulations state that requests "shall . . . allow bidders an adequate opportunity to prepare and submit their bids, giving due regard to the construction season and the time necessary for bidders to inspect the site, obtain subcontract bids, examine data concerning the work, and prepare estimates based on plans and specifications."[27] While the FAR states 30 days is usually sufficient,[28] large projects can require substantially

---

[25] 41 U.S.C. § 253a(a)(1) (1996); 10 U.S.C. § 2305(a)(1)(A) (1997).
[26] 41 U.S.C. § 253a(b)(1) (1996); 10 U.S.C. § 2305(a)(2) (1997).
[27] FAR § 36.213-3(a).
[28] FAR § 14.202-1(a).

more time. Again, private and public facilities should adhere to this instruction when drafting solicitations.

(i)   Specifications

In addition to the solicitation general terms and conditions and evaluation procedures, the solicitation should contain specifications describing the facility's desired end product. Specifications generally refer to any description of the physical or functional characteristics, or nature of the supply, service or construction item being purchased.[29]

The specification should include a clear description of any requirement for inspecting, testing, or preparing the supply, service or construction item -- the scope of work. The purpose of specifications is to provide a basis for obtaining a supply, service or construction item that meets the facility's needs in a cost effective and timely manner.

Many states and localities require public facilities to furnish specifications that promote fair and open competition. Because more competition will result in better priced and better quality bids it is also in the facility's interest to develop specifications that promote competition. To promote competition without sacrificing quality of performance, specifications must be unambiguous, accurate and complete. Defective or incomplete specifications will lead to costly changes, delays and disputes that may result in facility liability. Specifications that are made too restrictive by requiring more than the facility needs, however, result in limited competition, unfairness in the bidding process and lower quality bids.

The type(s) of specifications to be incorporated in the solicitation will vary depending on the facility's needs. For example, CICA provides

> [S]pecifications may be stated in terms of:
> (i)   function, so that a variety of products or services may qualify;
> (ii)   performance, including specifications of the range of acceptable characteristics or of the minimum acceptable standards; or

---

[29] MPC § 4-101 (1998) and Recommended Regulation R4-201.01.1 (1997).

(iii) design requirements.[30]

Functional specifications describe the work in terms of the facility's desired end-product and tend to be less particularized and restrictive than performance or design specifications. Any number of contractor proposed different solutions could satisfy the facility's needs.

Performance specifications are similar to functional specifications because they identify the facility's general operational requirements for the end-product without defining how it must be designed or constructed. "Where an item is purchased by performance specification, the contractor accepts general responsibility for design, engineering and achievement of the stated performance requirements."[31] Thus, there is no warranty of the adequacy of the specifications. The facility retains the right to reject the contractor's work upon final inspection.

Some design specifications by the facility set forth detailed and precise requirements. These design specifications allow the facility to control the approach and materials used to create the end-product. The facility can also base award solely on price because all bidders must use the same design. Design specifications can restrict competition and inflate the price, however, since other alternative -- less expensive -- approaches are excluded. Most important, design specifications increase the facility's liability by making the facility responsible for any design deficiencies and errors in the specifications. Consequently, most solicitations tend to combine design specifications with performance or functional specifications.

Another category of specifications is design-build specifications. Traditionally, these specifications are generated by the prime contractor, or an architect/engineer hired by the contractor, under a design-build contract (*see* discussion section 14.01(3), *infra*). In this situation the facility may provide functional or performance based specifications describing the end-product, but

---

[30] 41 U.S.C. § 253a(a)(3) (1996); 10 U.S.C. § 2305(a)(1)(C) (1997).
[31] *Monitor Plastics Co.*, ASBCA 14447, August 3, 1972, 72-2 BCA ¶ 9,626, at 44,971; *Stuyvesant Dredging Co. v. United States*, 11 Ct. Cl. 853, 860 (1987).

will generally not provide specifications setting forth precise measurements, materials, quality control and inspection require- ments, and other detailed information.[32] This arrangement is to the facility's advantage because the contractor assumes liability for defective specifications or errors resulting from misread specifica- tions. However, as mentioned above, frequently the facility will choose to provide detailed design specifications for customized work. In this case, the liability issue is less clear and costly dis- putes often result.

In addition to the specifications described above, there is a fourth category, referred to as proprietary, or "brand-name," specifications. Proprietary specifications identify a particular brand-name product to be used by the contractor. Using brand- name specifications may improve efficiency and quality assurance, but these advantages should be weighed against the goal of pro- moting competition. Facility procurement officials should consult the applicable state statutes and/or local regulations to ensure that the use of proprietary specifications is not prohibited. Proprietary specifications may violate a state statute requiring specifications to promote competition.[33]

(ii)   Protective Clauses

There are a number of commonly used protective clauses that public or private owners may use to avoid unnecessary costs and disputes. These clauses include: instructions to bidders; disclaimers; order of precedence clauses; and unbalanced bidding clauses.

With respect to instructions to bidders, most standard form contracts include language borrowed from federal procurement

---

[32] *Id.*

[33] *See, e.g.*, VA. Code § 11-49 (1993): Unless otherwise provided in the Invitation to Bid, the name of a certain brand, make or manufacturer does not restrict bidders to the specific brand, make or manufacturer named; it conveys the general style, type, character; and quality of the article desired, and any article which the public body in its sole discretion determines to be the equal of that specified, considering quality, work- manship, economy of operation, and suitability for the purpose intended, shall be accepted.

materially unbalanced. A bid is mathematically unbalanced when prices for some bid items are enhanced to compensate for items bid low. A bid is materially unbalanced if, as a result of mathematical unbalancing, there is reasonable doubt whether the facility will receive the lowest ultimate cost by accepting the unbalanced bid.[40] Mathematically -- not materially -- unbalanced bids may serve a legitimate business purpose by disguising a contractor's bidding strategy and preventing competitors from predicting future bids. Thus, an over broad prohibition of unbalanced bids may inhibit bidders from submitting otherwise legitimate low bids.

(iii)   Subcontractor Requirements

The facility's procurement official(s) should review applicable state and local law regarding whether (1) bidders must list potential subcontractors in their proposal and (2) whether that requirement creates a legal obligation for the contractor to hire the listed subcontractor upon award. These types of requirements are designed to prevent "bid shopping" after award. Even if the applicable law does not require bidders to list planned subcontractors, many state, local and private facilities will require bidders to list subcontractors so that a facility can evaluate the bidder's ability to perform, i.e., whether the bidder has identified enough qualified subcontractors to perform the work required, and the quality of planned subcontractors. Some facilities will also require bidders to obtain pre-award commitments from listed subcontractors to ensure there will be sufficient qualified labor available to perform the contract work. Thus, by requiring bidders to list subcontractors, some of the uncertainty and risk inherent in the solicitation process is replaced with increased control for the facility. A facility can further control the subcontractor selection process by specifying in the solicitation documents that the facility must approve potential subcontractors, but that privity of contract between the facility and subcontractor does not arise from the approval.

---

[40] *Sammy Garrison Construction Company, Inc.*, B-215453, November 21, 1984, 84-2 CPD ¶ 545; *General Construction Company/Reidel Int'l.*, B-208918, August 2, 1983, 83-2 CPD ¶ 152.

Consequently, the facility should require the eventual awardee to "flow down" these provisions to all subcontracts.

3.02   Special Characteristics of Negotiated Procurements

Because negotiated procurements are commonly used for more complex and/or expensive contracts and because the rules governing such procurements are often difficult to apply, we set forth below in detail some of the special characteristics of negotiated procurements.[41] The typical steps in a negotiated procurement are as follows:

1. Offers are solicited through a Request for Proposals ("RFP"), or Solicitation;

2. A pre-proposal conference is held for the offerors;

3. Depending upon the questions raised at the pre-proposal conference, the facility may send out written clarifications or amendments to the solicitation;

4. Offers are submitted to the facility;

5. Offers are reviewed by the facility's contracting officer to determine if

    a) The Response was timely;

    b) The Response meets each of the submission requirements in the RFP; and

    c) The Response contains omissions, erasures, alterations or additions.

6. Offers are then evaluated and scored;

7. An award is made if practicable. Otherwise, a competitive range is determined;

---

[41] *Cf.* MPC Recommended Regulation 3-203 *et seq.* (1997) and FAR Part 15.

8. Remaining offerors are invited to discussions and advised of their deficiencies;

9. Offerors are invited to submit BAFOs;

10. A final evaluation is made and final scores are determined;

11. The facility's contracting officer awards the contract and notifies the unsuccessful offerors; and

12. The unsuccessful offerors are debriefed upon request.

The key elements are discussed below.

(1)   Evaluation

Evaluation in a negotiated procurement is the process of rating proposals under the solicitation evaluation criteria. As stated above, under most governing rules and regulations, the solicitation must advise offerors of the evaluation criteria and their relative weights.[42] For example, a solicitation might provide that technical is the most important factor, followed by past performance, followed by cost. The solicitation should also inform offerors of all subfactors and provide a general description of the agencies needs through a statement of work or specifications. The facility evaluators then compare proposals to the stated criteria and assign numerical, adjectival or color ratings.

For facility evaluators, the basic process involves:

1. Reviewing the requirements of the RFP and the Source Selection Plan;

2. Reading the Proposals;

---

[42] *See* note 24, *supra*; FAR § 15.203(a)(4) (1998); and, MPC Recommended Regulations R3-203.13.1 and 13.2 (1997).

3. Identifying the deficiencies or areas where the offeror failed to meet the solicitation requirements;

4. Requesting clarifications;

5. Identifying the strong and weak points of each proposal;

6. Writing a narrative summary; and

7. Assigning a score to each proposal.

(2)   Award Without Discussions

Once the facility has evaluated all proposals, the facility must determine whether or not discussions with offerors are necessary. Under federal procurement rules, an agency cannot award without discussions unless the solicitation notifies offerors that the agency reserved the right to award without discussions.[43] A similar requirement may apply to state and local entities and provides a helpful guideline for facility procurement officials.[44]

The decision to award on evaluation of initial proposals alone is significant. On the one hand, awarding without discussions will save substantial time because the facility need not establish a competitive range, conduct discussions or evaluate BAFOs. On the other hand, awarding without discussions may not result in the most advantageous award for the facility. Discussions may result in lower prices or improved technical responses based on a better understanding of the facility's needs.

Under government contracts, once any discussions have been conducted, an agency may not award based solely on initial proposals. Accordingly, if an agency or facility plans to award based on initial proposals, it must use care in any communications

---

[43] FAR§ 15.306(a)(3); *see also* note 17, *supra*.

[44] *See, e.g., Appeal of Johnson Controls, Inc.*, No. 1155 (*MSBCA* September 21, 1983) (where procurement was complex, agency did not understand representations made in appellant's proposal and agency had not notified offerors that award might be made without discussions, the agency had a duty to negotiate prior to award).

with offerors after receipt of initial proposals to ensure that any such communications do not rise to the level of discussions. When award will be made without discussions, facilities may have communications with prospective offerors to address "clarifications."[45] Clarifications are appropriate to address minor irregularities and apparent clerical mistakes. Under the 1998 version of the FAR, agencies may also communicate with offerors regarding certain other limited aspects of proposals, i.e., the relevance of an offeror's past performance information and adverse past performance information to which the offeror has not previously had an opportunity to respond.[46] Clarifications do not give the offeror an opportunity to revise or modify its proposal, except to the extent that correction of apparent clerical mistakes results in a revision.

Facility procurement officials may address mistakes in a proposal through clarifications, communications[47] or discussions, depending on the magnitude and context of the mistake. However, if the facility suspects that an offeror has made a mistake in its proposal, the facility must strictly comply with any governing statutes, regulations or RFP provisions when addressing proposal revisions.

(3)   Competitive Range

If discussions are to be conducted, a facility must establish a competitive range consisting of those offerors with whom it intends to conduct discussions after evaluating initial proposals. The competitive range is that group of offerors who, based on the ratings of each proposal against all evaluation criteria, are the most highly rated proposals.[48] Prior to 1998, federal regulations required agencies to include in the competitive range all offerors that had a reasonable chance of award.[49] Under this standard, an agency was required to include an offeror in the competitive range, even if its proposal contained weaknesses or deficiencies, if the offeror had a reasonable chance of correcting those weaknesses or

---

[45] *Cf.* FAR § 15.306(a)(1) and (2).

[46] *Id.* This revision to the FAR was implemented on January 1, 1998 for most federal procurements. This rule will not apply to most state and local procurements unless their rules are amended to follow the FAR.

[47] *See* FAR § 15.306(b).

[48] FAR § 15.306(c).

[49] FAR § 609(a) (1997).

deficiencies through discussions.[50] In 1998, the regulations were amended to permit agencies to limit the competitive range to only "the most highly rated proposals, unless the range is further reduced for purposes of efficiency."[51] Most non-federal facilities will be governed by local statutes or regulations that likely incorporate the old FAR standard.[52]

(4)   Discussions

Once the facility has established a competitive range, it must conduct discussions with all competitive range offerors. Under the FAR, the intent of discussions is to allow offerors to revise their proposals so that the Government will obtain the best value based on the solicitation requirements and evaluation criteria.[53] This means that the agency or facility must discuss with each offeror "significant weaknesses, deficiencies, and other aspects of its proposal (such as cost, price, technical approach, past performance, and terms and conditions) that could . . . be altered or explained to enhance materially the proposal's potential
for award."[54]

(5)   Best and Final Offers and Award Determination

After the facility has concluded discussions, the facility should request that all remaining competitive range offerors submit BAFOs. After receipt of BAFOs, the facility will evaluate the offerors proposals based on the evaluation criteria specified in the solicitation.[55] Then, the responsible facility personnel must make an award determination based on "a comparative assessment of proposals against all source selection

---

[50] *DynaLantic Corp.*, B-274944.2, February 25, 1997, 97-1 CPD ¶ 10.

[51] FAR § 15.306(c). In order to limit the number of offerors in the competitive range for efficiency purposes, FAR § 15.306(c)(2) requires an agency to have notified all offerors of this possibility in the solicitation.

[52] *See, e.g.*, MPC § 3-203(6) (1998).

[53] FAR §§ 15.306(d) and 15.306(d)(2).

[54] FAR § 15.306(d)(3); MPC § 3-203(6) (1998) and Recommended Regulation R3-203.14 (1997); *see also Alliant Techsystems, Inc.*, B-260215.4; B-260215.5, August 4, 1995, 95-2 CPD ¶ 79.

[55] The cost proposal techniques set forth in FAR § 15.404-1 establish guidelines to ensure that the final agreed to price by an agency, or facility, is fair and reasonable.

criteria."[56] Often, the facility solicitation will provide for award to the offeror providing the best value or greatest value to the facility based on the specified evaluation criteria.[57] *Facilities must ensure that they follow the solicitation's evaluation criteria exactly in making the award determination.*

3.03   Protests and Protest Avoidance

(1)   Protest Procedures

Procurements conducted by most public entities are subject to review through an administrative or judicial bid protest process. Typically, the governing rules require disappointed offerors who wish to challenge the public facility's award decision to first pursue the matter through a protest to the awarding facility's contracting officer or to an agency board overseeing facility activities.[58] If the protestor is not satisfied with the results of a protest to the facility, most government agencies are then subject to judicial or administrative proceedings.[59] Obviously, each public facility will be subject to the unique rules governing the public entity that is responsible for the facility. However, there are a number of common protest procedures that are used in some form by most public owned or operated facilities. These include:

• The filing of a written protest to the contracting officer or the head of the purchasing agency within a set number of days after the protester knew, or should have known of the grounds for protesting;

• A stay of the procurement if the protest is filed within a set number of days and the contract has not been awarded;

• A decision on the protest from the contracting officer or head of the purchasing agency as expeditiously as possible;

---

[56] FAR § 15.308.
[57] *See* § 3.01(1)(ii) of this chapter, *supra.*
[58] *See, e.g.,* MPC Recommended Regulations R9-101.02 and .03 (1997).
[59] MPC §§ 9-505 and 9-510 (1998).

- If the protest is denied, the filing of a Request for Reconsideration; and

- If the party's Request for Reconsideration is denied, an appeal of that determination may be filed with the state's Procurement Appeals Board, or its equivalent.[60]

Typical substantive grounds of protest include: Failure to follow the solicitation evaluation criteria; failure to document the source selection decision and other critical source selection determinations; improper cost/technical trade-offs (i.e., ignoring the solicitation's stated relationship of the cost, technical and other factors); improper exclusion from the competitive range; lack of meaningful discussions; errors in the cost evaluation; improper disclosure of competitive information and unmitigated conflicts of interest. All of these protest grounds essentially rely on an allegation that the facility has failed to follow the published rules governing the procurement.

Accordingly, *it is essential that all facility evaluation personnel carefully review the solicitation and governing procurement rules and are instructed that they must follow both the letter and the spirit of the governing provisions.*

(2) Protest Avoidance

The protest process is time consuming and disruptive. If a protest is sustained, the public facility may be prevented from timely accomplishing its goals. Accordingly, the facility manager must exercise due care to avoid successful protests by insuring that procurements are conducted in accordance with legal requirements. In general, adhering to the following guiding principles should ensure that even if a protest is filed, it will not be sustained.

First, *the facility manager must make sure that personnel conducting the procurement follow the RFP evaluation criteria and award provisions strictly.* Protests are often sustained where personnel do not follow the published rules.

---

[60] *See id.* at §§ 9-101 and 9-505.

Second, *facility procurement personnel should document in writing all material strengths, weaknesses and deficiencies identified during the evaluation process.*

Third, *facility procurement personnel should prepare detailed narratives to support critical evaluation determinations, such as competitive range and award decisions.* Protests are often sustained where the agency fails to properly document the record.

3.04   Debarment

Many public entities include in their procurement regulations provisions authorizing the entity to debar or preclude a prospective bidder from participating in contracts awarded by that entity where the bidder has been convicted of criminal offenses involving fraud or otherwise found to be not presently responsible for purposes of doing business with a public entity.[61] These provisions vary widely in their scope, procedures and substantive provisions. In addition, public facilities may prepare their own debarment rules in addition to those of the relevant Government authority.[62] As with other areas of procurement law, the facility must ensure that if it determines to debar a prospective offeror, that it follows the applicable debarment regulations. Debarment decisions may be overturned where the agency has not followed the applicable regulations or has redeprived the offeror of procedural protections provided in the governing regulations.

---

[61] *See, e.g.*, MPC § 9-102 (Debarment or Suspension by the Chief Procurement Officer or the Head of a Purchasing Agency) (1998).
[62] *See* MPC § 9-102(2)(e) (1998).

Chapter 4

FACILITY LICENSE AGREEMENTS

By Turner D. Madden

4.00 Introduction

Much of our business concerns contracts. Therefore, the better understanding that we have of them, the more our facilities will benefit from on a short and long-term basis. The study of contracts in law school requires a year of intensive study, involving the rules and details of the contracting process, from formal, written contracts to simple, oral promises. We need not to cover all of a law school's contract curriculum in this Chapter, but will strive to give you a basic understanding of the formation of a contract and its ramifications. Defining the term "contract" in and of itself is difficult, due to the many forms a contract can take, and the many ways in which an offer to enter into a contract may be accepted. Without discussing the numerous technical aspects of a contract, it is sufficient to know that in its simplest form, a contract is the exchange of promises between two or more parties. In order for a contract to be legally enforceable in court, these promises must be supported by "consideration," or something of value. For example, if A asks B to wash his car for five dollars, the offer is the job of washing the car, and the consideration offered for performance of the contract is five dollars. If B accepts the contract, as stated, it becomes binding on both parties. If B, instead, asks for six dollars to perform the task, his request is deemed to be a counter offer, that A may now accept or reject. If A accepts the counter offer, the contract becomes binding, and if he does not, no contract exists. The above example is a very a basic contract, but more complex contracts take the same general format, differing only in the number of terms or conditions that must be satisfied to fully perform the contract.

4.01 Standard "License Agreement" Provisions

Below is a general list of contract provisions and a discussion of each provision included in standard license agreements for stadiums, arenas, performing arts centers, auditoriums, amphitheaters and convention centers. Please note that many of the agreements between facilities and their users are referred to as "license" agreements instead of "lease" agreements. The reason for this is that under the law of real property in most states, the lease creates a tenant's possessory estate for the lessee that has more rights to the land than a licensed space. Under a license, the licensee (the user) does not have any real property rights to the space. For example, under a license agreement, the applicable state law may provide that the licensee has no holdover rights that would prevent your next building user from moving into the facility. Under a license agreement, the real property laws of the jurisdiction would not be applicable to a licensee.

Many of these clauses may be used in short and long-term license agreements. Instead of including every facility rule or requirement in the primary license document, the facility may want to issue a set of rules and regulations that is in a separate document and incorporated by reference into the license agreement.

List of Standard License Agreement Provisions

Americans with Disabilities Act
Arbitration of Disputes
Assignment and
    Delegation
Cancellation
Choice of Law
Compliance with State & Federal
Laws
Compliance with Facility Regulations
Condition of Facility
Concessions and Novelties
Copyright Infringement
Discretionary Matters
Entire Agreement
Exclusive Service Contractors
Force Majeure
Indemnification and Hold Harmless
Insurance
Limitations on Liability for Facility

Name of Event & Purpose
Notice of Default
Period of Time and Use of Facilities
Radio & Television Broadcasting
Remedies Upon Default
Rental Amount
Reservation Deposit
Seating Capacity
Severability
Services Provided
Security
Simultaneous Events and Common
Areas
Stage Restrictions
Termination of Agreement
Ticketing and Box Office
Vacation of Premises
Waiver of Subrogation

Facility License Agreements

Below is a discussion of each clause listed above.

1)   Americans with Disabilities Act

As stated in Chapter 2, under the Americans with Disabilities Act, both the facility and the facility user are responsible for compliance under the ADA. However, the parties may allocate the obligations under the ADA through a license or other contract.[1] Therefore, the best way to protect your facility from a licensee's violation is to include a standard clause in your contract to protect your facility. For example, in a stadium arena or convention center license agreement, the standard clause should state that the facility is only responsible for compliance with the permanent building access requirements and the licensee or show management is responsible for compliance with the non-permanent accessibility requirements such as auxiliary aids and services. Auxiliary aids and services include sign language interpreters, closed captioning, conversion of documents into Braille, etc. However, in an arena or stadium, this clause may be inserted in the professional sports team facility license. An example of such a clause is as follows:

"Concerning the Americans with Disabilities Act and all the regulations thereunder ("ADA"), the Arena is responsible for the permanent building access requirements; such as, but not limited to wheelchair ramps, elevator standards, restroom standards, and internal hallways and doors. The Licensee is responsible for auxiliary aids and services and the non-permanent accessibility requirements, such as, but not limited to, assignment of seating accessibility, ticketing, assistive listening devices, sign language interpreters, signage and other auxiliary aids. The Licensee shall indemnify, defend and hold harmless the Arena from and against any and all losses, damages, costs, expenses, claims, and other liabilities arising out of, or otherwise attributable to, this Agreement and License granted hereunder, and Licensee's use and occupancy of the Arena."

2)   Arbitration of Disputes

Arbitration of disputes has become a major way of settling disagreements between parties while avoiding formal and expensive litigation. Many times contracts will contain a provisions indicating a third party mediator, such as the American Arbitration Association, is agreed by the

---

[1] 28 CFR § 36.201 (b).

parties to act as arbitrator in the event that they are unable to resolve disputes on their own. However, please be aware that many State and municipal governments prohibit arbitration in civil matters and thus you should check with local counsel regarding the arbitration regulations in your region.

3)   Cancellation
　　　　When a facility has been booked for an event, what happens if that event is cancelled? Does the reason for cancellation affect the parties rights under the contract? A facility manager will want to have a clause in their rental/license contract regarding their cancellation policy, and payment due to the facility if the booking is not kept. For example, if an event cancels over a year in the future, it is possible that the facility manager can find someone else to use the facility at that time, mitigating or lessening any damages they might incur. However, if an event cancels only a week or two before its scheduled license, the opportunity to book the facility for another client in that short time frame is next to impossible. In considering the needs of your specific facility, you might want to consider different levels of monetary damages, depending on the notice provided to the facility of cancellation of the event. An example of cancellation clauses are as follows:

"In no event shall Licensee terminate or cancel this agreement. Licensee understands, recognizes and agrees that the Facility will incur substantial damages if Licensee cancels or terminates this agreement and that Licensee will pay the Facility for said damages, plus a reasonable attorney's fees."

"Licensee covenants that if any default is made in the payment of the rent or any part thereof at the times specified, or if any default or violation is made in terms of the license, this license, at the option of the Facility shall cease and terminate and the Facility shall have the right to re-enter the premises with or without process of law and Licensee agrees to peaceably give up possession of the premises in such event and the Licensee shall, notwithstanding such re-entry, pay the full amount of said rental as herein agreed to be paid. In case of suit or action instituted by the Facility to enforce compliance with this agreement, Licensee agrees to pay all court costs and expenses of the Facility, including attorney's fees arising from such suit or action."

The second clause presented above covers not only cancellation in advance of the license date, but also any termination occurring during the license period as well. While having both a clause concerning advanced cancellation and Right of Re-entry upon Default are recommended, they do both cover similar ground. The advantage to specifying the terms is to make sure potential licensees are aware of the obligation they are undertaking, and to ensure that the facility can make full recovery for any damages incurred in the event of cancellation or default.

4)   Choice of Law
        Many contracts contain language regarding choice of law. This means that the parties agree to litigate or arbitrate any disputes between the parties under the laws of a particular state, and more often than not, in that specific state's courts. This can greatly minimize the costs incurred by a facility if a lawsuit occurs, by allowing all disputes to be settled in the courts and under the law of the state in which the facility is located. This issue mostly comes up when contracting with parties located out of state, such as national tours of performing artists, national expositions and shows, and other traveling events that are based in one state but travel between states or regions in the country. A sample choice of law or Forum Selection clause is as follows:

"The terms of this agreement shall be governed by the laws of the State of _____. Any dispute arising from this agreement shall be resolved in the Courts of _____. Licensee expressly consents to be subject to personal jurisdiction in all Courts located in the State of _____."

5)   Compliance with State & Federal Laws
        This clause is a "catch all" provision that requires the user to comply with federal and state laws as condition of the license agreement. Therefore, if the user violates the fire code or discriminates against a protected class of individuals, the facility may use this clause to either require compliance or terminate the license and sue for the balance of the license fee. An example of such a clause is as follows:

"The Licensee shall comply with the laws, regulations, rules and ordinances of the facility, the city or county, the state, and the United States that relate in any way to the event and the use of the licensed premises. Any material violation by the Licensee of any law, shall constitute a breach of this Agreement."

6)   Condition of Facility

In order to protect the facility, a manager of the facility and the licensee should walk throughout the facility prior to the licensee's moving into the facility. A checklist may be developed that identifies specific property locations where damage occurs to the building. A provision must also be included in the facilities standard license agreement that holds the licensee responsible for any damage to the facility.

In *Engel Stadium Corporation v. Chattanooga*,[2] the Corporation (Engel) and the city entered into a contract where Engel would license a baseball field in the city for a period of years and the city would expend $2 million dollars in refurbishing the facility.[3] The contract provided that the renovations were not to exceed two million, and that the improvements would comply with the standards set forth by Class AA baseball. The improvements were to take place in two phases, with the playing field to be improved in phase two at an expense of about $50,000.00. Engel sued the city for not properly improving the outfield, which had improper drainage causing postponement of games that could have been otherwise played, resulting in monetary losses in ticket sales, parking, concessions, and the like.[4] The Trial Court warded $475,000.00 to Engle, and the city appealed. The Court of Appeals held that the underground drainage system had been installed improperly, leading to ponding of water, and the soil/sand mix used was improper, leading to no natural percolation of water. While there were no written drainage standards for Class AA baseball, the oral standard was clear, the improper drainage was obvious, and the city clearly breached its license agreement with Engel. The Court of Appeals also held that the issue of actual damages suffered needed to be retried, because the figures given to the jury did not include amounts that would have been subtracted as overhead incurred by Engel.

---

[2] 1993 Tenn. App. LEXIS 398 (June 2, 1993).
[3] Id. at *2.
[4] Id. at *6.

In *Houston Oilers Inc. v. Harris County*,[5] the Houston Oilers football team licensed the Astrodome from Harris County for its football games. In a pre-season football game, a referee inspected the field and found it unsuitable for play. The game was delayed by 70 minutes while attempts were made to fix the field, but the game was eventually canceled.[6] The Oilers were fined over $325,000 for failure to furnish a proper field and had to pay the other team $440,000 in refunded ticket sales. The Oilers sued Harris County for failing to properly furnish the stadium in connection with its license, requiring the stadium be furnished with a playing surface as required by the National Football League. Harris County alleged that the cancellation of the game was done so the Oilers could negotiate a better license agreement and that because it was a domed stadium, the cancellation implied trickery, and the referee was incompetent. Harris County also counter-sued for slander, for disparaging remarks about the Dome's business and its ability to maintain the facility. The District court held that the NFL was not guilty of slander, conspiracy, tortuous interference with neither business nor fraud and would not be liable to Harris County for any damages suffered.

It is vital for a facility manager to make sure the premises are ready, available and in good condition for its tenants. If problems exist, the damage may extend to a further loss of future business, as the deficiencies of the facility are widely broadcast, it will be unlikely that the facility could prevail under claims such as slander or tortuous interference with business.

7)   Concessions and Novelties

Many facilities have exclusive contracts with vendors for food and beverage service, concessions and novelty sales. Even for those facilities without such a contract, a facility may want to control or prevent licensees from unfettered concession sales to prevent damage to the facility for the items sold or from the sellers of such concessions themselves.

Further, sales of concessions may provide an additional source of revenue for the facility, that it may choose not to share with a licensee. A license/rental agreement clause should address this issue to clarify it between the parties.

---

[5] 960 F. Supp. 1202 (S.D. Tex. 1997).
[6] Id.

An example of three such clauses are as follows:

"**Concession Rights:** All concession rights are reserved to the Facility and its assigns and the Facility or its agents shall have the sole right to sell, give away or dispense food, tobacco products, novelties, beverages, periodicals and other merchandise. The Facility furthermore reserves the right to conduct checkrooms, take photographs, and other privileges, and the Licensee shall not engage in or undertake any sale or dispensation of the aforesaid merchandise or similar articles or privileges without the prior written consent of the Facility. Neither Licensee nor Licensee's exhibitors shall give away or sell items under the terms of this agreement without express written consent of the Facility. The standard percentage for the sale of programs, records, and novelties is _____ percent (___ %) of gross proceeds from the sale of these and all other items sold at the Facility."

"All revenue derived from the sale of food and beverage concessions shall be retained by the Facility and shall be sold by the Facility or persons designated by the Facility. All revenue derived from the sale of novelties, souvenirs, record albums and programs, less the artist's share, shall be retained by the Facility and shall be sold by the facility or persons designated by the facility."

"The Facility reserves all food and beverage concessions and concession rights. Licensee shall have the right to sell through the Facility's licensed concessionaire such programs and novelties as are approved in advance by the Facility. No food or beverage shall be brought into the Facility by Licensee except as specifically permitted by express prior written consent by the Facility Manager. The Facility reserves the right to erect portable concession stands as needed for servicing of Licensee's patrons."

The first clause above is very strict about what is permitted in the facility, and specifies a percentage split in concession sales between the lessor and licensee. The second clause specifically addresses the financial issues and retains the majority of revenues gained from these sales for the exclusive use of the facility. In contrast, the third clause allows a licensee to negotiate sales of concessions through a facility-licensed concessionaire, with approval by the facility. This allows a facility manager to prohibit any potentially dangerous or disruptive novelties or concession items from being sold and used in the facility, while allowing such routine, harmless items to be sold. The best clause for your facility may involve a bit of each of these clauses.

8)   Copyright Infringement

Copyright infringement is of particular concern regarding music licensing. Under the trademark and copyright law, any music played in public on public address type systems or in a large area is subject to license fees. This means that any facility that is playing music over its public address system prior to a performance or during an intermission must be assured that such music is properly licensed. If the performer/event is playing the music, they should be responsible for paying the applicable licensing fees, but some facilities have been held vicariously liable for the unauthorized use of music by its tenants. In order to prevent such a problem, clauses like the ones below should be inserted into your license/rental contract with every licensee of the facility. For more information on copyright law refer to Chapter 13, Related State and Federal Statutes.

"Licensee will assume all costs arising out of or from the use of patented, trademarked, franchised, or copyrighted music, materials, devices, processes or dramatic rights used on or incorporated into an event. At the Facility's sole option, however, the Facility may elect to deduct such copyright fees from the Event settlement and pay such licensing fees on behalf of the Licensee. The Licensee agrees to indemnify, defend and hold harmless the Facility from any claims or costs, including legal fees that might arise out of or from the copyright infringement."

9)   Entire Agreement

This language is necessary to ensure that all parties know that only the written agreements between the parties are binding, and no oral agreements between the Facility's personnel or those of the Licensee are binding. This is very important, and avoids later confrontations regarding "But the manager said…" that cannot be verified. A sample of such a clause appears below:

"The terms and conditions of this agreement including the Facility's building rules and regulations, the Facility's basic equipment service and Labor Rates Brochure and the Facility's current Utility Service Order forms constitute the full and complete agreement between the parties. No other oral or written agreement shall, in any way, vary or alter provisions of this Agreement unless both parties consent to vary or alter the provisions of this agreement in a signed writing."

10)   Exclusive Service Contractors

Many facilities deal exclusively with one caterer, food and beverage company, service contractor, or security company. Thus, the licensee must either hire the in-house contractor or aquire the service through the facility. See the Concessions and Novelties clause above.

11)   Force Majeure

A "force majeure" provision or "act of god" provision specifies the category of incidents that may occur during the contract period that are not within the control of the parties. If the incident is not within the control of either party, and it is one of the enumerated incidents in the "force majeure" provision, then both parties may be released from their obligations to complete performance under the contract.

Warner Bros. Pictures, Inc. v. James Bumgarner[7] is a case that illustrates how a "force majeure" provision can be used to extend the contract. Warner Brothers had contracted with Bumgarner, also known as James Garner, for acting services in a contract signed in February of 1959. The contract contained a force majeure clause that stated if the producer could not prepare, produce or complete the motion picture, or if due to fire, flood, lockout, strike, accident, act of god, or any other "external force" beyond the control of the parties, the Producer was not obligated to pay the actor under the "casualty period" (duration of delay in production) and the actor was not obligated to render services during that time. If the casualty period was longer than eight weeks, the producer or actor could terminate the agreement, provided the actor provided notice to the producer of his wish to cancel the contract, at which time the Producer could opt to keep the contract in full force and effect by paying the actor his weekly salary.

In mid-January, 1960, the Writer's Guild of America went on strike against Warner Brothers and many other producers. The strike went on until June 20, 1960. On March 3, 1960, Warner informed Garner that the strike was covered within the force majeure clause of his contract and they

---

[7] 197 Cal. App. 2d 331 (1961).

would stop making weekly payments to him. Garner demanded payment of his salary on March 8, Warner refused the demand, and Garner opted to terminate his contract, stating Warner had materially breached their agreement by non-payment of salary.

Garner had been acting in the television series, "Maverick," in which he was one of the main characters. Warner sued on March 31, 1960, alleging it complied with its contract and had not made a material breach, and that Garner had been looking for an excuse to get out of his contract for some time. Garner cross-claimed, stating that the show "Maverick" had not been affected by the writers' strike, and that Warner could have also reassigned Garner to another production within the studio, rather than opt to discontinue his salary regarding the TV show. Warner also sought an injunction to prevent Garner from working on any other projects during this time.

At a bench trial, the trial court judge noted that Warner had not been forced to suspend production of the TV series involving Garner due to the strike. Further, the court noted Warner had at least 15 writers working during the strike under pseudonyms, at least one of whom was experienced in writing for the Maverick series. Production for a new season of Maverick was not scheduled to begin until May 1960 and at least one extra episode had been filmed in the prior season, leaving Warner Bros. in good position to meet its scheduling obligations for the 1960-61 season. The trial court concluded that the studio had wrongfully discontinued payments to Garner and ordered it to pay him $1,750.00 plus interest. On appeal, the court upheld the trial court's judgment, stating that Warner's decision to try to opt out of salary payments under the force majeure clause was ineffective, due to the fact that it had several scripts for Maverick ready or near ready, and that interruption of its production was unlikely. Further, the court noted that Garner then terminated the contract one week later, and thus was just owed one-week's salary under the terms of the contract.

✓ Operational Pointer – Be careful when you see language in a contract that is too broad. As the below case indicates, you may want to define the terms or clause so that it appears that each party considered the situation and agreed upon it.

In *City of Miami v. Joseph Robbie et. al.*,[8] the City of Miami sued the Miami Dolphins in a dispute over the rent owed to the City under a 1977 contract to play a minimum number of games in the city-owned Orange Bowl. The dispute arose due to the cancellation of games secondary to the NFL player's strike during the 1982 football season, where the City claimed rent was due for three unplayed games. The Dolphins claimed that they had agreed in settlement to play an additional home game in the Orange Bowl during the 1985 and 1986 regular season, or pay the City $30,000 if such game was, for any reason, not played. The City countered that the money was owed regardless of the fitness of the Orange Bowl for play, because the settlement was a payment for the breach in the 1977 contract. The Dolphins felt that the "for any reason" language did not include unfitness of the Orange Bowl for play by Act of God or public enemy. The trial court tried to enforce the Dolphins version of the settlement agreement, but the Court of Appeals held there had not been a meeting of the minds as to what "for any reason" meant under the settlement, and thus the Court was powerless to enforce the agreement at all, since no direct meeting of the minds had occurred.

12)   Indemnification and Hold Harmless

Indemnity agreements are agreements that provide for one party to hold another party harmless for a specified liability. For example, if Bob's Concerts, Inc. desires to book the XYZ Arena with a The Wild and Crazy Band, XYZ Arena will probably require Promoter Bob to indemnify and hold harmless the Arena for any injury to persons and damage to property caused by the promoter and the Band. Prior to drafting the indemnity agreement, the arena's attorney should consider the nature of the event, the practices and customs for that type of event, whether the promoter or show manager is a repeat customer, the other parties involved, the amount of insurance and level of coverage if any, the costs and overall risks to the facility.

Brenda Hamilton v. Facility Management of Louisiana, Inc. et. al.,[9] is a good example of how indemnity provisions in your standard license contract or license agreement can protect a facility. In *Hamilton*, the Louisiana Superdome was sued by Ms. Hamilton, an attendee at The General Conference of Seventh-Day Adventist (hereafter the "Church").

---

[8] 454 So.2d 606 (Fla. App. 1984).
[9] 545 So. 2d 1198 (La. App. 4th Cir. 1989), vacated 549 So.2d 316 (La.)

Ms. Hamilton left the Superdome and was walking to get her car when she was injured in the parking lot when a parking gate arm descended and struck Ms. Hamilton in the back of the head. Because the Louisiana Superdome had a broad indemnity provision in their license contract with the Church, the Church and their insurance carrier were responsible for the liability associated with the personal injury.

The Church claimed that because the injury did not occur on the licensed premises, but in the parking lot, the Church has no obligation to indemnify the Superdome. The indemnity provision in the Superdome license agreement states:

"A Licensee, by entering into said agreement, shall hereby waive any claim against and shall indemnify, save and hold harmless the HMC and its agents and employees for any damages to the premises, fittings, equipment. And furnishings of the facilities occasioned by or in connection with the use of the premises by Licensee during the time the premises are used or occupied under said agreement, and against claims of any and all persons for injury to persons or damage to property occasioned by or in connection with the use of the premises by Licensee."[10]

The Church raised the issue of whether there was an intent to indemnify the Superdome by the language of the contract. The Court cited two cases[11] which stated " Where the contract contains a general indemnity provision together with an agreement to provide comprehensive general liability insurance, it contains the language necessary to evidence an intent to indemnify the other for the other's negligence."

The Court held that the above indemnification language was clear and precise and that it designates that the Church shall indemnify the Superdome for any damages "occasioned by or in connection with the use of the premises by Licensee."[12]

---

[10] 545 So. 2d 1200.
[11] *Polozola v. Garlock*, 343 So. 2^d 1000 (La. 1977) and *Jennings v. Ralston Purina Co.*, 201 So. 2^d 168 (La.App. 2nd Cir. 1967).
[12] 545 So. 2d at 1200.

In *City of Montgomery v. JYD International, Inc.,*[13], an employee of JYD International was working as a temporary cash register operator during JYD's tenancy of the Montgomery Civic Center. Ms. Farris, the employee, entered the Civic Center from a service entrance and took a "short cut" through the Grand Ballroom to the River Room where she was to be on duty. While crossing the stage in the grand ballroom, she slipped and fell on an oily substance, fracturing her arm.[14] She then sued the Civic Center and JYD. Montgomery cross claimed against JYD demanding indemnification for any damages Montgomery might incur due to Ms, Farris' injuries. JYD then moved for summary judgment regarding Farris' tort claims against it, which was granted. Montgomery eventually settled the case with Ms. Farris before trial.[15]

Montgomery alleged that the indemnity provisions in its license contract with JYD for use of the Civic Center property described as the "River Room" used for JYD's rug sale covered the injuries incurred by Farris, JYD's employee. The Supreme Court of Alabama stated that when parties knowingly, evenhandedly, intelligently, and for valid consideration, enter into an agreement whereby one party agrees to indemnify another, including indemnity against the indemnitee's own wrongs, if expressed in clear and unequivocal language, then such agreements will be upheld.[16]

The Court then considered if JYD did agree to indemnify Montgomery, whether that agreement was valid when the injury that occurred happened well outside the rented space specified in the contract. The Supreme Court held that the broad language used in the indemnity agreement was so broad as to potentially make licensees responsible for accidents that occurred in the parking lots and sidewalks outside the Civic Center, clearly outside the scope of a licensee's control, and that when an indemnitee attempts to gain indemnity for its own negligent acts under these circumstances, the agreement was void as against public policy.[17]

---

[13] 534 So.2d 592 (Ala. 1988).

[14] Id. at 593.

[15] Montgomery and JYD then moved for summary judgment as to the cross claims between the defendants. The Court granted JYD's summary judgment request, in effect leaving Montgomery as the solely responsible party for the injuries incurred. Montgomery appealed.

[16] Id. at 596.

[17] Id. at 595.

The indemnification provision should also include any fire or theft that results from the negligence of the licensee. In *W.R. Winkler v. Appalachian Amusement Company*,[18] Winkler owned a building in Boone, NC that was licensed as a movie theater to the Appalachian Amusement Company. The license was entered into originally in 1938, with successors in interest taking over the agreement from their predecessors. In a small room behind the stage and screen, Appalachian operated a gas burner-powered popcorn machine. In January, 1950, a 16-year-old boy was popping corn in the room, having previously helped pop corn and having been instructed upon how to do it. The manager of the theater came down, took 25 boxes of corn with him, and instructed the boy to bring 25 more boxes up front. The theater was full at that time, waiting for the show to begin. The boy filled the machine to pop more corn as he left to help the manager. When he returned, flames were around the hopper, between the popcorn and the hopper and the wood under the popper was burning. The popper was on fire, and the boy unsuccessfully attempted to put out the fire by placing his coat over it and then left to get help. He returned with the manager and district manager, but by that time, the room was one large blaze, and was unable to be contained with the fire extinguisher. Due to the air ducts, the fire was able to rapidly spread throughout the theater.

The owner of the property sued for damages, alleging negligence on the part of the licensee, and pointed to the directions for the popper instructing that it never be left unattended while in use. The license stated that the licensee agreed to make repairs to the building at their own expense except if damaged by fire, and that the licensors agreed to keep the premises insured against fire or casualty, and that the licensees were responsible for repairing the premises if damaged due to fire. The building was valued at approximately $100,000 prior to the fire and $60-65,000 after the fire. The Plaintiff spent over $34,000 in repairing the fire damage to the building. In March of 1950, the parties cancelled the prior 1938 license and entered into a new agreement. The repairs to the building were made in part from money from fire insurance policies on the building and from money received from Appalachian under the new license agreement.

The Supreme Court of North Carolina considered the matter, and the doctrine that a licensee is not responsible for accidental damage by fire, but would be liable if the buildings were damaged by his own negligence.

---

[18] 79 S.E.2d 185 (N.C. 1953).

The Court held that sufficient evidence of negligence existed so that the matter should have gone before a jury, rather than dismissed by the lower court. The license provided that the licensor should repair a building damaged by fire, which he did, but the tenant was still potentially liable in this case because the fire was most likely directly caused by his negligence in leaving the popcorn popper unattended, contrary to manufacturer's instructions.

13) Insurance

Insurance clauses will cover both the insurance needed to be provided by the licensee of the facility, and what circumstances are covered by the facility's insurance. It is important to obtain a Certificate of Insurance from each and every licensee covering any mishap that might occur during a licensee's use of the facility, and indemnifying the facility from any responsibility for any injury that might occur. This is especially important when hosting high-risk events at a facility, such as wrestling, ultimate fighting, truck and tractor pulls, rodeos, and other events where the risk of injury to patrons or licensees is above the normal. This contractual language may also be called an indemnification and hold harmless clause. A few samples of such clauses are presented below.

"Licensee shall maintain the insurance hereinafter described at its expense naming the Facility as an additional insured. This insurance shall be in the amount of $_____ for death or bodily injury or loss sustained by one person in any occurrence; $_____ for death or bodily injury or loss sustained by more than one person, and $_____ for damages or loss of property in any one occurrence.

"Licensee shall indemnify and hold harmless and save the Facility from and against all claims, demands, actions, damages, losses, costs, liabilities, expenses and judgments recovered from or asserted against the Facility on account of injury or damage to person or property to the extent that any such damage or injury may be incident to, arise out of, or be caused either proximately or remotely, wholly or in part, by any act, omission, negligence or misconduct on the part of Licensee or any of its agents, servants, employees, contractors, patrons, guests, sublicensees, or invitees or of any other person entering upon the licensed premises or common areas with the express or implied invitation or permission of Licensee or when any such injury or damage is the result, proximate or remote, of the violation by Licensee or any of its agents, servants, employees, contractors, patrons, guests, sublicensees or invitees of any law, ordinance or governmental order of any kind, or when any such injury or damage may in any other way arise from or out of occupancy or use of the licensed premises or common areas by Licensee, or its agents, servants, employees, contractors, patrons, guests, sublicensees or invitees. This indemnification of the Facility by Licensee shall be effective unless such damage or injury results from the primary negligence of the Facility. Licensee covenants that if the Facility is made a party to any litigation or claim commenced against Licensee or relating to the Agreement or to the licensed premises, then Licensee shall pay all costs incurred by or imposed upon the Facility arising out of or incident to any such litigation."

These clauses basically state that the Licensee will protect the Facility from any liability for any injury occurring during the license period, providing the injury was not caused directly by the Facility's actions or failure to act. By mandating insurance coverage and the amounts of insurance required, this will further protect the facility from becoming the target of an injured party seeking "deep pockets" from which to recover a large settlement, since insurance coverage for such an injury will be in place. Insurance coverage for general liability, theft and fire should all be required. For more information on insurance see Chapter 5, Risk Management and Insurance.

14)   Liability and Limitations on Liability for Facility
This clause is different from the "indemnification" clause. First, a license agreement should state that the licensee is liable for their negligence and the negligence of their employees, contractors and guests. In a different clause, the "indemnification" clause should state that licensee shall indemnify and hold harmless the facility for any loss it may suffer because of the licensee's negligence.

This two-clause method provides the facility with better liability protection.[19] This clause passes the responsibility to the licensee to make sure that his or her sphere of liability is covered by insurance or managed properly or both. The licensee may then pass this liability down the line to each respective group. A "limitation on liability provision" limits the

---

[19] Please seek assistance from your legal counsel on all matters concerning the drafting or interpretation of facility license agreements.

amount of liability of one or both of the parties to a contract. For example, in many retail sales contracts, the manufacturer or seller attempts to limit their liability to the replacement value of the product. A facility may attempt to limit its liability for money damages in an amount equal to the payment for rental of the space.

In *Evans v. Valley Forge Convention Center,* [20] a child fell from an exhibit platform at a boat show at the Valley Forge Convention Center, and the parents sued for substantial and permanent injuries. The 23-month-old boy fell striking his head on the concrete floor four feet below the platform. The parents stated that the platform was negligently constructed and maintained, and that if a railing was properly placed, the child would not have been injured. The parents also sued for negligent infliction of emotional distress. The exhibitor claimed the parents failed to properly supervise their child, creating a situation in which the child could be injured. After reviewing several claims for summary judgment between the parties, the Court held that using a reasonable parent standard under Pennsylvania law would govern the exhibitor's claims, and was an issue to be determined by the court at trial. The Court dismissed the parent's claim for negligent infliction of emotional distress. The Convention Center sought to be dismissed from the complaint as not being in possession of the premises when the accident occurred, having licensed the premises to a promoter, who then sublet space to the exhibitors. The Court held that genuine issues of fact remained to be decided as to whether the convention center still retained control over the premises as the agreement provided that the Center had the ability to prohibit exhibitors or promoters from bringing any dangerous exhibits, materials, objects, vehicles or the like onto the premises, and was responsible for the maintenance of the Center, and thus the Court denied their motion for judgment.

✓ Operational Pointer – A limitation on liability clause for injuries and damages to property should be clearly stated in facility license agreements. The convention center in the above case left open the door to suit by maintaining significant control over what was brought into the facility and their standard maintenance concerns. It is possible to close this liability door with adequate indemnification agreements with show management, exhibitors and promoters. This case also hinges on the exact agreement between the

---

[20] No. 95-658, 1996 U.S. Dist. LEXIS 12091 (August 15, 1996).

boat show and the exhibitor, and a facility's contract should require the adequate indemnification and insurance provisions from an exhibitor or any other third party that sublicenses space from your licensee.

15)   Name of Event & Purpose

This clause requires the facility user to specifically name the event or events that will take place in the facility. The user must also state the purpose of the events. This clause prevents the user from switching the purpose for which he or she is using the facility. An example of such a clause is as follows:

"In consideration of the License Fee, the Facility grants the ABC Company, Inc. ("Licensee") permission to use the licensed premises, as described below, for a Sail Boat Show and for no other purpose."

16)   Notice of Default

A Licensee may become unable to use the facility as planned, due to its lack of funds, sickness of a performer, or for other reasons. If due to insolvency, the Licensee may wish to assign its license to a successor in interest, or may just choose to default upon the license agreement. A Licensee may also fail to make advanced payments as required, and thus leave the facility in a quandary. Should the facility demand payment and what should the facility do if the Licensee is unable to meet its obligations under the contract? A facility should have a notice of default provision in its contract, covering how a facility may notify the Licensee that the Facility is choosing to terminate its agreement, but still reserve the right to full payment, due to the Licensee's failure to live up to their end of the agreement. A sample of such a Notice of Default clause appears below:

"If before or during the terms of the Agreement (1) Licensee makes a general assignment for the benefit of creditors or takes the benefit of any insolvency act, (2) a receiver or trustee is appointed from Licensee or Licensee's property, (3) execution is issued pursuant to a judgment rendered against Licensee, (4) This agreement is assigned, passed to or devolves upon any person, firm or corporation other than Licensee or Licensee attempts to assign this agreement without prior written consent of the

Facility, or (5) Licensee defaults in the performance or observance of any of its obligations or agreements contained herein, including the agreement to make payments contained herein, then in any such event, this Agreement shall, at the Facility's option, expressed in a twelve hour written, telefax or telegraph notice to Licensee, terminate as fully and completely as if such date and time or termination were the date and time definitely fixed herein for the expiration of the term and of the Agreement, and Licensee shall then quit and surrender its right to the Facility, but Licensee shall remain liable as hereinafter provided."

17)   Period of Time and Use of Facilities
This clause is usually one of the first clauses in the contract. This clause is a detailed description of the facility area, halls, rooms, arenas and other areas that will be used by the licensee. The clause should have a move-in time, set-up days, event days and times, and a move-out time. If different areas of the facility have different move-in and move-out times, these times must also be stated in the license agreement. If the licensee is using the entire facility, the facility manager may still consider listing the specific areas licensed by the licensee. Many facilities contain areas such as a board room or conference area that may be licensed to a separate client without interfering with the larger event. Of course, as the manager of the facility you may want to inform and discuss the matter with the managers of both events.

✔ Operational Pointer – When stating any date in a letter, license agreement and booking sheet, always include the day of the week, e.g., "Friday, January 31, 2001." This practice provides you with a practical double checking procedure.

18)   Radio and Television Broadcasting
Many more events are being broadcast over radio and television than ever before. No longer are broadcasts of events limited to sporting events on major networks. Comedy acts performed in large theaters can be seen on television or heard on radio, antique shows held in convention and civic centers are shown on public television, concerts are shown on pay-per-view, and many more theatrical, operatic and dance performances are broadcast than ever with the proliferation of cable television. Even religious gatherings in facilities have been broadcast over the airwaves. By

including a clause regarding broadcasting of the Event in a license agreement, the facility can make sure that the facility gets credit in the broadcast over radio or television for hosting the event, and may be able to control the dissemination of the performance or event. Examples of broadcasting clauses are presented below:

"**Television and Broadcast Rights:** The Licensee shall not televise or broadcast any scheduled event to be presented at the Facility under the terms of the Agreement without prior written approval of the Facility Manager, and if the Licensee desires to telecast or broadcast any event, the Licensee agrees to pay the Facility an additional fee of _____ percent (____%) of the consideration received for the privilege of telecasting or broadcasting the event, in addition thereto, the Licensee shall pay all costs in connection with such broadcasting or televising of such Event.

"Neither the Licensee or Facility shall televise or broadcast the Event, whether live or recorded, without prior written consent of both the Licensee and the Facility. Any consent by the Facility shall be subject to, among other things, to the inclusion of this agreement of a "make whole" clause in favor of the Facility. Any broadcast of the Event shall be through the Facility's exclusive contractor (if any) at rates charges by such contractor. Licensee grants to the Facility and its tenants and designees the right to use and to authorize others to use the name or names of the Licensee of the Event or personalities appearing in the Event for the purposes of advertising and publicizing the Facility. The facility has the right to require advance payment for said broadcast privilege in addition to the rental fee. Such permission must be obtained in writing in advance of the broadcast date."

In either clause stated above, the facility has chosen to reserve the right to charge additional fees for the broadcast rights. Given the revenues generated by pay-per-view events alone, a facility should be particularly concerned with reserving the right to at least charge a fee for broadcast rights, if not request a percentage of the revenues generated from any such broadcast.

19)   Remedies Upon Default

Should a Licensee default under the agreement by failing to live up to the terms specified, a facility should issue a notice of default, provide the Licensee with a short period of time in which to cure the default, and then choose a remedy to the situation. If the tenant cannot cure the default, the facility will need to have adequate provisions for remedies or damages it wishes to recover in such cases. An example of such a clause, similar to that covering cancellations, appears below.

"Licensee covenants that if any default is made in the payment of the rent or any part thereof at the times specified, or if any default or violation is made in terms of the license, this license, at the option of the Facility shall cease and terminate and the Facility shall have the right to re-enter the premises with or without process of law and Licensee agrees to peaceably give up possession of the premises in such event and the Licensee shall, notwithstanding such re-entry, pay the full amount of said rental as herein agreed to be paid. In case of suit or action instituted by the Facility to enforce compliance with this agreement, Licensee agrees to pay all court costs and expenses of the Facility, including attorney's fees arising from such suit or action."

20)   Rental Amount

The rental or license amount must be stated in the agreement. If the amount is not known by the parties, the formula to calculate the rental amount when it is known should be stated the agreement. For example if the rate includes a percentage of the box office or if the rate is based of the use of exhibit space used or sold, these formulas must be stated in the agreement. Of course, just like a bank check, the amount stated in the license agreement should be written in words and numbers.

This clause should also cover any deposits that are required under the license agreement. This section of the clause states that the user of the facility shall pay a deposit in consideration for entering the license agreement. This clause should <u>not</u> state that if the licensee cancels the license agreement that he or she forfeits their deposit. This language provides the licensee an inexpensive way to cancel the entire license agreement. See the Cancellation Clause for more information.

21)   Seating Capacity

The seating capacity of a facility is derived not only from the number of seats available, but also by local fire code. Care should be taken so that the seating capacity of the facility is not exceeded. In part, by controlling the ticketing process, the facility also controls the seating and seating capacity. (Also see Ticketing and the Box Office clause and Chapter 9, Ticketing) An example of seating capacity clause is shown below:

"Licensee will not permit tickets or passes to be sold or distributed in excess of the seating capacity of the facility as determined by the Facility. The Facility will have the right to retain a certain number of seats as backup for problem seat locations. Licensee agrees that any tickets for seats with limited or impaired vision or any backstage seats that are sold will be clearly marked accordingly. Each person in attendance shall have a ticket for a specific seat. Standing in the aisles, vomatories, or steps is strictly prohibited."

22)   Security Protection

This clause addresses the security responsibilities of the parties. If the licensee must hire the in-house security personnel the policy should be stated in the license agreement. If the licensee may hire his or her own security, a security plan from the licensee should be submitted to the facility manager for his or her approval. Many facilities require the security company to submit a copy of their certificate of insurance with the security plan. This plan should be submitted at least thirty days prior to the event. This clause should also address the firearm policy of the facility. An example of a security clause where the licensee hires his or her own security is as follows:

"The Licensee shall be completely responsible for security in the facility (or if only part of the facility is being secured by the licensee than the licensed premises). The Licensee shall be solely liable for the acts and conduct of all persons for or on behalf of the Licensee and Licensee agrees to maintain at all times, at its own expense, security forces as are deemed necessary by the facility manager to maintain order and to protect persons and property."

23)   Security Interests – Uniform Commercial Code

The Uniform Commercial Code Article 9 (UCC) contains the basic rules regarding security interests in personal property and fixtures, sales of accounts, chattel mortgages and the like. Security interests basically relate to financing; for example, when you obtain a car loan, the bank or financial institution takes a security interest in the car, or uses it as collateral for the purchase, so that if you do not make your loan payments, they can take the car itself in lieu of payment. This is usually called a purchase money security interest in the property purchased. Inventory can be used to secure a loan, as can accounts receivable, equipment, and the like.

For a facility, this comes into play when the facility leases part or all of its space to a lessee that may not have enough money to pay the facility for the use of the space. For example, a facility may use the event ticket proceeds as security for the lease payment. A facility may also consider taking a security interest in equipment brought into a facility by an exhibitor or lessee of the facility to ensure payment of the rental/lease fee, in appropriate situations. To ensure a proper security interest in such property, an appropriate contract will need to be drawn up, and steps will need to be taken to "perfect that interest," to make sure there are no existing liens on the subject property that would lead to a facility not being able to collect or possess the property should the lessee default. If a facility is interested in this type of security interests, the manager should consult an attorney for the requirements and procedures necessary to perfect a security interest in your jurisdiction.

A security interest is also used against facilities. For example, if a facility desires to purchase a large piece of equipment like bleachers, and will be doing so by making payments over time. The vendor may take a security interest in the bleachers, allowing the debt to be secured by the equipment itself, and giving the vendor the right to take possession the bleachers if the debt is not paid. This is obviously an advantage to both parties; the facility need not come up with several thousand dollars or more up front to purchase an item, and the vendor does much more business by being able to sell his equipment while accepting payments over time, and he is assured "payment" in that he may repossess the equipment if the facility defaults. Other assets can be used to secure the purchase of a new item as well, not just the item purchased. Fixtures, accounts receivable, equipment, promissory notes, and the like can all serve as collateral for loans of money from a bank, or to secure the purchase of new items.

In *Klinger v. Pocono International Raceway, Inc.*, [21] First Penn-sylvania Bank (Bank), Klinger, and Pocono International Raceway (Poco-no) all had competing claims on ticket proceeds. On April 28, 1972, the Bank loaned five million dollars to Pocono, taking a security interest under Article 9 of the U.C.C. The loan agreement contained a security agreement and financing statements, later amended in 1976 in an Amendment to the Term Loan Agreement. The Klingers held a $50,000 Pocono judgment note due in 1971. Mr. Klinger died in 1977 and Mrs. Klinger caused the judg-ment, augmented by accrued interest to an amount over $70,000 to be revived by writ in 1978, and sought to execute on the judgment in July of 1978. Pocono was operating an auto raceway and the sheriff levied and took custody of $76,000 in ticket proceeds from the "Coca-Cola 500." The Sheriff went to the Raceway and had Pocono set aside the gate receipts over a three-day period, after which, the Sheriff picked up cash of approximately $76,000 for which a receipt was given. The Bank petitioned to intervene, seeking to set aside the Klinger levy, on the grounds that the Bank had a superior security interest and priority in the ticket proceeds due to its securi-ty agreement over the levy. The trial court judge refused to set aside the levy and the Bank appealed.[22]

The main question was whether ticket proceeds could be subject to an Article 9 security interest. The Bank's security interest covered all of the raceway's personal property and fixtures, without limit to all inventory, accounts receivable, contract rights and general intangibles, and proceeds therefrom. The Superior Court held that at the time of the levy, the Bank had a perfected, superior claim to the ticket proceeds under its security agreement signed in 1972 and amended in 1976. The ticket receipts were generated from the property secured under the agreement and constituted "identifiable proceeds," clearly covered under the agreement. The Court found that tickets were "personal property," and that personal property need not be tangible, such as trademarks, patents and the like. Tickets, being personal property, may have a security interest attached, and therefore proceeds from their sale are also subject to that security

---

[21] 433 A.2d 1357 (Pa. Super. 1980).
[22] Id. at 1359.

interest.[23] In their analysis, the Court found that when the Raceway held the tickets, it was "inventory" or a general intangible. When a customer bought the ticket, and it was sold, it became a license contract for the right to see an event on a certain date.

The raceway gets an account receivable converted into proceeds at the date of the event, when the contract is completed. Regardless of the form, the ticket remained subject to the security interest the Bank had put in place, by virtue of the language in its agreement with Pocono. Despite the fact that the Klinger debt pre-dated the original Bank security agreement, Klinger failed to perfect the debt until 1978, well after the Bank had its security agreement in place, and therefore, the ticket proceeds could not be subject to the levy to satisfy the Klinger debt.

The lesson from this case is that when a facility takes out a loan, and secures the loan with all of its assets, this will most likely cover tickets and ticket proceeds unless specifically exempted in the agreement. Priority in the liens will dictate who could levy against the property securing the loans, and whether such items like ticket proceeds could be seized. Priority of liens will also affect the willingness of subsequent lenders or suppliers to lend money or supply goods, as they will need to take a subordinate interest to the "senior" lien holders to secure their payment. This is best described in terms of the willingness of a bank to loan an individual money when there is already a first and second mortgage on a home. A bank may be unwilling to make a third mortgage loan, since the first two mortgagers will most likely be made whole should the house be sold, but the third mortgage holder's position is less secure, and more money may be owed than the home is worth. Likewise, subsequent lien holders, having "junior" priority, have a less secure position than senior lien holders, and may be less willing to take a security interest in property already subject to security interests.

24)   Services Provided

This clause states the basic services such as heating, lighting, and ventilation are provided by the facility that are included in the basic rental of the facility. Depending on the facility, "air conditioning" may not be included in the basic services provided to the license. The clause informs the licensee that any services provided in excess of the services listed will be billed at a specific hourly rate.

---

[23] Id. at 1361.

25)   Severability

This clause in a contract states that each and every clause acts as a separate contract. In basic contract law, if one clause was held to be invalid, the entire agreement could be thrown out because each clause depended on the other, much like how a vehicle depends on all individual parts to function in order for the whole machine to function properly as a unit. A severability clause, such as the one below, enables each clause to function completely on its own, and thus if one clause is held to be invalid for any reason, such as a change in law or interpretation by the parties, the remaining clauses will still function and constitute the agreement between the parties, preventing the whole agreement from being thrown out.

"Every provision of this Agreement shall be severable. If any term or provision is illegal or invalid for any reason whatsoever, such illegality or invalidity shall not affect the legality or validity of the remainder of this agreement."

26)   Simultaneous Events and Common Areas

This clause is usually for convention centers or multipurpose facilities. It informs the user that other events may be scheduled in the facility and for assignment purposes, all "common areas" are in the exclusive control of the facility manager. A facility manager may define the term "common areas" to include lobby space, registration areas, interior and exterior signage space, wall and hanging space, walkways, plaza areas and all other exterior areas of the facility.

27)   Ticketing and Box Office

This clause in most arena facility license agreements states that the facility shall control and direct the ticket office, ticket office personnel, and all ticket sales revenue from the time tickets are printed and are first on sale until the event has concluded. This provides the facility with some control over seating location, disability seating, ticketing policy and revenue. By controlling ticket revenue, the facility has a functional reserve from which to draw should the licensee not live up to its financial obligation to the facility under the license agreement.

A sample clause might read as follows:

"The facility shall at all times maintain control and direction of the ticket office, ticket personnel and ticket sale revenue until settlement.

A. Agencies: The facility shall have the right to offer tickets for sale at all of its regular agencies. Licensee may request that ticket sale privileges be extended to additional agencies, but Licensee assumes all responsibility for collection of funds from such agencies and will be liable to the Facility for box office or rental fee percentage of all tickets sold through such outlets. There shall be no consignment of tickets without the prior written consent of the Facility and payment to the facility of the full face price of such tickets at the time of consignment.

B. Charges: The Facility shall provide ticket office facilities. Licensee will pay as a reimbursable cost X percent (___ %) of the gross ticket sales less all applicable taxes, with a maximum box office charge being no more than _____ dollars ($). Said fee shall be separate and apart from the building's rent charge.

C. Tickets: At least ten (10) days before licensee desires the sale or distribution of the tickets and admissions to begin, Licensee shall deliver to the Facility all information required for such tickets and admissions for the Event and any information concerning the Event requested by the Facility, and the Facility shall cause such tickets and admissions to be printed. The Facility shall provide an accounting to Licensee for all tickets and admissions. All tickets must be ordered by the Facility with their cost being an additional charge to Licensee. Said charge shall be separate and apart from the building's rent charge. All ticket revenues shall be the sole property of the Facility until box office settlement.

D. Refunds: If any or all tickets sold for the Event are refunded, Licensee shall return to the Facility any ticket revenues received by the Licensee, and in addition, Licensee shall pay to the Facility its refund service charge for each ticket refunded.

E. Complimentary Tickets: Licensee agrees to provide _____ tickets to the Facility for each performance or day for any event, covered by this agreement on a complimentary basis. (Some contracts have this number as one percent of the total tickets available for the Event.)

F. Staging/Obstruction of View: If the Event is staged in such a way that the view from any Suite/Luxury Box is obstructed, Licensee agrees that the Facility shall make available to licensees of such suites/boxes the opportunity to purchase top-price tickets in the general seating area.

G. Settlement: All box office receipts after applicable taxes shall be held by the Facility and applied in payment of all sums of money which shall become due from the Licensee to the Facility hereunder or by reason of the

Licensee's use of the facilities provided herein, including all amounts becoming due for payments payable to Licensee to the Facility for personnel, services, materials and equipment furnished to licensee by the Facility under this Agreement, any agreement supplementing this agreement, Licensee's work orders and requests, or otherwise. The Facility will remit out of the box office receipts to all applicable governmental authorities on the Licensee's behalf, all sales, entertainment and other taxes. Any surplus remaining shall first be applied by the Facility in satisfaction of any remaining obligation or liability of the Licensee to the Facility under this license agreement or otherwise, including without limitation any damages whether stipulated herein or not, to which the Facility may be entitled by reason of breach of this License Agreement by Licensee. Rental settlement shall be made on (the closing night of the show/within 24 hours after conclusion of the Event) unless prior settlement is reached between both parties. A box office statement shall be furnished to the Licensee by the Facility within 24 hours after the conclusion of the Event, and at the Licensee's request, provisional settlement may be made as it deems required to assure proper final settlement. The Facility shall provide, within Fifteen (15) days following the Event, Licensee with a statement of all costs relating to the Licensee's use of the Facility and the application of box office receipts to such costs and shall pay to the Licensee any amounts that shall be due to the Licensee. Licensee agrees to examine such a statement and to notify the Facility in writing five (5) business days of any claimed error or objection. Unless Licensee notifies the Facility of any such claimed error or objection within five (5) business days, such statement shall be deemed to be a true and correct statement of account between the Licensee and the Facility. Licensee agrees to pay promptly any amounts shown to be due to the Facility on such statement which are not paid out of the application of box office receipts."

Settlement issues will arise between tenants and facilities on a frequent basis, so special attention should be paid to this clause. As indicated above, when a Facility is controlling the box office receipts, it will then be necessary to account for those receipts to the Licensee, as soon as possible following the event. Many facilities choose to undergo a preliminary accounting and estimate of costs, with a final settlement occurring at a specified later date. Other facilities may wish to make one settlement, rather than a preliminary and final settlement, depending on what the needs of the facility and licensee are under the circumstances.

Regardless of the timing of settlement, a statement should be provided to the Licensee with a date certain for any revisions before such statement becomes final. Otherwise, final settlement could be delayed for quite some time, which does not benefit either party. For more information on ticketing, see Chapter 9, Facility Ticketing.

28)   Vacation of Premises

Most facilities will be concerned not only with the Licensee's occupation of the facility, but with the event's prompt departure thereafter, so that subsequent tenants can be accommodated. If a tenant holds over, or fails to remove their possessions from the premises as agreed, a facility may be forced to assist them in such a departure to prevent any problems with incoming parties. Frequently, Time is of the Essence clauses will also be present, emphasizing the importance of prompt departure from the facility to the Licensee. Examples of hold-over and failure to vacate clauses are shown below.

"If Licensee fails to surrender the premises of the Facility at the expiration of the time periods for use stated herein, then the Facility may remove from its premises all effects remaining thereon and store the same wherever it sees fit at Licensee's cost, expense and risk. The Facility shall not be liable to Licensee on account of so removing and so storing such effects. For such additional periods as any effects of Licensee's remain at the Facility, Licensee shall pay to the Facility double the rate for the space involved. In addition, Licensee may be liable to the Facility for any claim of damages suffered by the Facility resulting from Licensee's failure to surrender the premises to the Facility as agreed."

"In the event that the Licensee fails, neglects or refuses to remove its property from the authorized areas of the Facility or related parking lots and driveways promptly upon a termination for default or after the time specified for removal thereof, said property shall be deemed abandoned and the Facility shall have the right to remove, place in storage or otherwise dispose of any such property at the sole cost and expense of Licensee.

Licensee hereby irrevocably constitutes and appoints the Facility as its special attorney-in-fact to perform all acts necessary in removing, storing and disposing of the said abandoned personal property and to execute and deliver a bill of sale therefore."

A highly occupied facility will at sometime need the "Time Is Of The Essence" language in their contracts to license the facility. This clause must be part of your standard license contract. The phrase "time is of the essence" has a definite legal meaning attached to it. It basically means that if a move-out time is specified (to the exact minute 11:59am) in the contract, the client will have fully vacated the premises by that point in time. If your facility's contracts are written so that one client is moving-out while another client is waiting to move-in, the "time is of the essence" language is important to you. As the facility manager you want to make sure that if any difficulties are incurred with a party being tardy in their vacating of the premises, monetary damages can be assessed against the hold-over client. The client moving-in may may attempt to hold the facility liable for any damages incurred because of the hold-over on the move-out of Client A.

Time is of the Essence is a legal term that fixes a period of time as vital to the performance of a contract. If the time period specified is not met, and that time period is crucial to the initial performance under the contract, then the duties under the whole contract can be discharged. Simply, this means that if under a contract in which time is of the essence work must be completed by January 1st, if that work is not completed by that date, the duty to pay the contractor may be discharged in full, meaning that no payment need be made on any of the work performed. This is best illustrated in real property cases like the one below.

In *Friendship Medical Center, LTD., v. Space Rentals*,[24] the area manager for Space Rentals made an invitation to Friendship to present it with a Sales Order Proposal Offer, under which Space Rentals would provide Friendship with a new medical center addition at Friendship's place of business at a cost of $143,647.00.

Friendship was to tender a 20% deposit to Space Rentals in order to finalize the offer. On May 11, 1973, prior to tendering the deposit, an addition to the sales proposal was made increasing the costs to $144,832.00. Because "time was of the essence," Friendship demanded and Space Rentals agreed to obtain the necessary permits for construction within 30 days of Friendship's offer so that Friendship could continue to serve its patients, maintain a high standard of medical practice within the community, fulfill its legal obligations to others, and maximize on its expenditures, specifically with Space Rentals through expanded operations, all of which was understood by Space Rentals. If the permits were not obtained in the time specified, Space Rentals was to return the 20% deposit to Friendship.[25] At the signing of the agreement, the deposit was tendered to

---

[24] 62 F.R.D. 106 (N.D. Ill. 1974).
[25] Id. at 108.

Space Rentals. Space Rentals did not obtain the permits within thirty days from the date of signing as required, and failed to return the deposit as specified in the contract. Friendship sought a refund of the deposit. Sales refused to do so, and as a result, Friendship lost profits, income, impairment of contracts with other parties, loss of patients, and loss of stature in the community, as well as the lost deposit, estimating its losses at $555,000 by Space Rental's failure to comply with the contract. Space Rentals alleged that in its complaint, Friendship failed to state a claim upon which relief could be granted by the Court. While the Court dismissed the complaint and allowed the Plaintiff Friendship to rewrite its complaint to specify its cause of action, it is clear that the Plaintiff lost money due to the breach of a "time is of the essence" clause, causing it to lose close to $555,000 and that the failure of Space Rentals to perform its duties under the contract in a timely manner may lead to the cancellation of the contract, refund of the deposit, and perhaps full reimbursement for damages suffered.

29)   Waiver of Subrogation

Subrogation is a legal term in which once an insurance company pays a claim of loss, it can then turn to the parties responsible for that loss, to recover the reimbursement it has already paid to the injured person. Likewise, the party who was injured, agrees to assign the insurance company any rights they may hold to sue the responsible party for the loss for which they were paid, preventing "double dipping" by the injured party. In a Waiver of Subrogation clause, the parties to the license agreement agree not to sue each other for any losses that are already covered by insurance policies, to the extent of coverage available. This means that if a patron is injured on an escalator during an event, and subsequently sues the Facility, the parties agree that applicable insurance shall pay the claim, and they shall not sue each other for the costs of the claim. If there is a deductible on the insurance policy, or the injury exceeds the amount of insurance available under the policy, these amounts may be the subject of litigation and dispute between the parties, because these would be non-covered costs. An example of such a clause appears below:

d) Stage Restrictions

Stage restriction provisions may be important to your facility, especially if space is restricted or if local safety or fire regulations determine the amount of room that can be occupied by a stage. Stage restrictions may also cover any additional charges a Licensee may incur if they desire additional equipment or modifications necessary for their event. An example of some of the clauses that might cover commonplace stage restrictions are as follows:

"Licensee shall file with _____ at least thirty (30) days prior to the commencement of the term of this permit, a full and detailed description of Licensee's requirements for the facilities, equipment or personnel to be used, including but not limited to all stage, sound, lighting, chair or table set-ups and such other information as may be required by the _____.
Additional frontal lighting supplied from the lighting bridge or side stage baffles is chargeable at the rate of $_____ per light per performance.
Maximum stage size, including sound wings and production equipment, cannot exceed _____ feet in width except when the first three rows of platform seats on the East and West sides are retracted, the maximum width cannot exceed _____ feet."

4.03 Overbooking and Double-Booking

In *Rainbow Travel Service, Inc. v. Hilton Hotels Corporation,* [26] Rainbow, a travel agent, booked hotel rooms at the Fontainebleu Hilton in Miami, FL in order to book travel packages for University of Oklahoma football fans to attend the Oklahoma-University of Miami football game scheduled for September 26, 1986. The Fontainebleu booked the requested number of hotel rooms and required Rainbow send them a significant deposit, covering the first-night's stay on the reserved rooms. Two Rainbow groups were to stay at the Fontainebleu. One group arrived and was immediately accommodated. When the second group arrived, they were told there were no rooms available, and were instead found rooms at the Seacoast Towers, some ten blocks away from the Fontainebleu.

---

[26] 896 F.2d 1233 (10th Cir. 1990).

Rainbow sued, and was awarded a jury verdict against the Fontaineblue for breach of contract and fraud, and the Fontainebleu appealed, alleging that the Oklahoma court did not have adequate jurisdiction over the out-of-state hotel, and in the alternative, that several errors were made by the trial court in admitting evidence. The Court of Appeals found that the trial court had personal jurisdiction over the out-of-state hotel, not only due to the numerous contractual contacts it had had with Rainbow, but also that it advertised within Oklahoma, and required that Rainbow partially perform its contract in Oklahoma by paying the large room deposit required. On the merits, the Court of Appeals upheld the jury's verdict for damages in the amount of $37,500 to the travel agent's good will, stating that the travel agent's whole business depended on good will with its customers, which had been damaged by Hilton's assurances to Rainbow that all rooms reserved would be available, and then by switching a number of people to another hotel at the last minute. While the Fontainebleu alleged that the damages to good will were speculative in nature, the Court held that such a determination of the value of this intangible business asset was properly left up to the jury to determine.[27] The Court also found that the jury's verdict on fraud was supported by the evidence that the hotel routinely overbooked itself by 15%; knew that due to renovations a large number of rooms would be unavailable that weekend; refused requests by other guests to extend their stay, yet represented to Rainbow's customers that a large number of guests extended their stay as a reason for having an inadequate number of rooms. The Hilton never let Rainbow know there was a risk of the hotel being overbooked and Rainbow's customers could get bumped. Rainbow was also able to show that a group from the University of Oklahoma was able to obtain a block of rooms that day, despite not having made advance reservations. While Rainbow also sought damages for breach of contract, hoping to provide its customers with a full refund to help repair the damage to its good will, the Court found that Rainbow did not have standing to collect damages on behalf of its customers, and had to be satisfied with the damages it received for injury to its reputation.

---

[27] Id. at 1239.

In *Ohio v. Cleveland*, [28] the Laramie Corporation offered to rent the Music Hall at the Cleveland Convention Center for June 25, 1980, to host the "Ms. Nude Ohio Beauty Pageant." The Convention Center was owned and operated by the City of Cleveland. The contents of the proposed show were outlined to the convention letter in a letter from the group, proposing to restrict admission to those over 21 years of age, and not sell nor permit the sale of food or beverages on the evening when the show was staged. The date was open and available for rental on the evening requested, and the City filed a lawsuit, seeking an injunction to prevent the show. In the meantime, the group could not make the arrangements necessary to ensure the show could go on as planned until it was assured it could rent the Hall as requested and sought a writ of mandamus, which would force the City to rent the Hall to the group. [29] The Court held that a writ of mandamus was inappropriate in this case, and that the group had an adequate remedy at law, by appealing the Court decision as to the injunction if it did not rule in its favor, despite the fact that time was running short before the date of the event. In a dissent, Justice Stillman stated that the Court's order had the effect of prohibiting the staging of the "Ms. Nude Ohio Beauty Pageant" and stated that Cleveland residents had seen "Hair," "Oh, Calcutta," "Equus," and "Marat de Sade," all containing nudity of male and female people to various degrees.

The City had objected to the pageant based on the illegality of nudity, despite the fact the pageant had been held in the City at another venue for several years without incident. The Judge stated the only reason to object was if the show was obscene, which was not alleged, and that the court's actions amounted to unjustified censorship.

4.04 Specific Cases on Stadium License Agreements

In *Golden West Baseball Company v. City of Anaheim*, [30] Golden West sued the City of Anaheim when it issued a permit allowing the construction of an office complex on part of the parking lot of Anaheim Stadium. [31] Golden West alleged that the permit violated its license agreement with the City by constricting or reducing the number of parking spaces

---

[28] No.42235, Ct. of Appeals, Ohio (Slip Opinion). June 2, 1980.
[29] Id.
[30] 25 Cal. App. 4th 11 (1994).
[31] Id. at 19.

available during Angel's baseball games from that required under the license. Anaheim initially entered into the agreement with Golden West in 1964, and in 1978, entered into another contract with ASA (a group that included the owner of the LA Rams football team) to commercially develop the parking lot in part to induce the Rams to move to Anaheim. In 1982, Golden West objected to ASA's development of the parking lot and sought an injunction to prohibit any of the proposed development.[32] The trial court held that Anaheim could develop a portion of the lot provided that ingress and egress were not interrupted, that the number of ground-level parking spaces guaranteed under the license remained. Golden West appealed the court's decision regarding partial development, and Anaheim appealed, stating that it could provide the number of parking spaces any way it chose, including by way of a multilevel garage if it so chose. The Court of Appeals reviewed the case and held that despite much dispute over whether the agreement between Golden West and Anaheim was an actual license or exhibition agreement, the parties sought for it to be a use agreement in order to avoid Orange County possessory interest taxes, and the interest conveyed was less than that of a licensehold interest.[33] The Court held that the interest was similar to that of an irrevocable license or easement, but that regardless of the type of interest, as long as at least 12,000 ground level parking spaces remained, [34] Anaheim was free to develop the lot according to proposed plans, and that a quiet title action quieted title in favor of the city, subject to Golden West's right to use the property. [35]

In *Fox v. Deese*, [36] a concert promoter sought to produce a two day outdoor concert in a city stadium. He met with the city manager and other officials, agreed to terms, and a contract was to be drafted by the city. In the meantime, the promoter was given a list of requirements, and was to enter into contracts with performing groups, stage hands, light and sound crews while the formal contract was drafted. The city delayed delivery of the contract until the promoter had made costly expenditures and when the contract was delivered, the terms varied significantly from what was agreed

---

[32] Id. at 20.

[33] Id. at 40.

[34] Id. at 42.

[35] Id. at 52.

[36] 362 S.E.2d 699 (Va. 1987).

toured the facilities in 1986 in order to explore holding its annual event at Valley Forge. Rosen held its first event at Valley Forge in February of 1986. In October of 1986, Valley Forge and Rosen executed a long-term license agreement and rider to license the center for the next 20 years with an annual rental payment of $75,600.00 for the first year and increasing with the consumer price index thereafter. The license payments were favorable for Rosen, mostly due to the other revenue the show would produce for the hotels, restaurants, and other entities at the facility. In a multiple property booking report, certain blocks of rooms were reserved at the hotels for each of Rosen's events for exhibitors and attendees. The events held by Rosen booked just about all of the facilities owned by Valley Forge, preventing it from renting out any of the facilities to others during the event period.[42]

The event took place through 1989, when Valley Forge petitioned for bankruptcy. Rosen did not contact Valley Forge after filing to see if there would be any effect on its contract.

Valley Forge sought to assume the contract. In the spring of 1989, Rosen sent a survey out to its exhibitors, including a slanted statement containing incorrect statements about the bankruptcy proceedings, not favoring Valley Forge, and 500 of the 800 exhibitors expressed a desire not to return to the facilities.[43]

In May of 1989, Rosen demanded to be let out of its license agreement, alleging that the event was too large for Valley Forge and that the event could be held more profitably in Atlantic City. Valley Forge did not agree to cancel the license, and Rosen began to threaten Valley Forge with damage to its reputation, contacting the press and to bring any litigation in the matter to the attention of the press. In a single letter, Rosen canceled its 1990 event at Valley Forge and said it was canceling its license agreement. Later it attempted to rationalize small problems like a missing shower cap in a room as its reasons for canceling the event. The Bankruptcy Court found these excuses transparent and weak, and that while Valley Forge was able to mitigate some of the damage caused by cancellation of the event by rebooking a small portion of the facilities, Valley Forge lost in excess of $290,000 from Rosen's actions. Rosen claimed that it was unaware that Valley Forge owned the hotels and surrounding facilities to the

---

[42] Id. at 896.
[43] Id.

Court in denying its responsibility for lost revenues at these facilities, yet in their survey, mentioned the joint ownership of the complex by Valley Forge.

The Court held that Rosen was aware or should certainly have been aware of the connection, and that damages for lost revenues at these facilities was a foreseeable[44] result of the cancellation of their license agreement. While the court held that the booking report itself created no independent liability where no separate license existed, here a license existed to hold events at the facility and the lost revenues from the hotel were foreseeable, irrespective of the booking reports. Valley Forge also claimed that Rosen defamed it in its slanted survey, and the Court agreed, awarding Valley Forge $1,000 in punitive damages, $1,000 for tortious interference of contract, $1,000 for disparaging Valley Forge, and $7,345.97 for failing to vacate the center in a timely fashion in 1989.[45]

Rosen was allowed to attempt to mitigate the damages by holding the 1991, 1992 or 1993 events at the facility, but regardless were still to pay $45,360 to Valley Forge for lost revenues in 1990. If unable to mitigate, Rosen was liable for $290,718.55 for breach of its license agreement, and was liable for the attorney's fees for the facility as well.

Clearly, this is a case where the facility won a decisive victory over an unhappy and dissatisfied licensee who wrongfully chose to cancel a license agreement, and in an attempt to justify their actions, defamed the facility leading to punitive damages.

In *Half-A-Car II, Inc., v. Interstate Hotels Corporation*,[46] the chief financial officer for Half-a-Car negotiated a sales contract with Interstate's national sales manager to provide rooms for Half-A-Car's annual convention in September of 1991. During the 1991 convention, the convention organizer discussed some concerns regarding services provided by Interstate with the same national sales manager, Mr. Karch, regarding Interstate's ability to host the 1992 convention, including the use of the master's ballroom. In October, 1991, Interstate Hotels sent Half-a-Car a proposal regarding the 1992 convention, requesting its immediate response. The chief financial officer initialed the changes made by the sales manager after talking with the convention organizer, made a few additional changes, and

---

[44] Id. at 903.
[45] Id. at 907.
[46] No. 93-5834, 1994 U.S. Dist. LEXIS 15223 (E.D. Pa. Oct. 25, 1994).

sent the contract back the same day. Shortly thereafter, Karch terminated his relationship with Interstate. There was no further contact between Half-a-Car and Interstate until February of 1992 when Half-a-Car called to make sure all arrangements had been made for the 1992 convention. Karch's replacement sent a Function Information Agenda to Half-a-Car, substituting the Heritage for the Masters Ballroom. Half-a-Car learned that the Master's ballroom had already been promised to another event several months earlier, and Half-a-Car decided to move its black-tie dinner to another location. In March of 1992, Interstate Hotels was notified that Half-a-Car would not hold its convention at the resort, and Interstate claimed that under the proposal Half-a-Car owed it $74,392.50 under the cancellation clause.

Arbitration proceedings were begun that were stayed, pending the Court's resolution of whether the two parties had a contract for leasing of the resort. In review of the proposal sent to Half-a-Car and the changes made by its chief financial officer, the changes to the proposal were a counter-offer to Interstate Hotels, and thus conditional acceptance of Interstate's first proposal for the convention. Interstate's actions subsequent to the counter-offer constituted acceptance of that counter-offer, and the actions of the parties conformed to the counter-offer. Half-a-Car alleges Interstate's actions were not acceptance of its counter-offer, saying any modification to the contract had to be in writing signed by both parties, but the Court stated this was only true after the parties had entered into a contractual relationship, not before. The rental of the Master's Ballroom was determined not to be a condition precedent to the formation of the contract, and the Court granted Interstate's motion for summary judgment and its motion to compel Half-a-Car to participate in arbitration as to the remaining terms of the agreement.

In *United States v. Bryant*,[47] Bryant and another person, Dalton, appealed their convictions of mail fraud and wire fraud in a scheme to bribe the Director of the Cervantes Convention Center in St. Louis for favorable treatment of their convention booking business, known as Showboard. Bryant and Dalton paid the Director over $26,000 from August 1979 to April 1980, in order to receive favorable treatment in leasing the Center for expositions and shows. The Cervantes Convention Center is a municipal Convention Center owned by the City of St. Louis, governed by a 21-member commission, and run on a daily basis by the Director. Commercial

---

[47] 766 F.2d 370 (8th Cir. 1985).

shows at the Center were only to be booked a year in advance, while non-commercial shows could be booked up to ten years in advance if the expected attendance was not local.[48] If local attendance was expected, the Center could only be booked 450 days in advance. In order to book an event more than 450 days in advance, a customer had to obtain the approval of the Convention and Visitor's Bureau, which would send a bulletin to the convention center for issuance of the licenses.

Bryant and Dalton received favorable treatment in three area sports shows, the Industry and Business Expo, and in the payment of bills. As to the Sports Show, it was an annual event held every year in February, and in 1980 was open to competitive bidding.

Rather than bid on the show, Bryant and Dalton attempted to monopolize the convention center space through non-commercial shows, and to do so, they formed a non-profit corporation and set out to convince the Visitor's Bureau that it was a legitimate organization with real members. They sought to license the convention center for its yearly non-commercial convention and trade show for five years during the prime dates for the commercial sports show. The manager at the center grew suspicious of the applications by this organization, its relation to Showboard, and the non-commercial status of its proposed events. Bryant and Dalton conceded that the organization had no members and that there was no alleged meeting of its board of directors, as they had set forth in a letter to the Visitor's Bureau. The admission supported one count of mail fraud.

The Director wrote the Attorney General asking for guidance, and the Attorney General suggested that if the faux corporation was commercial in nature, it should comply with the regulations for commercial shows; however, the Director, now receiving payments from Showboard, told Center personnel Showboard wasn't involved and issued the licenses for the years 1981 through 1984.

The initial license was mailed to the "president" of the faux corporation, Mathews, in Kansas City, forming the basis for an additional mail fraud count, but the other licenses were withheld due to suspicions of a Center employee. Mathews, at the direction of Bryant, sent a telegram to the Center about the remaining licenses, constituting one of the counts of wire

---

[48] Id. at 372.

exact dates reserved above and to be legally and contractually obligated to enter into the license agreement with the Facility. No oral modifications shall vary or alter this Agreement."

2)   PCMA's Contract Guidelines for Convention Centers

Convention center contracts generally and historically have been misunderstood and perceived by customers as instruments that are inflexible, inconsistent and generically written to cover all facility events. That's not surprising, since facility contracts were drafted by and for facility interests.

In 1992 PCMA President William Myers appointed a task force comprised of association executives, convention center management, convention bureau executives and industry attorneys to develop convention center contract guidelines that would improve relationships between facilities and their customers. On insurance issues the task force received counsel and guidance from an independent insurance consultant familiar with the industry.

The task force's charge was to review and analyze convention center contracts, and develop a set of consistent concepts to help make contracts fair, balanced, flexible, understandable and tailored to the industry. The task force recognized early on that all facilities have unique environments and that their customers have unique events as well, which precluded the creation of a model facility contract or language. The White Paper does not attempt to draft model contract language but rather provides guidelines of fair and equitable principals by which the customer and facility can conduct business. The task force identified the most common contract elements and developed corresponding guidelines for convention center contracts.

It is recommended that these guidelines form the basis for designing facility contracts for the convention and exposition industry. The task force also recommends that facilities design contracts specifically for convention and exposition events and that wherever possible contract language be user friendly without sacrificing the legality of the instrument. This later recommendation has been followed in drafting these guidelines.

Finally, the task force recognizes that the issues underlying the guidelines are dynamic and complex and they represent a starting point in resolving those issues.

1. Indemnification Insurance/Clauses

Arguably, the most controversial and least understood areas in Facility Contracts are indemnification clauses and the corresponding liability and necessary insurance. After consultation with legal and insurance experts, the task force recommends:

Guideline:

a. The customer shall furnish at his expense the primary event policy covering all claims of an event, except in cases of sole negligence, willful misconduct, acts or omissions of the facility, its employees, agents, subcontractors, etc. Sole negligence may include faulty equipment provided by the facility and defects in the leased premises.
b. The facility entity shall be listed as an additional insured on the primary event policy.
c. The facility lease shall spell out the terms and limits of customer's liability for fire and other damage to the facility's property and equipment under the customer's care, custody and control and such liability shall be limited to the amount of the customer's insurance as required in the lease; or, customer and facility may agree to mutual waivers of subrogation with respect to fire and property damage.
d. Indemnification clauses shall be clearly defined in the contract and may be subject to prevailing laws.

2. Condition of Facility Clauses

The task force formulated this guideline to protect the customer's best interest when a facility is not maintained between the signing of the contract and the start of the event.

Guideline:

The facility will provide the premises in a condition similar to or better than when the contract was executed or at the last inspection prior to signing the

7. Contract Interpretation Clauses

The task force determined that clauses specifying one party as the sole interpreter of the lease were unfair.

Guideline: Neither the customer nor the facility have sole power as interpreter of the lease terms.

8. Notice of Default Clauses

The task force determined contract breaches and litigation could be prevented by providing both parties reasonable time to solve contract defaults.

Guideline: The customer and the facility shall mutually agree to provide reasonable notice and time to cure or remedy a contract default with the exception of situations involving personal safety, immediate waste and damage to the facilities.

9. Cancellation Clauses

Standard contract forms should not contain stipulated damages. However, payment of damages as a result of cancellations is endorsed. It is recommended that those damages can best be determined through individual contract negotiations or option specified under Guideline 11.

Guideline: Should either party cancel for reasons beyond force majeure, the injured pain/shall be entitled to recover damages.

10. Reimbursement Cost to Enforce Lease Clause

It is important to include this provision in all contracts.

Guideline: In any dispute arising between the customer and the facility relating to the lease, the prevailing party shall be entitled to recover a reasonable attorney's fee and all related costs to
the litigation.

11. Dispute Resolution Clauses/Default/Breach of Contract

It is in the best interest of both parties to negotiate a comprehensive agreement that includes provisions for dispute resolution.

Guideline:
In the event of a contract dispute, the following procedures and sequence should be undertaken to remedy it:

a. Negotiation
b. CLC/Alternative Dispute Resolution
c. Litigation

Both the customer and the facility shall be entitled to reimbursement of all reasonable expenses and lost profits substantiated by the customer or the facility if cancellation is made or threatened by the customer or the facility in the performance of any of the obligations contained in the contract.

4.06 Specific Cases on Arena License Agreements

In *Florida Panthers Hockey Club, Ltd., v. Miami Sports and Exhibition Authority*,[51] the Florida Panthers, an NHL hockey team sued the Miami Sports and Exhibition Authority (MSEA), seeking a preliminary injunction and a declaration of its rights under a license agreement for the Miami Arena.

The MSEA, which owns the Miami Arena, the city, and Decoma Miami Associates, Ltd. (DMAL) entered into a land lease agreement for construction of the Miami Arena. DMAL then contracted with Leisure Management International, (LMI) to discharge some of its duties, including entering into rental agreements for the Arena.[52] In 1994, LMI entered into a license agreement with the South Florida Hockey Club, predecessors to the Panthers, providing a two hockey season license for use of the Arena, and allowed for four one-year options to extend the license.[53]

The license required that the Panthers renew their license for the 96-97 hockey season by August 1, 1995.

The Panthers decided not to exercise the option and did so by letter, dated May 31, 1995, indicating they would also consider

---

[51] 939 F. Supp. 855 (S.D. Fla. 1996); aff'd 116 F.3d 1492 (11th Cir. 1997).
[52] Id. at 857.
[53] Id.

renewing the license if they could negotiate a license similar to that held by the Miami Heat, a NBA team. Proposed amendments went back and forth, and a proposed agreement was reached between LMI and the Panthers. The MSEA then rejected many of the terms proposed by the Panthers as not in their best interest.[54] The MSEA then informed the Panthers that they were to vacate the Arena by July 15, 1996, at which point the Panthers sought an injunction and declaration of their rights under the license agreement signed with LMI.[55]

 The Panthers alleged that their presence continued to benefit MSEA and that the MSEA could not unreasonably withhold consent of the license amendments negotiated with LMI and DMAL. MSEA alleged that the amendments were a personal services contract and thus not subject to enforcement by injunction. The Court held that the license was in essence a license agreement and could be enforced with injunctive relief. The Court also held that since the MSEA had delegated the duties of negotiating and executing contracts to DMAL, DMAL and LMI were free to negotiate new licenses with the Panthers, although the Panthers had canceled their old license by letter to MSEA.[56] MSEA claimed it had unfettered right to cancel the proposed license to the Panthers, but the Court disagreed, stating the contract with DMAL specifically limited the MSEA's rights to disapprove of license agreements. The Court granted the injunction to the Panthers, stating disapproval of the license agreement was actually to MSEA's economic detriment and irreparable harm could be done to the Panthers if the Arena was not available to them, thus allowing the Panthers to play in the Arena and allow the Arena to reap the benefits from the games played there as well.[57]

---

[54] Id.

[55] Id. at 858.

[56] Id.

[57] Id. at 959.

SAMPLE CONVENTION CENTER LICENSE AGREEMENT

Event #: _____

THIS LICENSE AGREEMENT is made between the **XYZ Center** ("Center"), (insert address), telephone number (xxx) xxx-xxxx, facsimile no. (xxx) xxx-xxxx, and the **ABC Trade Association** ("Customer"), **Insert Address** and telephone number.

In consideration of the covenants and conditions contained herein, intending to be legally bound, the parties to this Agreement agree as follows:

1. **Grant Of License; Duration Of License.** The Center grants to Customer and Customer accepts a license to use, subject to the terms and conditions of this Agreement, the following described area(s) (the "Licensed Area") for **ABC Trade Show and Conference ("Event")** in the Convention Center for the period or periods specified below:

AREA	USAGE	START TIME	END TIME	DAY/DATE	FEE

Customer shall mail signed originals of this Agreement to: Center (address)

2.   License Fee; Deposits.

(a)   The License Fee is $_____. Customer is responsible for all incidental services incurred as provided in sub-section (e).

Deposit No.	Due Date	Amount
1	09/30/2008	$._____

Customer may make payments required by the Agreement by any of the following methods:

- **ia electronic fund transfer to: Insert bank name and code for transfer of funds. Each transfer should include the event code and event dates; or**
- **via Visa, MasterCard or American Express using the Center's Charge Card Verification Form, Exhibit I; or**
- **via check, sent directly to the Center (insert address)**

(b) If any part of the Licensed Area is identified in section 1 as exhibit space to be leased for a fee based on minimum net square footage ("NSF"), then the quoted license fee for that part of the Licensed Area is a minimum license fee. If the exhibits for this event occupy more than the minimum net square footage, then Customer shall pay the Center for the exhibit space actually occupied, at the rate per net square foot set forth in section 1. For the purposes of this section, "exhibit space actually occupied" shall not include aisles, columns, registration areas, or non-revenue producing exhibits or displays (to the extent that such exhibits or displays do not exceed 5% of the total net square footage).

(c) All deposits shall be non-refundable, except as otherwise expressly set forth in this   Agreement. Interest will not be paid, refunded or credited to Customer on any deposit(s) required of Customer. Failure to make deposit(s) on time shall constitute immediate breach of the Agreement by Customer.

(d) The License Fee is premised on the customer submitting to the Center in advance of the event a comprehensive Plan of Operation for use of all licensed space. The Plan of Operation must include; daily detailed schedule of events for entire license period; proposed exhibit floor plan; proposed registration and banner/sign hanging layouts; ballroom and meeting room set-ups; shuttle bus routes; list of contractors servicing the event; and other pertinent logistical information. All elements of the Plan of Operations must be submitted to the Center at least 21 days before the date of move-in, unless the Center requires an earlier submission in writing. The Customer shall be responsible for paying costs incurred by the Center, such as employee overtime, because of Customer's failure to comply with this requirement.

(e) The license fee does not include charges: (1) for food and beverage services, (2) utility services; (3) telecommunication services; (4) connections to the Center's audio and video distribution systems, and (5) other miscellaneous charges. Customer will be billed separately for all such charges. The charges for items (2)-(5) are set forth in the rate sheets attached to this Agreement as Exhibit II.

3.　　　**Use.** Customer agrees to use the Licensed Area for Event and for no other purpose.

4.　　　**Use of Common Areas.** All common areas of the center (including, but not limited to, the exterior, entrances, public concourses, lobbies that the Center makes available to the Customer may also be made available to other customers for concurrent access and use as required by their event activity. The Center will coordinate and schedule the use of common areas in order to best accommodate all customers.

The plan depicting Customer's public space layout must be submitted to the Center's Event Service Department no later than 60 days prior to your first move-in day. The plan must include banner dimensions, informational kiosks, directional signage, and all other information related to the use of the Center's common areas. All plans will be reviewed by the Center to insure that the use of public space does not interfere with the use of the Center by other customers occupying the Center at the same time. The Center reserves the right to make adjustments to the plan, if necessary, to accommodate the needs of customers who are using the same public areas. The Center shall notify Customer at least thirty (30) days prior to the move-in date if changes are made to your plan for the use of common areas in the Center.

5.   Security and Medical Services.

(a)   Customer shall provide security, which must be licensed and bonded in the City and County of _____, and medical services for the licensed area that meet or exceed the reasonable minimum requirements of the Center.

(b)   The Center shall, prior to the move-in date, review with the Customer the Center's requirements for security personnel deployment and medical services for **Event**.

6.   Exclusive Services.

(a)   The Center's designated providers have sole and total control over the following:

(1)   *Food Service Vendor* – service of food and beverages, including alcoholic beverages, at such time and location as the Center shall determine; and

(2)   *OEM Electric* – utility service (including electrical and water) Exhibit II;

(3)   *TJK Telecommunications* – telecommunications service (including local and long distance telephone service and internet service, both wired and wireless) Exhibit II;

(4)   **BCNC** *Projection* – for providing or operating any equipment that connects to the Center's audio and video systems.

(b)   Customer, its employees, agents or guests shall not give away, sell, resell or repackage any of these exclusive services, without the written approval of the Center.

7.   Compliance With Laws, Manual for All Building Users and Event Planning Guide. Customer agrees that its use of the Licensed Area will comply with all Federal and State laws and regulations. Customer agrees to comply with the Manual For All Building Users of the Center, attached hereto as Exhibit III and the Event Planning Guide, receipt of which is hereby acknowledged by Customer. The Center at all times shall have full access to the Licensed Area. The Center shall have the right to remove any person from the Licensed Area or the Center when necessary to ensure the safe and orderly operation of the Center.

8.   Insurance. Notwithstanding any indemnification provision in this Agreement, Customer shall secure, at its sole cost, for the duration of the license period (which license period shall include move-in and move-out), liability insurance, in at least the amounts described in Exhibit IV, for claims arising from injury or death to persons or damage to property and contractual liability. Customer shall, not later than twenty-one (21) days before the move-in date, submit a certificate of insurance evidencing the insurance coverage required herein, which certificate shall substantially conform to the form illustrated in Exhibit IV, and which shall expressly identify as additional insureds the Center and its Board of Directors and Officers.

9.   Notices. Any notices must be sent by Certified Mail, return receipt requested, to the addresses shown above, or by facsimile transmission to the above numbers, with written confirmation that transmission has been completed.

10.   Copyrights. Customer will assume all costs arising from the use or misuse of patented, trademarked, franchised or copyrighted music, materials, devices, and dramatic rights used in or incorporated in its event. Customer agrees to indemnify, defend and hold harmless the Center from any claims, damages or costs, including legal fees, which may arise from use of such material.

11.   Indemnification. Customer shall indemnify, defend and hold harmless the Center from and against any and all losses, damages, costs, expenses, claims, and other liabilities arising out of, or otherwise attributable to, this Agreement and License granted hereunder, and/or Customer's use and/or occupancy of the Convention Center. This indemnification shall not extend to any claims arising from the gross negligence or intentional acts of the Center or its agents, employees, or representatives. Customer hereby waives and releases all claims against the Center with respect to all matters for which the Center has disclaimed liability hereunder, including, without limitation, any and all liability for injury to Customer, its employees, agents, and the public.

12.   Return of Licensed Area. Upon the termination of the license period set forth in this Agreement, Customer shall vacate the Licensed Area and the Convention Center and return any equipment, all of which shall be in the same condition and repair as originally furnished to Customer, normal wear and tear alone excepted.

Customer is liable for any claim and/or damage, including but not limited to, rents or costs associated with infringement on the right of other customers resulting from its failure to surrender the Premises at the end of the Term. Should Customer fail to surrender the Premises, (1) Customer shall pay to the Center the customary rate for the space involved, and (2) the Center shall remove all Customer's effects from the Premises and treat the same as abandoned. All storage, if required, shall be at the cost, expense and risk of Customer.

13.   Assignment. This Agreement may not be assigned or transferred by Customer without the express, prior written consent of the Center which consent may be withheld in the sole discretion of the Center. In the event of any such assignment or transfer, Customer assumes full responsibility for the acts and conduct of any exhibitors or other persons admitted to the Licensed Area or any part of the Center by or with the consent of Customer or as an invitee of Customer or any of the invitees of exhibitors. Customer shall not under any circumstances license, sublicense, lease, rent, sell, or convey the Licensed Area or any part thereof. In the event the Customer has sublicensed, licensed, leased, rented, sold or otherwise conveyed the Licensed Area or portion thereof, then the Customer shall pay the Center its prevailing rate for the same, in addition to a service charge of $1,000.00.

14.   Americans With Disabilities Act. Concerning the Americans With Disabilities Act and all regulations thereunder, the Center shall be responsible for the permanent access accommodations, such as, but not limited to, wheelchair ramps, elevator standards, door width standards and rest room accessibility. Customer shall be responsible for non-permanent accessibility requirements, such as, but not limited to, auxiliary aids for the visually impaired, hearing impaired and mobility impaired, meeting room seating arrangements and exhibition accessibility.

15.   Default By Customer.

(a)   Customer is in default of this Agreement if it:
fails to pay any amounts due the Center under this Agreement;

(1)   breaches any material provision of this Agreement, including but not limited to the provisions for timely submission of rental amounts, or the required certificate of insurance, or evidence that Customer has retained the required security and medical services;

(2)   violates any applicable laws during the Term; or

(3)   becomes bankrupt or ceases doing business.

(b)   Should Customer default, the Center may:
(1)   declare the entire rent for the Term due and payable;

(2)   give notice of termination with twenty-four (24) hours for the Customer to resolve any alleged default. Any such notice of termination shall not excuse any breach of this Agreement. After such a termination, the relation between the Center and Customer is the same as if the Term fully expired and the Center shall retake possession of the Premises and the Customer shall pay the full amount of rental due under this Agreement together with all other reasonable costs, expenses and damages incurred by the Center as a result of the breach of this Agreement; and

(3)   seek other remedies available at law or equity. The use of any partial or single remedy shall not prevent the Center from using any other remedy.

16.   Default By Center.

(a)   The Center is in default of the Agreement if it:

(1)   fails to provide the Premises on the date(s) and time(s) set forth in this Agreement;

(2)   breaches any material provision of this Agreement; or

(3)   ceases doing business.

(b)   Should the Center default, Customer may:

(1)   receive the unearned rent paid to the Center under this Agreement;

(2)   give notice of termination with twenty-four (24) hours for the Center to respond to any alleged default; and

(3)   seek other remedies available at law or equity. Any such notice of termination shall not excuse any breach of this Agreement.

17.   Cancellation Damages. Should Customer cancel all or any portion of the Premises or Term, the Center is entitled to the full balance of Customer's rent, not as a penalty, but as liquidated damages to the Center. The Center agrees to make a good faith effort to relet the space. It is presumed that the Center has made such good faith efforts and Customer shall have the burden of proving otherwise. Should the space or any portion of it be relet, the amount received by the Center for such relet will offset Customer's liquidated damages. The Center agrees this Agreement shall not be canceled for the right of accommodating a meeting with another group.

18.   Force Majeure.
If the Licensed Area or all or any other part of Convention Center necessary to Customer's event is rendered unusable, or if the event is otherwise rendered commercially impracticable, by reason of acts of God, strikes against third parties, civil disorder, terrorism or acts of war, substantial curtailment of the transportation industry, or any reason beyond the control of either the Center or Customer, either the Center or Customer shall have the right to terminate this Agreement by delivery of notice to the other

party. In the event of such termination, the Center shall return all deposits made by Customer. Neither party shall be liable for any loss or damage suffered by the other party if this Agreement is terminated pursuant to this provision.

19. **Entire Agreement.** This Agreement contains the entire agreement of the parties with respect to the subject matter it covers, supersedes all prior or other negotiations, representations and agreements between the parties and their representatives. No other oral or written agreement shall vary or alter any provision of this Agreement unless both parties consent thereto in a signed Addendum.

20. **Applicable Law; Jurisdiction.** This Agreement shall be governed by and construed in accordance with the laws of the State. With respect to any suit, action or proceeding relating to this Agreement, Customer hereby irrevocably submits to the exclusive jurisdiction of the courts of the State and the United States District Court for the Region.

21. **Severability.** In the event any one or more of the provisions contained in this Agreement shall for any reason be held to be invalid, illegal or unenforceable in any respect, such event shall not affect any other provision of this Agreement, and this Agreement shall be construed as if such invalid, illegal or unenforceable provision had never been herein contained.

22. **Exhibits to Agreement.** The following EXHIBITS are attached hereto are hereby incorporated into and made a part of this Agreement:

> Exhibit I: Charge Card Authorization Form
> Exhibit II: Rate Sheets for services
> Exhibit III: Manual for all Building Users
> Exhibit IV: Insurance Requirements

23. **Special Terms and Conditions Other Than Space, Charges, or Credits.** The signed Agreement along with required deposits (if any), must be returned to the Center no later than *(30 days from issuance)*, or this Agreement is null and void and the reservation will be canceled.

IN WITNESS WHEREOF, the Center and Customer have executed this Agreement as of the date first written below.

CUSTOMER   **XYZ CONVENTION CENTER**

By:_____   By:_____
    (Signature)   (Signature)

Name:_____   Title: <u>CEO</u>_____
                                                (Printed)

Title:_____   Date: _____

Date: _____

Revised 5.15.04

To help serve you regarding compliance with the Center's insurance requirements, Exhibit IV, please provide the Center with the following information:

Name of Insurance Brokerage Company:

_____

Contact Person (if any):

_____

Address of Insurance Broker:

_____

_____

Phone: _____

Fax: _____

Chapter 5

Risk Management and Facility Insurance

By Turner D. Madden

5.00 Introduction

Risk management and the insurance process are an important and necessary part of the facility management. The facility manager properly takes on the responsibility to identify and assess the risk associated with each event. Because each event has its unique characteristics, the manager must identify and assess the potential risks and direct the planning to eliminate, reduce, or transfer the risk. With the right risk assessment, insurance coverage and planning, a manager should be able to avoid or reduce the probability of an accident, crises or other threat. Below are the four traditional solutions for managing risk in your facility. The key to the risk management process is to know what risks to avoid, reduce, retain, or transfer.

5.01 The Risk Management Process

1) Risk Avoidance – a facility may wish to avoid potential risks by carefully regulating the nature and character of the events held in the facility. An example of this might be choosing not to allow an event in your facility due to their inherent risks, or by forcing such a lessee to take all responsibility for any injuries caused during such an event. Risk avoidance is a broad category that covers prevention of injury or harm to any employee, lessee, or invitee (patron) of the facility.

In *Kahn et. al. v. Brown*,[1] James Brown, the "Godfather of Soul," had performed twice at the Baltimore Civic Center in 1964. In 1966, a promoter, again tried to book a performance for Mr. Brown at the Civic Center, but had the application denied due to prior "incidents of poor behavior" at the prior shows in 1964, and "problems in the community" during and after Mr. Brown's performances. Again in December of 1966, Kahn, a promoter sought to book a James Brown

---

[1] 259 A.2d 61 (Md. Ct. App. 1969).

performance for the spring of 1967, but was told the Bullets basketball team had first call for the proposed date, because of possible playoff games, although it was unlikely the team would get that far. The Bullets did not need the Center, and Kahn was informed that several acts would not be booked, including Mr. Brown. Kahn denied any such statement being made. In January, Kahn went to New York to arrange for Brown's appearance at the Civic Center on March 25, 1967. Brown's agent informed Kahn that there had been past problems in booking Mr. Brown into the Civic Center. Kahn nevertheless signed a contract to pay Brown $15,000 plus 55% of net receipts over $40,000 for one performance at the Civic Center on March 25, 1967. Kahn made an immediate payment of $7,500 to Brown as required under the performance contract. When it became clear on February 4 that the Bullets would not be in the playoffs, the director of the civic center sent a letter to Kahn confirming that the center was ready for rent. When learning that Kahn was to bring Mr. Brown for the performance, he wrote a letter to Kahn's attorney informing him that the Civic Center would not book James Brown due to prior problems incurred, and that they had made Mr. Kahn aware that they did not have the authority to book a James Brown concert at the Civic center. A deadline was set for Mr. Kahn to book an acceptable act for the March 25th date. Kahn then sought a writ of Mandamus to compel the Civic Center Commission to rent the center to him for the proposed James Brown concert, and included the fact he had already paid Mr. Brown a non-refundable $7,500 deposit to secure his performance on March 25.

Kahn tried to obtain another venue, and was rebuffed for the same reasons as the civic center. In early march, Kahn rented a large field in Baltimore County, intending to stage the show in a tent, and the zoning and police departments failed to give approval for the proposed tent show. March 25 came and went without a performance by Mr. Brown. Kahn sought a refund of his $7,500 , and the manager stated that Brown would perform for Kahn, whenever the land for the performance was first secured. Brown was scheduled to perform in June in Charles County, Maryland, and Kahn's attorney instructed the Sheriff of Charles County to attach $7,500 of ticket money, and brown filed an appeal of the attachment order, also claiming the $7,500 balance on the $15,000 contract he had entered into with Kahn. The trial court judge found that Kahn had taken a risk in signing Brown and that Kahn could not perform his end of the

✓ Operational Pointer – It is extremely important that for each lawsuit or claim that your facility receives, that you immediately notify your insurance broker and carrier of the claim in a written document. Your insurance policies most likely contain a timely notification clause. Numerous claims and lawsuits have been denied by insurance companies because the insured did not notify the carrier in a timely manner.

5.03 The "Additional Insured" Method of Risk Management

An "additional insured" is when another person or company is added to the insurance coverage so they are protected as if they were the party taking out the insurance policy. This may be easier to understand if we think about it in terms of adding a new driver onto an existing automobile policy; the sixteen year-old new driver becomes an additional insured on his parent's policy and is covered just as if he were the one who had taken out the policy.

As you can see from the below diagram, the convention center contract(s) must reflect not only the relationship between the client and the center but also the center and the other subcontractors and exhibitors that provide services in the center to the event. From this diagram you can see how many entities must provide the facility with a certificate of insurance and list the facility as an "additional insured" in the certificate. If we apply the same requirements to an arena, the professional basketball team should list the arena as an "additional insured" on all their insurance policies.

SHOW MANAGEMENT CONTRACTUAL ARRANGEMENTS

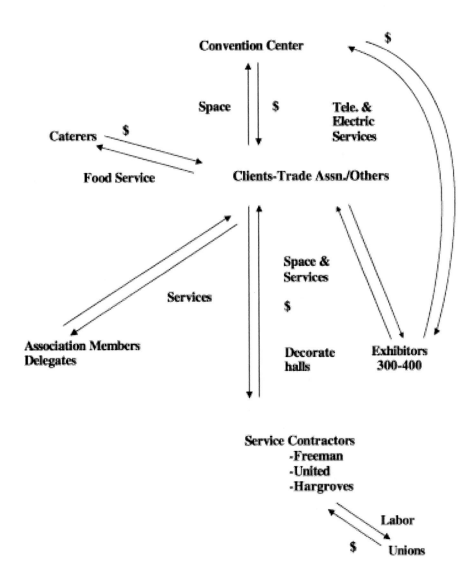

In *Bonner County v. Panhandle Rodeo Association, Inc.*[2], a woman fell from a bleacher seat while attending a rodeo sponsored by the Sandpoint Lions Club (Lions) and Panhandle on premises provided by Bonner County. Each year, beginning in 1974, the Lions and Panhandle put on a rodeo and were charged a nominal fee for use of the Bonner County Fairgrounds by the County. There was a paragraph in the agreement to use the Fairgrounds beginning in 1976 requiring the tenant to provide $250,000 per person and $500,000 aggregate liability coverage and third party coverage of $250,000 and provide proof of such coverage to the County.[3] The liability policy obtained by the Lions had an endorsement specifying the scope of coverage to "additional insured". The policy itself was not filed with Bonner, but a Certificate of Insurance was provided.[4] The personal injury action was filed against Bonner, which tendered the defense to Panhandle, the Lions, and its insurance company, Globe. Panhandle tendered to the Lions and Globe, who refused all tenders. At trial, the District Court held that the Lions and Panhandle were required to indemnify Bonner, Bonner and Panhandle were additional insureds under the Globe policy, and Globe was estopped from denying coverage. The personal injury action was settled, so only the insurance coverage issues remained, and the Idaho Supreme Court held that Globe could not deny coverage based on "sole negligence" exclusion in the policy.[5]

In *International Amphitheater Company v. Vanguard Underwriters Insurance Company*,[6] during a concert at the Amphitheater Company in Chicago several persons in attendance were allegedly attacked and sexually assaulted. This case was appealed from the trial court to the Appellate Court of Appeals. Four lawsuits were filed against the Amphitheater and other defendants, alleging negligent and willful conduct resulting in the injuries to the attendees. Vanguard Underwrites Insurance Company Amphitheater entered into an agreement to lease its premises to Rainbow Productions for a rock concert to be held on December 29, 1981.

Vanguard Underwriters Insurance Company, through one of its agents, issued a certificate of insurance to Talent Coordinators of America, Inc., a co-promoter (with Rainbow) of the concert. The

---

[2] 620 P.2d 1102 (Idaho 1980).
[3] Id. at 1103.
[4] Id. at 1104.
[5] Id. at 1105, 1106.
[6] 532 N.E. 2d 493 (Ill. App. 1988).

Amphitheater required to be listed as an "additional insured" as part of their standard requirements of the lease. After this lawsuit was filed, Vanguard denied insurance coverage to the Amphitheater. The Amphitheater filed a complaint[7] against Vanguard to be covered by the Vanguard policy. The Amphitheater included the fact that they did not receive a copy of the Vanguard policy but only the certificate of insurance.[8] Endorsement number 3 of the policy states:

> "IT IS HEREBY UNDERSTOOD AND AGREED THAT CO-PROMOTERS AND BUILDING OWNERS, MANAGERS LESSORS AND LANDLORDS SHALL BE COVERED AS ADDITIONAL INSUREDS, UNDER THIS POLICY BUT ONLY WITH RESPECT TO THE SOLE NEGLIGENCE OF THE NAMED INSURED'S OPERATIONS...."[9]

The trial court ruled that the above language covered the Amphitheater as an additional insured on all issues in the lawsuit. Vanguard on this appeal claims that the policy, endorsement Number 4, provides to the named insured (the Amphitheater) only upon the named insured's representation that it will not assume any obligations to provide security and crowd control.

In *Armstrong v. Ogden Allied Facilities Management Corp. et. al.,* [10] a woman was injured when she tripped over an unfastened cover to an electrical outlet recessed in the floor of the lobby of the Jacob Javits Center. Ogden managed the facility, and Larkin was the promoter of the trade show being held at the Center at the time of the accident.

The woman sued both Larkin and Ogden, and Larkin sought indemnity from Ogden, while Ogden cross-claimed against Larkin for breach of the license agreement for failing to provide insurance coverage in Ogden's favor, for indemnification, and contribution.[11] The accident

---

[7] Amphitheater filed a complaint for declaratory judgment seeking a declaration that pursuant to the certificate of insurance, Amphitheater was an additional insured.

[8] 532 N.E. 2d at 494.

[9] Id. at 494.

[10] 651 N.Y.S.2d 509 (N.Y. App. Div. 1ˢᵗ Dept. 1996).

[11] Id.

occurred in the public area of the building, not the rented exhibition hall located one floor below. The Court found that Larkin had provided a certificate of insurance to Ogden which was adequate proof that it had insurance coverage for the event. The Licensing Agreement between Larkin and Ogden contained broad indemnification language containing an exemption for acts attributable to the "sole negligence" of the licensor, and the Court found that since the accident occurred in the common area of the building, over which Ogden had control, there was no suggestion that anyone other than Ogden would be responsible for the injuries incurred. Both Ogden and Larkin also claimed that the Plaintiff was comparatively negligent. The Court held that for recovery under the indemnification clause, it was only necessary that the injury was not the result of Ogden's "sole negligence," and that should a jury find that the Plaintiff was comparably negligent, the indemnification clause would remain operative and Ogden could recover judgment against Larkin pursuant to their contract.[12]

In *Montgomery Elevator Company v. Building Engineering Services Co., Inc.,*[13] Building Engineering Services (BESCO) hired Montgomery Elevator to service and maintain the elevators and escalators in the Louisiana Superdome. Shortly thereafter, a sixteen-year-old girl was injured when the hem of her formal gown became enmeshed in the escalator, and a personal injury suit was brought against BESCO and Montgomery.[14] BESCO and Montgomery won the case, but Montgomery then sued BESCO for breach of contract, by failing to name Montgomery as an additional insured under BESCO's insurance policy, seeking to recover the attorney's fees it had to expend defending the personal injury suit.[15] The insurance clause in question required BESCO to maintain comprehensive liability insurance coverage, including bodily injury and property damage for use and operation of the equipment and to name Montgomery as an additional insured on the policy. Such insurance existed, but Montgomery was not named as an additional insured. The Indemnity clause required BESCO to indemnify Montgomery against all claims of liability asserted against Montgomery except for those attributed to Montgomery's negligence.[16]

---

[12] Id.
[13] 730 F.2d 377 (5th Cir. 1984).
[14] Id. at 379.
[15] Id.
[16] Id.

When the initial personal injury suit began, Montgomery mounted its own defense, and did not call attention to the contract clauses between it and BESCO. BESCO was dismissed by the trail judge in the personal injury case, and Montgomery won at trial. At no time did Montgomery cross-claim against BESCO.[17] The Trial Court ruled that Montgomery's failure to notify BESCO of the breach earlier prevented them from avoiding duplication of litigation expenses and extinguished its right to seek expenses from BESCO. The Court of Appeals affirmed this ruling stating that the breach of contract was a passive, rather than active or intention breach of the contract, and that Montgomery's failure to put BESCO in default, or notify it of the breach barred its ability to recover its $29,000 attorney fees expended in the personal injury suit.[18]

5.04 General Liability Insurance

The facility manager must obtain a certificate of insurance ("certificate") for each event in the facility. A certificate of insurance is a statement from an insurance company that insurance does exist, and states who and what acts are covered under the policy. A certificate of insurance is usually required by a facility from its licensee, stating that the licensee has adequate coverage to protect itself and the facility in the event a loss incurs, either through damage to the facility itself, or for personal injuries incurred during the licensed period. The certificate of insurance should be received at least 30 days prior to the event. Once the certificate is received by the facility, a manager must check it to make sure it contains the proper coverage for the event.

One of the recurring problems with certificates is that they are usually one-page forms that the underwriter or broker checks the appropriate block to indicate coverage. From just reviewing the certificate, you may think that all aspects of the event are covered by insurance. In order to see the entire coverage and all the exclusions, the manager must review the Policy of Insurance ("Policy"). However, most of the time, the Policy is not available for six to eight weeks. If you do not think the event is covered under the licensee's insurance, send a letter to the insurance broker that describes the event and the safety concerns. Ask the licensee's insurance broker if there is coverage for the event.

---

[17] Id. at 380.
[18] Id. at 383.

In the contract between the Northern California Roadster Racing Association and the Stadium, the Stadium agreed to be responsible for the condition and maintenance of the track. The Stadium also agreed to have public liability insurance naming both itself and the association as insureds (the Fireman's policy) while the association was to name the Stadium as an additional assured on its policy. This policy, however, contained restrictions that would not cover the stadium for an injury such as the one that occurred. The Court held that the Stadium had failed to adequately examine the policy, and that despite this fact, the restrictions were enforceable as written, as they were clear and distinct. In addition, the court found that the stadium failed to provide the additional insurer's with timely notice of the suit, and that the insurance companies found out about the suit when Fireman's made a demand on them for contribution. The Court granted a new trial, with the direction that the trial court enter a judgment for the insurers, denying liability under their policies.[24]

In *World Championship Wrestling Inc. v. City of Macon*,[25] a young girl was injured at a concession stand on the concourse level of the Macon Coliseum during a World Champion Wrestling (WCW) event. The girl and her family sued to recover damages for her injuries, and the City filed a cross-claim against WCW, claiming that under its lease agreement for the Macon Coliseum, it was required to provide liability insurance for the City's benefit, and moved for summary judgment. The trial court granted the City's motion, stating that the City should be exculpated by WCW up to $500,000 in the underlying injury action. WCW appealed the Court's decision, and the Court of Appeals held that under the lease agreement, WCW was required to provide liability insurance to insulate the City from liability should any injuries occur during the period in which WCW leased the space. WCW did not in fact obtain any such insurance, but argued that the injury occurred in association with the concession stands, and that this area was not specifically covered in the lease agreement. The Court of Appeals disagreed, noting that the "Arena" area mentioned in the lease agreement did not refer to only the seating area, but included the whole coliseum except the Monument Room, which was a separate facility. As such, WCW was responsible for injuries that occurred during its event in all parts of the Arena, including the concession area. Its failure to obtain

---

[24] Id. at 300.
[25] 493 S.E.2d 629 (Ga. App. 1997).

insurance then made WCW itself directly responsible for any damages accessed against the City, up to $500,000 in the underlying court action for injuries to the patron.

1) Errors and Omissions Insurance (Double Booking)

This type of insurance helps a facility to insulate itself in case of an error or omission on the part of its manager and staff for such things as accidentally double-booking events the facility. In the case below, we shall see that an insurance broker was held potentially liable for selling an insurance policy to a client offered by a non-licensed insurance company.

In *Cook County Bar Auxiliary et. al. v. Hyatt Corporation,*[26] Hyatt Regency Hotel was booked by the American College of Chest Physicians, in 1977, for its conference to be held October 23, 1983 through October 27, 1983.[27] The "hold" was placed on the function book incorrectly, indicating the events were to begin in the evening, rather than in the morning of October 23. In 1982, some five years after the hold had been placed for the use of the Hyatt's ballrooms by the College, the Cook County Bar Auxiliary contacted the catering manager at the hotel about reserving the space for its annual fashion show.

The manager thought the space was available and would not conflict with the College's use of the space. The Hotel told the Auxiliary the space was available, and they in turn forwarded a check as a deposit on the rental.[28] In May, 1983, several months later, the Hotel wrote to the College regarding the specific events to be held for the convention so that they could release any unused rooms to other interested parties. When the Hotel received the advance program, it realized the error and immediately contacted the College to see if it would release the rooms required by the Auxiliary on October 23, 1983 providing no information to whom the space was rented. The College refused to release the rooms and the hotel contacted the Auxiliary to discuss the problem. During the meeting, the Hotel explained that the College had booked the space five years prior, that the convention was logistically more complicated than the fashion show, and that the convention would bring the Hotel close to $1,000,000 in business versus the $25,000 from the fashion show. The

---

[26] No. 83 C 6384 1986 U.S. Dist. LEXIS 27639 (March 26, 1986).
[27] Id. at *1.
[28] Id.

not covered nor contemplated when the insurance policy was issued to the exhibitor.[37]

The Court in this case clearly holds that there is a limited scope to the insurance coverage mandated for exhibitors at special events, and this insurance will not excuse the State from any of its normal duties in making sure its premises are safe for all patrons.

In *United States Fire Insurance Company v. Kentucky Truck Sales, Inc.,*[38] a seller of new and used semi-tractor trucks loaned a semi-tractor truck to an event known as the Mid-America Truck Pull held in the coliseum of the Kentucky Fair and Exhibition Center.[39] The loaned truck was to be used as a tow-back truck. Kentucky Truck Sales was covered by a standard garage insurance policy issued by United States Fire Insurance Company (USFI) which specifically excluded coverage of autos used in any professional or organized racing or demolition contests or stunting activity.[40]

The truck pull was organized by three groups, and sold tickets to the public. The event consisted of competitions between trucks by class, including hot rod tractors, four and two wheeled modified class, in pulling a weighted sled down a specially constructed dirt track. The sled was able to increase or decrease its weight mechanically, and the truck from Kentucky Truck was used to pull the sled back into position for the next contestant. The truck was lent in exchange for advertising in the programs, PA announcements, and for having the truck there to be seen for the three-day event. This was also the first time Kentucky Truck had ever loaned a vehicle to the event.[41] An employee from Kentucky Truck was hired by the Pull to operate the tow-back truck for the last two nights of the event, although he had never participated in such an event before. The employee was instructed as how to operate the vehicle. A person who owned the vehicle scheduled to compete next walked onto the track between the sled and the tow-back truck when he was hit by the rear wheels of the tow-back truck and died of his injuries. The widow sued Kentucky Truck, the driver, and others for damages. USFI filed a declaratory action to seek a determination of whether its garage policy afforded coverage to Kentucky Truck, and the

---

[37] Id. at 1570.
[38] 786 F.2d 736 (6th Cir. 1986).
[39] Id. at 737.
[40] Id at 736.
[41] Id. at 738.

trial court declared that the insurance was not applicable in this instance, and Kentucky Truck appealed. The Court of Appeals held that a Truck Pull was a dangerous event holding increased risk for all, and that this was covered by the insurance exclusion regarding "stunting" activity, even though the truck was not itself competing in the event but just used in conjunction to the event.[42]

Insurance and applicable exclusions are crucial when holding an event. The owner of the loaned truck should have notified his insurance broker that there was a special event and that he would like to have "Special Event Insurance." Usually, for an ongoing business that has a complete insurance program, this type of insurance may be provided as a courtesy from the broker or the carrier. Even the seemingly innocuous loan of a truck in this case led to the death of a man and no insurance coverage, because a rider or other coverage was not sought prior to the event. Facilities may be extremely careful to make sure that all event participants are covered by adequate insurance, and have provided necessary certificates of insurance before an event takes place, to insulate them from any liability should injuries occur.

3) Alcoholic Beverage Distribution Insurance

Any facility that sells or serves alcoholic beverages must be concerned about alcoholic beverage distribution insurance. As we are all aware, alcohol is an intoxicating substance, and may lead to injury or death, either from drinking excessively, or from participating in dangerous behaviors while under the influence of alcohol. Many states allow "dram shop" suits, in which the server of the alcohol, namely bars and restaurants as well as others, can be held liable for the injuries subsequently caused by the person to whom the alcohol was served. Because many facilities serve alcohol during some or all events, serious consideration should be given to obtaining "dram shop" coverage insurance.

In *Maro v. Potash et. al.*,[43] Mrs. Maro was assaulted by a Mr. Potash at a Philadelphia Eagles game at Veteran's Stadium in Philadelphia on November 10, 1985. Mr. Potash subsequently harassed her again at another game, because the Maros and Potashs held season tickets and thus were seated again in the same vacinity in

---

[42] Id. at 740.
[43] 531 A.2d 407 (N.J. Super. 1987).

subsequent weeks. Dr. and Mrs. Maro, New Jersey residents, sued Potash, also a New Jersey resident, The Philadelphia Eagles, Spectraguard, in charge of security at the Stadium, and Nilon Brothers, the concessionaire at the Stadium for damages. The suit against Nilon Brothers was a dram shop case, alleging that Nilon had sold alcohol to Potash, leading to the assault and subsequent harassment of Maro. Nilon moved to dismiss, claiming the New Jersey courts did not have jurisdiction over them, as they operated solely within Pennsylvania and had had no direct business contacts with New Jersey since the 1960's. The New Jersey Superior Court held that jurisdiction over Nilon was proper, due to the vast number of New Jersey residents served at the Stadium every year. Also, as exclusive concessionaire, Nilon benefited greatly from business from New Jersey residents and from advertisements issued by other Stadium advertisers such as the Eagles, drawing spectators from New Jersey. The Court held that exercising jurisdiction would not pose an undue burden on Nilon, and thus the dram shop suit was not dismissed.

This case is a great example of where the server of alcohol at a stadium was held potentially liable for injuries to a third party, simply due to their act of serving alcohol. While the ultimate outcome of the case is unclear, the fact that the Court did not dismiss the case shows that potential liability existed, and that dram shop coverage would come into play should the concessionaire be held liable in this action.

4) Business Interruption Insurance

When a disaster strikes, like Hurricane Katrina, the survival of many businesses including public assembly facilities are contingent on receiving timely payments from their business interruption carrier. In general, "business interruption coverage operates to compensate the business for losses stemming from the business interruption: lost profits, loss of earnings, and continuing expenses during the period of repair or restoration of property damaged or destroyed by reason of a covered peril."[44] Coverage may extend for a reasonable period of time required to repair the facility.[45] An insured "is entitled to recover its actual loss of business income during the period of time necessary to restore the

---

[44] 11 Couch on Insurance (3d ed. 1998) § 167:9, p. 167-14.
[45] Id., § 167:18, p. 167-23; see Annot., Business Interruption Insurance (1996) 37 A.L.R.5th 41, 213-217, §§ 46-48

business premises."[46] Business interruption insurance is intended to return to the insured's business the amount of profit it would have earned had there been no interruption of the business or suspension of operations. In addition to business interruption insurance, we will also discuss related insurance provisions such as contingent business interruption coverage, civil authority coverage and leader property coverage. It is important to note, under what category of rights the courts may construe insurance policies. Insurance policies are construed under the well-settled law of contract claims. Whether the contract language in the policy is ambiguous is a question of law that a court may examine in the context of the entire agreement.

Under the general interpretation of business interruption insurance, the business is usually protected against losing "net profits." In other words, the facility or business must actually make a profit to collect on the policy. In many cases where the business did not produce actual "profits" including fixed charges and expenses, the courts will not put the business or insured in a better economic position from having its business interrupted than if no interruption had taken place.[47] Thus, facilities that receive appropriated funds (tax dollars), private contributions or donations from other sources may want to specifically define what income stream they want to insure. For instance, instead of "net profits" for a business interruption policy, a convention center may want to protect or insure "gross revenues generated from leased space and utilities" or other revenues.

Another required element of business interruption insurance is that there must be a suspension of business operations in order for the policy to cover the loss of profits. Some policies may cover the insured for a partial loss of business facilities but make sure you check the policy language before you pay the premium. Know what is covered under the policy. For instance, if the business remains open even though there is water damage or theft of major equipment, most courts will rule that the language in the policy requires the business to cease all operations.

---

[46] *Dictiomatic, Inc. v. U.S. Fid. & Guar. Co.* (S.D.Fla. 1997) 958 F.Supp. 594, 602.

[47] *Hotel Properties, Ltd v. Heritage Ins. Of America*, 456 So.2nd 1249 (Fla.App. 3 Dist., 1984).

In *Kearney Convention Center v. Anderson-Divan-Cottrell Insurance Inc. et. al.,*[50] the Kearney Convention Center sued its insurance broker for failing to obtain business interruption insurance with appropriate policy limits to adequately protect the Center.

The Center had previously obtained insurance from the same broker and had a $700,000 business interruption policy on an 80% co-insurance basis based upon the gross earnings of the Center. In January 1981, a fire occurred at the motel run by Kearney, resulting in part or all of the motel being out of business until June, 1981. The insurance company computed the lost gross earnings at $333,396 but determined that the motel had been underinsured and not within the 80% co-insurance requirement, so that the policy would only pay 36% or $119,472 of the loss incurred. The motel then sued its insurance broker for failing to use reasonable care to obtain adequate business interruption insurance, and failing to notify the motel that its coverage would only cover a small percentage of any potential loss. The motel sought to recover its loss for such negligence, and the trial court issued a verdict in their favor. The brokers defended their action by stating that the motel had failed to give them sufficient information to make an determination of appropriate coverage, but the motel stated they had provided the brokers with all information the broker requested from the motel. The jury awarded the motel the verdict. The motel appealed the verdict as to the calculation of damages due, and the instructions given to the jury for evaluating the actual loss. The Supreme Court of Nebraska agreed, and set aside the verdict amount and remanded the case for a retrial as to damages only, not as to liability for the error committed by the insurance brokers.

This is a good example of how business interruption insurance works, and why adequate insurance coverage was needed. Without assuring adequate coverage, the fire was going to place the motel out-of-pocket over $200,000, a devastating loss to a small business. By successfully suing the insurance brokers for failing to obtain adequate coverage, the motel would most likely recover most a substantial portion of its losses.

---

[50] 370 N.W.2d 86 (Neb. 1985).

5) Directors and Officers Insurance

This type of insurance covers the Directors and Officers of the corporate entity running the facility from personal liability if their decisions or actions lead to the harm of another. It is similar to Errors and Omissions insurance in the scope of liability, but will cover a different set of people. In today's lawsuit prone society, you may have difficulty attracting directors and officers to a non-profit corporation, unless Director's and Officer's insurance is offered.

6) Construction "Wrap-Up" Insurance

Construction wrap-up insurance is usually purchased by a general contractor or owner of a facility to provide worker's compensation insurance for all general and subcontractors participating in a construction project, in part to avoid any problems with liens caused by law suits for injuries suffered during the construction process.

In *Black et. al. v. Kiewit Construction*,[51] Black was working for Liberty Steel Erectors, constructing the Anacostia Parking Garage in Washington, D.C. when he was injured on the job. Washington Metropolitan Area Transit Authority ("WMATA") was the general contractor for the job, and subcontracted with Kiewit, who in turn subcontracted with Liberty. In the District of Columbia, all employers must have worker's compensation insurance for its employees. If a subcontractor fails to have the appropriate insurance, the general contractor is required to purchase such insurance for the subcontractor's employees. WMATA had a comprehensive "wrap-up" policy providing worker's compensation insurance for all contractors, subcontractors and their employees. Under this policy, when a general or subcontractor was hired, they were to be given certificates of insurance, naming them as insureds under the policy.

Black was injured following a fall into a hole at the job site. Black filed a claim and received worker's compensation benefits, but filed suit to recover further damages based on Kiewit's alleged negligence in maintaining safety on the job site. Kiewit moved for summary judgment, alleging it was immune from the subcontractor's suit. The Court reviewed a number of decisions including the Supreme Court's interpretation of D.C.'s worker's compensation law and held that

---

[51] No. 89-1834 (RCL), 1990 U.S. Dist. LEXIS 3951 (D.C. 1990).

Chapter 6

The Safe Operation of the Facility

By Turner D. Madden

6.00 Introduction

The safety of our attendees, patrons, spectators and event participants is of primary concern to the facility manager. Every operational detail must be monitored and controlled to accommodate the millions of people that attend events in our facilities. Each event, no matter how small, must be planned for the safety and enjoyment of the attendee. As managers know, the larger the event, the more planning is required by the facility and possibly by the city or state. This Chapter covers negligence the legal aspects of managing the safety of the facility.

6.01 Overview of Negligence

According to *Black's Law Dictionary*[1] negligence is the omission to do something which a reasonable man, guided by those ordinary considerations which regulate human affairs, would do, or the doing of something which a reasonable and prudent man would not do. Negligence is the failure to use such care as a reasonably prudent and careful person would use under similar circumstances; ..." This means that you are held to the standard of what a reasonably prudent and careful facility manager would do in like circumstances. Below are several cases that illustrate this point.

In *Joan McLaughlin v. Home Indemnity Insurance Company*,[2] Ms. McLaughlin fractured her arm when she slipped in a wet substance while descending a stairway at a rock concert in the Independence Hall in Baton Rouge, Louisiana. Ms. McLaughlin filed a lawsuit against Independence Hall, its liability insurer and the promoter of the concert. The Hall was arranged in a series of platforms that descend from the front entrance to the main floor. Each of the two aisles contained three steps between each platform. Chairs were on the platforms and festival seating

---

[1] Henery Campbell Black, M.A., West Publishing, Co. 1979.
[2] 361 So. 2d 1227 (1978)

was in effect on the main floor where no chairs were provided and the patrons sat on the floor.[3] All concert tickets were general admission tickets. Beer and soft drinks were sold on the main floor and the rest rooms were off the main floor. After the first band played and stopped there was an intermission. Ms. McLaughlin, who was seated in the platform area, attempted to go to the rest room during the intermission period. Ms. McLaughlin testified that it was dark and she could not see and she stepped into something wet and slipped and fell on the platform. As she attempted to right herself and proceed she slipped again and that was when she was injured.[4]

The trial judge found that the owners, operators, the promoter and the patrons were aware that drinks were being consumed on the main floor and in the platform seats and that people placed their drinks on the floor and they were being spilled. There were approximately fourteen policemen, four firemen and three "housemen" on duty that evening.[5] The trial judge concluded that he was unable to find any particular thing wrong that the defendants, the owners and operators of the Hall and the promoter, allowed to occur that created a hazard that was a surprise or unknown to the plaintiff, Ms. McLaughlin. Therefore, the trial judge ruled that the defendants were not negligent. On appeal to the Court of Appeal of Louisiana, the trial judge was reversed and the Court of Appeal found that the defendants were negligent. The Court of Appeal agreed with the trial judge that it is extremely hard to inspect and clean up during the course of the performance but "that the risk created by defendant's failure to turn the lights on during intermission was unreasonable." The Appeals Court further stated that:

> "It is during this period of time that patrons are expected to move about either for the purpose of obtaining refreshments or to go to the rest rooms. The danger of someone slipping and falling is the prime risk to be guarded against. Precaution against such a risk is minimal to say the least."

---

[3] Id. at 1227.
[4] Id at 1227.
[5] Id. at 1229

In *Chelton v. Tallahassee-Leon County Civic Center Authority,*
[6] Chelton and a friend went to the Civic Center to attend a concert. When they arrived, the concert had started, and the house lights were off. They asked an usher to show them the section where their seats were located, and he pointed to the section. Chelton and her companion went to the section indicated, gave their ticket stubs to another usher, and inquired as to the location of their seats. The usher indicated a general direction, but gave no specific answer. Chelton and her friend went down a stairwell to look for the seats when Chelton lost her footing, fell forward and smashed her lips on the concrete stair steps. Chelton felt the grade and steepness of the stairs helped contribute to her fall and injuries.

The Civic Center opened in 1981. The facility initially received many complaints about the steepness of the stairs, and subsequently installed handrails, patterned after those at the Omni Complex in Atlanta. Despite continued accidents, the manager of the Center felt the handrails helped reduce the number of accidents, but he had posted no signs warning patrons to watch their step. Stairwell lights on the seats are available, and ushers carry flashlights to help illuminate the area. The usher's duties are to assist people to their seats. While they do not walk every person to their seat, if a person is having trouble, they are instructed to physically walk the person to their seat, and to use their flashlights when doing so.

Chelton filed suit against the Civic Center, alleging that the illumination on the stairwells when the house lights were down was inadequate, that there were an inadequate number of ushers to supervise and safeguard patrons, and the Center was aware of the dangerous conditions of the stairway and failed to warn the patrons of the hazard. The Trial Court granted the Civic Center's motion for summary judgment, and Chelton appealed. The Court of Appeals reversed the Trial Court's grant of summary judgment, stating that issues of whether the Center had taken adequate steps to ensure the safety of its patrons, and whether the installed handrails were adequate to protect most patrons from injury was a matter to be settled

---

[6] 525 So.2d 972 (Fla. Ct. App. 1988).

by a jury, and the Civic Center's motion was not so strong as to allow dismissal of the suit without a trial.[7]

In *Filmore v. Convention Center & Visitor's Bureau,*[8] several people became ill while attending a banquet at the Cleveland Convention Center and sued the Center, the catering service, the Bureau, Bond Court and the City of Cleveland, who operated the Convention Center.[9] On examination, it appeared that the people actually became ill due to carbon monoxide (CO) poisoning, and not from food poisoning, and conditions existed at the convention center to reasonably conclude this was the cause of the illness. The report from the Ohio Department of Health went on to indicate that CO monitoring should be used before and after events of more than 400 people at the Center and that use of internal combustion engines in the center should be controlled to prevent increased CO levels before or during events. The Court of Appeals held that the Bond Court and Bureau were properly dismissed from the case, as was ARA, the caterer, but the City was not, due to its role as operator of the Convention Center. CO is a very dangerous and potentially fatal gas may build up in a convention center, from emissions of vehicles used in and around the facility, and perhaps even from parking areas, making it necessary for a prudent facility to check CO levels at regular intervals if vehicles are frequently used in the facility.

In *Maldanado v. Louisiana Superdome Commission,*[10] a man left his job working as a cook for the Hyatt Hotel to attend a football game at the Superdome, which adjoins the hotel by way of a shopping center and adjoining walkway. On his way into the Superdome at Gate C, about three steps in from the doorway, the man slipped in a large puddle, injuring his back, neck and left arm. The man informed a nearby ticket taker of his fall, and the man was taken to the first aid center. The man had many problems with his back following the incident, and this eventually led to his dismissal from his job. The ultimate diagnosis was a herniated disc in the man's lower back. He then sued the Superdome for not promptly cleaning up the accumulation of spilled beer that caused the fall. In a bench trial, the court awarded the man $175,000 in damages and $119,000

---

[7] Id. at 975.
[8] 1992 Ohio App. LEXIS 5493 (October 29, 1992).
[9] Id. at *2.
[10] 687 So.2d 1087 (4th Cir. LA 1997).

in special damages, from which the Superdome appealed. The Court of Appeals held that the Superdome had constructive notice[11] of the hazard, since it was the duty of ticket takers to notify housekeeping of any spills so they may be taken care of promptly; that patrons were required to throw out drinks prior to entering the stadium and often drinks were thrown on the ground and not into containers, and Gate C often experienced this problem because of the high traffic due to its link with the Hyatt. The man had arrived at the game well after the initial rush of patrons. The trashcans were overflowing at Gate C at the time of the fall. The hazard had most likely existed for some time, and the Superdome employees had not properly inspected the area.[12] There was also supposed to be a janitor stationed at Gate C to try to take care of any problems as they arose. There was ample evidence provided that the Superdome had constructive knowledge of the spill, time to correct the condition but did not and that the injuries of which the man complained were more likely than not directly related to his fall. The man was not comparatively negligent, and therefore the Court of Appeals upheld the trial court's verdict.

In *Williams v. 312 Walnut Limited Partnership,*[13] a man left the Cincinnati Reds stadium by a pedestrian walkway and turned onto a skywalk along side the 312 Walnut building. In order to avoid walking around a trash container and bumping into people on the crowded walkway, the man chose to vault over the trash can, but instead, he fell over the railing to the street below, causing severe injuries that eventually led to his death.[14] The man's family sued, claiming negligence in design of the walkway, placing of the trashcan, and other claims. For a negligence claim to be successful, the plaintiff must show that the Defendant had a duty to protect the plaintiff from injury, that the defendant breached that duty, and that the breach of that duty was the proximate cause of the Plaintiff's injury.[15]

---

[11] Constructive notice is defined as " the existence of facts which infer actual knowledge." Id. at 1091.

[12] Id. at 1092.

[13] No. C-960368, 1996 Ohio App. LEXIS 5887 (December 31, 1996).

[14] Id. at *6.

[15] Id. at *9.

The issue in this case rested upon whom owed a duty to the plaintiff to keep him safe from the injury he incurred. Experts testified that the walkway had been negligently designed by failing to provide alcoves for the trashcans. The City was sued as well because they had an easement agreement with 312 Partnership for the use of the walkway. The Court of Appeals affirmed the trial court's grant of summary judgment to all defendants, stating that under all possible scenarios, there was no breach of a duty owed to the injured man, and that the trash can was an open and obvious obstacle which he unfortunately chose to avoid by vaulting, leading to his eventual death.

While this case clearly lays out the rules of negligence, it also shows a facility manager that they should be aware of any possible dangers on walkways adjacent to their facility, and attempts should be made to make these passageways free of obstacles to prevent any similar unfortunate accidents. Although the facility was not held liable for the injuries in this case, a manager should still be aware of any similar problems they may encounter and an attempt should be made to remove any dangers that may be present.

In *Gunther v. Charlotte Baseball, Inc.,*[16] a woman was struck in the face and severely injured by a foul ball while attending her first baseball game. While oral warnings were issued about possible injury due to foul balls, the woman arrived after the game had begun, missing the first warning and was hit prior to the issuing of any additional warning.[17] Additionally, no warning was printed on the tickets.[18] The woman claimed to have been distracted by a foul ball that had just shattered the press box glass, when a subsequent foul ball hit her, causing serious injuries to her face and her eye orbit.[19] While the Charlotte Knight's stadium was described as "state of the art," it had had prior problems with foul balls shattering the press box glass, and subsequent to the woman's injuries discussed the possibility of installing shatterproof glass.[20] The court stated that the overwhelming weight of authority had held that baseball patrons assumed

---

[16] 854 F.Supp. 424 (D.S.C. 1994).
[17] Id. at 426.
[18] Id.
[19] Id.
[20] Id.

the risk of being struck at games, and that while the woman was a novice spectator, her ignorance of the game was no excuse.[21] The court stated the hazard of being struck by a foul ball will always exist and that such risk is held to be assumed by spectators, providing due care has been exercised by erecting a screen or the like and it is up to the fan to decide whether to sit within the protected area or not.[22] While the woman alleged that her injury was due in part to the negligence of the stadium in failing to install shatterproof glass in the press box, causing her attention to be distracted, the court noted that there are a variety of distractions at a ball park, from mascots, to vendors, scoreboards and raffles, and that any distraction was as foreseeable to the spectator as to the owners, and thus the stadium was not liable for her injuries.[23]

Similarly, in *Singerman v. Municipal Service Bureau*,[24] a man was hit in the eye by a hockey puck, sustaining serious injuries, while on the ice at Westland Sports Arena. The plaintiff was playing pick-up hockey at the rink, rented by Mr. Eller for a pre-season skate-around.[25] Singerman, an experienced hockey player and on the coaching staff at Eastern Michigan University Hockey Club, had been invited the day before to join Eller's group. Singerman was on the ice with no protective gear and passed pucks with players while warming up.[26] The players then broke into a scrimmage. Singerman saw the player take a shot at the goal which struck him, but maintained that poor lighting at the arena prevented him from reacting properly in order to avoid the puck.[27] Singerman then sued the City of Westland, the Westland Sports Arena, and others. The claims against the arena were dismissed on the grounds of governmental immunity and Singerman appealed.[28] Singerman claimed he was a business invitee, and that the improper maintenance and design of the lighting in the arena resulted in his injury.[29]

---

[21] Id. at 427.

[22] Id. at 428.

[23] Id. at 430.

[24] No. 103715, 1997 Mich. LEXIS 1590 (July 15, 1997).

[25] Id. at *2.

[26] Id. at *3.

[27] Id. at *4.

[28] Id. at *4.

[29] Id. at *7.

The Supreme Court of Michigan held that the inadequate lighting was not a hidden harm that was undiscoverable, that Singerman chose to engage in a known hazardous sport without adequate protection, and thus assumed the risk of injury and therefore the trial court's dismissal of claims was upheld. In dissent, several justices felt that the Arena could have foreseen that the inadequate lighting would cause an injury, that several memos regarding corrections to the lighting had been written prior to the injury, and that while Singerman may have been comparatively negligent, this did not relieve the Arena from maintaining the premises in a safe condition.[30]

In *Lowe v. California League of Professional Baseball*, [31] a fan was injured when struck by a foul ball during a professional baseball game. The game was being played at the Epicenter and the team mascot, "Tremor," a dinosaur with a long tail, had been performing. The mascot was touching the fan and distracting him, and as the fan began to return his attention to the game, he was struck by a foul ball, unable to react in time to avoid injury. [32] Very serious injuries resulted, leading to this lawsuit. The Court of Appeals addressed whether the mascot's performance constituted negligence by increasing the inherent risk to the fan from foul balls under normal circumstances, and reversed the lower court's dismissal of the case, stating there were issues of fact to be resolved before a jury.[33] It is quite possible that given the actions of the mascot, distracting the fan by an actual touching, that the fan may prevail at trial, since the mascot increased his risk of harm above the risk normally associated with attending baseball games.

6.02 General Crowd Control

Prior to each event, especially first time events, a plan should be developed to determine how the patrons should be staged for ticketing, where they will enter and safely exit the event. Plenty of bullhorns and other crowd control equipment should also be on hand to provide security personnel with the proper equipment.

---

[30] Id. at *17.
[31] 56 Cal. App. 4th 112; 1997 Cal. App. LEXIS 532 (July 1, 1997).
[32] Id. at *2.
[33] Id.

The movement and attitudes of people (crowds) can rapidly change depending upon the event participants, the weather conditions, if alcoholic beverages are served and with the perception of the organizers of the event.

In *People of the State of New York v. U.S.T.A. National Tennis Center, Inc.,*[34] the City of New York served summons on the USTA tennis center during the U.S. Open Tennis tournament for allowing the entrances and exits to the center to become blocked with people, in violation of the Administrative Code of New York.[35] The USTA had ushers prohibit people from entering the stands above the tennis courts until "odd games" when the players exchanged ends of the court, to prevent distraction of the players during the game. People often waited for up to 25 minutes to be allowed to go to their seats, and this caused a great number of people to block the exits, causing a very serious hazard should the stadium need to be emptied in a short period of time. The USTA defended its actions as being necessary for the players, that the statute in question failed to provide adequate notice, and was being selectively enforced, violating the USTA's constitutional rights.[36] The court held that the Code was clear and unequivocal on its face, and that despite the USTA's interest in protecting players from distraction, it was in fact putting 10,000 to 20,000 spectators at risk by blocking the exits and entrances. The court stated that:

> "Blocked exits are a primary cause of injuries and often death when disasters occur at public events involving the assemblage of large numbers of people. This is especially true in the instant case. Here 10,000 people were engaged in watching tennis matches. ... The evidence shows that it would not be feasible to evacuate the stadium in the event of an emergency with the stairwells and passageways being impassable with people ...
>
> History is replete with catastrophes involving the loss of many lives due to hazards presented by improper

---

[34] 544 N.Y.S.2d 458 (1989)
[35] Id. at 459.
[36] Id.

policing of access and exit facilities at public events."[37]

Thus, the court found the USTA guilty on all counts.

In *Bowes v. Cincinnati Riverfront Coliseum,*[38] eleven people were killed during entrance to a concert by "The Who," during which festival seating was available. Damages for wrongful death and personal injuries were filed by the families of the dead patrons against the City of Cincinnati, the facility, the directors, concert promoters, and the group themselves, among others.[39] In multiple motions to dismiss various parties involved, the Court of Appeals held that the Directors and Officers of the corporation who operated the coliseum could be held liable for the decisions that were made to employ festival seating when they were aware of previous problems with this first-come first-served seating arrangement, and that they were potentially liable for punitive damages as well. The City was not released from its responsibility to the coliseum, nor were any of the others who were sued. This case clearly points out both the need for facility managers and directors to protect themselves from potential personal liability by having applicable directors and officers insurance, as well as pointing out the clear hazards posed by festival seating arrangements. Although many states now prohibit festival seating by law, it is important to realize that open seating arrangements could still pose a hazard due to the crush of fans if adequate controls are not in place.

In *Gibson v. Shelby County Fair Association,*[40] Gibson, a seventeen year old spectator at an auto race at the fairgrounds operated by the Shelby County Fair Association (Association), was injured and permanently paralyzed when a wheel became detached from a speeding racer, broke through the wire fence beside the track and struck him. The Association had leased the fairgrounds to Dale Swanson for hot rod and stock car auto races. The cars usually had the gears for the rear wheels locked, to prevent the differential from operating, causing increased stress on the axle of the cars. The track itself was dirt, originally built for horse racing, but was made a little wider and sloping for the car race.

---

[37] Id. at 460, 461.
[38] 465 N.E.2d 904 (OH 1st App. 1983).
[39] Id. at 906.
[40] 65 N.W. 2d 433 (Iowa 1954).

OSHA had been intending to make a general inspection after the convention center came up on their list, when they received a complaint from an employee of another primary contractor regarding safety conditions at the site.[48] The OSHA inspector decided to act on both the employee complaint and complete a general inspection at the same time.[49] When the OSHA inspector arrived at the site, the project manager for yet a third contractor who acted as construction superintendent, called together representatives from all the contractors to request cooperation with the inspection.[50] When representatives from Beiro arrived, they refused to allow access to any part of their work area without a warrant, and physically blocked the inspector's access to the site. The inspector then left the site, and returned the next day with two compliance officers, after being notified by the D.C. government official that the legal problems had been resolved and the government, owner of the worksite would consent and fully cooperate with the inspection.[51] The OSHA team began with Beiro, accompanied by their legal counsel and project manager. Beiro received several serious and non-serious citations which they contested, alleging their fourth amendment rights were violated because the inspection or "search" took place without a warrant and that they were a victim of selective and vindictive prosecution.[52] The court held that the D.C. government had the authority to consent to the inspection of the construction area, shared among several contractors, and that Beiro had no privacy expectation to that general area.[53] While Beiro did not willingly consent to the inspections, the OSHA officers acted upon their authority to inspect granted by the DC Government, the owners who had control over the site, and thus Beiro was legally subject to the inspection without an administrative warrant having to be issued. However, inspections of Beiro's tool trailer and change shed were not open to the naked eye and violations regarding this inspection were vacated.[54] The OSHA inspectors were allowed to inspect everything in plain sight and further inspect

---

[48] Id.
[49] Id.
[50] Id.
[51] id.
[52] Id. at 898.
[53] Id. at 899, 900.
[54] Id. at 902.

areas in which they had a suspicion that a violation existed. The court further held that because several other contractors were also cited during the inspection, and that the fines imposed were not at the maximum allowed, Beiro's contention regarding vindictive prosecution was invalid.[55]

In *Brennan v. Gilles*,[56] a subcontractor's employees were killed when scaffolding collapsed plummeting the workers and almost 400 pounds of window glass onto the ground below the fourth story addition being made to the NASA Goddard Manned Space Flight Center in Greenbelt, Maryland.[57] OSHA charged both the subcontractor and the general contractor, Gilles, with serious violations of safety regulations pertaining to scaffolds, and issued a citation to each.[58] Gilles contested their liability for the citation and $550 penalty, stating that although Gilles submitted an accident prevention plan and the responsibility for job site safety was that of the Gilles superintendent, the scaffolding in question was furnished, maintained and used solely by the subcontractor's employees. The Administrative law judge found that Gilles was responsible for the accident because its workers, as well as those of the subcontractor, had access to the hazard and could have been in a position to suffer injury from the collapse, and that they had the overall responsibility for safety at the job site.[59] Under the Act, where there is a substantial probability of death or serious physical harm, a violation is denominated serious unless the employer did not, and could not with the exercise of reasonable diligence, know of the presence of the violation.[60] The act also requires the assessment of a fine for all serious violations.[61] The Court of Appeals, affirming the Commission's reversal of the Administrative Law judge's findings, held that Gilles did not act as a joint employer of the subcontractor's employees, although this was a factual determination to be made upon the circumstances existing, not a general pronouncement of all general

---

[55] Id. at 905.
[56] 504 F.2d 1255 (4th Cir. 1974).
[57] Id. at 1257.
[58] Id. at 1256.
[59] Id. at 1258, 1259.
[60] 29 U.S.C. sec. 666(j) subsec 17(k).
[61] *Brennan v. Gilles*, 504 F.2d at 1256.

contractor-subcontractor relations under the act.[62] The court also held that Gilles' employees did not have access to the zones of danger created by the faulty scaffolding, and thus they were not held liable for the violations of the subcontractor under these facts.

(1) Bloodborne Pathogens

As we all are aware, personal hygiene is important, and hygiene in general becomes more important when we are discussing public facilities. If a food employee neglects to wash their hands, they can transmit bacteria and disease to others, and it can become wide spread in a short period of time. Moreover, with the large number of people entering facilities daily, there can be a risk for exposure to bloodborne pathogens, or diseases through blood or other bodily fluids. OSHA has addressed this risk by promulgating regulations geared toward controlling the potential spread of disease.[63] While public facilities are not hospitals, there is a small risk that disease could be spread by contact with bodily fluids from the large number of people using a facility on a day to day basis. Of primary concern is the spread of the Hepatitis B virus (HBV) a very serious liver disease that can be fatal, and the Human Immunodeficiency virus (HIV) the virus that leads to AIDS, but many other diseases from the common cold through bacterial infections can be spread through mucus, fecal material, urine, and other bodily secretions. Many facilities have first aid stations on hand, the nurses or other staff should be well-versed in universal precautions. Likewise, security personnel, who will most likely have first contact with an injured person, should be advised of universal precautions, should someone who is bleeding need assistance. It is the facility's or subcontractor's responsibility to supply gloves and other protective equipment to all employees that may encounter blood or other bodily fluids,[64] and insure the accessibility and use of such protection. The employees most in need of such protection would logically cover security, first aid personnel, and cleaning staff.[65]

---

[62] Id. at 1261.
[63] 29 C.F.R. 1910.1030 et. seq.
[64] 29 C.F.R. 1910.1030 (d) (3)
[65] 29 C.F.R. 1910.1030 (d)(4), regulating housekeeping.

Facilities should still encourage employees who may come in contact with bodily fluids to get vaccinated for Hepatitis B as a precaution.[66] Training in bloodborne pathogens should be conducted for all personnel subject to exposure, as a part of their ongoing job responsibilities.[67]

As we may all be aware, contact with blood from an infected person on an employee who has an area of open skin could lead to infection. Although HIV is not easily transmitted in normal course of contact, 24 cases of health care workers infected with HIV through patient contact had been confirmed by 1991.[68] Hepatitis B, much more infectious that HIV, can survive on a piece of clothing or other material for a week and can be spread by dirty laundry; there are approximately 113 to 129 deaths annually from health care workers from HIV and the death rate rises to 187 to 197 if the deaths of non-healthcare workers exposed by health care workers is included.[69] It is thus clear why OSHA promulgated regulations to minimize exposure, which can be as simple as ensuring security personnel have a pair of rubber gloves with them and use them if they encounter someone who is bleeding and needs assistance.

In *American Dental Association et. al. v. Martin, et.al.,*[70] the American Dental Association challenged OSHA's regulations regarding bloodborne pathogens. The court thoroughly reviewed the potential risks to dental workers versus the burden placed on them by ensuring use of universal precautions, and stated that OSHA did not attempt to access the risk of disease transmission industry by industry, but neither was it required to.[71] The rules deal with practices to prevent contact with potential fatal disease, certainly a rational course of action. The court held that the regulations were valid, as a reasonable

---

[66] 29 C.F.R. 1910.1030 (f)

[67] Several videos with post-tests are available for training purposes, and can be purchased through several companies. Please check the World Wide Web by using "bloodborne pathogens" in your web browser for access to company's web site and library of training materials.

[68] *American Dental Association et. al. v. Martin et. al.*, 984 F.2d 823, 824, 825 (7th Cir. 1992).

[69] Id.

[70] 984 F.2d 823 (7th Cir. 1992).

[71] Id. at 826.

attempt to control disease in accordance to the standards set forth by the Centers for Disease Control.[72]

2) Elevator Safety

Elevators, like escalators, are used in many facilities to aid in passenger transportation between floors. Elevators have been known to cause injuries to passengers through malfunctions, ranging from accidental falls in elevator shafts due to ill-timed door-opening/freezing mechanisms, closing of doors on passengers, failure of the car to level with the floor, and defects in the car itself. While we will see from the following cases that facilities may avoid liability for elevator malfunction if they have an appropriate service/maintenance contract, prompt reporting, responding, and restriction of access to defective elevators, will be necessary. A prudent facility manager should be aware of the hazards posed by both freight and passenger elevators and the need to keep them in good operating condition at all times.

In *Wyatt v. Otis Elevator Company*,[73] Wyatt was found dazed and bleeding near the doors of a passenger elevator of an office building in Mobile, Alabama. Wyatt claimed that as he exited the elevator, the closing door struck him on the back and injured him. Wyatt sued the owners of the building and Otis, who was under contract to update and maintain the elevators with the building's owners. The jury returned verdicts in favor of Wyatt and the building's owners, but denied the owner's claims for indemnity against Otis. Otis and the building owners appealed.

Elevators contain two sets of doors- one for the car itself, and one set for the floor/hoistway. When a passenger crosses the threshold of either set of doors, if the doors are in the process of closing, an automatic electronic detector is supposed to reverse the closing of the doors and reopen them to prevent injury. Otis' electronic detector was supposed to work in this fashion, with two separate independent devices present to trigger the retraction system: a sensor and electronic eye, both mounted on the car door. Otis claimed that there was no witness to Wyatt's injury, and that examination of the electronic mechanisms showed they were in proper working order.

---

[72] Id. at 831.
[73] 921 F.2d 1224 (11th Cir. 1991).

There also was no other evidence to indicate any other cause for Wyatt's injury other than closing of the elevator doors. The Court of Appeals concluded that the jury was presented with ample evidence to conclude that the injuries had been caused by a malfunctioning door, and that the injury may have been caused by the hallway door, where no sensor was located.

Alabama treats elevators as common carriers, much like buses, trains or subways, and thus requires that they meet the highest standard of care to its passengers.[74] The trial judge had permitted evidence from others in which the doors did not operate as intended, including an incident in which a small child had his hand injured by the closing door. Otis had received notice regarding problems with the elevators, and one had been inspected earlier on the day of Wyatt's injury and repaired for a malfunction. The Court of Appeals ruled that the judge did not abuse his discretion in allowing this testimony, and upheld the jury's verdict in favor of Wyatt. The court further reversed the judgment as to the owner's potential collection of attorney's fees and remanded it to the lower court for reconsideration.

Clearly, proper notice of elevator malfunction was a keystone in this case. It was also important that the State considered an elevator a common carrier, and thus held the company to the highest standard of care under the law. As stated above, the owners of the building had reported problems with the elevator that had been allegedly fixed prior to the passenger's injury, alleviating them of the responsibility for the accident. Had the malfunction not have been promptly reported to the company, the building owners could have been held responsible for the injuries caused to the passenger.

In *McKenna v. Insurance Company of North America*,[75] McKenna, a nineteen-year-old laborer, suffered serious injuries to his right ankle and heel when his foot became entangled between a freight-passenger elevator and its shaft wall. A jury returned a verdict for McKenna for two hundred and fifty thousand dollars, and the Insurance Company filed for a new trial. The plaintiff alleged his injury was due to negligent inspection of the elevator, and that the elevator was operable with its gate open.

---

[74] Id. at 1227.
[75] 11 Phila. 617 (Phila. Ct. of Common Pleas 1984).

If the gate had been fully closed, his foot could not have come in contact with the shaft and he would not have been injured. The accident occurred when freight and passengers were squeezed into the elevator. McKenna squeezed into the back of the elevator near the gates, found his foot being pulled downward and caught as the elevator began to move.

These injuries were permanent in nature and required extensive surgery to try to remedy the injury that occurred. A new trial was granted because evidence existed that the elevator could have been tampered with by employees to allow it to run with the gate open rather than fully closed, thus exempting the inspection company from liability for the injuries received.

✓ Operational Pointer – These cases indicate that freight and passenger elevators must be maintained in safe condition, and no "jerry-rigging" should be tolerated, for whatever purpose. Any such "on-site modifications" may nullify the product warranty and any insurance coverage the facility has, thus making the facility directly liable should an injury occur. This point should be reviewed with newly hired maintenance personnel and on a regular basis with current employees. A policy against any such "jerry-rigging" should also be included in Building Maintenance Policy Manuals.

In *White v. Milner Hotels, Inc.*,[76] a guest at the hotel took an elevator to her room. When the elevator stopped, it was four inches above the actual floor and the guest fell and received injuries when she stepped out of the car. The hotel was aware that the elevator had been stopping frequently above the floor level, at which time a serviceman was called who would adjust the elevator so it stopped nearly level to the floor. The guest sued the hotel, for failing to maintain the elevator in a safe condition and failing to solve the continual leveling problem, although they were aware of the hazard. A jury returned a verdict for the hotel, and the plaintiff appealed. The Supreme Court of Oregon reversed the decision and remanded for a new trial, stating that the court had improperly instructed the jury as to the duty of care owed to elevator passengers. The court advocated a standard of care that required the hotel to exercise a degree of reasonable care under the circumstances and risk for injury involved.

---

[76] 518 P.2d 631 (Ore. 1974).

In *Dowis v. Continental Elevator Company, Inc.,*[77] a two-year-old child was injured in a fall down a freight elevator shaft. The Dowis family was moving belongings into an industrial building, using the freight elevator. There was a ten by fourteen-inch hole near the rear door and side of the elevator car. The child, running ahead of the adults onto the elevator, entered the opening at the rear of the elevator and fell sixteen feet to the bottom of the elevator shaft, causing severe injuries. The parents of the child sued, alleging that Continental, in charge of maintenance of the elevator, failed to maintain the elevator in good condition, and failed to fix the hole although they were aware of it. They also alleged that Continental also did not warn anyone of the hole in the car. The trial court had granted a summary judgment for the elevator company and the Dowis family appealed. In review of all the evidence presented, the Supreme Court of Nebraska felt there were genuine issues of fact that needed to be resolved at trial, and that the trial court had improperly issued a summary judgment.

✓ Operational Pointer – Because we have many contractors and subcontractors in our facilities using the freight elevators, the same level of care required for passenger elevators in the "front" of the house should be used for the freight elevators in the back of the house.

3) Escalator Safety

Escalators are used in many facilities for the efficient movement of patrons from one level to the next. Escalators are often an "attractive nuisance," meaning they attract the attention of children and can be seen as a toy rather than a potential danger to their safety. Proper function and safety devices may prevent almost all escalator accidents, and it is important that a facility manager be aware of the accident potential surrounding this piece of equipment and the absolute necessity to maintain the equipment in top working order. While the appropriate maintenance contract may prevent any loss due to injury on escalators, a facility manager will still be responsible for reporting any malfunction, broken parts or other sources for potential injury to the maintenance firm/company at the earliest possible time to ensure no mishap occurs.

---

[77] 486 N.W.2d 916 (Neb. 192).

Jack-In-The-Box. Jack-In-The-Box and its franchisees sued the suppliers in California Superior Court, alleging negligence, breach of contract, and other claims including loss of business based on the adverse publicity following the outbreak of illness. The case made its way to the California Supreme Court in *Vons Companies, Inc. v. Seabest Foods, Inc. et. al,*[94] wherein Vons alleged the Jack-In-The-Box franchisees had failed to cook the hamburgers at proper temperature, leading to the outbreak of illness. In its analysis of the case, the court focused on whether jurisdiction of the case was proper in California, and ruled that there were sufficient contacts between all parties involved to allow jurisdiction by California Courts over the entire case, overruling the prior Court of Appeals decision.

While the ultimate outcome of this case has yet to be decided, it is clear that food contamination is a very serious matter, as are appropriate cooking and handling procedures. A facility manager or his caterer must make sure all concession personnel are well aware of appropriate food handling and cooking techniques, to avoid the potential for injury due to food contamination/poisoning. In any mass gathering where food is present, tainted food can cause wide spread illness in a short period of time. Symptoms can be mild discomfort, vomiting or can be as severe as death, as in the Jack-In-The-Box hamburger contamination cases, which killed several young children. Therefore, all necessary food handling regulations should be enforced at all times.

In *Feldt v. Marriott Corporation,*[95] a young woman and her date went to a cafeteria style restaurant following a school dance. After standing in line, paying for food, sitting down, and eating, a restaurant employee noticed the woman was not wearing shoes.

The manager of the shop told her she would have to leave because she was not wearing shoes, and the woman said she would, after she finished her food. No sign to that effect was posted, but the manager stated it was company policy to refuse service to those without shoes. The manager continued to insist that she leave, and she continued to state she would do so once finished. The manager did not offer to refund the money spent on the food, nor did the woman ask for a refund. The manager left and returned with a police officer, who informed the woman she was violating the unlawful entry statute by refusing to leave when asked. The officer took the woman's arm and

---

[94] 14 Cal. 4th 434 (Cal. 1996).
[95] 322 A.2d 913 (App. D.C. 1974).

began to escort her out of the restaurant. The woman began to struggle and the officer arrested her. After going through fingerprinting, photographing, and the like, she was later released on her own recognizance and the charges dropped when she appeared in court the next day. The woman then sued Marriott, the operator of the restaurant, for false arrest.

The trial court found for the restaurant owner and the woman appealed. On appeal, the court examined the status of restaurant patrons, following service and payment for the service rendered. In this case, the woman had borrowed her sister's shoes that were uncomfortable after a long night of dancing, and left them in the car when she entered the restaurant. Due to her long gown, no one noticed her bare feet until after she was seated and eating her meal. The court noted that the woman could have been lawfully refused service before the sale itself had taken place, but the question arose as to whether she had a lawful right to remain on the premises to eat the food she was served after being asked to leave. The Court found that the situation was similar to that of a theater patron, having received a ticket and then having that "license" revoked, was left only with a breach of contract claim against the theater. When the woman was asked to leave, her license to sit in the restaurant was revoked, and the officer was justified in arresting her under the unlawful entry statute when she refused to leave. The only claim she could bring against the restaurant was one for breach of contract, not false arrest, and thus the court affirmed the trial court's decision.

6.05 Hazardous Materials

Facilities use industrial chemicals to clean, lubricate and maintain the large HVAC systems. Convention centers and exposition centers and other similar facilities may have exhibitors that use industrial chemicals in the presentation of their machinery and equipment. The exhibitors usually dispose of these used chemicals immediately after the trade show. Facilities may either take possession of the waste by subcontracting a waste management company to properly dispose of the waste or the facility may require the exhibitor to dispose of the waste through their own waste management company. Either way, because the waste was physically generated on facility property, the facility is partially responsible for the proper disposal of the waste. The production, use and disposal of hazardous materials are highly regulated by the state and federal government. Hazardous chemicals are tracked by the exact quantity from production, use and disposal. This concept is called "from cradle to grave" tracking.

6.06 Unusual Events

In *Semaphore Entertainment Group Sports Corp. v. Gonzalez*,[96] Promoters sought to hold an "Ultimate Fighting Championship" in Bayamon Municipal Coliseum, but the Secretary of the Department of Sports sought to enforce a cease and desist order to prevent the event from occurring. "Ultimate Fighting" is a full contact martial arts fighting contest, where athletes from different sports combining techniques from sumo, kick boxing, tae kwon do, jiu-jitsu, karate, Greco-Roman wrestling, shoot fighting and kempo. There are few rules and mandatory protective gear, and medical testing is required of all entrants. This type of event is also known as Extreme Fighting.

The Promoter, Semaphore Entertainment Group (SEG) and Sports and Entertainment, Inc, (SEI) negotiated to present the event in Puerto Rico, and entered into an agreement with the Director of Sports and Recreation in Puerto Rico to lease the coliseum. SEG then entered into subsequent contracts to have the event broadcast by pay-per-view in the United States, suppliers of transmission equipment, and contracts to promote the event and videos of the event. SEI made similar expenditures, and tickets went on sale, with thousands of tickets being sold. The necessary equipment had already been shipped to the coliseum, when the Secretary of Sports began investigating allegations that the event was excessively violent.[97] SEG asked whether the hearing was investigative or adjudicative and was told that it was a public hearing that was investigative in nature. Almost immediately after the hearing examiner issued his report, the Assistant Secretary for Sports submitted an administrative complaint with request for immediate action and two hours later, the Department issued a cease and desist order to prevent the event from occurring. SEG & SEI alleged wrongful administrative procedure and sought to enjoin the Secretary of Sports from enforcing the order, alleging it would interfere with the contracts SEG and SEI had already entered into regarding the event. The court noted while the parties were represented at the administrative hearing, they did not receive the required notice of proposed action and were

---

[96] 919 F. Supp. 543 (D.C. P.R. 1996).
[97] Id. at 547.

denied an opportunity to respond.[98] Additionally, at the time the contracts were entered into, Puerto Rico had no law or regulation that would have prohibited the event. The court found that SEG and SEI had shown that they would be irreparably harmed if the cease and desist order was enforced. The court ruled that SEG and SEI were likely to succeed in court on the merits of their case, and the court then issued the injunction allowing the event to occur.

In *LaFrenz v. Lake County Fair Board*,[99] a woman with a "pit pass" at a demolition derby was injured and subsequently died from those injuries after a car left the track and crashed through the retaining wall.[100] The woman had been to prior derbies, knew of their nature, and had signed a "waiver and release of liability and indemnity agreement" before being allowed in the pit area. The administrator of her estate sued for damages, the trial court awarded a judgment for the defendants, and the administrator appealed.

The Appellate Court upheld the lower court's decision, stating that even if the form had just been presented rather than be explained to the woman completely, there was not enough evidence presented to preclude judgment for the defendants.[101] In these cases, we clearly see that demolition derbies can be very dangerous events, leading to injuries whether you are in the stands or in the pit area. Most importantly to facilities who may consider putting on these events, is the insurance issue. By making people wishing access to the pits sign waivers and releases of liability kept the fairgrounds from being found liable for the death of a young woman. The failure of having any event insurance led to the participant's auto insurance to come into play to cover injuries caused to spectators at an event. A prudent facility should carefully examine all liability issues and get appropriate insurance when holding these events.

---

[98] Id. at 549.
[99] 360 N.E.2d 605 (Ind. App. 1977).
[100] Id. at 607.
[101] Id. at 609.

The Safe Operation of the Facility

In *Rosenberger v. Central Louisiana District Livestock Show Inc. et. al.,* [102] part-time rodeo contestant was injured while participating in a bare-backed bronco riding contest when his left knee struck part of the gate as the assigned horse attempted to go through the partially opened gate. The injury required surgery and left the Plaintiff with some degree of permanent disability. [103] The Rodeo took place at the Rapides Parish Coliseum, and was conducted by the Central Louisiana District Livestock Show (Central). The lease of the coliseum to Central prevented Central from subletting the coliseum and required Central obtain insurance to cover any injuries or claims arising out of use of the facility. [104] Central obtained the insurance required from Southern Farm Bureau Casualty Company. The trial court found Central negligent along with the person who furnished the livestock and was to supervise and organize the rodeo, with no assumption of risk or contributory negligence on the part of the rider, granting a judgment for $33,679.54. The Court of Appeals reversed the trial court's decision, finding for Defendants on the basis of assumption of risk.

The Supreme Court of Louisiana in review agreed that bronco riding is an inherently dangerous sport, that the Plaintiff assumed the ordinary risks involved, but that the negligent operation of the premises by the operators of the rodeo, by leaving a gate partially open, was not a risk assumed by the rider. It was the failure of the operators to properly secure the gate that led to the rider's injuries, and that Central was liable via respondeat superior[105] for the negligence of the operators it hired. [106]

---

[102] 312 So.2d 300 (La. 1975).

[103] Id. at 302.

[104] Id.

[105] Legal doctrine that states that when an employee causes injury to someone in the course of their employment, the employer may be held liable, since the employee was acting on behalf of the employer and furthering his business at the time of the injury.

[106] Id. at 305.

In *Creel v. Washington Parish Fair Association et. al.,* [107]a woman was injured when a bronco threw its rider out of the arena and on top of the spectator.[108] The Washington Parish Fair Association (WPFA) had control and supervision of the arena at the time of the accident, and the trial court awarded damages in the amount of $97,000 to the woman. WPFA and its insurer, Alliance, appealed. WPFA had contracted with Jackson, a producer of rodeos, to hold a rodeo in 1983. The rodeo committee was guaranteed the first $15,000 in ticket sales and any sales in access of $35,000 would be distributed with the committee receiving 30% of the sales over $35,000.[109] A pipe and wire fence was installed during the rodeo, and seating in bleachers was provided on a concrete platform. At the time of the accident, additional folding chairs had been placed to increase seating in a new "boxed seating" area. This arrangement had been approved by WPFA. The person injured had purchased the box seats and were seated fairly close to the fence. During the course of a performance, the horse tossed a bronco rider over the fence and onto the woman who suffered ruptured cervical discs. The trial court concluded that the accident occurred, not due to a low fence height, but to placement of the "box seating." The court found that WPFA was vicariously liable and Jackson was negligent in placement of the chairs in such a manner that led to the woman's injury.

On appeal, the court stated that placement of the chairs was not a defect in the arena, but that WPFA was negligent in approving the box seating, and that while the rider was not liable to the spectator, WPFA had a duty to protect spectators from harm and could be held liable, as it could have prohibited the box seating or provided a different fence that may have protected the spectator.[110]

---

[107] 597 So.2d 487 (La. Ct. App. 1st Cir. 1992).
[108] Id. at 488.
[109] Id.
[110] Id. at 491, 492.

In *Dunbar v. Latting et. al.,* [111] several people were injured when bleachers collapsed at a rodeo. The court granted a summary judgment to the Village of Hopkins Park and Latting Rodeo Productions, and the Plaintiffs appealed.[112] The plaintiffs had attended a rodeo in a park when the bleachers collapsed, and the township of Pembroke was dismissed from the suit with prejudice. The Village contended it was not its responsibility to maintain the bleachers at the park, and the Rodeo likewise contended it was involved in the rodeo only to the extent of its contract with Pembroke Rough Riders Rodeo Productions. The Village had liability insurance, but the Village claimed it was immune under the Tort Immunity Act.

Evidence showed that the rodeo was a yearly event wherein the bleachers were put up prior to and taken down after the rodeo. Wooden bleachers were used that year. A local company not named in the complaint constructed them. The Village also entered into a contract with Pembroke each year to put on the rodeo, but Pembroke did not require proof of liability insurance, although insurance was required under the agreement. Latting Rodeo provided rodeo equipment to the rodeo, not including the bleachers, and no employee of Latting was ever near the bleachers.

The Court of Appeals held that under the Tort Immunity Act, the Village could only be held liable for willful and wanton conduct, and that while the Village may have been negligent, its behavior was not willful nor wanton.[113] The court further found that Latting had no duty to inspect the bleachers itself, being only responsible for providing animals and rodeo equipment, and thus had been properly been granted summary judgment by the trial court.[114]

In *Russo v. the Range, Inc.,*[115] Russo went down a giant slide ride located at The Range Amusement Park, and injured his back, causing compressed fractures in his vertebra. Russo sued the Range for his injuries, alleging that while using the sack provided to slide down the slide, he left the slide a bit during the dips in the slide, and despite attempts made to slow his progress, continued to speed up. Coming back down on the slide was alleged to have caused the injury.

---

[111] 621 N.E.2d 232 (Ill. 3rd Dist. 1993).
[112] Id. at 234.
[113] Id. at 237.
[114] Id. at 239.
[115] 395 N.E.2d 10 (Ill. App. 1979).

The Range defended its actions, stating that the tickets contained assumption of risk language on the back, notifying all purchasers that they were responsible for any injury occurring due to their use of the amusement rides, and a sign appeared at the top of the slide, informing patrons they were sliding at their own risk. A sign also told patrons not to attempt to slow their descent and showed the proper sliding position. Russo admitted that he saw these signs and understood them. The trial court had granted summary judgment to the Range, and Russo appealed. The Court of Appeals reviewed the doctrine of assumption of risk, and stated that it presupposed that the danger incurred was one normally associated with the activity and that the injured party knew or should have known of the risk involved and decided to take that risk on, despite the chance of injury. Assumption of risk functions as a defense for those sued by injured parties in three circumstances. The first situation is when a plaintiff signs a written document to relieve the defendant of any obligation of conduct towards him. The second case is when the plaintiff implies consent to excuse the defendant from a legal duty to protect the Plaintiff that would otherwise exist. The third case is a situation in which the plaintiff was aware of the danger created by the defendant's negligence, and without any further relationship between the parties, the plaintiff chooses to voluntarily to encounter the hazard. This third example is most often used in product liability cases. The Court of Appeals held that the circumstances surrounding Russo's "consent" to relieve the Range of any legal duty towards him or assumption of the risk involved were issues to be presented before a jury, and were not proper for summary judgment. The court then reversed the trial court's findings and directed the court to proceed with the case, in order to evaluate whether the "flying in the air" that occurred here was unusual or unexpected and thus Russo may not have been able to assume the risk, not knowing that such an event would occur.

6.07 First Aid Services

In *Kleinknecht v. Gettysburg College*,[116] Drew Kleinknecht died of cardiac arrest on September 18, 1988 while a student at Gettysburg College during a lacrosse team practice. His parents filed a wrongful death and survival action against the College and the College moved for summary judgment, which the District Court denied, but granted on reconsideration in January of 1992. The court held that the College had no duty to anticipate and guard against the student's fatal arrhythmia in an otherwise healthy, young athlete. The Plaintiffs appealed, alleging that the College had failed to implement measures to provide prompt assistance in event an athlete suffered from cardiac arrest, that the employees of the College breached their duty of care, and that the College and the student trainer were not entitled to immunity under the Good Samaritan Act. The student was a 20-year-old college sophomore, recruited to play on the lacrosse team. Prior to Drew's death, no athlete at the college had ever experienced cardiac arrest while playing a sport. Two full time athletic trainers were employed by the College at the time and were required to be certified in CPR and standard first aid. Twelve student trainers were also employed and stationed at the two training room facilities. Student trainers were assigned to cover practices and games in the spring, and fall practices were held for "skills and drills" purposes, with no student trainers assigned. During the fall practice session, beginning at 3:15 p.m., both coaches were in attendance, and the practice took place outside one of the training facilities, with the nearest telephone 200 yards away in the training room. Neither coach had CPR training, nor had discussed how to handle an emergency during the training session. Drew was participating in a drill when he suffered cardiac arrest, stepping away from play and dropping to the ground, for no apparent reason. The teammates and a coach ran to his side, and he was lying in an awkward position. No one knew what occurred, but some suspected a spinal problem. The team captain noticed funny gurgling sounds, and that Drew began to turn blue in color.

The Coach tried to access the situation and called for team members to get a trainer and get help. The coach then ran to get help himself. The Plaintiffs allege that the coach sent two players to a dorm for help, and the other coach did not remember the head coach sending for help.

---

[116] 989 F.2d 1360 (3rd Cir. 1993).

The Plaintiffs allege that the Coach did not follow emergency procedures, and that the players who ran for help did so on their own accord rather than at directions from the Coach. A student trainer was located by a team member, and was the first to reach Drew, saw his labored breathing, but did not attempt CPR, only monitoring his condition. By the time the coach returned, an ambulance had been called, and the head trainer arrived in a golf cart, saw Drew was not breathing and then began CPR. A student with emergency medical technician experience, who had by chance arrived on the scene, assisted the trainer in providing CPR until the ambulance arrived. Drew was defibrillated and given drugs, but despite repeated efforts, could not be revived and was pronounced dead at 4:58 p.m. The College estimated the ambulance arrived within 8 to 10 minutes of the collapse, while the Plaintiffs allege the actions taken by the College and students took significantly longer than the College's estimates. The student had no prior history of health problems and had been examined by the College doctor in January of 1988 and found healthy and able to practice. It was determined that Drew died of cardiac arrest following a fatal arrhythmia, although no cause of the arrhythmia could be found despite several extensive post-mortem examinations, and no evidence was found of contact with a stick or ball that could have induced the problem. In a similar case in Ohio, a trial court held that there was no duty as a matter of law for the College or other sponsor of athletic events to have ambulances, emergency vehicles, trained help or doctors present during the playing of a lacrosse game or other athletic events, and the failure to do so did not constitute negligence as a matter of law.[117] The court of appeals reversed, determining it was a question of fact for the jury to determine as to whether the failure to have an ambulance present or to provide quick access to the field in event of an emergency was reasonable.

The Court of Appeals held that in this case, like the case above, Drew was participating in a College-organized sports team practice, and that a special relationship existed between Drew and the College to impose a duty of reasonable care on the College. Because Drew was not acting as a private student, but as a member of a College-sponsored sports team at the time of his collapse, for which the College had actively sought his participation, he was owed a duty of care above that owed to a college fraternity football game or intramural sports. The

---

[117] Id. at 1366, citing *Hanson v. Kynast*, No. CA-828 (Ohio Ct. App. June 3, 1985), rev'd on other grounds, 494 N.E.2d 1091 (Ohio 1986).

court predicted that the Supreme Court of Pennsylvania would rule that the College owed a special duty of care to Drew as well. While the lower court had held that Drew's injury was not foreseeable, the Court of Appeals held that the incident was generally foreseeable, and that the coaches and student trainer were all aware of instances where athletes had died during athletic competitions. The College owed Drew the duty of taking reasonable precautions against the risk of death while he was participating in the college's athletic program. The court held that the College owed a duty to Drew to protect him from the risk of harm by providing adequate preventative emergency measures, but the question as to whether the College breached its duty at all was for the jury, as was the question as to whether the breach of this duty was the proximate cause of Drew's death. Additionally, while the parties agreed that neither coach was entitled to immunity, the College argued it was entitled to immunity as a corporate person, but the court held that the legislature could not require a corporation to have CPR training, which can only be taken by an actual person under the Good Samaritan Act, and thus the College was not entitled to immunity under the Act and could still be held liable even if immune, as vicariously liable for the acts of its agents, including the student trainer. The Court of Appeals then reversed the district court's holding that the College acted reasonably, did not owe a duty of care to Drew and that the College was entitled to immunity under the Good Samaritan Act, and remanded the case to the district court for further proceedings.

Public Assembly Facility Law

Chapter 7

Facility Security after September 11, 2001

By Turner D. Madden

7.00 Introduction

In any large gathering of people, security for the safety of those present becomes a concern. Likewise, to ensure the safety of patrons, search and seizure issues can come into play. Can a facility "frisk" patrons? Can metal detectors be used? If illegal contraband is found on cursory searches, is a facility obligated to inform authorities? If off-duty police officers are employed for security purposes, are they obligated to make an arrest? What regulations and prohibitions can a facility make and legally enforce? These complicated questions deal with our Fourth Amendment guarantees against unreasonable search and seizure. We will attempt to answer some of these questions in this Chapter, and give an overview of the responsibility of a facility for the safety and control of the crowds it attracts on a regular basis.

7.01 The Fourth Amendment and State Action

In general, all guarantees in the Bill of Rights are guarantees that the federal government will not make unwanted intrusions into the lives of the citizens. Through the Fourteenth Amendment of the Constitution, the guarantees in the Bill of Rights are further applied to guarantee the citizens of every State that the individual State governments will also refrain from violating any of the provisions of the Federal Constitution.

The Fourth Amendment states:

> "The right of the people to be secure in their persons, houses, papers and effects against unreasonable searches and seizures shall not be violated, and no warrants shall issue, but upon probable cause supported by oath or affirmation and particularly describing the place to be searched and the persons or things to be seized."

The doctrine of State Action prohibits the State, either federal or local, or any of its representatives, acting under the color of law, from violating the civil rights of the citizens.[1] This means that the guarantees of the Fourth and Fourteenth Amendments of the Constitution apply to the state and federal governments, but not to private citizens against each other. In every day terms, this prevents individuals from suing each other for prohibiting their freedom of expression, or in the extreme, from children suing their parents for unwarranted searches of the bedrooms.

When applied to facilities, if facilities are owned or operated by the State, or if local police officers are in charge of enforcing the regulations of a facility, they can then also be held liable for any violation of the civil rights of any of its patrons. If a facility can be deemed an "arm" of the State through its creation or operation, it is said to be acting "under the color of law". Likewise, we could all agree that local police officers are acting on behalf of the State or local government when performing their duties, and thus are likewise acting "under the color of law" when performing security duties at facilities, whether on duty or off-duty at the time.

1) Search and Seizures at Facilities

Searches are commonplace in many facilities, mostly to regulate what the patrons may or may not bring with them to an event. Given that patrons have brought weapons, alcohol, drugs, bottles and cans into facilities, and such objects have caused injuries to other patrons. The facility has a clear interest in protecting the safety of the people it has invited to its premises, and thus a direct interest in controlling such items.[2] The extent to which security personnel are allowed to search individuals, and what items they may take from individuals has been the subject of litigation for many years.

There have been many cases where patrons have challenged the right to search attendees or manner in which such searches have been conducted at facilities.

---

[1] See 42 U.S.C. § 1983.
[2] See generally 28 A.L.R. 4th 1250.

In *Stroeber v. Commission Veteran's Auditorium,*[3] three patrons sued the manager of the facility and the commissioners in charge of instituting the search policy at Veteran's Auditorium in Des Moines, Iowa. It was felt that due to alleged prior incidents of property damage, personal injury, alcohol, drugs and "general rowdiness" at rock concerts, more stringent security measures were required for these events.[4] The Auditorium Commission employed off duty police officers to act as security guards, and such officers were permitted to arrest patrons in their capacity as police officer, although the Commission itself brought the actual charges against any arrested patrons.[5] Officers were permitted by the Police Commissioner to wear their uniforms for such duty,[6] leaving little doubt that any action pursued by the officers acting as security guards occurred under "color of law." One sign was posted in the lobby of the Auditorium, informing patrons that security guards would check for and confiscate or detain any contraband, including controlled substances and alcoholic beverages.[7] In addition, a tape-recorded message was played continuously in the lobby informing patrons of this warning, but the patrons testified that on the night in question, no message was heard.[8] Bags and purses were sometimes opened and checked; male patrons were occasionally subjected to pat down searches. Confiscated items were marked and could be reclaimed after the show, but patrons were often arrested if contraband drugs were found.[9] Security guards also admitted that not everyone was checked, and visual search or surveillance of all patrons was impossible.[10] It was also not clear whether patrons were informed of their right to refuse the search and have their ticket price refunded prior to being searched, nor were clear specific guidelines for conducting searches in place.[11]

---

[3] 453 F.Supp. 926 (S.D. Iowa 1977).
[4] Id. at 929.
[5] Id.
[6] Id.
[7] Id. at 930.
[8] Id.
[9] Id.
[10] Id.
[11] Id.

The Court evaluated the search procedures in light of Supreme Court guidelines set forth in numerous cases[12] and felt that the stop and frisk procedures in place at Veteran's Auditorium were conducted with less than probable cause and were done not to discover weapons that could pose a hazard to the officers, but in order to discover controlled substances.[13] While consent to search can be permissible, it requires voluntary consent, free of coercion, express or implied.[14] Thus the District Court held that the searches conducted at Veteran's Auditorium were invalid as violations of the patron's fourth amendment rights,[15] due mostly to the lack of notice of what search would take place, the scope of the search, and permission to refuse the search and obtain a refund.

Likewise, in *Jensen v. Pontiac*,[16] a patron sued the municipal operator of a stadium after being asked to open her purse for inspection by a guard at the facility. The stadium personnel conducted the searches in the attempt to prevent injury from thrown projectiles, by prohibiting bottles and cans from being brought into the stadium. The guards stopped any person with a container large enough to house any of the items prohibited. Any person refusing the visual search could dispose of the containers or return them to their vehicles. If the patron refused inspection or disposal of the packages, they were refused admission to the facility. Signs were also posted at each gate describing the objects prohibited from the stadium and the search procedures themselves.

In this case, the patron was first asked permission to visually inspect the container, her purse, and was informed by the guard that she could refuse the request. The guard then inspected the purse as requested. The Court ruled that such a warrantless search was reasonable due to the necessity to protect patrons, and that visual inspection was not as intrusive as physical searches allowed in other cases. While no written guidelines had been established to the minimum size of container for which patrons could be stopped potentially limiting the effectiveness of the searches, modified procedures were recommended by the Trial Court requiring all patrons be searched would

---

[12] See *Katz. v. United States,* 389 U.S. 347 (1967), *Terry v. Ohio,* 392 U.S. 1 (1968), *United States v. Chadwick,* 433 U.S. 1 (1977) and *Schneckloth v. Bustamonte,* 412 U.S. 218 (1973).
[13] *Stroeber* at 932.
[14] Id.
[15] Id. at 933.
[16] 317 N.W.2d 619 (Mich. Ct. App. 1982).

be even more effective in preventing dangerous objects from entering the facility.

In *Nakamoto v. Fasi*,[17] a city-owned Arena mandated inspection of spectators for bottles and cans prior to admission into the facility, after several patrons had been injured by thrown bottles and cans, by broken bottles, and by use of bottles in fights at rock concerts. Men's and women's coats, jackets, and purses were inspected if such items could conceal bottles or cans. Private security guards visually inspected the items, and if bottles or cans were found, the patron was asked to leave them outside the Arena to be retrieved after the performance, or if the patron refused the request, they were denied entry. In this case, a woman was asked to open her purse for inspection, but no sign was posted regarding inspection policy. Since the patron was not informed of her ability to refuse such inspection, the search in this case was held to be invalid, since the patron had no way of knowing that she had any alternative other than submitting to the inspection if she wished to attend the concert. The "consent" to the search was in effect coerced and not voluntary. Too much discretion was left to the security guard on duty to decide who was to be searched, and there were alternative procedures available that could be used instead, that would be less intrusive to the privacy of the patrons. It should be noted that subsequent to this event, signage regarding the search policy was posted at all entrances to the arena, and a notice regarding the search procedure was printed on the back of all tickets sold to rock concerts.

In *State v. Carter*,[18] a pat down search of a patron as he entered an auditorium for a rock concert yielded controlled substances. The search was held to violate the patron's Fourth Amendment rights, and led to a reversal of his conviction for possession of such substances. As in the prior cases, past incidents at the auditorium involving alcohol and drugs led the auditorium, in cooperation with the police department, to institute security procedures that were indiscriminate in their scope of searching patrons before permitting entrance. Signs announcing the prohibition of bringing controlled substances into the auditorium were posted in the lobby and a taped message was broadcast continually stating controlled substances were not permitted. Spectators were made aware they would be checked to make sure the policy was enforced. Twenty-five security guards were employed to

---

[17] 635 P.2d 946 (Haw. 1981).
[18] 267 N.W.2d 385 (Iowa 1978).

search all patrons, but many people avoided searching due to the press of the crowd at the entrances. In addition, some patrons were only subjected to a visual search while others received the pat down. The search in question in this case was alleged to have been routine and not initiated by prior suspicion. The defendant had not seen the signs nor heard the message, and nothing was said before he was searched. The Court held that the search had been conducted without consent, and that the search, later justified by the defendant's attempt to escape, could not be converted from an illegal search to a justified one merely by subsequent events after the search was underway.

In *Jacobsen v. Seattle,*[19] a highly intensive pat down search by police officers of patrons seeking admission to an arena for a rock concert violated patrons Fourth Amendment rights. As seen previously, such procedures were instituted to prevent dangerous items and controlled substances from entering the facility, this had presented a problem in the past. Purses and bags were searched and any bottles, cans or controlled substances were seized at the discretion of the officers. The Court held that the intrusive searches conducted were much more invasive than required, given the potential danger to others posed by prohibited objects entering the arena. The Court further held that irreparable injury could occur to the mostly young and juvenile patrons in understanding their constitutional guarantees to be free from unwarranted searches and seizures in the future.

2) When is a Facility Free From State Action?

A facility may allow more invasive search procedures if it is not subject to State Action, ie., when there is no involvement by the State in either the institution or enforcement of security procedures and the State is not otherwise involved in management of the facility. This category would mainly cover privately owned facilities, who do not employ off-duty police officers for their security needs.

---

[19] 658 P.2d 653 (Wash. 1983).

In *Gallagher v. Constable*,[20] a concert promoter leased a facility at the University of Utah for a Neil Young concert, and hired a private security firm to provide security services for the concert. The University Public Safety Department provided some of the security for the event as well, and the promoter paid the University for the services of its officers.[21] The University did not have its security personnel perform pat down searches at either this event or any other university-sponsored event.[22] The private security service, however, routinely conducted full pat-down searches at rock concert events, and did so at the event at the University of Utah.[23] University officials were notified that pat-downs would occur shortly before the concert as part of security procedures.[24]

Upon entering the facility, fliers were passed out to patrons informing them of the items prohibited from the facility. Patrons were informed of the pat down by security personnel, and that if the patron wished to refuse the pat down, they could obtain a refund of the ticket price, although several patrons reported they were not informed of the opportunity to receive refunds. The searches conducted involved a patron complaining of being patted down their arms and legs, groin, underarms and torso, and a woman, six months pregnant, being patted down on the stomach at least twice, while the guard insisted her stomach was "too hard".[25] While at first blush it would appear the patrons would have claims for fourth amendment violations for the intrusive and offensive nature of the searches conducted, the Court of Appeals held that while the searches were observed by University Police officers and that the director of the facility, a University employee, knew of the searches, there was no actual participation by the State in the searches, nor did the University somehow maintain a symbiotic relationship between the security personnel hired or the concert promoter who leased the facility, nor could the Court find some concerted conspiracy between the State and the security guards in violating the patron's civil rights.

---

[20] 49 F.3d 1442 (10th Cir. 1995).
[21] Id. at 1445.
[22] Id.
[23] Id. at 1445, 1446.
[24] Id. at 1445.
[25] Id. at 1446.

Without being able to show state action or prove the involvement of the State in the searches, the claims of the patrons were dismissed.

7.02 Permissible Searches and Guidelines for Facilities

When considering instituting guidelines for searching patrons for items prohibited in a facility, please consider the following:

- The minimally invasive search necessary to locate and re-move prohibited items from a patron's possession should be employed. In many cases, a simple visual search without any actual touching of the patron's person or effects should be sufficient.
- Adequate signage and notice should be given to patrons re-garding the search and their right to refuse any search. They should also be notified at the time of search that they need not comply, but that they may also be prohibited from en-tering the facility if the search is not conducted.
- Patrons must be treated as equally as possible, with every-one being subjected to the same search procedures, rather than allowing security personnel to be selective in whom they search and the rationale for such a search.
- Employment of private security personnel by someone oth-er than the facility (if municipally or state owned) may in part absolve the state from any fourth amendment viola-tions committed by the security personnel.

Should the facility choose to use more invasive searching procedures or decide to be more selective in choosing whom to search, they are at serious risk of violating the search and seizure rights of the fourth amendment. It must also be stressed, however, that facilities that are not state or municipally owned, nor employ police as security agents, may not be violating the fourth amendment if they institute more invasive procedures, due to the lack of state action.

7.03 Crowd Control

In all public facilities, crowd control or maintenance is vital. By human nature, when large crowds of people are gathered, a "crowd" mentality can set in, giving patrons "permission" to act in way they might not otherwise. We have all seen news footage of fans storming a field after a particularly exciting sporting event, pull down goal posts after a football game, throwing trash and the like onto the field of play, etc. Crowds have also been known to push and storm exits, occasionally causing injuries and death by crushing after rock concerts, soccer games, and other events. Due to the dangers posed by mass gatherings of people at facilities, crowd control is a major concern for facilities and their security teams. From controlling entrances and exits of the facility, to maintaining order during events, a facility must be aware of the potential risks posed by mass gatherings and take the necessary steps to ensure the safety of the patrons and the compliance with facility rules and regulations.

In *DeFulio v. Spectraguard, Inc.,*[26] a man attempted to enter Veteran's Stadium in Philadelphia without a ticket to see a rock show by climbing a fence.[27] As the man neared the top of the fence and grabbed the concrete platform above him, a security guard stepped on the man's hands, causing him to fall 15 feet onto the concrete concourse and broke both ankles.[28] The man sued Spectraguard, who provided the security officers and Electric Factory Concerts, who promoted the event, stating they were vicariously liable for the guard's actions. The guard was employed to prevent people without tickets from entering the stadium, as required under the lease from the city to Electric Factory.[29] The jury awarded the man a total of $165,000 and the Court awarded additional delay damages, bringing the net award over $200,000. The defendants requested the Court to overturn the verdict, which it denied. The defendants tried to allege the guard's actions were outside the scope of his employment, and thus the employer was not liable for his acts.

---

[26] No. 6199, 1995 Phila. Cty. Rptr. LEXIS 40 (June 23, 1995).
[27] Id. at *2.
[28] Id.
[29] Id. at *4.

The Court stated that under the legal doctrine of respondeat superior, an employer is responsible for the negligence of its employees that may be imputed to the employer. In other words, since the guard was acting within the scope of his employment, by trying to keep out trespassers, clearly part of his job, the employer was liable for the injuries he caused by trying to keep the man out of the Stadium, even though excessive force was used and caused injury. In fact, the force used, stepping on the man's hands, was "not unexpected".[30] There was an admission during the case that the guards would not have grabbed the man while he was climbing up the fence, and that such an act would have been contrary to all of their instructions.[31] While the guard showed lack of judgment, it did not absolve the employer from liability, and the jury's verdict was upheld.[32]

This case is a good example of how trying to control the entrance of unauthorized patrons into a facility caused injury, and that security personnel were responsible for the damages caused. This helps point out how important it is to have properly trained and experienced security personnel, have detailed procedures for handling gate crashers, and how easy it was to use excess force causing injury to a "patron".

In *Ramirez v. Texas*,[33] a man was caught vandalizing a stall set up for a trade show at the Dallas Convention Center.[34] Mr. Hulme, a center employee, told Mr. Ramirez to drop the spray can and get out, which he did. Mr. Hulme followed, but lost sight of Mr. Ramirez. Seconds later, Mr. Ramirez was spotted banging on the wall hollering "to a better Jesus" at which time he was again asked to leave, and then he ran out of the hall.[35] Mr. Hulme followed Mr. Ramirez and began yelling for security. Mr. Ramirez began banging on the doors where another gathering was being held, at which time security guards overtook him and threw him to the ground. Dallas police arrived and the struggle continued with the uniformed officers.

---

[30] Id. at *7
[31] Id.
[32] Id. at *10.
[33] No. 05-95-00688-CR, 1997 Tex. App. LEXIS 239 (Jan. 23, 1997).
[34] Id. at *1.
[35] Id. at *2.

The officers subsequently tried to gain control of Mr. Ramirez and being unable to do so, sprayed him with mace. Having little effect, they then gave a chokehold, and Mr. Ramirez made an attempt to grab the officer's gun. The officer then increased the chokehold until Mr. Ramirez passed out. Mr. Ramirez struggled and fought throughout his detainment and transfer to the police car. Mr. Ramirez defended himself at trial, stating he was just trying to get information on setting up a booth at the Convention Center when Mr. Hulme approached him. Mr. Ramirez stated that he did spray jewelry on display with spray jewelry cleaner, but was not vandalizing the booth.[36] Mr. Ramirez also alleged his acts with the officers occurred while trying to explain himself, and he was not trying to get the officer's weapon. Mr. Ramirez was indicted on charges relating to the attempt to take a weapon from a peace officer, was found guilty and sentenced to 2 years in jail, five years probation and an $800.00 fine.[37]

Crowd control goes beyond just regulating large crowds, but also regulating general access to a facility and the importance of maintaining proper security for the safety of all.

In *State of Ohio v. Kuehne*,[38] Judy Kuehne, her son Sandy, and a friend attended a Cincinnati Reds baseball game at Riverfront Coliseum. After the sixth inning, an usher saw Sandy consume part of a hotdog that had been partially consumed by another patron and drink from several beer cups left around the Stadium, and asked to see his ticket. Sandy swore at the man and left. The usher reported the incident to the police officer working off-duty detail at the Stadium. The supervisor of security, Mr. Estes, was advised that two patrons were creating a disturbance on the green level. Estes approached the patrons accused of causing the disturbance, and asked to see their ticket stubs. The request made to Ms. Kuehne and Sandy was met with hostility and neither could produce their ticket stubs as requested. Two officers then approached the Kuehnes, and stated that unless they could produce proof they were at the Stadium lawfully, they would have to leave. Both of the Keuhnes began screaming, directing profanities towards the officers, and were generally uncooperative.

---

[36] Id. at *5.

[37] Id. at *7.

[38] No.C-910454, C-910455, 1992 Ohio App. LEXIS 2128 (1st Dist. April 22, 1992).

The officers persuaded the Keuhnes to accompany them to the plaza level to discuss the matter without disturbing others. Ms. Kuehne was very difficult, allegedly hit one of the officers, and was arrested for disorderly conduct. After being handcuffed, she screamed and doubled over on the ground. The other officer ejected Sandy from the Stadium, and returned to assist the officer in removing Ms. Kuehne. Ms. Kuehne was being walked out of the Stadium when Sandy reappeared, was informed he was under arrest and resisted, slapping and shoving the officers. The Kuehnes were then taken to the police room at the Stadium, and were charged with disorderly conduct and resisting arrest. At trial, the disorderly conduct charges were dropped, and a jury found both Kuehnes guilty of resisting arrest. The Kuehnes appealed. Ms. Kuehne alleged that joinder of the trials prejudiced her case, especially when Sandy was cited for contempt of court and fined $400.00. The Court of Appeals held that the Kuehnes should have been tried separately, since their arrests occurred for separate instances and the defendants may have prejudiced the jury's decision against each other. The Kuehnes also alleged they were denied ineffective assistance of counsel and that the jury was not given adequate instructions about the charges, both of which the Court of Appeals found had been adequate at trial. However, due to the Trial Court's error in joining the cases, the judgment of the Trial Court was reversed and new, separate trials granted.

The facility in this case acted appropriately in its actions, and the trouble-makers were arrested, more for the commotion they caused and resisting arrest than for actual criminal activity. This case can act as a guideline for appropriately handling those causing a disturbance to those around them in a large gathering, and the appropriate use of force under the given circumstances.

7.04 Who Is Responsible for Injuries to Patrons?

In *Townsley v. Cincinnati Gardens, Inc.*, [39] a seventeen-year-old boy went to the Gardens to see a Harlem Globetrotters basketball game. During the game, the boy went to a rest room on the second level containing one toilet, one urinal and a sink. Inside, the boy was confronted by several older and larger men who asked him for

---

[39] 314 N.E.2d 406 (Ohio Misc. 1973), rev'd 314 NE2d 409 (Ohio App. 1974).

money and then assaulted him, knocking out two front teeth and beating him until he was barely conscious. When the boy entered the washroom, there were no guards or ushers nearby, and the washroom was dimly lit.

At trial, the head of security at the Garden testified five guards were on duty that night. Two were stationed on the main level, and the remaining three were to provide services to the rest of the arena. Patrols were supposed to check the hallways and rest rooms. The Court held that the Garden knew or should have known of the danger in the rest room on the night in question, and awarded a judgment to the victim for a total of $2,477 to compensate him for both the dental work needed and the injuries caused by the negligence of the Garden's security personnel in failing to ensure the safety of its patrons. On review, the Ohio Court of Appeals reversed its decision, holding that the facility could not reasonably be held responsible for the actions of its patrons under these circumstances and could not have known of the danger posed in its restrooms.

While the Court of Appeals reversed the lower court decision, it remains clear that a facility should take every step reasonable to ensure the safety of its patrons and that patrolling of secluded areas by guards should be completed on a regular basis. Likewise, installation of "rape alarms" or similar notification devices in bathrooms or other places within the facility may aid the security department in rapidly responding to any disorderly conduct or danger posed or incurred by patrons. Further, keeping all restrooms adequately lit and patrolled will assist in preventing incidents.

In *Ptasnik v. Johnston,*[40], a hockey player employed by the Detroit Hockey Club got into a fight with a paying customer at a hockey game. The customer sued the player, the Club, and the Olympia Stadium Corporation. The player cross-claimed against the Club and Stadium, who then moved for summary judgment, which was granted, dismissing the player's suit against his employer and the Stadium, and he appealed.

The player alleged that the Stadium did not provide safe facilities for the enjoyment of a hockey game, resulting in the player's being assaulted by the customer. The player hit the customer with a hockey stick.

---

[40] 234 N.W. 2d 548 (Mich. Ct. App. 1975).

The player said he was acting within the scope of his employment when the fight occurred. Therefore, the Hockey Club had a duty to compensate him for any damages assessed against him in the customer's suit for assault and battery. The Court stated that the player's defense of self-defense against the customer's actions would not necessitate compensation from either the Club or Stadium, because he would not be assessed any damages, and if he was found guilty of assault and battery, an intentional tort, indemnity was improper due to the intentional nature of the crime. The Court did find, however, that the player could be entitled to recover his costs and attorney's fees from the Club in defending the action, and allowed this claim to stand but upheld the trial court's dismissal of all other claims.[41]

In *Rowley v. Mayor and City Council of Baltimore*,[42] a female security guard was battered and raped while on duty at the Baltimore Convention Center. The guard then sued the city and convention center, claiming that her injuries were due in part to negligence on the part of Facilities Management, Inc.("FMI"), an independent contractor that operated and managed the convention center. The guard claimed that the city and convention center failed to repair a lock on an exterior door to the convention center that allowed the assailant to enter and attack her. The city had originally hired Hyatt Management Corp. ("HMC") to operate and manage the convention center, while the city maintained an oversight authority, the day to day running of the center was in the hands of the management company. HMC eventually assigned its rights and duties under the contract to Facility Management, Inc. with the city's acquiescence.[43] FMI's duties included full responsibility for management and direction of the convention center, including building operations and maintenance. Security personnel were employed on a mid-night shift, and were supposed to notify the Baltimore City Police of any potentially dangerous situation, and thus they were not issued any weapons themselves. While on duty one night, Rowley heard an unusual noise and left the security office to investigate. She was immediately attacked by an assailant who had gained entry to the convention center through a door with a broken lock.

---

[41] Id. at 549.
[42] 484 A.2d 306 (Md. App. 1984).
[43] Id.

- The Safety Act provides a comprehensive approach to risk management and litigation management by allowing the user of approved products and services to receive the same protections as the manufacturers or sellers of anti-terrorism products and services.

The above protections are awarded by DHS only after the manufacturers or sellers of anti-terrorism technologies complete an application and DHS performs a comprehensive and rigorous review of the product or service. In recognition of the broad range of threats and possible countermeasures, the Safety Act applies to design services, program management and integration services, vulnerability assessments, camera services, software, guard services and other analyses relevant to U.S. Homeland Security. Almost any product or service that has an anti-terror purpose is eligible for the protections under the Safety Act. The CERTIFICATION category is more applicable to products used by the Department of Defense. In addition to the benefits provided under Designation, Certification allows a seller of an anti-terrorism technology to assert the Government Contractor Defense for claims arising from acts of terrorism. Technologies that receive Certification will be placed on DHS's Approved Products List for Homeland Security.

We need your feedback. The International Association of Assembly Managers is trying to determine if it would be cost effective and attractive to facilities within the United States to create a "block" designation under the Safety Act. Hopefully, the IAAM "block" designation would streamline the application process and incorporate the IAAM Best Practices for Safety and Security as the anti-terrorism technology. For more information about the Safety Act including an application, the final regulations and approved products and services, go to www.safetyact.gov.

7.06 Pre-Employment Screening for Security Purposes

The nature and importance of pre-employment information has changed dramatically since the tragic events on September 11, 2001. For example, on February 27, 2002, federal officials charged 20 employees at Boston's Logan International Airport with giving false information in order to obtain jobs and security badges. All of those arrested were immigrants, and 15 of the 20 were in the country illegally.[44] This follows the dismissal of over 271 workers at Salt Lake City International Airport in December for falsifying employment applications, and other arrests at major airports throughout the country for similar violations.[45]

Security concerns have come to the forefront throughout the country. Besides the use of security badges and identifications in more and more businesses, federal buildings have maintained restricted access, including the cessation of tours at several federal buildings, including the U.S. Mint in Philadelphia, for an indefinite period. Even Walt Disney World and Sea World have instituted routine bag checks prior to entering the parks, a step never before taken. Public Assembly facilities are likewise included in the areas receiving additional security scrutiny. Super Bowl XXXVI at the New Orleans Superdome and the Salt Lake Winter Olympic Games were deemed by the White House Office of Homeland Security as "national security special events," meaning the United States Secret Service led the coordination of all security with help from the National Guard. At Super Bowl XXXVI and the Olympics, all employees, subcontractors, vendors, sponsors, and anyone that was planning to work the event, underwent a background check by the Secret Service. Picture identification badges with limited access codes were issued to each employee and contractor. Employees and contractors still had to undergo security screenings whenever entering the secured perimeter around the facility.

---

[44] New York Times, www.nytimes.com/2002/02/28/national/28LOGA.html.
[45] Washington Post, www.washingtonpost.com/ac2/wp-dyn/a14401-2002Feb27?language=printer

conviction for theft, burglary, robbery, or embezzlement, for example, could be an automatic disqualification for any position involving the handling of money.[47]

- *Military Discharges:* There are four common types of military discharges: honorable, general, undesirable, and dishonorable. Undesirable and general discharges are given for a variety of reasons, and may or may not indicate that the discharged individual was found guilty of an offense. A dishonorable discharge, on the other hand, is given only to individuals whose guilt has been adjudicated. The EEOC and the courts treat less-than-honorable discharges resulting from an adjudication of guilt the same as a conviction. That is, there should be a review of the length of time since the discharge, the nature and seriousness of the underlying offense, and the relationship of the nature of the offense to the particular job applied for. If, however, an individual has received an undesirable or general discharge but has not been convicted of an offense, the discharge is, like an arrest, not an indication of guilt, and may therefore not be used as an employment disqualification.[48]

A facility manager should require all subcontractors to verify the information of its employees. For example, six of those arrested at Logan Airport were employed by the Airport's private security firm. Every subcontractor, including concessions, security, vendors, exhibitors, and promoters should be urged to screen their employees as well. For large events and multiple events, the number of part-time workers increases substantially, but the need to thoroughly screen these employees does not. For more information, you may go to the Equal Employment Opportunity Commission website at http://www.eeoc.gov .

---

[47] See id. at 345
[48] See id. at 346

Chapter 8

Antitrust Law

By Turner D. Madden

8.00   Introduction - Basic Concepts of Antitrust Law

The term "Antitrust" is commonly used to refer to the four principal federal antitrust laws, they are the Sherman Act, the Clayton Act, the Robinson-Patman Act and the Federal Trade Commission Act. These laws are based on the proposition that the public benefits from vigorous competition. Vigorous competition will increase the supply and reduce the price of goods and services. A single violation of the Sherman Act is a felony. Individuals that violate the Act may be imprisoned for up to three years and fined not more than $350,000 for each offense. The statute provides fines of up to ten million dollars for corporations. The antitrust laws include civil penalties. Those injured by violations may recover damages as much as three times their losses, plus their legal fees. Below is a brief summary of the four federal antitrust statutes.

> a) The Sherman Act of 1890 prohibits contracts, combinations of businesses, and conspiracies designed to restrain free trade (Section 1 of the Act). The Sherman Act also prohibits any firm, acting alone or with another, from illegally monopolizing or attempting to monopolize a particular product or service. (Section 2).
> b) The Clayton Act prohibits tying arrangements and certain exclusive dealing arrangements. This Act also prohibits mergers or acquisitions which may substantially lessen competition or tend to create a monopoly.
> c) The Robinson-Patman Act forbids a seller from discriminating in price between competing customers, or favoring one customer over another in granting of promotional services, facilities or allowances when the discrimination adversely affects competition. This is a highly narrow statute that is subject to a number of defenses.

d) The Federal Trade Commission Act makes unlawful unfair methods of competition and unfair or deceptive practices such as false or misleading advertising.

The objective of antitrust laws is to keep business competition truly free. Fair competition is fundamental to the free enterprise system. The antitrust laws are based on a simple principle: "Do not monopolize or unreasonably restrain U.S. trade or commerce." The actual application of the law is more complicated than this straightforward statement. The antitrust law is both specific in some areas and vague in others, with exact interpretation often being uncertain. Legal advice should be obtained whenever there is any question as to the lawfulness of any contemplated course of action or proposed transaction. While a facility cannot expect all of its employees to be experts on antitrust law, it should expect and insist that each employee learn what actions are specifically required or prohibited by antitrust law; and to recognize areas where antitrust law problems can arise so that advice of legal counsel may be sought.

In large companies, especially those with varied business interests, antitrust claims are easily brought. It can be very expensive to defend an antitrust claim. Individual employees may even be subject to fines, and criminal penalties including jail terms. Violations of antitrust laws should be taken as a very serious matter.

The suggested policy below, adopted from those in place at several major corporations, is intended to help you understand the principals of competition which must be followed when conducting facility business.

It is the policy of X Facility that each employee compete vigorously and ethically in the conduct of business matters, but always in compliance with the United States and State antitrust laws. Beyond compliance, employees are expected to avoid conduct that could appear to be a violation of the law. Any employees who have dealings with foreign countries must also comply with the competition laws of those countries.

The term antitrust is used to refer to the most significant federal laws: the Sherman Antitrust Act, the Robinson-Patman Act, the Clayton Act, and the Federal Trade Commission Act. These laws deal with unfair competition and practices as well as -agreements "in restraint of trade" such as price fixing and tie-in sales, for example.

Guide for Compliance

- Price fixing - an agreement with a <u>competitor</u> (another facility) to fix or otherwise affect prices, terms, or conditions of sales, rental or lease of the facility.
- Production restrictions - agreements with competitors to limit or restrict production to keep supplies limited and prices high. As applied to facilities, this would include any agreement with a competitor to artificially restrict availability of the facility to allow one or both facilities to charge higher fees.
- Quality restrictions - agreements with competitors to limit competition based on product quality.
- Market division - agreement with a competitor to divide markets by allocating sales territories, product lines, or division of customers or suppliers.
- Refusals to deal - agreement with a competitor to boycott or not deal with a third company.
- Resale price maintenance - agreement with a customer to fix, or otherwise affect prices terms or conditions of resale (sublease).
- Exclusive dealing - agreement that prohibits a customer from dealing with a competitor's products.
- Tying in contracts - an agreement where the sale of one product to a customer is conditioned on the sale of another product.
- Full line contracts - an agreement forcing a customer to purchase a full line of products in order to be entitled to purchase an individual product from that line.
- Reciprocal dealing - any agreement with a customer that says, "I will buy from you provided that you will buy from me."

Certain other business transactions and prices may violate antitrust laws if they unreasonably restrain trade or damage a competitor. The application of antitrust laws in these areas is very complex, particularly when trying to determine what is "reasonable" and what is not. Please consult counsel regarding the following:

- Monopolization - any business transaction or practice that may result in the facility acquiring a substantial share of sales in any channel of trade or any geographic area.
- Mergers and Acquisitions - any purchase of a business or share of a business, especially if the business purchased is related to any of the company's existing businesses.
- Below cost selling - selling products or services below their actual cost, especially when the purpose of doing this could be "predatory," i.e., designed to damage a competitor or drive a competitor out of business.
- Unfair or deceptive practices - any unfair business method or any business practice which may deceive a customer.
- Requirement contracts - an agreement which requires the customer to buy all supplies for a given product from the company, with the result that the customer is prevented from purchasing competitive products from other companies.
- Territory or customer restrictions - an agreement that restricts the customer's right to resell a product to a particular geographic area or to a particular class of customers.

Another category of antitrust offenses involves discrimination which harms customers or competitors. Violations can occur both in selling to customers or purchasing from suppliers. If a competitor is harmed, it does not matter under the law whether the selling price or terms were reasonable or unreasonable. Please consult legal counsel before publishing any price lists containing volume discounts and before offering any discriminatory prices or sales terms that could harm a competitor. Specific examples of problem areas are:

- Price discrimination - charging customers different prices for the same product except if the differences are "cost justified" or is a good faith effort to meet competition.
- Special allowances - offering special services, payments or other assistance to one customer which are not offered on a proportionately equal basis to that customer's competitors.
- Buyer's liability - any transaction where the company knowingly receives or tries to receive discriminatory prices or sales terms from a supplier.

The Sherman Act[7] in part prevents illegal "tying." Tying occurs when the seller of a product has exploited its control over another product, the "tied" product, to force the buyer to purchase the tied product which the buyer may have preferred to purchase elsewhere on different turns. For tying to be illegal, there must be a tying arrangement between two distinct and separate services, the seller must have sufficient economic power in the tying market to restrain competition in the market, and the amount of commerce affected must not be "insubstantial." The Visitor's Bureau contended that the hotel minimum they require is a sales objective, not a requirement for leasing the Convention Center, and that they lacked sufficient market power to enforce a tying agreement. The tying was a disputed factual issue, and the court could not conclude that illegal tying was not occurring. The Visitor's Bureau alleged it did not force lessees to buy services it did not want, but that out-of-town conventioneers tend to stay in the area and need hotel rooms, but locals who lease the center itself may not need hotel rooms in connection with a show or convention, and out-of-town conventions that may not fill all hotel rooms, will be forced to reserve a set number of rooms in order to lease the Convention Center.

The District Court stated that a refusal to give competitors access to an "essential facility" is a type of anti-competitive conduct that can support a monopolization claim. The Defendants alleged that Hart could not bring this type of claim because they were not a competitor with the facility, which the court found questionable. The Visitor's Bureau also claimed that they were immune under the state action immunity doctrine from such claims, but the court held that they were not entitled to Summary Judgment on the basis of these claims. The court held that Hart's suit was valid and denied the Visitor's Bureau's motions for summary judgment and the case was settled prior to trial.

---

[7] 15 U.S.C. § 1 & 2.

8.02   The Essential Facilities Doctrine

Under the essential facilities doctrine, one who is in possession of a facility that cannot practicably be duplicated by potential competitors must allow such facility to be shared on fair terms. A facility is
essential if duplication of the facility would be economically infeasible
and if denial of its use inflicts a severe handicap on potential market
entrants. A refusal to provide competitors access to an essential facility is
one type of anticompetitive conduct that will support a monopolization
claim.[8] Section 2 of the Sherman Act[9] forbids a person to " ... monopolize, or attempt to monopolize, or conspire with any person or persons, to
monopolize any part of commerce among the several states."

In *Flip Side Productions, Inc., v. Jam Productions, Ltd., et. al.,*
[10] Flip Side alleged that Jam and its associations controlled the Rosemont
Horizon, an "essential facility," for the promotion and booking of pop
rock and R & B concerts in the Chicago metropolitan area in violation of
the Sherman Act.[11] Flip Side also contended that the defendants violated
the Racketeer Influenced and Corrupt Organizations Act (RICO)[12].
Generally, promoters contract with artists for their services, and the
promoter in turn is responsible for advertising the concert, selling tickets,
and obtaining a suitable facility to hold the event. In Chicago, concerts
are presented at facilities in three size categories: arena-level, seating
10,000 people or more; mid-level facilities, seating 3,000 to 4,500; and
lower-level seating, at approximately 1,000. Thirty-five lower-level and
16 mid-level facilities are located in the metropolitan Chicago area. Two
arena-level facilities competed with each other for business–the Chicago
Stadium, seating 19,000, and the International Amphitheater, seating
10,500. The amphitheater was built in 1930 and closed its doors in 1982.
The Stadium, as well as hosting professional sports teams, also hosts
events such as boxing, ice shows, circuses, and other entertainment
events, including 21 concerts between 1979 and 1983. Only three of
these concerts were attended by less than 10,000 patrons, and

---

[8] *Hecht v. Profootball, Inc.*, 570 F.2d 982 (D.C. Cir. 1977), cert. Denied,
436 U.S. 956 (1978).
[9] See 15 U.S.C. Sec. 2.
[10] 843 F.2d 1024 (7th Cir. 1988).
[11] 15 U.S.C. Sec. 1 & 2.
[12] 18 U.S.C. Sec. 1961 et. seq.

the Stadium is only currently available to promoters with the ability to provide the owner with satisfactory profit.[13] Since 1980, three additional arena-level facilities were constructed, including the Rosemont Horizon, the Pavilion, and Poplar Creek.

In order to build the Rosemont Horizon, bonds were issued and long-term contracts were entered into with Ringling Brothers, Tempo International, and Araserv, for the exclusive use of the Horizon, with Tempo to provide at least 50 (reduced subsequently to 32) concerts annually, Ringling Brothers to perform their circus there every year, and Araserv to provide all concessions. Each of these contracts provided annual licensing fees to the Village of Rosemont. The Pavilion, operated by the University of Illinois, contracted with Jam Productions to stage concerts there, granting Jam the exclusive right to present at least 30 concerts a year at the Pavilion, guaranteeing the University $250,000 in exchange for the use.

In 1982, Flip Side alleged that Jam entered into exclusive leases with both the University of Illinois and the Village of Rosemont to promote concerts at the two "essential facilities," leading to a monopolization of concert promotion in the Chicago metro area, and Jam countersued, contending that Flip Side had also violated the Sherman Act entering into an exclusive contract with the International Amphitheater, purported to be an essential facility before the construction of the Horizon. Flip Side also alleged Jam had exclusive contracts with the Aragon, a mid-level facility and the Riviera and Park West, "essential" lower-level facilities. The court granted Jam's motion for summary judgment as to the mid-level and lower-level facilities, due to the number of facilities of that size in the area. The judge then dismissed the University of Illinois from the complaint, finding there were over 100 available dates for concerts and Flip Side had never inquired as to the availability of the facility, let alone ask for permission to hold events there. Jam moved for summary judgment in 1984 and the judge denied that motion. Jam later alleged that Flip Side's owners were indicted by a federal grand jury for mail and wire fraud in a scheme to defraud rock performers, by falsifying ticket and expense information in order to retain the excess funds as profit.

---

[13] 843 F.2d at 1026.

This allegation concerned four concerts at Soldier's Field. The owners eventually pleaded guilty to these claims. Jam and Tempo eventually moved for summary judgment, alleging the Horizon was not an essential facility. The District Court granted the motions, based on the availability of the Pavilion, Stadium, and Poplar Creek. Flip Side appealed. The court of Appeals reviewed the record, and determined the essential question was whether Jam's control of Horizon had the market power to create a "bottleneck" by excluding competitors from an essential facility. Further, agents stated performers preferred the Horizon, and that the Pavilion served about one-half as many patrons, not making it a true competitor with the Horizon. However, the Court of Appeals affirmed the District Court's decision, finding that the Horizon was not an essential facility for arena-level concerts. Flip Side failed to produce facts establishing a genuine issue for trial.[14] Even under the best circumstances, Flip Side failed to show any antitrust injury caused by Jam or Tempo. The court further rejected Flip Side's standing to bring a RICO claim, because the claim rested on allegations of Jam's agreements between its performers, and Flip Side was not injured by any such action.

8.03 University Agreements

In *United States v. Brown University et. al.*[15] the Antitrust Division of the Department of Justice sued the eight Ivy League universities and M.I.T., alleging violations of the Sherman Act for agreeing to distribute financial aid to students based solely upon need and to collectively determine the amount of assistance commonly admitted students would be awarded. The trial court entered a judgment in favor of the Antitrust Division.

The Ivy-overlap group was formed by the Ivy League schools in 1958 to, firstly, eliminate merit-based aid to students, and then to award financial aid on a needs basis, ensuring that the packages available to students admitted to the schools within the league would be comparable. This differed from the methodology applied by the College Scholarship Service (CSS), or Congressional Methodology, in which when two children in a family were attending college, CSS would attribute parental contributions evenly between

---

[14] Id. at 1033.
[15] 5 F.3d 658 (3rd Cir. 1993).

students, whereas the Ivy methodology would distribute parental contributions based on the relative costs of the colleges attended. When parents are divorced, CSS expects contributions only from the custodial parent, whereas the Ivy Method assumes contributions from both parents. These deviations resulted in less generous aid packages than those available solely under the CSS method. This led to compromises between aid packages at different schools for commonly admitted students, to even the package offered without making an effort to genuinely assess the student's financial circumstances.

Stanford became one of the only institutions then competing for the highest qualified students, and the Ivy group attempted to get them to join the group, but Stanford declined, allowing it to still offer scholarship based on achievement rather than solely on need. The Antitrust Division sought an injunction to prevent these practices, and shortly thereafter, signed a consent decree with all schools except MIT, who proceeded to trial. The trial court determined the Ivy Group's conduct constituted trade or commerce under the Sherman Act, rejecting MIT's claim that financial assistance was pure charity, and characterized the process as one of setting a selective discount to educational services, constituting price fixing.

The trial court entered a broad permanent injunction to prevent MIT from participating in this type of price fixing behavior based in financial aid, tuition or the like, and MIT appealed.

The Court of Appeals noted that just because the school was not compelled to offer any financial aid did not make the aid offered charity. By offering aid to needy students, MIT can gain more of the "cream of the crop" students than if it were forced to only admit students that could pay the cost of attending the school, approximately $25,000 per year. The Ivy Overlap group, by fixing prices, effectively prevented each of the schools from having to respond to market forces regarding the setting of tuition prices and benefits offered at different institutions. By leveling the playing field, so to speak, the only difference between schools was their character, academic and social outlets, not the cost or aid associated with attending the school. The court held that financial assistance to students was part and parcel of the tuition setting process and thus a commercial transaction subject to regulation under the Sherman Act.

In evaluating whether the agreement between schools in the Overlap group was reasonable, the Court of Appeals directed the District Court to apply a full rule of reason analysis, implying that the broader access to high-quality education for needy students was offered by the leveling of financial competition between the institutions involved, and that it was up to the Antitrust Division to show that a reasonable, less restrictive alternative exists to achieve the same end result, and whether the free market can achieve the same result.

Do's and Don'ts:
* Do understand the antitrust laws and their possible application to your job. Ask questions, should any concern arise.
* Don't take chances! Play it smart. Do seek legal advice if you have any doubt.
* Do avoid any unnecessary contacts with competitors.
* Don't share pricing information with outsiders.
* Do report any overtures, suggestions or innuendoes with legal counsel.
* Don't write any document that suggests the company has an understanding with any competitor regarding pricing or other competitive variable.
* Don't engage in any market sharing, splitting or price setting with any other facility.
* Do compete independently and vigorously at all times.
* Do avoid any advertising, marketing or other programs which could be objectively viewed as unfair or deceptive.
* Don't enter into any agreement, understanding, gentlemen's agreement, or even discuss with a competitor on prices, profits, costs, market shares, bids or intentions to bid or termination or selection of classes of customers.

for lost, stolen, or damaged property. The holder is admitted on condition, and by use of this ticket agrees, that the holder will not transmit or aid in transmitting, in whole or in part, any description, account, picture, reproduction, or result of the football game or related events to which this ticket admits the holder. Breach of the foregoing will automatically terminate this license and may result in legal action against the holder. The holder agrees that the holder's image or likeness may be used as part of any live or recorded video display or other transmission, reproduction, or depiction in any media now or hereafter existing of all or any part of the event to which this ticket admits the holder. Spectators who are in possession of a wheelchair-designated ticket must be physically challenged and using a wheelchair or be a designated companion. This ticket may not be resold or offered for resale at a premium in excess of the amount allowed by law. There will be no refunds and no exchanges other than as provided herein. Tickets obtained from sources other than representatives of the National Football League or its Member Clubs may be lost, stolen, or counterfeit tickets and in such cases will not be honored. This ticket cannot be replaced if lost, destroyed, or stolen. This ticket may not be used for advertising, promotion, or other commercial purposes (including contests, sweepstakes, and giveaways) without the prior express written consent of the National Football League."

As we can see from the language appearing on the back of tickets, the "contract" formed between the purchaser of the ticket and the vendor has become complex, creating a detailed relationship between the parties. Even every day movie theater tickets have waivers and limitations of liabilities on the reverse side of the ticket.

In some patron admission situations, the facility may require participants and patrons to actually sign a waiver to enter a dangerous area near the event. In *Valley National Bank v. NASCAR*,[3] a woman was injured after two cars crashed in a stock car race, left the track, and hit another driver's trailer, causing severe head injuries to a woman seated near the trailer. The woman and her husband (the Prays) were acquainted with one of the drivers in the races and were invited down to the races by the driver, Mr. Rees. Mr. Pray was very familiar with car racing and had been to hundreds of racetrack facilities. He had often been in pit areas and had been a race car driver as well as a member of NASCAR. His wife was also very familiar with racing, although she had never been a direct participant.

The Prays went to the fairgrounds on the night in question, and chose to sit in the pit areas rather than in the grandstands, so as to be closer to their friend, Mr. Rees. NASCAR rules were in place that evening, which prohibited any spectators from the pit area. The Prays had gone to the pit booth to buy tickets for the pit area, for which a premium over normal grandstand prices were charged. People wanting to enter the pit booth area needed to sign a "benefit plan registration – release and indemnity agreement" (BP) form. Both of the Prays signed this form. The attendant at the booth did not ask them if they were merely spectators, nor did they volunteer this information. The BP was checked for signatures and two additional forms were signed, a release of liability and a pit pass. All three documents were required before they were permitted in the pit area.

The BP signed contained a medical benefit plan and a release and indemnity agreement that release NASCAR, racetrack promoters and NASCAR employees from any liability due to their negligence in consideration of being allowed into the speedway or raceway. Both the Release of Liability form and the pit pass contained release of liability language.

After reading and signing the required documents, the Prays entered the pit area protected by jersey barriers and sat on stools near the hot dog stand to watch the races. Because of the size of the race that night, the designated pit area was full and some drivers, including Mr. Rees were pitted about 200 feet from turn one of the half-mile track, an area not protected by jersey barriers. Because of the danger posed, drivers had been asked prior to the race to remove their cars from this area.

---

[3] 736 P.2d 1186 (Ariz. App. 1987).

The Prays left the main pit area to see Mr. Rees near his trailer. Mrs. Pray was seated next to Mr. Rees' trailer in a lawn chair when the collision and subsequent accident occurred, leaving her with severe brain injuries.

The Prays sued for damages, and the trial court found for the NASCAR. The Prays appealed, alleging that the releases were invalid as a matter of law and that the trial court had erred in instructing the jury on express and implied assumption of risk.

The Court of Appeals considered the releases and held that there was no public policy reason for holding that the releases were invalid. The Prays had voluntarily and knowingly entered the pit area. The Prays argued that because the releases were not intended for spectators, there had been no meeting of the minds, but the Court of Appeals found that credible testimony had been presented that the Prays were aware of the danger posed through their years of experience with racing and that they would have entered the area even had they read the releases carefully. The Court of Appeals held that the Prays had not been prejudiced by any other action of the court, and upheld the jury's verdict in favor of the defendants.

9.02   Municipal and State Control of Scalping

Scalping, or the resale of tickets at a price higher than that initially asked at the box office, has been occurring at least since the turn of the century. State laws and local ordinances controlling or outright forbidding scalping are fashioned either to prohibit scalping unless regulated by the state through special licensing procedures, or to prohibit outrageous price mark-ups on the secondary market for tickets. For very popular events, scalpers have even begun to produce fake tickets in order to capitalize on the eagerness of consumers to attend these events. State and local authorities have enacted statutes and ordinances to regulate the place, manner and price at which tickets are sold, and many are fashioned as consumer protection statutes. Despite the regulation imposed, most laws also recognize the right of a person to dispose of a ticket to an event if they are unable to attend, but also limit the amount for which the ticket can be sold to its face value. Please refer to the table below for a comparison between the scalping and ticket broker laws for several selected states.

Selected State Scalping Law Comparisons

State	Statute Requirements	Ticket Brokers/ Price Restrictions	Punishment
Arizona A.R.S. §13-3718 (1997)	Cannot resell ticket for above imprinted price plus tax and fee from original vendor within 200 feet of event or in parking lot.	May not change imprinted price on ticket w/o permission.	Petty offense
California Cal. Pen. Code § 346 (1997).	Cannot resell ticket for above imprinted price while on the grounds of, or in the vicinity of the facility where event occurs, without permission of owner or operator of venue	Not covered in Penal Code	Misdemeanor offense
Connecticut Conn. Gen. Stat. § 53-289 (1997).	Cannot resell ticket for above imprinted price	Brokers allowed with permission of facility; Service fee of three dollars and tax allowed	Misdemeanor offense, with escalating punishment for each subsequent offense; each ticket sold is a separate offense
Florida Fla. Stat. § 817.36 (1997)	Cannot resell ticket for over $1.00 of price imprinted	Instate licensed travel agents exempt from provisions	Second degree misdemeanor; second offense is first degree misdemeanor
Georgia O.C.G.A. §10-1-310 et. seq. (1997).	Cannot resell ticket above imprinted price	Agents allowed and must specify any service charge on their tickets; maximum service fee of three dollars	Misdemeanor
Illinois 720 IL.C.S. 375/0.01 et. seq. (1997)	Cannot sell tickets above imprinted price	Ticket brokers allowed if meet statutory regulations; Reasonable service fee allowed	Class A Misdemeanor and fine up to $5,000 for each offense; tickets subject to confiscation

Massachusetts Mass. Ann. Laws Ch. 140 §185A (1997)	No resale of tickets allowed without license, wherever conducted	Agents must have a license under statute; reasonable service charge only	
Missouri R.S. Mo. §578.395 (1997)	Cannot resell tickets above imprinted price	Reasonable service charge allowed	Misdemeanor with escalation of punishment with each subsequent offense
New Jersey N.J. Stat. §56:8-27 (1997)	Cannot resell tickets without license.	Resale of tickets only through established, licensed businesses	Not mentioned in licensing statute
New York NY CLS Art & Cult. Affr §25.03 (1997)	No resale of tickets without license; exception for one-time resale at face-value by individuals	Brokers/Agents allowed with licensure only; reasonable delivery charge only	Punishment not specified in licensing statute
Pennsylvania 4 P.S. §202 et. seq. (1997)	No purchase of ticket with intent to resell at a price higher than that imprinted without license	Brokers allowed with appropriate license; must post established price & price being charged to consumers; no charge above maximum premium allowed	Fine of $300 for first offense or 30 days in jail; second offense is second degree misdemeanor

In a very old case, *In Re F.A. Dees*, [4] the San Francisco police sought to force a company who sold theater tickets out of its news-stands in the large hotels in San Francisco to obtain a ticket peddler's license, and it was held that the tickets did not properly fall under the definition of "sale of second hand goods;" therefore a license was not required. We can see from this case, that ticket scalping has been a concern for over 70 years, and the government has been attempting to regulate ticket speculation for at least this long.

---

[4] 194 P. 717 (1920).

In *Loska v. Superior Court of Los Angeles County*,[5] the Plaintiff challenged the constitutionality of the Los Angeles municipal code forbidding the selling of tickets to places of public assembly in public places. The Plaintiff had attempted to sell tickets to a Dodgers game approximately ¼ mile from the Stadium. The court reviewed the ordinance, its history and rationale and concluded that while the State had a legitimate purpose in trying to curtail curbside ticket sales, due to the mounting problem of counterfeit tickets defrauding the public, the ordinance also had the effect of preventing a one-time holder of an extra ticket from disposing of his ticket without making a profit.[6] The court stated that it offended its sense of fairness to impose criminal penalties on a citizen who at one time disposes of an extra ticket on the streets of the city without making a profit, and that the Plaintiff could raise this defense, if it was not his practice to sell tickets to make a profit.[7] Otherwise, the ordinance was held to be constitutional insofar as its reasonableness to reach and effect "commercial ticket sellers" seeking to make a profit from such sales and resales.[8]

In *Latino v. Kaizer*,[9] two men were charged with violating the Chicago Municipal code which prohibited ticket scalping and then sued the police officers that arrested them for false imprisonment and arrest without probable cause. In contested facts, police officers thought they overheard the men trying to sell tickets to an NBA playoff game and arrested them, confiscating the tickets, while the men stated they were just trying to find other members of their business to give them the tickets and that they had refused an offer to sell or trade the tickets. The trial judge vacated the original jury verdict, as he felt the officers' testimony was perjured, as it was unlikely the men would sell playoff tickets and the District Court in review granted a new trial. The Court of Appeals in review held that the initial jury verdict for the police officers needed to be reinstated because the trial judge had overstepped his authority in vacating the jury's verdict and that it was in fact possible that the men were trying to sell the tickets at a profit.

---

[5] 188 Cal. App. 3d 569 (1986).
[6] Id. at 580.
[7] Id. at 580, 581.
[8] Id. at 584.
[9] 58 F.3d 310 (7th Cir. 1995).

In *People v. Shepherd,* [10] an individual attempted to dispose of three extra tickets to a football game at face value, and was arrested for violating an ordinance forbidding sale of tickets without permission at a public park. The conviction was upheld, with the court holding that the State had a viable interest in crowd control, and although the single sale was not a problem, the large-scale problem posed by many sellers was. The court held that the defendant was entitled to dispose of his tickets, but could not do so at the public park.

In a slightly different decision, in *People of the State of New York v. Johnson,* [11] an individual took out an ad in the Village Voice newspaper, to attempt to dispose of some opera tickets she was unable to use. [12] Two police officers saw the ad which did not specify a price, met the woman while "undercover," and arrested her once they agreed on a price for the tickets at twice the face value and the money exchanged hands. The judge in this case stated that the woman was totally unaware of the law preventing resale of tickets, and that punishing her with a misdemeanor offense that could perhaps hurt her chances of getting a renewed visa served no purposes. Additionally, the Metropolitan Opera's policy that unused tickets could be returned, but not for a refund but as a forced donation to the Met was not in the best interests of the public. [13] While the Judge noted that the statute was enacted for legitimate public purposes, its application to this individual would result in unjust treatment as this was a one-time disposal of extra tickets, not a business or regular practice of ticket speculation, which were the cases specifically addressed in the statutory regulation. [14]

From this line of cases, we can see that municipalities seem to have quite a lot of leeway in controlling scalpers, particularly their setting up of business in and around the facility. Should a local ordinance prohibit scalping, facility managers may wish to encourage the enforcement of these regulations both to protect their interest in legitimate ticket sales, and in facilitating the smooth flow of traffic around their facility. However, it seems clear that the occasional one-time disposal of tickets by an individual in a non-public place is seen as a *de minimus* violation and will be permitted.

---

[10] 74 Cal. App. 3d 334 (1977).

[11] 278 N.Y.S.2d 80 (1967).

[12] Id. at 81.

[13] Id. at 82.

[14] Id. at 85.

9.03 Scalping and Ticket Fraud

The existence of a valuable commodity, tickets to a popular event, will, by its nature, spawn those who wish to profit from the limited supply of tickets and high public demand for this commodity. The eagerness of certain individuals to capitalize on this "secondary market" has caused them to engage in illegal behavior in order to profit from the supply-demand equation posed by tickets to events.

In *United States v. Mount*,[15] the judge made an interesting observation:

> "Ticket scalpers, like arbitrageurs in stock markets and dealers in gems, move assets in scarce supply towards those willing to pay the most for them. If promoters of an opera or rock concert underestimate the demand for tickets and set prices too low, the initial buyers will make a profit, while scalpers receive compensation for the service of moving the tickets from those who first acquire them to those who value the more highly. Promoters lose nothing from scalping in such cases, and everyone else may gain. …Scalping raises the effective price to the final customer without producing income for the promoter, so if the promoter's interests lie in holding the price below the short-term market-clearing level, the promoter will oppose scalping."[16]

In this case, an individual offered 30 strips of tickets to Minnesota Twins post-season games to a ticket broker, with each strip having a face value of $400. The broker was willing to pay $1000 per strip, even though he was unsure of how many post-season games, including the World Series, the Twins would actually get to play. The catch here is that the Twins did not sell strips to brokers, only to season ticket holders, then the press and the opposing team. After these groups receive tickets, then the tickets were released to the public with strict limits on how many tickets may be purchased. The broker knew that the offer for tickets must be fraudulent, and in fact the individual had ob-

---

[15] 966 F.2d 262 (7th Cir. 1992).
[16] Id. at 263.

beneficiaries of the contract, even if their separate contract with the promoters based compensation in part upon ticket sales. The court then dismissed the claim against Ticketron on the basis that no third party beneficiary contract existed.

Because of the above ruling, facilities may want to insert a clause in their contracts with ticketing agencies that the ticketing agency is solely responsible for their actions to the facility for lost, stolen or misappropriated tickets.

In *Connecticut v. Leary,* [23] the Supreme Court of Connecticut addressed the problem of a ticket broker selling tickets at a price over the three dollars above face value allowed by statute as a handling or service fee on tickets.[24] The trial court had held that the "premium" charged above face value was based on location of seats and desirability of the event, not on actual fees incurred to obtain or deliver the tickets, but was a subterfuge for the scalping of tickets.[25] The brokers claimed that the statute violated their equal protection and due process rights under the constitution and that the statute was unconstitutionally vague. The statute did permit owners and operators of the facilities where events were held to authorize a person to sell tickets at prices above the three dollars over face value, but without specific authorization by the facility, any such premium on sale was considered scalping. The court held that such a statute allowed the performers, promoters, and facilities to realize the profits from "enhanced" ticket prices, a legitimate purpose, thus not a violation of the equal protection rights of the brokers. The statute was promulgated as a consumer protection statute, to prevent the gouging of consumers at the expense of the facilities, promoters and artists, by ticket brokers not authorized to make such sales. As such, the court determined the statute was constitutional and that the ticket agency involved was held to the statutory standard in any ticket sales it made.[26]

In *Commonwealth v. Santangelo,*[27] the owner of a variety store, having a license to resell tickets, was convicted of scalping. Unable to obtain Celtics tickets from the box office, the defendant obtained the tickets from a ticket broker for $45 and resold the tickets for $50, well above the printed ticket price on the ticket. Although the $5 over his cost

---

[23] 587 A.2d 85 (Conn. 1991).
[24] Id. at 86.
[25] Id. at 87.
[26] Id. at 90, 91.
[27] 520 N.E.2d 1340 (Mass. App. Ct. 1988).

was reasonable and within the premium allowed by statute, the $45 cost paid for the tickets was not allowed to be recovered. The court held that the purpose of the statute to safeguard the public against exorbitant rates and abuses, and that if allowed to pass on his gouging by the vendor to his customers, the defendant would in fact be eviscerating the purpose of the statute, as the public would be no more protected from inflated prices than if he himself inflated the price.[28]

Thus even if properly licensed, a ticket reseller may still violate the law if he charges a price that exceeds that allowed by law. Clearly, should a facility manager wish to deal with ticket brokers, they should do so under contract and be keenly aware of the law regarding enhanced ticket prices. In most statutes present in the case law, there are exceptions for facilities contracting with brokers and agencies to handle ticketing, and it behooves a facility manager to be well versed in the statutory and regulatory requirements.

9.05 Season Tickets

Season tickets are sold to many sporting events and theatrical venues across the country. The ability to gain season tickets and retain the option to season tickets in the future are seen as valuable rights by those who have them. Season ticket holders are willing to go to great lengths to preserve these rights, as seen below. The way season tickets are construed by the courts is also vital to the right of renewal professed by many seeking to retain season ticket rights.

In *Soderholm v. Chicago National League Ball Club, Inc.,*[29] Soderholm sued the Chicago Cubs to require the Cubs to sell him 18 season tickets for the 1991 baseball season. The trial court had dismissed his complaint and he appealed. In 1985, Soderholm had purchased 24 season tickets to the Cubs games, held in his name and the name of his business, Eric Soderholm Batting Schools. At the end of the 1985 season, the Cubs sent Soderholm an invoice offering him the same tickets for the 1986 season. Soderholm accepted by sending in money for the tickets, and this relationship continued through the close of the 1990 season. At that time, Soderholm held 18 season tickets to the Cubs games. In January of 1990, the Cubs had heard alleged rumors that Soderholm had been selling his season tickets at inflated prices above face value. The team

---

[28] Id. at 1342.
[29] 587 N.E.2d 517 (Ill. Ct. App. 1992).

then sent Soderholm a letter stating that the Cubs would not sell tickets to people who resold tickets at inflated prices, and that they had received security reports that he had repeatedly sold tickets at above face value prices, and that should this practice continue, his account was in jeopardy of not being renewed for 1991.

After the 1990 season, the Cubs informed Soderholm that they would not offer him 1991 season tickets due to his violation of the ticketing policy. Soderholm went ahead and sent a check to the Cubs for 1991 season tickets, which the Cubs returned. In December, 1990, the Cubs offered to sell 6 season tickets to Soderholm for 1991, subject to the Cubs season ticket restrictions, including the resale policy, without the usual accompanying right of first refusal or renewal. Soderholm then sued in 1991, demanding that the Cubs provide him with all the season tickets he had requested, and injunctive relief to force the Cubs to sell him the tickets. He argued that he had a contractual right to the season tickets, and the Cubs stated no such contract existed, and that Soderholm came to the court with 'unclean hands'[30] and thus was not entitled to the remedy he sought. On appeal, Soderholm alleged he had an option contract with the Cubs to purchase the tickets sought, and the Court of Appeals held that there was no evidence of assent by both parties to such a contract. Considering the history between the parties, Soderholm felt that the Cubs were obligated to sell him 1991 tickets, but the court held that the invoice sent to prior season ticket holders at the end of the season was merely an offer to sell tickets, with an acceptance of the offer and formation of the contract for tickets only forming after the deposit for the tickets was sent in with the invoice in a timely manner. Since the Cubs never sent an invoice to Soderholm for 1991 tickets, no offer had been made, and thus they had properly returned the deposit sent in by Soderholm. Further, the court held that no option contract or contract for first refusal existed. Soderholm tried to construe his season tickets as a lease, creating a periodic one-year tenancy or right to the specific seats, and alleged the Cubs gave him improper notice of termination of the tenancy. The court disagreed,

---

[30] A legal doctrine where a court will not grant an injunction or specific performance, in this case, ordering the Cubs to sell him tickets and guarantee that he will have the right to renew or refuse the tickets for subsequent seasons, to those that appear before the court having committed illegal or immoral acts themselves, in this case, having sold his season tickets to others at a premium above face value.

holding that the tickets were a revocable license, revocable at any time at will by the Cubs, the licensor. The court found that by issuing season tickets, the Cubs did not grant a leasehold, but merely a series of revocable licenses, and that a ticket merely entitled the holder to a license to enter the ballpark and watch the event on the date indicated, no more and no less. Thus, the court granted summary judgment for the Cubs, dismissing Soderholm's complaint.

A very interesting case involves *In re: Harrell.*[31] In this case, a person declared bankruptcy, and among his assets were four Phoenix Suns season tickets. The Suns felt that the sale of the current season's tickets by the bankruptcy trustee was acceptable, but resisted the trustee's attempt to also sell alleged rights to playoff tickets and to future season tickets, as violating the Sun's policy of only transferring the right to playoff tickets and season tickets to family members or from a controlled business entity.[32] The trustee saw the right to purchase playoff and future season tickets as a valuable property right that could be sold to pay off the debtor's outstanding obligations. The trustee claimed that the Sun's policy restricting transfer should not be recognized by the Bankruptcy Court.[33] The court held that the trustee could sell the tickets by lottery, and that the Suns were obliged to honor the right to future season tickets and playoff tickets to the new owner, despite their policy to the contrary.[34] The Suns promptly appealed the case. The Suns had tried to enforce a strict no-transfer policy, but it was found that on at least one prior occasion, permission had been granted to transfer tickets with all associated privileges to a non-relative third party.[35] In a thorough analysis, the District Court held that the "expectancy" of renewal rights was not property, and the Sun's limitation of transfer of ticket rights limited any expectancy, thus the trustee could not sell the right to future tickets, but only the tickets already purchased by the debtor.[36]

---

[31] No. CIV 93-0854-PHX-SMM 1994 U.S. Dist. LEXIS 7188 (Ariz. April 6, 1994).

[32] Id. at *2

[33] Id. at *3.

[34] Id.

[35] Id at *9.

[36] Id. at 25, 26.

The court in *Re Harrell* contrasted the policy of the Suns with that of the Pittsburgh Steelers *In Re ID Craig Serv. Corp.*[37] The Steelers granted permission to the transfer of season tickets with the paying of a small transfer fee. This allowed the debtor himself to sell the tickets, and thus would also allow the trustee to sell the tickets in his stead. Clearly, the message sent by the courts is that should a facility or team wish to restrict transfer rights, it must do so completely. Without complete restriction on transfer, any subsequent sale of season tickets must be accompanied by the "right" or license to tickets in the future.

In *Texas Stadium Corporation v. Morris,*[38] a patron had entered into a contract in 1986 with Texas Stadium to lease the "Crown Suite," a luxury box through 2008. The contract obligated Morris to purchase ten tickets to pre-season and regular season games to see the Dallas Cowboys play at the stadium, and also gave him the right to purchase three parking passes per game, with language in the contract stating the tickets and parking passes were to be "available for purchase ... on the same basis as such tickets are offered to owners of possessory rights to other Crown Suites or Circle Suites" at the stadium.[39] Beginning in 1989, the stadium began offering package deal contracts that included tickets and parking passes in the overall price of the suite, with some contracts containing the language of Mr. Morris's contract, and others stating there is no charge for these items.[40] Morris filed a breach of contract claim in 1992, claiming that he should be reimbursed for tickets he purchased after 1989, and should receive free tickets and parking in the future for the duration of his contract. The trial court agreed and entered a judgment granting Morris reimbursement for past tickets paid, and a declaration that all future tickets and parking would be at no additional charge. Texas Stadium appealed, alleging that in all post-1989 contracts, the price of tickets and parking were figured into the cost basis of the suite, which had not been done for Morris's suite. The Court of Appeals sent the case back to the trial court, stating that there were genuine issues of material fact to be settled, and that the trial court's grant of summary judgment was inappropriate.[41]

---

[37] 138 Bankr. 490 (Bankr. W.D. PA 1992)
[38] No. 05-95-00833-CV 1996 Tex. App. LEXIS 3086 (July 19, 1996).
[39] Id. at *3.
[40] Id.
[41] Id. at *6.

In *Reed v. Cleveland Browns,*[42] a fan sued the Browns for refund of his season tickets costs after it was announced that the team would be leaving Cleveland, stating that he just could not enjoy the games, knowing the team was leaving. The Trial Court granted him relief, and the Browns appealed. The Appellate Court stated that:

> "Consider too the purchaser of season tickets for a baseball team. That the Chicago Cubs turn out to be the doormat of the National League would not entitle the ticket holder to a refund for the remaining games, any more than the star tenor's laryngitis entitles the opera attendee to a refund when the understudy takes over the role."[43]

The Appellate Court held that despite that damage to fan morale and disappointment felt, the season ticket holder was not entitled to reimbursement for season tickets not used after the announcement.[44]

In a series of decisions in 1972-1973, United States district courts held that professional football teams were not guilty of anti-trust violations or illegal tying arrangements by requiring season ticket holders to also buy pre-season tickets, that the patrons alleged they would not have purchased otherwise.[45] Since in each case, some tickets were available to each regular season game, this enabled a purchaser of season tickets to decide to either purchase a season-long ticket, including pre-season games, or individual game tickets, where no tying problems would exist, thus allowing the teams to avoid anti-trust liability.

---

[42] No. 95-L-194, 1996 Ohio App. LEXIS 5797 (December 20, 1996).

[43] Id. at *16, *17, quoting *Seko Air Freight Inc., v. Transworld Systems, Inc.* (7th Cir. 1994) 22 F.3d at 774.

[44] No. 95-L-194, 1996 Ohio App. LEXIS 5797 (December 20, 1996), at *17.

[45] See *Coniglio v. Highwood Services Inc., et. al.,* 1973 Trade Cas. (CCH) p.74, 795 (W.D. NY 1973); *Pfeiffer v. New England Patriots Football Club, Inc.,* 1973 Trade Cas. (CCH) p. 74, 267 (D. Mass. 1972); *Driskill v. Dallas Cowboys Football Club, Inc.,* 1973 Trade Cas. (CCH) p. 74, 544 (N.D. Texas 1973); *Laing v. Minnesota Vikings Football Club, Inc.,* 1973 Trade Cas. (CCH) p. 74, 601 (D. Minn. 1973).

In *Kully v. Goldman,*[46] Kully sued Goldman, asking the court to enjoin Goldman from withholding the transfer to Kully annually of four season tickets to the University of Nebraska Cornhuskers football games, to force Goldman to continue to receive the tickets from the University and to act as trustee of the tickets for Kully's use. Kully alleged that he entered into an oral agreement with Goldman in 1961, where Goldman was to acquire 8 season tickets to the Cornhuskers games, four for himself and four for Kully. Kully alleged that this contract created a trust or agency agreement to purchase or transfer tickets, or that there had been a breach of the oral contract to purchase and transfer the tickets. The parties settled the matters between themselves as to the 1979 season tickets, but the question as to Kully's entitlement to future season tickets through Goldman remained. The trial court had found that an implied trust had been created between the parties.

The court stated that if Kully provided $500 security and paid Goldman up front for the tickets, Goldman would be manditorily enjoined and required to obtain tickets to all future seasons of the University of Nebraska's football team for Kully.

Goldman appealed to the Supreme Court of Nebraska. The Supreme Court ruled that the ruling as to 1979 tickets was proper, but that as to future seasons, the trial court had erred. While the court found that the parties had a valid agreement from 1961 through 1979 for Goldman's purchase of tickets for Kully and reimbursement for same, nothing existed to form a trust between the parties, and that Kully could not seek specific performance on an agreement that could be nullified at any time by a third party, in this case, the University. Goldman never had a contractual right with the University for the purchase of season tickets. Because he was on the University's annual purchaser list, his prospects of obtaining season tickets was extremely good, but it was not an enforceable property right. Kully had sought to get the seats transferred to his name in 1971, but the University had refused, noting that the seats were in the east stadium which had been reserved for students and that the University had a policy not to issue any more season tickets in that section to new holders. The University thus held an option not to honor future reservations for tickets, and that any promise to acquire future

---

[46] 305 N.W.2d 800 (Neb. 1981).

season tickets was a promise not supported by consideration[47] and thus the court could not grant Kully the relief he sought.

In *Richman et. al. v. The Chicago Bears Football Club, Inc.,* [48] season ticket holders for the Bears games sued, alleging that the player's strike during the 1982 season had led to an unreasonable delay in refunding ticket sales to season ticket purchasers, and that they were entitled to interest on the funds collected from the date of the strike through the date reimbursement was finally made. The trial court dismissed the complaint and the Plaintiffs appealed. The Plaintiffs had all purchased season tickets prior to the start of the 1982 season for all home games.

Due to a player's strike, four games were eventually canceled: games to be played on October 3, 10, 24, and November 7, but the games were not "officially canceled" until the strike was resolved on November 16, 1982. One game was rescheduled and played out of town on January 3, 1983. In a letter to season ticket holders dated November 26, 1982, the Bears offered refunds of $12.50 per ticket or credit towards the purchase of 1983 season tickets. The Bears began paying refunds to those that requested them on December 10, 1982. The plaintiffs alleged they were entitled to any profit the Bears might have made on funds received for games not played and not refunded until December 10, 1982. The Court of Appeals held that the Bears had no contractual obligation to hold the games on a certain date, especially since the season tickets were purchased ahead of the issuing of a schedule for the season. The obligation to present games was suspended during the strike, and the court held that the Bears had acted promptly to offer refunds or credit to season ticket holders, and that such an action was not necessary until the games had been officially canceled the day the strike was settled. The Court of Appeals affirmed the Trial Court's ruling and dismissed the Plaintiff's complaint.

This case is important in showing that a team or facility's prompt action in the refund process is vital. The interest sought was not recoverable in this case, because the team had acted in a prompt manner. It is possible that had the team delayed its actions until the end of the resumed season or longer, that the court would not have looked so

---

[47] Consideration is a legal notion of the thing or reason a contract is formed; the exchange of value between the parties, most often, money. All contracts require, and offer, acceptance of the offer, and consideration to be held to be valid and enforceable contracts.

[48] 468 N.E. 2d 487 (Ill. Ct. App. 1984).

favorably on their case. When refunds are due in the event a game or event is canceled, such refunds should be made available as soon after the event as practicable.

In *Wagner v. Wagner*,[49] a couple obtained priority to purchase two season tickets to the University of Kentucky basketball games. When the couple separated, in advance of subsequent divorce proceedings, they agreed to split the tickets, each getting one-half of the home game tickets or some variation thereof. The ticket order form continued to come to the wife's residence in the husband's name. After the wife had remarried, the husband changed his address so the form came directly to him. The husband would copy the form, send it to his former wife, who would then send him a check for one-half the purchase price.

This process went smoothly from 1976 through 1988, when the wife had misplaced the form and was ten days late with her check to the husband. The husband then refused to honor the agreement. The following year, the wife sent her check early to the husband, but the husband returned the check with a note that their age-old agreement was not a lifetime commitment and that he was terminating it. The wife then sought to have the agreement enforced by the Court and force the husband to deliver one-half of the tickets. At a hearing, both parties testified as to the agreement, and the husband stated he felt he had no legal obligation to honor the agreement, while the wife testified it was her understanding that the agreement was to continue ad infinitum. The judge held that the agreement was enforceable, and that the parties were to share tickets through the 1991-92 season, at which time the tickets would be solely the husband's, stating that the parties were entitled to terminate their relationship and fifteen years was long enough for this type of arrangement. The wife asserted that the court had erred in terminating the agreement after the 91-92 season, without evidence of a time frame from the parties themselves, and that the judge had unfairly awarded the tickets to the husband thereafter. The Court of Appeals agreed, stating the court had improperly inserted terms into the agreement between the parties not inserted by them on their own. The Court also held that the award of the tickets to the husband over the wife was an arbitrary decision, and that the tickets were joint property at separation, had value, and thus had been most likely bargained for in the divorce and separation agreement. While the Court of Appeals agreed with the trial judge that the parties were entitled to end their agreement if they wished, it needed to be done with

---

[49] 821 S.W.2d 819 (Ky. Ct. App. 1992).

one party purchasing the other's interest to the tickets, rather than the outright grant of ticket rights by the trial court judge.

While this case might seem only tangentially related to facilities, it certainly shows to what lengths people will go to preserve their season ticket rights, and how valuable individuals see this commodity. This couple not only shared season tickets for fifteen years following divorce, they also went to court twice, doubtlessly spending as much in attorney's fees as the season tickets cost in total. It is testimony to the seriousness of this issue to patrons and that when considering the transfer of season ticket rights to others upon death, divorce, or any other such occasion, a facility should be cautious and perhaps ask for evidence of an agreement for such a transfer if appropriate.

In a similar case, *State Block, Inc. v. Poche*,[50] a corporation and a former officer disputed the ownership of eight season tickets to Louisiana State University (LSU) football games. After leaving the company, the officer had asked LSU to transfer ownership of the tickets into his name, and it complied. The former employer alleged that it had always paid for the tickets, which had been used primarily by the officer for business entertainment purposes. The trial court had ruled that the tickets belonged to the officer, and the employer appealed. The Court of Appeals ruled that the employer had owned the tickets due to their actual purchase over the years, but that since LSU had not been included in the suit, the Court had no power to award the tickets to the employer, and thus the officer, who had LSU change the address on the renewal form so it would go directly to him, still maintained the rights to renewal of season tickets.

Facilities may learn from this case, in that they can be pulled into litigation over season tickets as a third party and forced to make transfers by a court. It may be necessary for facilities to clarify the ownership of its tickets or any ownership policies.

---

[50] 444 So.2d 680 (La. Ct. App. 1984).

disabled that was not required of the non-disabled, and held the policy to be a violation of the ADA.

In a recent case which was cited above in Chapter 2, *Independent Living Resources v. Oregon Arena Corp.*,[53] disabled individuals sued Oregon Arena Corp., the owners of the Rose Garden Arena in Portland, Oregon, which opened to the public in 1995. The Rose Garden serves as home for the Portland Trailblazers and the Winterhawks hockey team and hosts a variety of other events throughout the year. The disabled individuals maintained that the wheel-chair accessible seating in the Rose Garden was limited to either "nose-bleed" seats or "end-zone corner" seating, functionally limiting the accessible seating to the least desirable seats in the house, violating the requirements under Section 4.33.3 of the ADA that require adequate dispersal of accessible seating. The patrons further maintained that there were not enough disability seats available, and that many of the seats shown by the Rose Garden as accessible seats had been in-filled with seating for long-term non-disabled season ticket holders, making many of the accessible seats in the plans for the Rose Garden non-existent in reality. The Magistrate Judge, in an extremely detailed opinion, found that Rose Garden had violated standard 4.33.3 by failing to adequately disburse and integrate accessible seating, both vertically and horizontally, into the permanent seating plan, but instead inappropriately clustered wheelchair seating into less desirable areas. This problem had been further complicated by the Trailblazers selling long term season tickets for four and five year periods to ambulatory patrons and in-filling accessible seating areas with risers to accommodate ambulatory patrons, freezing disabled patrons out of blocks of accessible seating in desirable areas of the Arena, and instead having ticket agents steer disabled patrons into less desirable areas of the Arena. The Judge reviewed the huge financial advantage this held for the Arena, replacing 33 accessible seats and their companion seating with 1,028 ambulatory seats, leading to an extra $2 million in ticket revenues over a basketball season alone. The Arena had maintained that they were allowed to in-fill once a particular class of tickets were sold out, where the Department of Justice maintained that the appropriate requirement regarding in-fill was that all tickets must be sold out before in-fill into wheelchair accessible seating is allowed. The Judge did not rule on the in-fill and ticket sale policy, but

---

[53] No. 95-84-AS, 1997 U.S. Dist. LEXIS 18349 (D. Or. Nov. 12, 1997).

instead requested further information from both sides before rendering a decision on the issue.

In *Kennedy Theater Ticket Service v. Ticketron, Inc.,* [54] Kennedy, an independent ticket broker sued Ticketron, alleging that Ticketron received benefits not available to independent ticket brokers, such as discounts in ticket-purchase prices, permission to return any unsold tickets, being granted exclusive ticket allotments to events, promoters inform the public that tickets to the event are available through Ticketron outlets, providing advertising, and being allowed to collect a service charge on each ticket sold, along with compensation for each sale from the subscriber, putting independent brokers at a competitive disadvantage and granting Ticketron a monopoly of sorts, leading to this anti-trust suit. [55] Ticketron alleged that the tickets it sold were in effect on consignment from promoters and facilities, and Ticketron acted as an agent of its principal, exempting it from liability under the law. The Court rejected this argument, and the characterization that Ticketron gave its business did not bind the court. The Court noted that tickets were revocable licenses for admission to events, and that under the Robinson-Putnam Act, although a ticket was a memorandum of the license agreement to see the event for which the ticket was purchased, this did not turn the ticket into a commodity under the meaning of the act, and the Court dismissed the Plaintiff's complaint as to the count of violating the Robinson-Putnam Act.

In *Washington National Arena Limited Partnership v. Comptroller of Treasury,* [56] the Comptroller assessed the Washington National Arena (WNA) for over $185,000 in admission taxes for the period of January 1978 through August, 1981. Under Article 81 Sec. 402, admission to any place by a single ticket, season ticket, or subscription, including cover charges for tables was subject to having a tax levied upon it. WNA operated the Capital Centre, which hosted the Washington Bullets Basketball team and the Washington Capitals Hockey team, as well as other sporting events, conventions and other productions. Abe Pollin, a general partner in WNA, conceived to turn the worst seats in the house into luxury seats by installing sky suites, loges, and portal boxes, which included plush seating, liquor cabinets, bathrooms, closed circuit TV, stereos and other amenities. Use of these luxury seats is obtained

---

[54] 342 F.Supp. 922 (E.D. Pa. 1972).
[55] Id.
[56] 519 A.2d 1277 (Md. Ct. App. 1987).

through a fixed-term lease, of which the price includes the amenities listed, preferred parking in a reserved section, and membership to the Capital Club, a restaurant located in the Centre. All of these items come together in the package, and are not negotiated for separately. The agreement also provided for the furnishing of an appropriate number of tickets for each event at the Centre along with the required number of parking passes.

WNA appealed the Comptroller's tax assessment, where it argued that the value of the amenities available in the luxury seats, apart from admission, should not be assessed and only the cost of admission should be used in assessing the tax, if any, owed.

The Tax Court affirmed the Comptroller's assessment of the tax based on the gross received from leasing the luxury boxes, and WNA appealed. The circuit court judge permitted that allocation of costs among admission prices and the amenities provided was permissible.[57] The Comptroller then appealed. The Court of Special Appeals held that the lease price constituted a single admission price and was fully taxable, and the Court of Appeals granted certiorari.[58] The Court stated that the circuit court judge had correctly determined that the Article permitting taxation was silent as to allocation of amenities "included" in ticket purchase prices. The Comptroller argued that the package was taxable as a single admission price, but the Court disagreed, stating that if WNA chose to set up packages allowing people to get a bus ride to the Centre, see a game, spend the night at a hotel and receive meals, the Comptroller would view that as taxable in whole, which would allow taxation of unrelated amenities, which did not seem to be the legislative intent when enacting the article allowing tax on admission tickets.[59] The Court held that allocation of the lease amount to the various amenities and admission was permissible, but also that the parking fees and club membership could possibly be included as taxable admission costs.[60]

In *MacLean v. First Northwest Industries of America, Inc.*,[61] two couples sought admission to a Seattle Supersonics basketball game on a "Ladies' Night" promotion evening. The two men in the group

---

[57] Id. at 1279.

[58] A writ issued by a court of superior jurisdiction to review the decision of the lower court for error.

[59] 519 A.2d at 1280.

[60] Id. at 1282.

[61] 600 P.2d 1027 (Wash. Ct. App. 1979).

sought admission at the one-half regular admission price given to women on "Ladies' Night," for themselves as well as their spouses, but the ticket seller refused to sell him discounted tickets for the two men in the group. MacLean then filed a class action suit against First Northwest Inc. (FNI) and the City of Seattle, seeking damages, injunctive relief and costs.

FNI operated the Seattle Supersonics and was responsible for setting admission prices to the games, while leasing the Coliseum from the City.

FNI established "Ladies' Night" at basketball games ten years earlier at the public coliseum, in the hopes of attracting women fans and hoping to encourage family attendance. Ladies' Night used to be every weeknight game, but was later changed to Sunday home games, and was enlarged in 1977 to cover all classes of tickets, where before it did not cover the top price bracket tickets. MacLean tried to allege this policy violated the Washington State Equal Rights Amendment but the trial court denied his request to amend his complaint. On appeal, the Court of Appeals considered the Equal Rights Amendment (ERA) issues sua sponte[62] and found that the half-price tickets available only to women on designated nights violated the ERA of the Washington State Constitution, and constituted sex discrimination. The Court found that the sex discrimination by FNI in its ticketing policy was seen as state action, as the City under its lease to FNI required FNI to comply with all state and federal laws, and the City of Seattle did nothing to change the ticketing policy despite the change in the law (passage of the ERA) that required a change. The Court reviewed a similar case involving the New York Yankees where the judge suggested that a Community Day offering reduced prices to everyone would perhaps better serve the purposes for which "ladies'day" was instituted, in a non-sexist manner.

The Court also reviewed the Law Against Discrimination, and found that the ticketing policy also violated this law. The Court suggested that a "Black's Night" or "Hispanic Night" would be similar in nature, but would never occur because of its blatant discriminatory nature, but the difference between such a policy and a "Ladies' Night" was negligible. [63] The Court reversed the trial court's grant of summary judgment to

---

[62] on its own volition or accord.
[63] Id. at 1032.

Chapter 10

Equal Employment Opportunity Law

By Allen G. Siegel and Henry Morris, Jr.

10.0   Introduction

Equal employment opportunity is a major concern for employers today. Over the past three decades, federal, state and local governments have passed numerous laws, ordinances and administrative regulations prohibiting employers from discriminating on the basis of race, color, sex, religion, national origin, age, disability, or veteran status, with respect to every employment action, including decisions to hire, test, train, promote, transfer or discharge employees. Moreover, not only are employers prohibited from discriminating, in some instances, they are required to take affirmative steps to aid minorities, women, disabled individuals and veterans in employment.

Such laws and regulations are a fact of business life. And they serve as the basis for numerous complaints and lawsuits. Regardless of personal ideology, all would agree that lawsuits are an unnecessarily expensive and time-consuming method of achieving compliance with established law. Nevertheless, many employers do not yet follow a systematic approach to complying with the numerous laws prohibiting discrimination in employment. Discrimination charges can be *very* costly and embarrassing. A class action, claiming a pattern of discrimination against groups of persons, can result in a judgment against a company of several millions of dollars. Even if the company proves that it did not discriminate, it may have to spend a lot of money, and much valuable time, in defending itself and its reputation against a discrimination claim.

This Chapter presents a general overview of the equal employment opportunity laws and their major principles, and how those principles apply to day-to-day situations. You, the supervisor, are most often the person who deals directly with applicants and employees, and as the company's personal representative, your acts are often considered the acts of the company. This places you in an excellent position to promote and effectuate the company's interest in hiring and retaining qualified individuals, consistent with the legal and regulatory requirements of providing equal employment opportunity.

The purpose of this Chapter is to provide you with a quick and reliable reference tool for everyday use. By referring to its Guidelines and suggestions as various situations arise, you will be able to protect the best interests of your company, and stay in compliance with the law.

10.01 Overview of Equal Employment Opportunity Laws

The major federal laws governing equal employment opportunity in the private sector are listed and briefly described in Appendix A of this Chapter. Generally, these laws prohibit discrimination in employment on the basis of race, color, religion, sex,[1] national origin, age, physical or mental disability, or veteran status (the "protected groups"). The laws cover employers, labor unions, and employment agencies, and apply to each and every stage of the employment relationship, from the recruiting, hiring and assignment of new employees, to benefits, layoff and discharge.

This Chapter will focus on the principles of the federal equal employment laws, since the federal requirements apply to almost every employer in the country. You should always keep in mind, however, that most states and many local governments also have equal employment laws, which are often even more stringent and far-reaching than the federal legislation.

---

[1] While several states have passed legislation to ban discrimination based on sexual orientation, Congress has not proscribed such discrimination on the national level.

the company's employment practices have a discriminatory intent or impact.

Assume, for example, that the population of Metropolis, where ABC Company is located, breaks down as follows:

Whites	70%
Blacks	25%
Hispanics	3%
Asians	1.5%
Native Americans	.5%
Men	49%
Women	51%

If the EEOC or the OFCCP examines ABC Company's workforce, the agency will look to see whether a breakdown of the workforce reflects this population breakdown, not just as an overall matter, but at every level of employment, *e.g.,* that 25% of management employees are black, that 25% of clerical employees are black, that 25% of production employees are black, that 51% of management employees are women, that 3% of clerical employees are Hispanic, and so forth. To the extent that the statistics show a significant deviation from the "ideal" model, the agency might use this as evidence that ABC Company has discriminatory employment practices.

As stated earlier, statistics may also be used to show adverse impact. In the janitor example above, for instance, the plaintiff in a lawsuit may prove adverse impact by showing (a) the percentage of blacks in the relevant labor market who have completed high school; and (b) the percentage of whites in the relevant labor market who have completed high school. If these statistics show that (a) is much smaller than (b), and if this statistical disparity is reflected in ABC Company's workforce, the diploma requirement may be found to have an adverse impact on blacks.

The EEOC has issued guidelines on employee "selection procedures," which provide, generally, that a "selection procedure" will be considered to have an adverse impact if it results in a selection rate for members of one group which is less than 80% of the selection rate for the group with the highest rate, the so-called "80% rule." The phrase "selection procedures" includes tests, applications, interviews, evaluations, or any other method used to select employees for hire, promotion, layoff, discipline or discharge.

> *Example:* All applicants for employment with ABC Company are required to take a general aptitude test. 75% of white males, the group with the highest rate, pass the test, but only 50% of black males pass the test. The black pass rate is less than 80% of the white pass rate (50/75 = 66-2/3); therefore, the test has an adverse impact under the EEOC's guidelines.

It should be noted that this "80% rule" is a rule of thumb, and does not *always* indicate adverse impact. If, for example, a company has so few applicants that a percentage comparison is not statistically significant, the rule would probably not be applicable.

Statistical evidence also contributes to making intent irrelevant, since by using statistics to prove discrimination an individual complainant can sometimes avoid introducing *any* subjective proof that he or she, personally, has been discriminated against. Moreover, statistics can be used to convert individual discrimination claims into class actions. In a class action, an individual plaintiff claims that he or she is a representative member of a "class" of persons of a particular sex or minority group, all of whom have been discriminated against by the defendant company. The "class" may consist of as few as 10 persons, or it may consist of thousands of individuals, *e.g.*, every woman and black who has ever applied for a job with the company, considered applying for a job with the company, worked for the company, or been discharged by the company. The individual plaintiff may present statistics to show that members of the class have not been hired or promoted in numbers proportionate to their representation in the labor market, and if the company cannot explain why, it may lose the case. This can happen even if the company may have had legal and justifiable reasons for the employment action that it took with respect to the individual plaintiff. Thus, the importance of statistics cannot be overemphasized.

Although statistics are most often used by plaintiffs and the EEOC in an attempt to prove that a company has discriminatory employment practices, an employer also may use statistics to demonstrate that its employment practices are *not* discriminatory. In one case, for example, in which the employer was accused of discriminating against Latinos, the employer successfully defended itself by introducing statistics which showed that the percentage of Latinos in its workforce compared favorably with the percentage of available qualified Latinos within the relevant geographic range of the employer's place of business. Thus, while plaintiffs and the EEOC can use statistics as a sword, facilities may also use statistics as a shield.

A final note on statistics. While the courts have often relied heavily on statistical evidence in individual and class action discrimination cases, the usefulness of statistics varies with the surrounding facts and circumstances of each case. Courts will not credit statistics which are irrelevant, meaningless, segmented, particularized, or fashioned to obtain a desired result. The statistics presented must be correct, complete, and comprehensive before a court will give them substantial weight. The sample from which they are compiled must also be sufficiently large to support the conclusion offered. Courts are scrutinizing statistical evidence more and more closely to determine if it is useful under the particular facts and circumstances of each case.

3) Job-Related

The major exception to the adverse impact rule exempts employment practices which are job-related and consistent with business necessity. Even though a practice has an adverse impact on women and minorities, if it is clearly job-related and consistent with business necessity it will not constitute illegal discrimination.

Example: Easy-Fly Airlines requires its pilot candidates to have 2,000 hours of flying time. The requirement has an adverse impact on women and minorities, who have had fewer opportunities to gain experience in the aviation field. Nevertheless, the requirement will be acceptable if the airline can show that it is the minimum experience necessary for safe and efficient job performance. An important factor in this showing is the human and economic risks associated with poor job performance.

The high school diploma requirement for janitorial positions in the earlier example, on the other hand, probably would not pass muster. Even though the company might want to have an educated workforce, a high school education will rarely be necessary to the successful performance of janitorial duties, and therefore, would not be necessary to the efficient operation of the company's business.

The United States Supreme Court and the Civil Rights Act of 1991 have outlined the proper method of analysis for "adverse impact" discrimination cases as follows: First, the plaintiff must prove that an employment practice has an "adverse impact." This may be shown by statistics, or by other kinds of evidence, and usually involves the "80% rule," discussed earlier. Then, the company must show that the practice is job-related and consistent with business necessity. Generally, this requires evidence that the practice is predictive of, or has a significant correlation with, successful job performance.

The EEOC guidelines on employee selection procedures require that job-relatedness be proven by a process called "validation." To validate a selection procedure, a company must conduct a study to illustrate a statistical correlation between the selection procedure's measurement of skills, abilities and aptitudes for the job in question and successful performance of the job. With a few simplistic exceptions, *e.g.,* validating a typing test requirement for a prospective typist, a company will often have to engage the services of a professional to "validate" a selection procedure adequately.

Companies may also be responsible for the discriminatory conduct of their supervisors and other management employees. This may be true even if the company is unaware of the conduct, and even if the conduct is contrary to express company policy, since, often, the acts of supervisors and other management employees are considered to be the acts of the company.

With regard to some kinds of conduct, particularly harassment, a company may also be legally responsible for the acts of non-supervisory employees and even non-employees. If a company has knowledge of such improper conduct by non-supervisory employees or non-employees, or should have had knowledge of such improper conduct, and fails to take prompt and appropriate corrective action, it may be legally liable for these acts also. See the discussion in this Chapter entitled Sexual Harassment.

In some circumstances supervisors and other employees may also be *personally* liable for their improper conduct. Even in this event, however, the company may still retain responsibility for any discrimination that has occurred.

9) Double Jeopardy

A basic principle of American jurisprudence is the ban on double jeopardy, *i.e.*, that no person should be tried twice for the same crime. Although this doctrine is generally relevant only to criminal proceedings, there are analogous doctrines pertinent to civil proceedings which protect individuals from having to defend themselves against repeated charges and complaints based on a single incident.

This doctrine, however, does not always apply in the area of employment discrimination law. An aggrieved applicant or employee has numerous forums in which to seek redress for his or her alleged injury, and the employer's victory in one such forum will not necessarily preclude the complainant from filing another complaint–and winning–elsewhere. A typical case might proceed as follows:

Juan Juarez files a complaint with the state civil rights office, alleging that ABC Company refused to promote him because of his national origin. The state office investigates and determines that Juarez was not qualified for the promotion. The complaint is dismissed.

Juarez then files a charge with the EEOC. The EEOC investigates and issues a "no cause" determination, which means that it, too, does not believe ABC Company discriminated against Juarez. The EEOC, however, also issues Juarez a "right to sue" letter, which permits him to file suit in federal court.

Juarez then files a lawsuit in federal court, claiming that ABC Company has discriminated against not only him, but also against all individuals of Hispanic origin. He presents statistics showing that 35% of the local labor market is made up of individuals of Hispanic origin, but only 5% of the ABC Company's workforce consists of individuals of Hispanic origin. ABC Company is unable to submit a convincing explanation for this disparity, and loses the suit.

Even if Juarez had lost in federal court, he might then have been entitled to file a lawsuit in a state court, depending upon the provisions of state law. And, if he were covered by a collective bargaining agreement, he might also have been entitled to have his union file a grievance with the company, thus bringing the matter to arbitration.

10) Consistency
Consistency is a principle which is of particular importance in dealing with employees on a day-to-day basis. Inconsistent treatment of individuals who happen to be of a different sex, race, religion, etc., is a major source of discrimination claims.

Example: Jack Smith, who is white, arrives for work late five different times during a one-month period, and is given a written warning and a three-day suspension. Joe Jones, who is black, is discharged for the same conduct. Joe will likely claim that the difference in treatment was based on his race, and unless the employer comes up with a very good explanation for its inconsistent treatment of the two employees, Joe will win.

There may, of course, be legitimate reasons for treating employees differently. In the preceding example, for instance, Joe Jones might also have been performing poorly, while Jack Smith might have had the highest production rate in the plant. If such other reasons exist, an employer is certainly entitled to use them in making employment decisions. The EEOC and most courts, however, will assume, given the facts in the example, that the inconsistent treatment is the result of discrimination. So, an employer must be well prepared to justify such treatment on alternate grounds.

Inconsistent treatment may violate Title VII even if it does not affect traditional terms and conditions of employment, such as promotions or rates of pay. For example, a court has ruled that a retail store which required female sales clerks to wear a smock over their street clothes but did not require male clerks to do so was discriminatory, because it was demeaning for one sex to wear a uniform when members of the other sex did not.

11) Documentation

The importance of documentation cannot be overemphasized. Proper documentation can establish and support both the objectivity and consistency of a company's employment practices, and can mean the difference between victory and defeat in an employment discrimination lawsuit or administrative proceeding.

When a discrimination charge is filed with the EEOC or a state agency, the first thing that an investigator normally will request is any and all available documentation with respect to the incident. If the charge relates to a hiring decision, for example, the investigator will want to see a job description, application forms, and any written evaluation of or reasons for rejecting the individual who has filed the charge. If the available documentation is complete, and reflects objective and proper reasons for the rejection, the employer may have to proceed no further. If, on the other hand, the charge relates to a discharge decision, and the company has *no* written warnings or other records of prior disciplinary action, the company is likely to be in for a long and hard fight.

A general overview of the kinds of things that should be documented, and of the kinds of documentation that should be maintained, can be found in the section of this Chapter entitled Record-Keeping. Additional references to documentation, including when and where it is appropriate or required, will also appear throughout other sections of the Chapter.

10.02 The Employment Relationship

With this very general background, it is now appropriate to proceed to a more detailed discussion of the equal employment opportunity laws as they relate to the various stages of the employment relationship.

A. Hiring

The obvious goal in the hiring area is to attract and employ the most competent and qualified individuals. With knowledge of a few simple concepts you can achieve this goal without running afoul of the various laws and regulations prohibiting discrimination in employment.

1) Job Descriptions

The very first step in the hiring process always should be the preparation of an accurate and detailed description of the position that you want to fill. Since you seek to find employees whose qualifications fit the job, it is essential that the requirements of the job be clear, precise and objective. A good job description will also assist you in defending the legality of your selection procedures, should that become necessary. If you have established in advance the objective requirements of a job, it will be very difficult for a rejected applicant who does not meet those requirements to charge discrimination.

In preparing a job description, you should:

- Include all of the essential functions and other duties of the job, and indicate how often each must be done. Be specific.
- Enumerate in detail the skills and abilities necessary for successful job performance. If current employees are performing adequately, do *not* require skills or abilities greater than what they possess.
- Avoid overly broad requirements. Specify only those requirements that are really necessary to the job. If, for example, the job requires a knowledge of basic geometry, do not say that applicants must have a high school diploma. Say that they must have completed a course in geometry.
- Be sure that the qualifications you specify are the minimum *required* for the job. You may specify that additional qualifications would be helpful, but if you *require* more than is necessary, you may discourage individuals who could later prove that they were capable of performing the job.
- Avoid stereotypes. If, for example, you are describing a job that requires heavy lifting, do not assume that a woman or older person cannot do the job, and say "must be a young man." Instead, say "must be able to lift 80 lb. boxes 30 times a day," or whatever the specific requirement might be.

2) Advertising and Recruiting

Some of the same concepts that apply to job descriptions also apply to job advertising. If you use advertisements to attract applicants, you should be sure that the language of the ad describes only *necessary* job requirements, without "loaded" phrases. For example, if you are looking for an individual to sell your company's product, say "sales person" — *not* "salesman" or "saleslady." If there is no neutral title for the position, indicate in the advertisement that persons of either sex will be considered. This may be done by adding the phrase "Equal Opportunity Employer — M/F" at the end of the ad. You should also avoid phrases like "recent graduate," "young and aggressive," "boy," or "girl," which implicitly discourage older applicants.

If you use newspapers or magazines to advertise, always place your ads in the general "Help Wanted" column — never in a column for "Help Wanted — Female" or "Help Wanted — Male." In addition, if you advertise for employees through an employment agency or union hiring hall, you should make sure that the agency or hiring hall does not list your ads in any sex-segregated manner.

As mentioned earlier, there are certain limited situations in which age, sex, religion or national origin may be a bona fide occupational requirement. In those situations, the specific BFOQ may be mentioned in an advertisement for the position. For instance, an employer casting the role of a teenage girl in a play could require all applicants to resemble such a character without violating the ban on age or sex discrimination. BUT REMEMBER, this exception to the general prohibition on discrimination is very narrow, and it NEVER applies to race.

Some facilities also recruit by word-of-mouth advertising or referrals from current employees. While there is certainly nothing illegal about these recruiting methods, they may place unnecessary limitations on your applicant pool and increase the likelihood of a discrimination charge. If, for example, you rely on your present employees to "spread the word" about a job opening, and most of your present employees are white males — chances are, most of the applicants for the job will also be white males. Accordingly, you may be charged with discouraging female and minority applicants. Even worse, a class action may be filed, based on statistics showing the underrepresentation of certain groups in your workforce as compared to their representation in the relevant labor market.

If you wish to use your employees in recruiting, you should monitor the results in terms of the applicant flow from the various groups comprising the local labor market. If you are not getting a significant number of applicants from one or more protected groups, you should consider supplementing your word-of-mouth recruitment methods with newspaper advertisements and/or the services of an employment agency. You may also encourage your employees to seek out women, minorities and disabled individuals among whom to "spread the word." And, you may actively seek referrals from protected group members already in your employ.

Regardless of the method that you use to attract and recruit potential applicants, you should establish and maintain an applicant flow chart to monitor your results in terms of sex and racial and ethnic groups. A sample Applicant Flow Chart is contained in Appendix B to this Chapter. If the chart indicates that a disproportionately low number of women and minorities is applying, you may want to consider taking affirmative action to recruit them, even if you are not otherwise subject to affirmative action obligations. For specific suggestions about how you might do this, see the section of this Chapter entitled **Affirmative Action**.

3)   Employment   Applications   and   Other Pre-Employment Questions

Once a job description has been prepared and applicants have been recruited, the next step in the hiring process is ascertaining which applicants are qualified for the job. This is normally done by asking each applicant to complete an employment application, which is sometimes followed by a personal interview.

Regardless of whether questions are contained on an application form, or are asked in an interview, the general rule is the same: *only* job-related questions should be asked. The EEOC takes a dim view of facilities that request information from job applicants that is not strictly job-related. The agency apparently believes that if such information is solicited, it might be used unlawfully in making an employment decision. Moreover, certain kinds of questions might imply the existence of a non-job-related prerequisite which has been previously established to have an adverse impact on members of certain protected groups. See *Tests and Other Employment Prerequisites.* Generally, all questions that inquire, directly or indirectly, about an individual's race, color, sex, religion, age, national origin or disability must be avoided. You *may ask* an applicant's age, sex, religion or national origin if the characteristic is a bona fide occupational requirement, but you should again keep in mind that this exception to the discrimination laws is *very* narrow, and thus will apply only in unusual circumstances. You should also keep in mind that this exception *never* applies to race.

The immigration laws make it unlawful for an employer to hire an undocumented alien, and impose on employers strict verification requirements. You *must* verify whether a job applicant is authorized to work in the United States.

Frequently, you may require information about an *employee* that would violate the general rule on preemployment questions to *applicants.* If you carry group life insurance on your employees, for example, you may need to know an individual's age, sex, or marital status. If such information is necessary, it is better not to ask about it until after an applicant has been hired. The rule with respect to post-employment inquiries is somewhat more lenient than the rule with respect to pre-employment inquiries. And, at that point, you can demonstrate a legitimate need for the information.

Appendix C contains a list of permissible and impermissible questions which sometimes appear on employment applications, with suggestions about how necessary information might be obtained without raising inferences of discrimination. Appendix C also contains a sample employment application form illustrating the concepts discussed, which you may be able to tailor for use in your company.

4) Pre-Employment Physical Examinations

Using pre-employment physical examinations to evaluate applicants sometimes raises adverse impact issues, *e.g.*, hypertension occurs far more often in blacks than whites, and is not related to successful performance of many jobs, but more frequently raises issues of discrimination against the disabled. The Americans with Disabilities Act of 1990 (ADA) and other federal and state laws and regulations contain rules and requirements with respect to pre-employment physical examinations.

To ensure that physical examinations comply with *all* relevant requirements of the ADA, the following steps should be taken:

a. The physical examination should be job-related. In other words, the examination should assess such factors as mobility, endurance, uses of senses and mental capacity, or the ability to withstand various working conditions and environments. It should not result in conclusory determinations about diseases or disabilities which do not specifically address an individual's job capabilities.

b. All entering employees in the same job category must be subject to examination, and not just those with a disability or perceived disability.

c. A physical examination cannot be performed before making a conditional job offer to an applicant. Accordingly, the results of the physical examination must be the last factor evaluated before the final decision to make an offer of employment is made.

d. The results of the examination may not disqualify applicants currently able to perform essential job functions with or without a reasonable accommodation because of unsubstantiated speculation about future risk.

e. The results of the examination should be specific and objective so as to be susceptible to review by an independent medical evaluator. The results should also be transmitted to the applicant at the same time they are transmitted to you, if the applicant so requests.

f. Information obtained during the examination must be maintained separately and treated as a confidential medical record. However, such information may be shared with supervisors who need to be informed regarding work restrictions and necessary accommodations, first aid and safety personnel, and government officials investigating compliance with the ADA.

g. The results of the examination must be used only in accordance with the ADA. In other words, the employer may not use the examination to discriminate against a disabled worker.

5) Non-Medical Tests and Other Employment Prerequisites

Non-medical tests and other employment prerequisites are subject to the EEOC guidelines on employee selection procedures. These guidelines say that any selection procedure that has an adverse impact must be justified by business necessity, or the adverse impact must be eliminated. To show that that procedure is justified by business necessity, it must be "validated."

The guidelines describe three types of validation: criterion-related validity, content validity and construct validity. All three types of validation require that a company demonstrate that the criteria, content, or constructs measured by a selection procedure have a significant relationship to the actual day-to-day performance of a job, and that by measuring these factors, success on the job can be accurately predicted. If there is not a significant statistical correlation between the results of the selection procedure and successful job performance, the selection procedure is not "valid" and, therefore, may not be used. The guidelines make the assumption that if a selection procedure cannot be validated, it is not job-related, and that the adverse impact which results from its use is unnecessary and illegal discrimination.

The guidelines' validation requirements are extremely rigid and technical. As a result, few facilities have been able to comply with them to the satisfaction of the EEOC or reviewing courts. Accordingly, it is a good idea, if possible, to eliminate any test or employment prerequisite that has an adverse impact and that is not essential to the conduct of your company's business.

Since it is sometimes necessary to use tests and other employment prerequisites, it will be helpful for you to know how certain commonly used requirements have been treated by the courts and the EEOC.

c. Experience Requirements

Experience requirements are most frequently challenged because the specific experience required is in a field or position that historically has been closed to women and minorities. As with any other requirement, an experience requirement may be imposed if it is shown to be necessary to successful job performance, and therefore job-related. This is rarely found to be the case, however, in connection with non-skilled and non-professional positions. Courts often take the view that experience requirements for such positions are merely a pretext for excluding women and minorities. On the other hand, experience requirements for highly skilled or professional positions are usually acceptable, particularly if the degree of skill that the job requires is high and the economic and human risks of poor job performance are great.

To avoid problems in this area, you should make sure that experience requirements are *necessary,* and not just preferable. Even though you might like to have someone in a job who has prior experience, if the job can be performed capably without such prior experience, you should not require it. This is especially true if the skills or abilities which would be reflected by prior experience can be picked up on the job in a relatively short period of time.

d. Arrest, Conviction and Military Discharge Records

Statistics show that members of certain minority groups have a disproportionately high number of arrests, convictions, and less-than-honorable military discharges. As a result, the use of these factors to disqualify individuals for employment will automatically have an adverse impact on these minority groups. Whether such an automatic disqualification is, nevertheless, permissible depends upon the circumstances.

Arrests: An arrest is only an accusation. And, in our society persons are considered innocent until proven guilty. Therefore, an arrest is not an indication of guilt, and an employment decision may not legally be based on whether or not an applicant has been arrested. In fact, the EEOC and some state civil rights agencies say that it is illegal for an employer even to ask about an applicant's arrest record, since the inquiry may discourage otherwise qualified applicants.

Convictions: A conviction *is* an indication of guilt. Thus, convictions *may* legally be an employment disqualification. Generally, however, it may not be a good idea always automatically to disqualify someone for a job because of a prior conviction. You should examine the type and seriousness of the crime, the length of time since the conviction, and how the type of crime might be related to the particular job.

> *Example:* Jack Smith, a 30-year-old black man, was convicted of petty theft when he was 19 years old, and has had a spotless record since then. He is applying for an assembly line position in your company's production department. Based on the length of time since the offense, the relative lack of seriousness of the offense, and the kind of job for which Smith is applying, use of this conviction as a disqualification to employment could be considered evidence of discrimination.

In some instances, however, convictions for certain crimes *may* be used as an automatic disqualification for certain positions. A conviction for theft, burglary, robbery, or embezzlement, for example, could be an automatic disqualification for any position involving the handling of money. Even in this case, however, it is a good idea to consider the length of time that has passed since the conviction, and the applicant's record during the interim.

Military Discharges: There are four common types of military discharges: honorable, general, undesirable, and dishonorable. Undesirable and general discharges are given for a variety of reasons, and may or may not indicate that the discharged individual was found guilty of an offense. A dishonorable discharge, on the other hand, is given only to individuals whose guilt has been adjudicated.

The EEOC and the courts treat less-than-honorable discharges resulting from an adjudication of guilt the same as a conviction. That is, there should be a review of the length of time since the discharge, the nature and seriousness of the underlying offense, and the relationship of the nature of the offense to the particular job applied for. If, however, an individual has received an undesirable or general discharge but has not been convicted of an offense, the discharge is, like an arrest, not an indication of guilt, and may therefore not be used as an employment disqualification.

e. *Subjective Criteria*

Employment decisions are often made not on formal criteria, but on the subjective judgment of supervisors who know the candidates and the positions to be filled. These supervisors may have discriminatory motives, or subconscious stereotypes and prejudices. The Supreme Court thus ruled in 1988 that subjective selection criteria that have a disparate impact on a protected group can, like standardized tests and other objective criteria, be discriminatory even if they are facially neutral and not accompanied with discriminatory intent.

The Civil Rights Act of 1991 has increased the employer's burden in a disparate impact action, requiring an employer to justify a facially neutral practice that may have an adverse impact. After the plaintiff has shown that a particular employment practice has an adverse effect on a protected group, the employer must now show that the challenged facially neutral practice is "job-related to the position in question and consistent with business necessity." And the practice will still be unlawful if the employer refuses to adopt a different practice with a lesser impact. The Act does not define what constitutes a valid business necessity.

6) Testers

In the employment context, "testers" are individuals who pose as job applicants for a job that they do not intend to accept for the sole purpose of uncovering unlawful discrimination. While testers have been used for several years in the fair housing area, the use of testers in the employment area has only recently become popular.

The EEOC has issued an internal policy guidance memorandum stating that it would endorse the use of "testers" to uncover evidence of employment discrimination. According to the EEOC, testers have standing to sue under Title VII as "aggrieved persons" because of their right not to be rejected for employment on the basis of their race, color, creed, sex or national origin. The agency reasons that even though testers have no actual desire to secure employment, they have suffered an injury through the discriminatory rejection.

10.03 Salaries

From the viewpoint of an employee, salaries are probably the most important aspect of the employment relationship. Although inconsistent treatment of employees in the salary area might subject your company to discrimination claims under almost all of the equal opportunity laws, there is also a specific federal law relating to wage discrimination on the basis of sex with which you should be familiar.

That legislation is the Equal Pay Act of 1963 (EPA). The EPA prohibits wage discrimination on the basis of sex among employees performing equal work in the same establishment under similar working conditions. There are three key factors: "equal work," "same establishment," and "similar working conditions." If all of those factors are present, male and female employees must be paid "equal wages."

Equal work does not mean identical work; it is enough if the work is of substantial equality. Equal work does, however, mean more than merely comparable work. In addition, in evaluating whether work is substantially equal, the actual duties of the jobs in question are controlling, not the job titles or classifications.

The statute specifies three separate criteria for defining equal work. The first is equal skill, which requires an exploration of such factors as experience, training, education, and ability. These factors are only important, however, if they are actually used in performing the job. You are *not* justified in paying a man more than a woman simply because he has more education, for example, if he is not actually using his education in the particular position.

The second criterion for defining equal work is equal effort. This is a reference to the physical and mental exertion required in performing a job.

Male and female employees may be paid differently for different *levels* of effort, providing the work does not merely involve different *kinds* of effort.

The third criterion is equal responsibility, which requires consideration of employee accountability and the relative importance of a position, including whether it involves the exercise of supervisory authority or independent judgment. In one court case, for example, a bank

10.04 Promotions

Companies sometimes use tests and other objective criteria in making promotion decisions. If such procedures are used, and if they have an adverse impact on protected groups, the EEOC guidelines require that they be "validated" to show that they are job-related. (See *Non-Medical Tests and Other Employment Prerequisites.*)

More frequently, however, promotional decisions are made on the basis of subjective evaluations by supervisors. Making decisions on the basis of subjective evaluations is not automatically illegal, but if decisions are made on this basis and adverse impact results, a court may presume that the procedure is discriminatory unless certain steps have been taken.

To avoid a claim that promotional decisions based on subjective evaluations are discriminatory, you should do the following:

- Have written standards and guidelines for making promotional decisions. The standards should be clear, objective, as detailed as possible and consistently applied.
- Evaluations should be in writing, and should indicate why the candidate for promotion does or does not meet the written standards. Be specific.
- The standards and your evaluation should reflect the *important* aspects of job performance. If, for example, particular skills are rarely required for a job, neither the standards nor your evaluation should assign undue weight to the employee's level of performance of those skills.
- If possible, the subjective evaluation of a candidate for promotion should be only *one* factor in the promotion decision, and not the sole basis for it. This might mean, for instance, that you would want to combine the subjective evaluation with a performance test, in making the decision about whether or whom to promote.

Perhaps most important, your promotion system should have some type of safeguard against discriminatory bias, either intentional or inadvertent, by the person in charge. One type of safeguard would be a review process, whereby the employee's evaluation is discussed with him or her by an objective third party, who would solicit comments from the employee as to whether he or she agrees with the evaluation. This third party would then seek to resolve any disagreements by discussing the evaluation with the evaluator, or with the employee's co-workers or others having knowledge of his or her work.

As with hiring decisions, the key to making justifiable promotional decisions is to show that they are based on an individual's job-related qualifications and prior performance. Promotional decisions should *always* be made on that basis, and should always be thoroughly and accurately documented.

10.05 Transfers and Job Assignments

A potential source of discrimination charges is the transfer or assignment of protected group members to inconvenient locations or undesirable positions. All transfers and job assignments should be made on the basis of well-documented objective reasons.

A specific practice that has frequently caused problems is the assignment of individuals of a particular race to serve customers or clients of that race. This might occur, for example, if a company assigned black salespersons to the predominantly black portions of a sales territory, and white salespersons to the predominantly white portions of a sales territory. Assignments made on this basis have been found unlawful.

Likewise, it has been found unlawful to assign minority employees to dirty and confining jobs where non-minority employees are not also given such assignments. If, however, it can be shown that the assignment is based on other factors, such as a poor work record, a lack of ability, or the employee's choice, the assignment would not be illegal.

It should be emphasized that there is no law that requires that employees be assigned to positions for which they are not qualified. All that the law requires is that assignments be made on the basis of non-discriminatory, job-related factors.

10.06 Seniority and Layoffs

As a general rule, it is not unlawful to base employment decisions on an established seniority system, but there are two exceptions to this rule. First, the rule may not be applicable if the seniority system was adopted for discriminatory purposes. Second, the rule may not be applicable to a seniority system that continues the effects of past discrimination by locking women and minorities into inferior positions, unless the system was clearly entered into in good faith. A bona fide seniority system established in good faith, however, will insulate an employer from a Title VII challenge even if it has an adverse impact on protected groups, absent evidence of intentional discrimination.

If, on the other hand, an employer engages in discriminatory employment practices, a court may order that retroactive seniority rights be granted to the victims of the discrimination even if the seniority rights of other employees are affected. This can be viewed as a kind of "affirmative action," which is discussed in more detail in a later section of this Chapter.

An issue that frequently arises is whether seniority rights may be used as a basis for layoffs without violating equal employment opportunity laws. Women and minorities have, in recent decades, made significant gains in the employment area. Because this is a relatively recent phenomenon, however, they frequently have earned considerably less seniority than their white male counterparts. As a result, the EEOC has expressed concern about seniority systems that require that the last employees hired be the first to be laid of, since this type of system often has an adverse impact on women and minorities. Most courts that have considered the question, however, have upheld the legality of this kind of system, if the system was established in good faith and for non-discriminatory reasons.

10.07   Discipline and Discharge

Nothing in the equal employment opportunity laws prohibits an employer from taking any necessary disciplinary action against an employee, provided that the discipline is not motivated by a discriminatory purpose, or administered in a discriminatory fashion. Disciplinary actions must be taken without regard to an employee's race, sex, religion, age, national origin, veteran status or disability. Imposing discipline for a good reason is always permissible. If, however, a company has no specific objective guidelines for imposing discipline, discrimination may be suspected.

The following are examples of disciplinary actions found to be lawfully based on good reasons, even though imposed upon members of protected groups:

- Demotion of a black employee for proven incompetence
- Demotion of a female for unsatisfactory work performance
- Suspension of an Hispanic employee for excessive absenteeism and tardiness
- Suspension of an older employee for an on-the-job accident

Examples of disciplinary actions found to be unlawful discrimination include:

- The demotion of a black cashier for cash register shortages where cash register shortages of other employees had not resulted in demotion
- Demotion of a female for "poor supervisory ability and public relations," where this "reason" was really a cover for sex bias
- Suspending a black employee for five days for "flagrant loafing," where other employees were given a three-day suspension for the same conduct

Fourth, any time you give an employee a disciplinary warning or take any other kind of disciplinary action, you should ask the employee to acknowledge the discipline with his or her signature. If the employee refuses to sign, it is a good idea to make a notation of this in his or her file.

Fifth, always document your *reasons* for taking disciplinary action. If an employee is ultimately discharged, documentation of each and every prior disciplinary action will be invaluable, in the event a discrimination charge is subsequently filed.

Sixth, consider giving an employee about to be discharged the option of resigning. Although this will not, necessarily, prevent a charge of discrimination from being filed, it may lessen feelings of hostility which could otherwise lead to the filing of a charge. In addition, it may make it easier for the employee to obtain new employment, and an individual who is working is, as a practical matter, much less likely to file a discrimination claim than one who is not employed. Moreover, even if the employee files a claim and wins, the backpay award will be reduced by his or her interim earnings.

Seventh, it is helpful to have a system of progressive discipline for repeated violations.

Eighth, it is a good idea to establish a policy that all serious disciplinary actions, particularly discharges, must be authorized by a least two persons. If you believe that an offense warrants discharge, for example, you might review the facts of the situation with *your* supervisor or another company official, *e.g.*, the personnel director, and make it clear to the employee that the discharge is the joint action of both of you.

This could prevent a claim that the decision was based on your individual bias or favoritism.

As with all other employment decisions and practices, the key to avoiding problems with discipline and discharges is evenhanded and *consistent* treatment. Disciplinary decisions based on objective, well-documented, and job-related reasons should withstand legal challenge.

10.08 Special Discrimination Problems

1) Sexual Harassment

Sexual harassment is now recognized as a form of illegal sex discrimination.

The EEOC has issued guidelines on sexual harassment. They define sexual harassment to include unwelcome sexual advances, requests for sexual favors, and other verbal or physical conduct of a sexual nature, where:

- submission to the conduct is made a condition of employment, either explicitly or implicitly. For example, "If you're going to be successful here, you and I will have to become 'intimate' friends."
- submission to or rejection of the conduct is made the basis for an employment decision. For example, "If you sleep with me, I'll see to it that you get that promotion. If not. . ."
- the conduct seriously affects an employee's work performance, or creates an offensive or hostile work environment. For example, repeated lewd remarks, pinching and grabbing, the passing around of sexually explicit pictures or cartoons, or other similar sexually oriented behavior.

A key word in the definition of sexual harassment is "unwelcome." Sexual harassment does *not* mean consensual sexual activity, unless it affects the workplace in some manner. It is important to keep in mind, however, that a great many sexual harassment claims stem from an "affair that goes sour."

Example: Joe Smith has an affair with his secretary, Jane. Jane decides she wants to end the relationship, but Joe resists, and threatens to fire her if she does not continue with the affair. Jane may file a discrimination charge, and her earlier willingness to participate in the affair will *not* be a defense to the claim. Once the conduct becomes unwelcome, it becomes sexual harassment.

You should also be sensitive to the fact that what might be an innocent gesture to one person might be offensive to another. Some male supervisors, for example, attempt to gain rapport with their employees by casually draping an arm over an individual's shoulder while talking to him or her. A female employee may mistakenly interpret this innocent gesture as a sexual advance and claim sexual harassment.

Although most of the court cases to date have involved female "victims," conduct need not be directed toward a woman for it to be sexual harassment. It is also possible for a man to be the victim of sexually harassing conduct by female supervisors or co-workers. Also, some courts have held that homosexual advances directed toward employees of the same sex constitute sexual harassment. More importantly, however, the "victim" of sexual harassment could be someone who is only indirectly affected by improper conduct.

> *Example:* John is eligible for a promotion which Sue gets instead because she is having an affair with the boss. John might successfully claim to be the victim of sexual harassment since the promotion decision was based on sexual conduct rather than job qualifications.

Under certain circumstances, a company may be liable for sexually harassing conduct engaged in by its supervisors or agents, regardless of whether or not it has any knowledge of the conduct.

A company also may be responsible for sexual harassment by non-supervisory employees or non-employees, such as customers or salespersons, if the company knows or should know of the conduct and fails to take immediate and appropriate corrective action.

If an employee comes to you with a complaint of sexual harassment, a sure way of inviting trouble is to take the complaint lightly or to suggest that the employee is being overly sensitive or just silly. *Every* complaint of sexual harassment, or even idle gossip about improper conduct, should be taken seriously and promptly investigated.

There are several steps that a company should take to minimize liability for sexual harassment in the workplace:

- The company should institute and disseminate a strong, written policy prohibiting sexual harassment. The policy should communicate to employees that sexual harassment will not be tolerated and that the company's policy against sexual harassment will be aggressively enforced. The policy should spell out the forbidden behavior in detail, including such conduct as catcalls, innuendoes, and sexual jokes. Appropriate sanctions also should be stated, up to and including discharge.
- The company should make sure that supervisors thoroughly understand the policy against sexual harassment. Periodic meetings with supervisors to review the policy can be useful in that regard.
- The company should establish a clearinghouse for receiving sexual harassment complaints, and should encourage employees to report any improper conduct. To be effective, the people who receive complaints should be individuals with whom employees feel comfortable speaking freely. Also, the company should not require the employee to complain to the offending supervisor.
- The company should investigate all reports and complaints of sexual harassment as quickly and thoroughly as possible, and should advise complaining employees of the results of the investigation.
- All investigations should be conducted as confidentially as possible to reduce the risk of slander and invasion of privacy claims. Information should only be divulged to people who have a need to know of the investigation or the allegations.
- Employees must be assured that they will suffer no retaliation for using the company's internal complaint procedure.
- The company should take prompt and appropriate disciplinary action against any employee found to have engaged in sexual harassment.

whose employees were required to wear respirators to protect against toxic gases in the workplace. A Sikh employee, whose religion proscribed shaving, was unable to achieve a gas-tight seal because of his beard. When he refused to shave his beard, the employer suspended him without pay, but offered him other positions in the company. The employer also promised to return him to his former position if and when a respirator was developed that he could use safely. The employee sued, arguing that the law entitled him to his original job. The court, however, disagreed and found that the employer had made a good faith effort to accommodate the employee. Thus, the company had not engaged in unlawful discrimination.

Another religious practice frequently requiring accommodation is an employee's belief that it is wrong to join or pay dues to a union. Federal law provides that an employee in this situation may *not* be required to join the union or pay union dues.[4] Since, however, the employee will nevertheless enjoy most of the benefits provided by the union, he or she *may* be required to donate a sum equivalent to the union dues to a charitable organization, and the union may charge the employee with any representation costs incurred in processing a grievance upon the employee's request.

Requiring an employee to compromise on his or her belief by asking the employee to seemingly endorse a religious holiday may also be discriminatory. For example, one case involved a receptionist who was fired for refusing to answer the telephone with a "Merry Christmas" greeting. As a Jehovah's Witness, she felt the greeting would violate her religious beliefs. The court found that the employee had established a case of religious discrimination and awarded her backpay and damages. In another case, an employer was found to have violated Title VII by forcing its employees to attend a weekly prayer service at its plant.

---

[4]   Under this law, in contrast to the EEOC Guidelines, the religious practice must reflect the tenets or teachings of an established religion or sect which has traditionally been opposed to joining or paying dues to a labor organization.

4) Accommodating Veterans and the Disabled

Prior to the enactment of the Americans with Disabilities Act (ADA), federal legislation prohibiting discrimination against the disabled applied only to certain federal contractors, and subcontractors of federal contractors, and to certain recipients of federal financial assistance. Such protections for disabled individuals were and remain available under the Federal Rehabilitation Act of 1973 and the Vietnam Era Veterans Readjustment Act of 1974.

Federal law prohibiting discrimination against veterans covers veterans of the Vietnam era and disabled veterans of any era. A disabled veteran is defined as a person who has a disability rated at thirty percent (30%) or more by the Veterans Administration, or who was discharged or released from active duty due to a disability incurred or aggravated in the line of duty.

Certain federal contractors and their subcontractors are required under federal law to establish a written affirmative plan for veterans and the disabled. Moreover, employers covered by the laws prohibiting discrimination against veterans are required to list certain job openings with state and local employment agencies.

Unlike the Vietnam Era Veterans Readjustment Act of 1974 and the Federal Rehabilitation Act of 1973, the ADA covers all employers with 15 or more employees. Moreover, while the ADA's major provisions are similar to state anti-discrimination statutes and federal statutes regulating government contractors and recipients of federal financing assistance, they reach beyond current law and are more specific.

The ADA prohibits discrimination against a qualified individual with a disability with respect to all aspects of employment, including job application procedures, hiring, advancement, discharge, compensation and job training. A qualified *individual with a disability* is an individual who, with or without *reasonable accommodation*, can perform the *essential functions* of the position held or desired.

a) Individual with a Disability

The ADA defines an individual with a disability as one who (1) has a physical or mental impairment that substantially limits one or more major life activity; or (2) has a record of such impairment; or (3) is regarded as having such impairment. Thus, a disability includes, for was unable to show that his performance was satisfactory. The Court then granted the Big Ten summary judgment as to the discrimination claims under Title VII.

As to the ADA claim, Clemons had to show that he was treated as disabled by the Big Ten due to his obesity, affecting a major life activity. The Court found that the Plaintiff had the ability to work, and did so consistently at a regular job, in addition to his football officiating duties, and his weight did not effect his ability to perform at those jobs.

Clemons was unable to show that the Big Ten or Parry perceived him as disabled due to his weight, or disabled in being able to perform major life activities, and granted the Big Ten's motion for summary judgment as to the ADA claim, dismissing the suit against the Big Ten.

b) Reasonable Accommodation

Essentially, reasonable accommodation involves altering existing facilities or procedures to make them readily accessible to disabled employees. This may include, for example, job restructuring, part-time or modified work schedules, alteration of the physical environment, acquisition or modification of equipment or devices, permitting a disabled employee to take unpaid leave and the provision of qualified readers or interpreters.

An accommodation is not considered reasonable if it imposes an "undue hardship" on the employer's operations. Whether an accommodation imposes an "undue hardship" is determined on a case-by-case basis. "Undue hardship" includes significant difficulty or expense in light of such factors as (1) the nature and cost of the accommodation required; (2) the overall financial resources, size and number of employees of the employer and the specific facility; and (3) the impact of the accommodation on the operations of the facility making the accommodation.

c) Essential Functions of a Job

"Essential functions" of a job refer to fundamental, rather than marginal, job tasks. An employer is prohibited from denying an individual a job or a promotion because his disability interferes with his ability to complete a task which bears only a marginal relationship to the particular job, or a task that can easily be transferred to another employee without adversely affecting the employer's operations.

Under the Act, an employer may still devise physical and other job criteria and tests for a job so long as the criteria and tests are job-related and consistent with business necessity. Thus, for example, an employer may adopt a requirement that an applicant be able to lift fifty pounds, *if* that ability is necessary to perform the essential functions of the job in question.

It is important, however, for the employer actually to impose such requirements in fact and not merely on paper.

Evidence of whether a particular function is essential includes, but is not limited to (1) the employer's judgment as to which functions are essential; (2) written job descriptions prepared before advertising or interviewing applicants for the job; (3) the amount of time spent on performing the functions; (4) the consequences of not requiring the employee to perform the functions; (5) the terms of any applicable collective bargaining agreement; (6) the work experience of past employees; and/or (7) the current work experience of employees in similar jobs.

d) Employee Benefits

The ADA's non-discrimination rules also apply to health insurance and other employee benefits. Accordingly, an employer may not expressly exclude disabled persons from benefit coverage, or apply special coverage rules to disabled employees, simply because they are disabled. For example, under the ADA an employer may be prohibited from establishing a general maximum lifetime medical benefit cap of $1,000,000 while at the same time imposing a special maximum benefit amount of $5,000 upon persons with AIDS. If an employer provides insurance or other benefit plans to its employees, it must provide the same coverage to its employees with disabilities.

Greater uncertainty exists with respect to benefit plan provisions that simply *result* in discrimination against disabled employees. In general, the Act permits employers to place limits on certain treatments, or to impose relatively low lifetime benefits caps, provided that the limitations apply to *all* plan participants. If, however, an employer fails to impose the new limit or new cap until a disabled person(s) actually approaches or exceeds the limit or the cap, a question of intentional discrimination will arise. Because numerous questions exist as to how the ADA will be enforced with regard to health insurance and other benefit plans, facilities are advised to consult with counsel regarding the provisions of their employee benefit plans.

In sum, the ADA is having a significant impact on American businesses. Moreover, because many states have enacted legislation prohibiting discrimination against the disabled, you should always consult with company counsel to determine the laws of your particular state. There are several general steps, however, that should be taken to minimize problems with discrimination against the disabled and veterans:

- The company should designate an employee representative to coordinate efforts to comply with the laws barring discrimination against veterans and disabled individuals.
- Pre-employment inquiries as to the nature and severity of any disability should be eliminated. Inquiries should focus on specific job requirements.
- Employment criteria should be reviewed and revised to ensure that they do not tend to screen out qualified veterans or disabled individuals. Any test given should reflect job skills and aptitudes rather than sensory, manual or speaking skills, unless the latter types of skills are what the test purports to measure.
- Pre-employment physicals should not be given until after a conditional offer of employment has been made, and only then if such examinations are given to all employees in the same job category. Information obtained from pre-employment physical examinations must be kept confidential.
- Serious consideration should be given to accommodations for disabled employees which would not impose an undue hardship on your business. Any accommodations made should *always* be documented.

5) National Origin Discrimination

Although discrimination on the basis of national origin is subject to the same rules and principles as discrimination on the basis of race, age, or sex, it also raises a few unique issues and concepts of which you should be aware.

National origin discrimination is defined as the denial of equal employment opportunity because of an individual's, or his or her ancestors', country of origin, or because an individual has the physical, cultural or linguistic characteristics of a particular national origin. This includes the denial of equal employment opportunity because:

- an individual is married to a person or associates with persons of a particular national origin;
- an individual is a member in, or associated with, an organization identified with or seeking to promote the interests of national origin groups;
- an individual attends or participates in schools, churches, temples, or mosques generally used by persons of a particular national origin; or
- an individual, or the individual's spouse, possesses a surname which indicates a particular national origin.

Until the enactment of the Immigration Reform and Control Act of 1986 (IRCA), it was lawful to discriminate against non-citizens, although a citizenship requirement might nevertheless have been unlawful if it had the purpose or effect of discriminating against individuals on the basis of national origin. Under IRCA, it is now unlawful for employers knowingly and intentionally to discriminate against individuals based on national origin or citizenship.

To reconcile Title VII with IRCA, the EEOC issued a policy statement in April 1989 declaring that Title VII will continue to protect illegal aliens from employment discrimination. Remedies that discourage future discrimination, such as posting of notices, corrective measures and affirmative recruitment remedies, remain unaffected. Because IRCA, however, prohibits the employment of undocumented workers, the traditional make-whole backpay remedy may be excluded where the employer claims it simply acted to comply with the new immigration law.

The EEOC has issued "Guidelines on National Origin Discrimination." These guidelines contain at least two potentially significant provisions.

First, the guidelines list several selection procedures that have been shown to have a tendency to exclude individuals on the basis of national origin, and that will, therefore, be scrutinized closely. The list includes:

- height and weight requirements;
- fluency-in-English requirements, where employment opportunity is denied because of an individual's foreign accent or inability to communicate well in English; and
- training or education requirements that deny employment opportunities because of foreign training or education, or which require foreign training or education.

Second, the guidelines prohibit companies from adopting a rule requiring employees to speak only English at *all* times in the workplace. A company is permitted to have a narrowly-drawn rule requiring that employees speak only English at certain specified times or locations, but only if it can show that the rule is justified by business necessity. Moreover, if such a rule is adopted, employees *must* be informed of the exact circumstances and times when it is applicable, and of what discipline will be imposed if they violate it. If a company makes an employment decision on the basis of such a rule without having given employees effective notice, the rule will be considered evidence of national origin discrimination.

One federal court of appeals, however, disagreeing with the EEOC, held that Title VII does not protect the ability of Hispanic workers to express their cultural heritage at the workplace, as long as these employees are bilingual. According to the court, bilingual employees can readily comply with the English-only rule, and such a rule does not impose on them a burdensome term or condition of employment. Notwithstanding this decision, employers should be cautioned that an English-only rule will be subject to close scrutiny by the EEOC.

6) **Pregnancy Discrimination**

In 1978, Congress enacted an amendment to Title VII, common-ly known as the Pregnancy Discrimination Act. Under this legislation, discrimination on the basis of pregnancy, childbirth, or related medical conditions is considered to be discrimination on the basis of sex. The effect of this legislation is that pregnancy and pregnancy-related conditions must, in the employment area, be treated the same as any other temporarily disabling condition.

In its simplest application, this general principle means that if your company has health or hospitalization insurance, the insurance must cover pregnancy and pregnancy-related conditions of your employees to the same extent, and on the same conditions, as it covers other disabilities of your employees. In addition, if your company provides medical insurance coverage for its employees' spouses and dependents, this coverage also must include benefits for pregnancy and pregnancy-related conditions of the employees' spouses and dependents.

Another issue is paid and unpaid maternity leave. If a company maintains a temporary disability or paid sick leave plan, maternity must be treated the same as any other disability. That is, if an employee required to miss work because of a non-pregnancy medical condition is paid under the plan until he or she is medically able to return to work, a pregnant employee must be paid under the plan for the period of time that she is medically required to be away from work.

A more difficult issue is the question of unpaid leave. Clearly, if a company grants unpaid leave for other disabilities, it must also grant unpaid leave for pregnancy. However, what if the employer has *no* policy for granting unpaid sick leave? The EEOC takes the position that even if an employee would not otherwise be granted unpaid sick leave for a disabling medical condition, a refusal to grant a pregnant employee unpaid sick leave is illegal. In situations where there is a need for an immediate replacement and it is impossible to find a temporary substitute worker, the employer must offer the employee leave with the understanding that she is entitled to return to the first available opening for which she is qualified. And the Supreme Court has ruled that states may require employers to provide unpaid pregnancy leave and reinstatement to employees even though they may offer no comparable benefits to disabled workers generally.

A third issue which has arisen in connection with maternity is whether the company may *force* a pregnant employee to take leave. Generally, a policy requiring a pregnant employee to take a maternity leave of arbitrary duration, unrelated to the individual's actual ability to work, is unlawful. Both the EEOC and the courts take the position that a decision about when to take maternity leave, and how much, should be left up to the woman and her physician, based on her continued fitness to perform her job. This means that the approach must be individualized, and an across-the-board policy is consequently illegal.

With the growing concern over the exposure of pregnant women and their unborn children to hazardous substances, many companies have adopted fetal protection policies limiting or excluding fertile women from jobs which may be harmful to fetuses. Employers have generally sought to justify fetal protection policies by asserting that such policies are essential to workplace safety and that without a policy to protect fertile women, the employer may be found liable under state tort law for prenatal injuries. The Supreme Court has rejected these arguments where a company, which manufactured automobile batteries, adopted a policy excluding fertile women from jobs exposing them to lead. The Court noted, among other things, that since lead exposure has been shown to have a debilitating effect on the male reproductive system, a policy which gives fertile men, but not fertile women, a choice as to whether they wish to risk their reproductive health for a particular job is obviously biased. While the Court unanimously found that the fetal protection policy at issue violated Title VII, there was not unanimous agreement on the impropriety of such policies in all cases. Thus, the legality of fetal protection policies remains a somewhat open issue.

Once the issues relating to leave are resolved, the next issue is reinstatement after the leave. Here again, pregnancy must be treated the same as any other temporarily disabling condition. If jobs are held open for employees who are temporarily disabled for other reasons, the job of a woman on pregnancy disability leave must also be held open for her return. If she cannot be reinstated immediately due to job unavailability, she must be given preferential consideration for future openings.

Although post-leave reinstatement may be denied on the basis of particular business-related facts, such as an overall cutback within the company, or the employee's poor work record, it is clear that an employer may not refuse to hire a returning female employee simply on the basis of her former pregnancy. An employee returning after a pregnancy may not be treated less favorably in any respect than a person returning from sick leave for an illness.

Although there is some necessary flexibility allowed as to rehiring, the requirements relating to seniority are quite fixed. The seniority of an employee who takes maternity leave *must* be calculated from the time of her original hiring, and not from the date of her return to work after pregnancy. Whether the employee must also receive seniority credit for the period of the pregnancy leave depends on how persons taking other kinds of sick leave are treated. If they continue to accrue seniority during the period of their leave, a pregnant employee must also be allowed to do so.

Note: The preceding discussion pertains to a *medical inability to work* resulting from pregnancy. Accordingly, you may wish to require a statement from the employee's physician certifying the length of pregnancy leave medically necessary for the employee. It is only with respect to *that* period of time that you must treat the employee the same as employees with other temporary disabilities.

It is important to recognize that leave allowed for pregnancy disability and leave allowed for child care are separate issues. According to the EEOC, leave allowed for child care and bonding has no relationship to health, and must be offered to men and women on the same basis. Therefore, employers who grant liberal parental leave to new mothers, but not to new fathers, may be violating Title VII.

The preceding discussion relates to the Pregnancy Discrimination Act and the EEOC Guidelines and rulings issued under that Act. Many states also have laws and guidelines on pregnancy and maternity leave, and in some cases, these state requirements are even more stringent than federal requirements. In addition, Congress and several states have enacted family and medical leave laws which provide for a period of unpaid leave — twelve weeks under the federal law — to parents of newborn or adopted children and to employees who need time to attend to a family member with a serious health condition or to recover from their own serious health condition. A discussion of those laws is beyond the scope of this Chapter. They should, however, be consulted whenever you address questions concerning leave related to an employee's health or the health of the employee's family members.

7) Age Discrimination

The Age Discrimination in Employment Act (ADEA), as amended in 1990 by the "Older Workers Benefits Protection Act," makes it unlawful for employers, unions or employment agencies to discriminate against individuals aged 40 and over. The prohibition applies to hiring, firing, promotions, benefits, and other employment decisions, and extends not only to discrimination against employees in the protected age group in favor of younger employees, but also to discrimination against employees in the protected age group in favor of other employees in the protected age group.

The ADEA contains a number of exceptions to its general prohibition against age discrimination. First, like Title VII, the ADEA allows age to be considered in an employment decision if the employer can establish that age is a *bona fide occupational qualification* (BFOQ). Also like Title VII, however, this exception is very narrowly construed. The EEOC guidelines on age discrimination, which have been endorsed by the Supreme Court, state that an employer asserting a BFOQ defense has the burden of proving (1) that the age limit is reasonably necessary to the "essence of the business," *and* either (2) that all or substantially all of the individuals excluded by the age limit are in fact not qualified, or (3) that some of the individuals excluded by the age limit possess a disqualifying trait that cannot be ascertained except by reference to age. Clearly, this burden will be very difficult to meet in the majority of cases.

A second exception to the general ban on age discrimination is for actions which differentiate on the basis of "reasonable factors other than age."

The scope of this exception is unclear; however, the EEOC guidelines provide that it may not be used to justify an employment practice which uses age as a limiting criterion. The guidelines further provide that if a test is claimed to be for a "factor other than age," and has an adverse impact on individuals within the protected age group, it must be justified as a business necessity, pursuant to the guidelines on employee selection procedures.

A third exception is for actions taken pursuant to a *bona fide* seniority system, although not even a legitimate seniority system may be used to require or permit an individual to be involuntarily retired. In addition, under the EEOC guidelines, while a seniority system may be qualified by factors such as merit or ability, it must be based primarily on length of service in order to qualify for the exception. The guidelines also require that the seniority system be communicated to employees and that it be applied to employees uniformly, regardless of age.

Although the ADEA generally bans the compulsory retirement of employees, there is an exception for "*bona fide* executive or high policy making employees," who may be compelled to retire at age 65. Summarized very briefly, the exception applies to an individual who (1) for two years prior to retirement is employed in a very high management-level supervisory position, and (2) will be entitled, upon retirement, to nonforfeitable retirement benefits from a plan or plans of the employer totalling at least $44,000 per year.

Employers often attempt to avoid age discrimination problems by offering early retirement incentives to employees who are willing to waive their rights to sue under the ADEA. Although the Act allows *bona fide* voluntary early retirement plans, these plans must incorporate a number of safeguards. Indeed, the Older Workers Benefit Protection Act (OWBPA) sets forth specific rules governing voluntary early retirement incentive plans and the method by which employees may waive age discrimination claims. For example, under the OWBPA, employees who waive their rights under the ADEA must, among other things, be advised in writing to consult with an attorney before signing, be given at least 21 days to consider the early retirement agreement, and have at least seven days after signing to revoke the agreement.

Employers should keep the requirements of the OWBPA in mind when designing and implementing workforce reduction incentive plans.

The OWBPA also requires that age-based distinctions in employee benefit plans other than minimum age provisions for voluntary early retirement programs be cost-justified. Accordingly, an employer is required to provide older workers with benefits at least equal to that for younger ones, unless it can prove that the cost to the company is greater for older employees.

Most states and some local jurisdictions also have laws prohibiting discrimination on the basis of age, and these laws are in several instances far more restrictive than the ADEA. Under many state laws, for example, the protected age group encompasses *all* individuals over the age of 18. Where a state law prohibiting age discrimination exists, a plaintiff may not bring an action pursuant to the ADEA until at least 60 days after proceedings have commenced under the state law. However, once an action is commenced under the ADEA, it supersedes any state action.

10.09 EEOC Proceedings

Despite everything you and your company might do to avoid a violation of the equal employment opportunity laws, a disgruntled individual may accuse you of discrimination. This accusation might be made with the EEOC, the OFCCP, or a state civil rights agency. Most typically, however, it will be made with the EEOC. Accordingly, it will be helpful for you to know what is involved in EEOC proceedings.

The following discussion is, of necessity, very general. As you read it, you should be aware that different offices of the EEOC sometimes follow slightly different procedures, and that the office located in your area might also have additional procedures not discussed here. In addition, the procedures of state civil rights offices often vary substantially from those of the EEOC. Thus, it is always important that you familiarize yourself with the procedures of the specific entity with which you are dealing. General EEOC procedures, however, are as follows.

1) The Charge

EEOC proceedings are started when an employee, applicant, or former employee files a "charge" with the agency, alleging discrimination. The EEOC will send you a copy of this "charge," but it will frequently consist of no more than one or two paragraphs telling you in very general terms what you are charged with doing wrong.

If there is no state or local law prohibiting discriminatory employment practices, a charge must be filed with the EEOC within one hundred and eighty (180) days after the allegedly discriminatory incident.

If there is an applicable state or local law, the complaining individual must file the charge with the EEOC within three hundred (300) days after the alleged discrimination, or within thirty (30) days after the individual received notice that state or local proceedings have terminated, whichever is earlier.

When it sends you the charge, the EEOC may offer you the "opportunity" to engage in "pre-determination conciliation." The EEOC will want you to reach a settlement with the complaining party, so that it will not have to investigate the charge.

Although a conciliation at this stage might be useful if you have a very bad case, it is generally not a good idea. By entering into a settlement at this point, you are supposedly not admitting to a violation of the law, but you will probably have to take actions in order to settle which will make it appear as if you are admitting a violation. Moreover, it is not a good idea to allow your company to look like an "easy mark," particularly if you feel that you have done nothing wrong. If you develop a reputation for quickly settling every case that comes along, you may invite a lot of frivolous charges.

Even if your preliminary investigation reveals that you have a bad case, and if you feel that it might be appropriate to settle, you should nevertheless consult with company counsel before doing so. Counsel might see a potential defense to the charge that you are not aware of, or may have valuable advice to offer concerning the terms of the settlement. Assuming you decide to settle, however, it is essential that you obtain from the individual charging you with discrimination a complete release from all liability.

Whether or not you decide to engage in pre-determination conciliation, the period immediately following the filing of a charge can be fraught with danger if not handled properly. The EEOC has a large backlog of cases, and after you receive a charge, it may be weeks, months, or even years before they pursue it. As a result, you may be lulled into complacency, and fail to take any action with respect to the charge. Do *not* let this happen! As soon as you receive a charge, you should undertake an immediate investigation of the facts. Why?

Equal Employment Opportunity Law

- If the EEOC takes no action within 180 days after the charge is filed, the complaining individual may bring a private lawsuit without waiting for the EEOC to do something.
- Any backpay liability will continue to run throughout any period of delay, despite the fact that the delay is caused by the EEOC.
- By the time the EEOC gets around to you, witnesses helpful to you may be unavailable, or may have forgotten the facts surrounding the incident, and helpful records may be missing or difficult to reconstruct.

In short, it is important that you undertake an investigation immediately so as to be prepared for any contingency. Moreover, with an immediate investigation, you can be ready to mold and present your case in its most favorable light.

2) The Investigation

Immediately after receiving a charge, there are four things you should *always* do.

1) Notify and consult with your attorneys or the persons in the company responsible for these kinds of matters;

2) Undertake a thorough investigation of the alleged discrimination;

3) Gather together all company records having anything to do with the charge, including any notes made during an interview, application forms, disciplinary slips, customer complaints, supervisory reports or evaluations, and any other documentation which might support the employment action taken; and

4) Try to anticipate the areas that the EEOC may get into in addition to the specific incident described in the charge. If, for example, the charge involves a failure to hire a woman, you can expect that the EEOC will examine your company's history of hiring and promoting women in general.

There are also two things you should *never* do:

1) Never get angry and fire off a hot, emotional letter to the EEOC. The letter may contain damaging admissions which can be used against you, and even if it does not, it will do you no good.
2) Never fire or take any other retaliatory action against an employee who has filed a charge. Retaliation is a violation of the law, even if there is no merit to the charge of discrimination. Although you may be angry or upset with an employee who has filed a charge, it is essential that you not treat the employee any differently as a result of the action that he or she has taken. This does not mean that you cannot continue normal disciplinary policies, where appropriate, but you should be very careful that any disciplinary action is justified and well-documented.

At some point after you receive notice of the charge, the EEOC will usually send you a lengthy list of written questions (sometimes called "interrogatories"). Frequently, these questions will request far more information than is relevant to the charge. In connection with a charge of race discrimination, for example, you may be sent numerous questions asking about your employment practices with respect to women.

Although you are not required, unless subpoenaed, to supply all of the information that is requested, you should always supply any available information which is not damaging, since an outright refusal to supply information will likely be held against you. If the questions request more information than appears to be necessary, or request information which would be overly burdensome and time-consuming to prepare, you may try to talk with the EEOC investigator assigned to your case to see if it is possible to limit your responses, or to eliminate some questions. For example, there might be a question asking you to list the name, race and sex of every employee discharged for the past 10 years. If the charge alleges race discrimination against an employee recently fired, you may seek to limit your response to the name and race of employees discharged within the past 12 months.

Many of the questions might also relate to statistics. Without misrepresenting facts, you should always be careful to select the statistics which most accurately reflect your employment practices yet present them in the best light. If necessary, you may want to consider securing a professional to assist you in this area.

Usually, one of the EEOC questions will ask for the company's position regarding the charge. In most cases, you will want to take this opportunity to present the EEOC with a detailed statement of your position and arguments. You should never do this, however, without assistance of counsel, since anything you say in this statement may be used against you later.

The EEOC sometimes will also schedule a fact-finding conference at this point. Both you and the complaining individual (and your attorneys, if you wish) will be asked to meet with the EEOC investigator to discuss the alleged discrimination. Each side will be given an opportunity to present its story, and the investigator will try to determine which facts are in dispute, and which are not.

Sometimes, the EEOC's investigation will end at this stage. Based on your answers to written questions, and the fact-finding conference, the EEOC will issue a determination as to whether or not it believes there was discrimination. Other times, the investigator will want to go further and interview all potential witnesses to the alleged discrimination.

Supervisors and company officials should always insist that company counsel be present if they are interviewed. You may also request that an attorney be present in interviews with non-supervisory employees; however, if the employee or the investigator objects to this, you should not press the point. Moreover, you should normally allow interviews to be done on company time, since an employee may be more apt to say negative things if he or she is interviewed at home or elsewhere away from the workplace.

If you have not submitted a detailed position statement in response to the EEOC questions, then, following the interviews (or following the fact-finding conference, if there are no interviews), you or your attorneys should prepare and send to the EEOC a written memorandum outlining your position and arguments. In fact, even if you previously have submitted a detailed position statement, it often is advisable to submit a second statement at the close of the investigation. By marshalling all of the facts the investigator has heard in the light most favorable to you, you may convince the investigator to make a decision in your favor.

3) The Determination

After the investigation is completed, it may take quite a while for you to get a decision, called the "determination." This determination will either say that there is "probable cause" to believe that discrimination has occurred, or that there is "no probable cause" to believe that discrimination has occurred.

A "no cause" determination is a victory, but it is not always a final victory. A "no cause" determination means that the EEOC will not sue the company, but it does not prevent the charging party from suing the company. When the determination is issued, the EEOC also will issue a "right to sue" letter, which allows the complainant to file suit in federal court. However, a complaint must be filed in court within ninety (90) days after the letter is received.

If the EEOC issues a "cause" determination, it will be accompanied by an invitation to "conciliate." The EEOC will, on behalf of the charging party, try to get you to settle the case.

In its initial settlement offer, the EEOC will usually ask for everything possible. It will demand that you reverse the allegedly discriminatory employment decision, and pay the charging party any lost wages and/or provide additional compensatory relief. It will also request that you sign a conciliation agreement, which might require you to agree to hiring quotas, to open-door investigation rights (permitting the EEOC to come in at any time), to detailed reporting, or to expensive training programs.

Nothing in the law requires you to settle the case at this point, but you should usually try to do so. You can often negotiate the settlement down, by, for example, demanding that any lost wages be offset by unemployment compensation, or by wages from interim employment. (To assist you in this negotiation process, you should ask for copies of the individual's tax returns and unemployment compensation records, and for information about interim jobs and the individual's search for interim work.) You can also often negotiate many of the other items out of the conciliation agreement, such as the provisions relating to hiring quotas or training programs.

4) Litigation

If a settlement is not reached, the next step in the process is litigation. The EEOC may itself bring a lawsuit, but traditionally this has only happened if the case was very big or very serious. If the EEOC does bring a lawsuit, it will often bring a class action, alleging a pattern or practice of discrimination by your company.

If the individual sues, the EEOC will refer him or her to a private attorney. The private attorney will normally get assistance from the EEOC, and he or she might also expand the case to a class action. If the individual complainant wins a lawsuit, the company will be required to pay the fees for this private attorney.

Losing a discrimination lawsuit can be very serious. If the case has been expanded to a class action, the company may be liable for backpay for thousands of individuals who were discriminatorily refused hire or promotion, or who were discharged on discriminatory grounds. Also, since these cases often run on for years, millions of dollars in backpay can accumulate during the time between the alleged discrimination and the end of the lawsuit.

Reinstatement is, along with backpay, the most obvious form of relief. However, reinstatement may not always be an appropriate remedy. The position may no longer be available, or reinstatement may displace an innocent incumbent employee. Often, the hostility engendered by litigation makes reinstatement ill-advised. In such cases, courts often support an award of "front pay" to successful plaintiffs, a prospective award designed to compensate the plaintiff for economic losses that will be incurred after the court decree, as the plaintiff moves toward a new place in the job market.

Discrimination plaintiffs may also seek an award of compensatory and punitive damages. Prior to the enactment of the Civil Rights Act of 1991, compensatory and punitive damages were only available to remedy racial and ethnic discrimination. The Civil Rights Act of 1991 permits victims of intentional sex, religious and disability discrimination also to recover compensatory and punitive damages.

Unlike the damages traditionally available in cases of racial and ethnic discrimination, however, the 1991 statute sets caps on the amount of compensatory and punitive damages available based on the size of the employer's workforce. Specifically, damages are capped at $50,000 for employers with 15 to 100 employees, $100,000 for employers with 101 to 200 employees, $200,000 for employers with 201 to 500 employees, and $300,000 for employers with more than 500 employees.

Compensatory damages include compensation for future pecuniary losses, emotional pain, suffering, inconvenience, mental anguish and loss of enjoyment of life. To be eligible for punitive damages, an employee must prove that the employer discriminated with malice or with reckless indifference to the employee's civil rights. And, under the 1991 Act, a party to a discrimination lawsuit may demand a trial by jury for claims for which compensatory and/or punitive damages are sought.

In addition to the foregoing, a court may also order the company to establish a burdensome affirmative action plan with quotas, to set up expensive training schools or programs, and/or to maintain extensive records of its employment practices. And in all cases, if the company loses it will have to pay the plaintiff's attorney's fees and costs. In a complicated class action, attorney's fees alone can be hundreds of thousands of dollars, and may even exceed the amount of damages.

5) Involving the Union

If your company is a party to a collective bargaining agreement, you may want to try to involve the union if you receive a charge from the EEOC or are sued for discrimination. This may be particularly true if the alleged discrimination is related in some way to the collective bargaining agreement or might otherwise have some relationship with the union.

There are at least three reasons for involving the union. First, if the discrimination arises from the collective bargaining agreement or from some action of the union, you may be able to force the union to pay part of any backpay award. Second, the union may have some influence over its members, and may be able to help you settle a charge or get it dropped. Third, if you do not involve the union, you may end up in a position where the EEOC or a court is ordering you to do one thing, and the union contract requires you to do another. Accordingly, this is a step that should not be overlooked.

10.10 Affirmative Action

Affirmative action is a phrase used to describe special efforts taken to recruit, hire, advance, and promote members of protected groups. The nature and extent of these special efforts depends upon the reason affirmation action is undertaken.

A company might undertake a program of affirmative action for one of three reasons:

a.   Because it has been ordered by a court to do so;
b.   Because it is required by law to do so; or
c.   Because it voluntarily decides to do so.

1) Affirmative Action Ordered by a Court

If a lawsuit is filed charging a company with discrimination, and the company loses, the court can impose affirmative action requirements as a part of the remedy for the discrimination. A court has broad discretion in fashioning this type of remedy, and in the past, courts have used this discretion to order companies to establish and meet quotas, goals, and timetables with regard to hiring, promotion and other aspects of the employment relationship.

2) Affirmative Action Required by Law

Facilities having contracts with the federal government (including subcontractors of federal contractors) are required to take certain kinds of affirmative action, depending upon the size of the contract.

a.   More than $2,500. Employers having a federal contract or contracts totaling more than $2,500 in any 12-month period are required to take affirmative action on behalf of handicapped individuals. Such affirmative action might include the following:

- A review of personnel processes, particularly job qualification requirements, to ensure that any procedure which tends to screen out qualified handicapped individuals is job-related and consistent with business necessity and the safe performance of the job;

- A consideration of the reasonable accommodations which could be made for handicapped individuals without undue hardship;
- Enlisting the assistance and support of recruiting sources, including state employment agencies, state vocational rehabilitation agencies, college placement offices, labor organizations, and organizations of or for handicapped individuals, in recruiting and hiring handicapped individuals;
- Recruiting at educational institutions which participate in training of the handicapped, such as schools for the blind, deaf, or retarded;
- Establishing contacts with appropriate social service agencies or vocational rehabilitation agencies for advice, technical assistance, and referral of potential employees;
- Reviewing employment records to determine whether the potential skills of current handicapped employees are being fully utilized or developed;
- Including handicapped workers when employees are pictured in advertising; or
- Making handicapped employees available for participation in career days, youth motivation programs, and related activities in the community.

b.   More than $10,000. An employer having a federal contract or contracts totaling more than $10,000 in any 12-month period is also required to take affirmative action on behalf of disabled and Vietnam-era veterans, and to take affirmative action to ensure that individuals are hired, and treated during employment, without regard to their race, color, religion, sex, or national origin.

The affirmative action required to be taken on behalf of veterans includes listing all suitable employment openings with an appropriate local office of the state employment service. The only exception to this requirement is for openings which the employer proposes to fill from within its own organization or pursuant to a customary and traditional employer-union hiring arrangement. The employer is also required to file at least quarterly reports with the local office of the state employment service indicating the number of individuals hired during the reporting period, the number of non-disabled veterans of the Vietnam era hired, the number of disabled veterans of the Vietnam era hired, and the total number of disabled veterans hired.

Other affirmative action which might be taken on behalf of veterans includes:

- Enlisting the assistance and support of recruiting sources such as the local Veterans Employment Representative, the Veterans Administration Regional Office, the veterans' counselors and coordinators on college campuses, the service officers of national veterans' groups, or local veterans' groups and veterans' service centers;
- Contacting the office of the National Alliance of Businessmen in order to cooperate in the Jobs for Veterans Program;
- Establishing contacts with appropriate veterans' service organizations for such purposes as advice, technical assistance and referral of potential employees;
- Evaluating the selection process, including training and promotion, to ensure that it is free from stereotypes which might limit the access of disabled and Vietnam-era veterans to jobs for which they are qualified;
- Participating in veterans' "job fairs";
- Including qualified disabled or Vietnam-era veterans on the personnel relations staff; or
- Using all available resources to continue or establish federally assisted apprenticeship and on-the-job training programs.

Employers in the $10,000 and more category are also required to take affirmative action to ensure that applicants are considered, and that employees are treated during employment, without regard to their race, color, religion, or national origin. Such affirmative action must be taken in connection with initial employment, promotion, demotion, transfer, recruitment or recruitment advertising, layoff or termination, rates of pay or other forms of compensation, and selection for training, including apprenticeship. The employer must state, in all solicitations or advertisements for employees, that all qualified applicants will receive consideration for employment without regard to race, color, religion, sex, or national origin.

     c.   More than $50,000 and more than 50 employees. An employer having a federal contract or contracts totaling more than $50,000 in any 12-month period, and employing more than 50 persons, is required to have a written affirmative action plan for handicapped individuals, for disabled and Vietnam-era veterans, and for women and other minorities.

     The affirmative action plan for veterans and handicapped individuals must be made available for inspection by any employee or applicant upon request. The employer is also required to invite all applicants and employees who wish to benefit under the affirmative action plan to identify themselves.

     A written affirmative action plan for veterans and handicapped workers should include the following components:

- A policy statement;
- A section on the procedures to be used to disseminate the affirmative action policy through outreach, positive recruitment efforts, and internal and external publications;
- A section detailing the responsibility for implementing the policy;
- A section on the development and execution of action programs;
- A section detailing the procedures to be followed in issuing the invitation to veterans and handicapped individuals to take advantage of the affirmative action plan;
- A section detailing procedures to be used in reviewing personnel policies to ensure careful consideration of the qualifications of handicapped individuals and veterans, including the scheduling of a review of all mental and physical job qualifications;
- A section detailing the procedures and practices to be followed in considering and making reasonable accommodations for veterans and handicapped individuals; and
- A section detailing procedures to be used in setting compensation and in using sheltered workshops, apprenticeship programs, and on-the-job training.

The requirements of a written affirmative action plan for women and minorities are even more extensive. The first step in its development must be a detailed analysis of the employer's present use of women and minority group employees. This must include both a workforce analysis, which is a listing of each job title, ranked by pay, and the total number of males, females, and minorities in each; and a utilization analysis, which is a determination of whether there are fewer women or minorities in particular job groups than would reasonably be expected, based upon their availability in the relevant labor market. If women and minorities are "underutilized," the affirmative action plan must include goals and timetables for remedying the "underutilization."

Other elements which should be included in an affirmative action plan for women and minorities include:

- A policy statement;
- Procedures for formal internal and external dissemination of the policy;
- The establishment of responsibilities for implementation of the affirmative action plan;
- An identification of problem areas (deficiencies) by organizational unit and job group;
- An action-oriented program designed to eliminate problems and to attain established goals and objectives;
- An internal audit and reporting system to measure effectiveness of the total program; and
- Policies and programs for attaining the active support of local and national community action programs and community service programs, designed to improve the employment opportunities of minorities and women.

Although it is permissible to combine the written affirmative action plan for veterans and handicapped individuals in the same document with the written affirmative action plan for women and minorities, it is probably not a good idea to do so. The latter requires the establishment of goals and timetables, while the former does not. More importantly, however, the affirmative action plan for veterans and handicapped individuals must be made available for inspection by applicants and employees, whereas the affirmative action plan for women and minorities need not be made available for such inspection. Consequently, it is often worth the extra time and effort to establish two separate plans.

3) Voluntary Affirmative Action

Occasionally, a company will voluntarily decide to establish an affirmative action plan, even though not required to do so by law or court order. The company may do this as a preventive measure, to enhance public relations or because it has analyzed its workforce and found itself deficient in its hiring and advancement of protected group members. Such voluntary plans often resemble the elements of court-ordered plans or plans required by law. Though well-intentioned, employers should recognize that adopting such plans may expose them to liability for reverse discrimination.

4) Reverse Discrimination

Because affirmative action plans and programs frequently include quotas, they often raise the issue of "reverse discrimination." If an affirmative action plan requires that a specified number of women or minorities be hired to a certain position, for example, qualified white males will necessarily be limited in their opportunity to attain that position. A white male denied a job or promotion because of such a quota might file a charge of "reverse discrimination."

If affirmative action requirements are imposed by law, a claim of reverse discrimination probably will be unsuccessful. If affirmative action efforts are imposed by court order, a reverse discrimination claim also should be unsuccessful, at least insofar as the order is based on a finding or admission of discriminatory conduct.

Whether a voluntary affirmative action plan is entitled to judicial deference is less clear. However, the United States Supreme Court rejected a reverse discrimination claim that challenged a voluntary affirmative action plan because the company's voluntary affirmative action plan was temporary and did not unnecessarily disrupt the interests of white workers. The Supreme Court also has ruled that employers may, in certain circumstances, favor women over more qualified men in order to comply with the terms of a voluntarily-adopted affirmative action plan. The EEOC has issued guidelines designed to protect companies from charges of reverse discrimination stemming from voluntary affirmative action efforts. These guidelines extend EEOC approval to voluntary affirmative action plans under the following circumstances:

1) The plan is in writing;
2) The company has undertaken a self-analysis which shows that existing or planned employment practices have an adverse impact, and are unjustified by business necessity;

3) A comparison of the employer's workforce with the labor force shows the effects of prior discriminatory practices; and
4) The available group of qualified minorities and women for hiring or promotion is artificially limited as a result of historic restrictions by employers, labor organizations, or others.

In short, a finding that a voluntary affirmative action plan results in reverse discrimination may be avoided if the employer has good documentation of its reasons for undertaking the plan, if the terms of the plan are reasonable, and if the period of time for which the plan is to be effective is consistent with the objectives to be attained. Still, this area of the law is fraught with difficulty. No employer should implement or modify an affirmative action plan without advice of counsel.

10.11 Record-Keeping

The importance of documentation has been emphasized and reemphasized throughout the preceding sections of this Guide. The following is a brief overview of the kinds of documentation that should be maintained:

- Written job descriptions which accurately and completely describe necessary job qualifications;
- An applicant flow chart, to provide you with information about your applicant pool (see Appendix B);
- Carefully drafted employment applications, requesting only job-related information (see Appendix C);
- Written evaluations of applicants for employment prepared pursuant to specific, objective, written guidelines;

- Written records of the reasons for hiring or rejecting applicants for employment, with specific reference to job qualifications and the aforementioned written guidelines and evaluations;
- Written records of any decision made during the course of employment, including salary decisions, promotions, transfers and job assignments, and layoffs. Subjective evaluations leading to any such decision should also be in writing, and should be based on specific, objective, written guidelines;
- Written records of all disciplinary actions, copies of which should be signed by the employee;
- Termination reports, explaining in detail the reason(s) for any discharge;
- Memoranda with respect to any accommodations made or considered for religious practices, or for veterans and the disabled; and
- A written affirmative action plan, where appropriate.

In addition to all of this protective documentation there are a number of specific types of records which you are *required* by federal equal employment opportunity laws to maintain. The following is a very brief summary of those requirements.

Title VII
1) Employers with 100 or more employees are required to file, annually, an Employer Information Report EEO-1. The EEOC may also require additional reports to be filed, if it believes them necessary to effectuate the purposes of the law.

2) There are no *specific* requirements for other employers, but the EEOC has reserved the right to impose record-keeping requirements on individual employers or groups of employers. Moreover, if any personnel or employment record is made or kept by an employer (such as application forms, disciplinary records, etc.), the record must be preserved for at least one year.

3) If a charge of discrimination is filed against an employer, the employer must preserve all personnel records relevant to the charge until final disposition of the charge. "Personnel records relevant to the charge" include not only records relating to the complaining party, but also records of other employees holding positions similar to that held or sought by the complaining party.

Americans with Disabilities Act

The ADA incorporates Title VII's provisions on record-keeping requirements, except that where an employer does keep personnel or employment records, such as application forms or requests for reasonable accommodation, then records must be kept for a period of *one year*.

The EEOC has reserved the right to impose record-keeping requirements on individual employers or groups of employers.

When a charge of discrimination has been filed, the employer must preserve all records relevant to the charge until final disposition of the charge.

Uniform Guidelines on Employee Selection Procedures

The Guidelines require employers to maintain and have available for inspection records which will disclose the impact that tests and other selection procedures have upon employment opportunities of persons by identifiable race, sex, or ethnic group. If the selection process for a particular job has an adverse impact, information must be collected and records maintained until after the adverse impact has been eliminated and remains eliminated for at least two years.

Age Discrimination in Employment Act

1) Employers must maintain and retain for at least three years a record for each employee including name, address, date of birth, occupation, rate of pay, and compensation earned each week.

2) Personnel or employment records made in the regular course of business and relating to job applications, promotion or discharge, job orders submitted to employment agencies or labor organizations for recruitment, test papers, results of physical examinations considered in connection with personnel action, and advertisements, must be kept for at least one year.

3) Employee benefit plans must be kept for at least one year after termination.

4) Application forms for positions of a temporary nature must be kept for at least 90 days.

Executive Order 11246

1) Covered employers must maintain a written affirmative action program and supporting documentation, including the required workforce analysis and utilization evaluation.

2) Covered employers must also maintain other records and documents relating to compliance with the applicable EEO non-discrimination and affirmative action requirements, including records and documents on the nature and use of tests, the validation of tests, and test results.

Rehabilitation Act of 1973

1) Covered employers must maintain and update annually a written affirmative action program.

2) Covered employers must also maintain records regarding complaints and any action taken with respect thereto.

Vietnam-Era Veterans Readjustment Assistance Act of 1974

1) Covered employers must maintain and update annually a written affirmative action program.

2) Records regarding complaints and the action taken with respect thereto must also be maintained.

3) Periodic reports must be filed with local offices of state employment services regarding employment openings and hires.

Immigration Reform and Control Act of 1986

1) Employers must verify the employment eligibility of every new applicant.

2) Completed INS Form I-9 must be retained for three years after date of hire or one year after the employee is terminated, whichever is later.

3) It is recommended, although not required, that employers keep a copy of any document presented by the individual to comply with the verification requirements.

10.12 Overview of Preventive Measures

Of primary importance in preventing problems in the equal employment opportunity area is an understanding and awareness of the concepts and principles outlined in this Chapter. In addition, specific preventive measures have been suggested throughout the Chapter. The following is a brief overview and summary of those specific suggestions:

Hiring

1) Prepare a written job description for each position in your company, being specific as to essential job requirements.

2) Avoid sex- or age-based language in advertisements, e.g., "young girl," or "salesman."

3) Monitor your applicant flow, and if few women or members of minority groups are applying for jobs, consider special recruitment efforts.

4) Review your employment application forms, making sure they request only job-related information.

5) Train interviewers as to proper interviewing techniques, and assist them in becoming sensitive to discrimination issues.

6) Do not administer a medical examination until after a conditional offer of employment has been made. Administer physical examinations to all entering employees within designated categories, not just those with identifiable mental or physical limitations.

7) Avoid the use of general aptitude tests. If other tests are used, review them to ascertain whether they disqualify disproportionate numbers of women or members of minority groups. If so, make sure they test only job-related skills and abilities.

8) Review other employment prerequisites, particularly education and experience requirements, to make sure that you are not requesting more than is necessary for successful job performance.

Salaries

9) Review your wage schedules and classifications to verify that, unless there is a very good reason for a difference, men and women performing equal work are receiving equal pay.

Evaluations

10) When using subjective evaluations for promotions or other employment decisions, do the following:

a) Establish written standards for the decision to be made. These standards should be clear, objective, job-related, and as detailed as possible.

b) Require that evaluations be in writing, and that evaluations specify the extent to which the employee does or does not meet the written standards.

c) Make sure that the standards and the evaluation reflect and emphasize the significant aspects of job performance, and do not assign undue weight to minor elements of the job.

d) If at all possible, use subjective evaluations only in conjunction with other evaluative techniques.

e) Establish a review process whereby an employee can discuss his or her evaluation with a third party and can challenge any part of the evaluation he or she believes to be incorrect.

Discipline and Discharge

11) Develop and disseminate a personnel manual outlining work rules and disciplinary procedures.

12) Follow your stated procedures faithfully. Treat employees consistently, particularly as to discipline, unless a very good reason exists to justify inconsistent treatment.

13) Put all disciplinary actions in writing and state your reasons for each action taken. Ask disciplined employees to acknowledge the disciplinary action with their signatures.

14) Consider establishing a system of progressive discipline for certain offenses so that employees cannot claim they were not warned.

15) Establish a policy that discharges must be authorized by at least two people, *e.g.*, the employee's immediate supervisor and the personnel director.

16) Consider a policy whereby an employee about to be discharged is given the option of resigning.

Miscellaneous

17) Designate an EEO officer to receive complaints about harassment and other discriminatory conduct, and to coordinate your compliance efforts. Ideally, the EEO officer should be someone removed from the workplace, such as an individual in the personnel office.

18) Make sure that all employee complaints are promptly and thoroughly investigated, and that appropriate disciplinary action is taken against anyone engaging in discriminatory conduct.

19) Determine the types of reasonable accommodations which can and should be made for applicants and employees with disabilities. Such accommodations may include, for example, job restructuring, part-time or modified work schedules, making facilities readily accessible to disabled individuals, acquisition or modification of equipment or devices, modification of examinations, allowing disabled employees to take leave and the provision of qualified readers or interpreters. Document any studies made or any actions taken in this area.

20) Review your insurance programs and personnel policies to make sure that pregnancy is being treated the same as other temporary disabilities.

21) Monitor your statistics as to ratios of hire, promotion, layoff, discipline and discharge. Take action to remedy any deficiencies.

EEOC Proceedings

22) If a complaint is filed with the EEOC, undertake an immediate and thorough investigation.

23) Gather and preserve any and all records relating to a charge of discrimination.

24) Do not take any retaliatory action against an employee who has filed a complaint of discrimination.

25) Cooperate with the EEOC, but be careful not to allow the agency to take advantage of you.

General
    26) Any time you are in doubt about any aspect of equal employment opportunity law, consult with your EEO Officer, other company officials, or company counsel.

10.13 Conclusion
    The equal employment opportunity area has expanded rapidly in recent years, and now extends to virtually every part of the workplace and to every aspect of the employment relationship. It is essential that you take these matters seriously. Far too many companies fail to take EEO matters seriously until they get a complaint, and then it is often too late.
    One final word of caution. Because this is an area which has grown rapidly, many of the legal principles are still changing almost daily. This Chapter covers many of the important principles of equal employment opportunity law as they have been interpreted as of this date. The principles are likely, however, to continue to evolve. Moreover, it was impossible, in preparing this Chapter, to touch on *every* problem that might arise. Accordingly, if you are confronted with a situation you are not sure how to handle, talk to your supervisors. They can check with company counsel as to what to do. Generally, however, if you are caught in an emergency, rely on common sense and good judgment. By treating employees fairly and consistently, you should be able to resolve most problems that might arise, and will be able to protect your company and yourself from a charge of employment discrimination.

      Allen G. Siegel   Henry Morris, Jr.

Appendix A
MAJOR FEDERAL EQUAL EMPLOYMENT
OPPORTUNITY LAWS

1)   **Title VII of the Civil Rights of 1964.**

Title VII bans all discrimination in employment because of race, color, religion, sex, or national origin. It covers all terms and conditions of employment, and applies to all employers with fifteen (15) or more employees. It is administered and enforced by the Equal Employment Opportunity Commission (EEOC), and makes the employer responsible for *any* discrimination within its organization.

2)   **The Civil Rights Act of 1991.**

The Civil Rights Act of 1991 reverses a number of Supreme Court decisions, and expands the rights and remedies available to victims of discrimination under existing laws. For example, it gives all prevailing employment discrimination plaintiffs the right to recover expert witness fees as part of their costs, and reduces the plaintiff's burden or proof in "mixed motive" and "disparate impact" cases. Moreover, it gives victims of discrimination the right to a trial by jury and allows recovery of up to $300,000 in compensatory and punitive damages depending upon the size of the company.

3)   **The Equal Pay Act of 1963.**

The Equal Pay Act is a part of the Fair Labor Standards Act, and covers all employers covered by that Act. The Equal Pay Act requires that men and women performing substantially equal work in an establishment of the employer under substantially equal circumstances receive equal pay. This law is also administered and enforced by the EEOC.

4)   **The Age Discrimination in Employment Act.**

This Act applies to any employer with twenty (20) or more employees, and prohibits employment discrimination against individuals aged 40 and over. The EEOC is also responsible for the administration and enforcement of this law.

5)   The Civil Rights Act of 1866.

This Act, passed in the aftermath of the Civil War, prohibits any form of race-based discrimination. The Act applies to all employers without regard to the number of people they employ and is enforced by the federal courts upon the filing of a lawsuit. In 1987 the Supreme Court expanded the scope of this Act to protect individuals from discrimination because of their ancestry or ethnic characteristics. It thus held that Arabs and Jews are protected from discrimination under this Act.

6)   The Civil Rights Act of 1971.

Much of this Act requires some type of governmental involvement (*i.e.*, "state action") and is thus not applicable to the majority of private sector employers. However, one part of the Act, codified as 42 U.S.C. §1985(3), has been interpreted not to require state action. This statute prohibits conspiracies for the purpose of depriving a person, or a class of persons, of equal protection or of equal privileges and immunities under the law, and is enforced by the federal courts upon the filing of a lawsuit.

7)   The Rehabilitation Act of 1973.

This Act requires that any employer having federal contracts or subcontracts totaling more than $2,500 in any 12-month period take affirmative action to hire and advance qualified handicapped persons. The Act also applies to recipients of federal financial assistance, who are prohibited from discriminating against qualified handicapped individuals. Employers covered by the Act are required to make "reasonable accommodations" for the physical and mental limitations of handicapped applicants and employees, and if they have 50 or more employees and contracts worth at least $50,000, they are also required to prepare a written affirmative action program for the handicapped. The Rehabilitation Act is enforced by the Office of Federal Contract Compliance Programs (OFCCP), the Department of Health and Human Services (HHS), and each federal agency which gives out federal assistance.

8)	**The Vietnam-Era Veterans Readjustment Act of 1974.**

This Act also applies to employers having federal contracts and subcontracts, but in this case the value of the contracts must be more than $10,000 in any 12-month period to make the Act applicable. The Act requires covered government contractors to take affirmative action to hire and promote Vietnam-era veterans and disabled veterans of any era. Covered employers must list most job openings with the state or local employment office and, if they have 50 or more employees and a contract of $50,000 or more, they must also have a written affirmative action plan for veterans. This Act is administered and enforced by the OFCCP.

9)	**Executive Order 11246.**

This presidential directive requires equal employment opportunity and affirmative action by federal contractors and subcontractors having contracts of more than $10,000 in any 12-month period. The Order also applies to contractors and subcontractors performing under federally-aided construction contracts. Covered employers with at least 50 employees and contracts of at least $50,000 in any 12-month period must establish a written affirmative action plan that includes goals and timetables for the increased utilization of minority persons and of women. Executive Order 11246 is enforced by the OFCCP.

10)	**Immigration Reform and Control Act of 1986.**

The Immigration Reform and Control Act of 1986 (IRCA), which makes it illegal for employers knowingly to hire or continue to employ illegal aliens, at the same time prohibits discrimination based on national origin or citizenship status, if the discrimination is knowing and intentional.

11)	**Employee Polygraph Protection Act of 1988.**

This Act prohibits most private employers from using lie detector tests to screen applicants or to test current employees, except as part of an ongoing investigation of workplace theft or other incident causing economic injury to the employer, where there is reasonable suspicion that the employee to be tested was involved in the incident and had access to the property that is the subject of the investigation.

12)   **Americans with Disabilities Act.**

The Americans with Disabilities Act (ADA) prohibits discrimination in private employment against physically and mentally disabled people who, with or without "reasonable accommodation," are capable of performing essential job functions. The Act requires an employer to reasonably accommodate otherwise qualified employees or job applicants, unless to do so would cause the employer "undue hardship." The ADA, which also prohibits discrimination against disabled people with regard to public accommodations, transportation and telecommunications, prohibits both intentional discrimination and acts of omission which have the effect of discriminating.

13)   **Older Workers Benefits Protection Act.**

The Older Workers Benefits Protection Act, enacted in 1990, prohibits employers from discriminating in employee benefits on the basis of age. Under this Act, employers must provide older workers with benefits at least equal to those provided to younger workers, unless the employer can prove that the cost of providing an equal benefit is greater for an older worker than for a younger employee.

The Act also establishes minimum standards which must be met in order for individuals such as retirees to waive their rights under the ADEA. Among other things, they must be given at least twenty-one days to consider signing an early retirement agreement and at least seven days after signing an agreement to revoke it. They must also be advised by the employer in writing to consult an attorney before signing the agreement.

14)   **The Family and Medical Leave Act.**

This Act requires employers with 50 or more employees to allow eligible workers up to 12 weeks of unpaid leave during any 12-month period for one or more of the following:

(1) the birth of a son or daughter of the employee and in order to care for him or her;

(2) the placement of a child with the employee for adoption or foster care;

(3) to care for a spouse, child or parent with a serious health condition;

(4) because of the employee's own serious health condition which makes the employee unable to perform the functions of his or her job.

Appendix C
Pre-Employment Questions

The following discussion applies not only to questions on applications, but also to questions in an interview or elsewhere in the pre-employment context. The sample employment application following the list of questions illustrates the concepts discussed.

1. Age? Date of Birth?

Pre-employment questions about age should be avoided unless age is a *bona fide* occupational requirement, which is rare. Most states, however, have child labor laws, and certain jobs *(e.g.,* retail liquor sales) also require individuals to be of a minimum age. Accordingly, it is entirely appropriate to ask whether an applicant is at least a required minimum age.

2. Citizenship? Place of Birth?

Since the Immigration Reform and Control Act of 1986 prohibits discrimination based on citizenship status, questions as to citizenship are prohibited unless they are job-related. (If, for example, your company performs work related to national security, federal security laws might prohibit your having non-citizen employees in certain positions.) Under IRCA, however, you are prohibited from hiring an illegal alien. Accordingly, you *must* verify whether an applicant has the legal right to work in the United States.

Asking about an applicant's place of birth might likewise imply that you will discriminate on the basis of national origin or citizenship. Since an individual's place of birth is rarely related to how well he or she will perform a job, this question also should not be asked.

3. Color of Eyes? Hair?

These types of questions do not belong on a job application. Eye and hair color are almost never job-related and may tend to identify individuals as to race or national origin.

4. Height? Weight?

Questions about height or weight should be asked *only* if height or weight is clearly related to job performance. The fact that such questions are asked might imply that there is a minimum height or weight requirement for the job, and such prerequisites have been clearly established to have an adverse impact on women and individuals of certain national origins. Furthermore, minimum height and weight requirements are very rarely found to be job-related. (Courts have rejected, for example, the assumption that height is related to physical strength or forcefulness.)

5. Physical or Mental Handicap?

An employer may ask an applicant to describe or demonstrate how, with or without reasonable accommodation, the applicant will be able to perform specific job functions. Such a request, however, should be made of all applicants in the same job category. An employer may not make a pre-employment inquiry during an interview or on an application form regarding an applicant's disability or perceived disability. For example, if the employer is hiring someone who must drive a car, the employer may ask if the applicant has a current driver's license, but may *not* ask whether the applicant has a visual impairment. An employer may ask an applicant with an apparent disability to describe or demonstrate how the applicant will perform specific job functions, regardless of whether the employer makes such a request of all applicants in the job category. For example, an individual with one leg who applies for a position as a washing machine repairman may be asked to demonstrate that, or explain how, with or without reasonable accommodation, he would be able to transport himself and his tools down basement stairs. On the other hand, if an apparent disability will not interfere with or prevent the performance of a job-related function, the employer may only request a demonstration or explanation by the applicant if the employer routinely makes such a request of all applicants in the same job category. And, whether or not the apparent disability will interfere with the performance of a job-related function, an employer may *not* inquire as to the nature or severity of the applicant's disability.

Pre-employment application forms should not be used which ask an applicant to list or check any of the impairments which he or she might have. Moreover, applicants should not be asked about any prognosis regarding a condition or whether the applicant will need special leave or treatment because of a disability. On the other hand, it is permissible to state the attendance requirements of the job and inquire whether the applicant can meet these requirements.

6. Marital Status?

Federal law does not prohibit discrimination on the basis of marital status. But, the laws of several of the states specifically prohibit employers from discriminating on this basis.

Whether or not a person is married is rarely relevant to successful job performance. Moreover, asking a woman whether she is married may raise suspicions about the many stereotypes discussed earlier in this Chapter. Therefore, this type of question should *not* be asked on a pre-employment basis. If the information is necessary for insurance or other fringe benefit purposes, the question may be asked, but only after an offer of employment has been made and accepted.

7. Maiden Name? Prior Married Name? Spouse's Name?

All of these questions might be considered indirect inquiries as to marital status. In addition, this type of question sometimes raises an inference of discrimination on the basis of religion or national origin, and is not relevant to job performance.

On the other hand, it is permissible to ask whether an applicant has ever been known by another name if this information is necessary in order to check an applicant's references or prior work history.

8. Education?

The permissibility of education *requirements* is discussed in the section of this Chapter entitled *Non-Medical Tests and Other Employment Prerequisites.* Generally, how much education may be required for a particular position depends on the extent to which education is related to successful job performance. Pre-employment inquiries as to education should be similarly limited. If a position does not require a high school diploma, for example, information about high school and college should not be requested. Even if you do not use this information in making an employment decision, the appearance of such questions on an employment application, where unnecessary, might discourage otherwise qualified applicants.

Since questions as to education should be tailored to particular jobs, it is a good idea to have different employment applications for different categories of employees. The sample employment application form included in this Appendix contains suggested alternative education questions for (a) manual labor positions, (b) administrative or clerical positions, and (c) executive positions.

Even if an education requirement is job-related and subject to inquiry, there is another pitfall of which you should be aware, *i.e.,* asking about graduation dates. Requesting the date an applicant graduated from grade school or high school is an indirect way of ascertaining his or her age, and age inquiries are generally impermissible. If it is relevant whether or not the individual graduated from a particular educational institution, it is preferable simply to ask "Did you graduate?"

9.   Prior Work Experience?

Prior work experience is relevant to an individual's qualifications for a position, and questions intended to elicit this kind of information are certainly permissible. There is also nothing wrong with asking about the reason for leaving prior employment, or asking for a description of specific duties on previous jobs.

10.   Arrest or Conviction Record?

As discussed under *Non-Medical Tests and Other Employment Prerequisites,* an arrest may never legally be used to disqualify someone for a job. As a result, the EEOC has taken the position that pre-employment questions about an applicant's arrest record are illegal.

A conviction, on the other hand, *may* be used as basis for denying employment, if it is related to performance of the particular job. (See *Non-Medical Tests and Other Employment Prerequisites.*) For example, an employer is not required to consider for employment as a cashier a person who has been convicted of embezzlement. Likewise, a hotel would not be required to consider a convicted burglar for the position of porter, where he or she would have access to the rooms and personal belongings of guests.

If a conviction might be relevant to positions within your establishment, you will want to include a question about convictions on your application form. If so, you should also ask for an explanation of any "yes" answer.

11.   Military Record?

Questions about military service are permissible, to the extent that they seek to obtain information about relevant experience and/or training for a job. Questions about the type of discharge received, however, can raise problems. As discussed in more detail under *Non-Medical Tests and Other Employment Prerequisites,* aless-than-honorable discharge may be similar to either an arrest or a conviction, depending on the surrounding facts. Only a "dishonorable discharge" is *always* an indication of convicted guilt, however, and thus it is probably advisable to limit an application question to "Did you receive a dishonorable discharge?" As with a conviction question, the applicant should be told that the dishonorable discharge will not be an absolute bar to employment, and should be given an opportunity to explain the nature and seriousness of the underlying offense.

12.   Available for Saturday Work?

As discussed in more detail under **Accommodating Religious Practices,** the rules regarding religious discrimination require an employer to make "reasonable accommodations" for an employee's religious observances or practices, where it can do so without undue hardship. Several religions prohibit their adherents from working on Saturday, a normal work day for many businesses. Unless the nature of your business is such that it would cause you undue hardship to accommodate an individual who could not work on Saturday, this question should not be asked since it might tend to discourage such individuals from applying for a job, and might leave the impression that you will unlawfully base an employment decision on the response. (The same principle would, of course, also apply to other days of the week, including Sunday.)

You may, however, state your normal work hours, and without inquiring as to religious practices, ask whether the applicant is *otherwise* available to work these hours. The question of accommodation can then be addressed after a preliminary offer of employment has been made.

13. Credit Records (Charge Accounts? Own Your Home? Own A Car?)

Statistically, certain minority groups are at lower economic levels than whites. As a result, using an applicant's credit record or home ownership as a factor in an employment decision may have an adverse impact on such minorities. Further, an individual's credit record or home ownership is rarely relevant to his or her ability to perform a job.

On the other hand, ownership of an automobile *can* be job-related. Where an employee is required to use his or her personal automobile in the course of employment, such as for deliveries or sales, a question about car ownership is clearly job-related, and may be asked. Similarly, it is permissible to inquire whether an applicant has transportation to work, particularly if your establishment is not located near public transportation.

14. Bondable?

Individuals with arrest or conviction records often find it difficult or impossible to obtain fidelity bonds. As discussed earlier, minority groups often have a disproportionately high number of members with arrests and convictions, and as a result, requiring applicants to be bondable may have an adverse impact on minorities. This means that you should *only* ask applicants if they are bondable if the job for which they are applying requires bonding.

15. Garnishment Record?

Again, statistics show that members of certain minority groups have had their wages garnished more often than others. It might also be assumed, from a practical standpoint, that an individual who has a prior garnishment record will be more likely than an individual without such a record to have his or her wages garnished again. However, although wage garnishments are an administrative inconvenience for employers, this inconvenience is probably not sufficient to permit prior garnishments to be a job-related disqualification. Consequently, this question should not be asked.

[Sample Employment Application]
[Name of Company]

[Name of Company] is an equal opportunity employer. [Name of Company] seeks and employs qualified persons in all job classifications and administers all personnel actions without discrimination on the basis of race, color, religion, sex, age, national origin, handicap, veteran status or any other unlawful bases. Disabled applicants may request any needed accommodation to participate in the application process.

EMPLOYMENT APPLICATION
(PLEASE PRINT PLAINLY)

Date: _____

Name: _____

_____

      First   Middle   Last

Present Address:

_____

      Street   City   State

Last Previous Address:

_____

      Street   City   State

Social Security Number:

_____

Applying for Position as:

_____

When Available:

_____

431

Are you 18 years of age or older? ☐ Yes ☐ No

Are you legally entitled to work in the United States? ☐ Yes ☐ No

Person to notify in case of accident _____

Telephone No. _____

REFERENCES

Name two people who have known you at least two years (do not include relatives, former employers, personnel of this company, or persons whose affiliation may reflect your race, religion, or natural origin).

Name:_____

Address:_____

Business &
Position:_____

Telephone (if known):_____

Name:_____

Address:_____

Business &
Position:_____

Telephone (if known):_____

****

[OPTIONAL]

School activities —— honorary, social, sports, etc.*

_____

_____

_____

What positions of leadership or responsibility have you held in school, work, or elsewhere?

_____

_____

_____

Of what civic, technical, trade, professional or other organizations are you are member?*

_____

_____

_____

Publications or patents

_____

_____

_____

Public Assembly Facility Law

Any outside business activities? Describe.

_____

_____

_____

List foreign languages ☐ read   ☐ spoken   ☐ written

_____

_____

_____

*Please exclude any organization the name or character of which may reveal the race, religion, or national origin of its members.

believes that a union has committed an unfair labor practice, the employer may file a charge.

The NLRB decides whether an unfair labor practice has actually been committed. The Board is also responsible for holding secret ballot elections among employees when requested to do so.

11.01 The Union Drive to Organize Your Employees

1) The Roots of an Organizing Drive

Why does a union generally seek to organize a company, and why are certain employees receptive to these efforts? Employee dissatisfaction is one of the main reasons unionization drives begin. Workers frequently are concerned about job security, wages, fringe benefits, communication with management and general working conditions, all of which are within the control of their employer. Many times wages are not the chief issue.

Employees are often concerned about the quality of their supervision and the way they are treated by their first-line supervisor such as yourself. Ineffective supervisors are often more likely to contribute to unionization than the paid union organizers themselves. On the other hand, many union organizational campaigns have been stopped at their inception through the efforts of a single first-line supervisor who was highly respected and well-liked by his/her workers. Therefore, it is very important for you to treat your employees fairly, to make them feel appreciated and secure, and to make yourself accessible to them so that they will feel free to discuss their problems with you.

Although there are many important characteristics of a good supervisor, listed below are some of the major characteristics which have been shown to minimize the chances of unionization:

- A good supervisor treats his/her employees with *respect* and *dignity*.
- A good supervisor is *accessible*. The employees feel free to discuss their problems with him/her.
- A good supervisor is *impartial*, and does not show favoritism.
- A good supervisor is *firm* but *fair*. He/she maintains reasonable discipline but does not punish unfairly.

- A good supervisor has *good communication* skills: he/she communicates clearly and accurately, asks questions, and listens.
- A good supervisor is *responsive*: he/she provides feedback, shows appreciation for an employee's good work, rewards initiative, and gives credit where it is due.
- A good supervisor is *honest* and *clear*: he/she keeps employees informed, gives them clear and advance notice of changes, and does not make promises he/she doesn't keep.

2) Early Warning Signals of Unionization

Despite your best efforts, however, a union may attempt to organize your employees. Early warning signs may include the following: You may notice workers talking in hushed tones with one another. Possibly you may hear rumors of union activity, find union literature lying around, or see strangers talking to employees outside the building. You may also notice that employees will communicate less with you. You should not bring up the subject of the union with your workers at this stage. Instead, pay attention and keep your superiors informed about the union's activities. It is important, however, to avoid actual surveillance of the employees or creating the impression of surveillance. If an employee wants to discuss the union with you or ask questions about it, make note of the questions asked, but defer all answers and discussions until you have spoken to your superiors. Find out the answers and get back to the employee as soon as possible. Some guidelines about what you can and cannot say and do in these circumstances appear in Section II(F) below.

3) Handbilling, Solicitation and Card Signing

Typically, during the early phases of an organizational campaign, the union will begin distributing pro-union literature and soliciting employees to join the union. Before union activity starts, the company, on advice of its attorneys, may post rules governing union solicitation of employees and the distribution of literature to them. Employers should be cautious about initiating such rules while the union is organizing, because the Board may consider it evidence of the employer's intent to interfere with the employees' right to organize.

The NLRB has established guidelines on so-called "no solicitation" and "no distribution" rules which balance a union's organizational rights with an employer's management and property rights. It is important for you to be aware of these guidelines because you may be enforcing the company's rules.

Generally, an employer may prohibit the solicitation of union membership during the time in which employees are supposed to be performing job duties, because union activity while employees are actually working obviously interferes with their work. However, the employer may not prohibit solicitation by employees, even on company property, during periods when the employees are not working, such as lunch breaks, rest periods, and coffee breaks, even though the employees may be paid for these time periods. The Board currently considers rules which prohibit employees from engaging in solicitation during working time presumptively valid. However, rules prohibiting solicitation during "working hours" or "company time" are presumed to be invalid, because they could be deemed to cover time when the employees are not working. Therefore, to ensure that a "no solicitation" rule will not be considered unlawful on its face, the employer could incorporate in the rule a clear statement that the restriction does not apply during break periods and mealtimes, or other periods during the workday when employees are properly not engaged in performing their work tasks.

"No solicitation" rules generally are valid only if they are applied against all solicitations, including those for charitable, religious, civic or similar purposes. The Board may permit some limited exceptions for charitable solicitations identified by the company, but the company should consult with counsel before relying on such exceptions. Therefore, if your company has a "no solicitation" rule, be sure to enforce it even-handedly and at all times, not just during an organizational campaign.

The guidelines on "no distribution" rules are somewhat different. The employer may prohibit distribution of union literature and handbills in *working areas* during both working and nonworking time. A rule prohibiting distribution is presumed valid unless it extends to activities in nonworking areas or to activities during time in which employees are not actually working. The employer may restrict distribution in nonworking areas, however, if necessary to maintain production or to prevent safety hazards. Again, be on the lookout for union organizers distributing literature and report it to your superiors immediately. However, as with "no solicitation" rules, "no distribution" rules must also be enforced consistently against distribution of both union and non-union literature.

Valid "no solicitation" or "no distribution" rules will generally not be invalidated solely because they are published at the inception of an organizing drive. However, an employer should, if possible, implement such rules before organizing activities begin at its place of operation. If such activity has already begun, the employer should implement universally applicable "no solicitation" an "no distribution" rules which do not refer specifically to the union. Be aware that non-employees can be prohibited from soliciting or distributing literature on company premises at all times, as long as there are other methods of communication available to the union to reach employees, and as long as the prohibition is enforced consistently. However, off-duty employees generally may return to non-working areas of the company to solicit and handbill, unless their activity interferes with production, discipline or safety.

Along with distributing literature and urging employees to support the union, organizers typically will be trying to gather proof that a majority of your employees support the union. Under the NLRA, an employer must bargain with the union when it in fact represents a majority of the employees in an appropriate unit and when it makes a demand upon the employer. The union commonly attempts to achieve "majority status" through union authorization cards, signed by a majority of employees. By signing one of these authorization cards, an employee usually joins the union, designates it as his/her exclusive bargaining representative, and authorizes the employer to deduct union dues from his/her wages. In addition, the union may attempt to demonstrate the extent of its representation by union membership applications, petitions, proxies, and other documentary evidence.

4) Union Demand for Recognition

After collecting proof of support from employees, the union may demand that the employer recognize it as the exclusive bargaining representative of the employees. Usually, the union sends the company a letter claiming that it represents a majority of employees and demanding that the employer immediately recognize the union as the employees' bargaining agent. An employer may legally refuse to recognize a union at this point, and instead demand that the union prove its claim of majority status in an appropriate bargaining unit through an NLRB-conducted election. The company must exercise caution in this regard and should not meet with the union until it has consulted its attorneys.

If a union organizer contacts you, demanding recognition or seeking to show authorization cards to you, refer him/her to your superior or the company's labor relations official. Unless you have express authorization from your company, you generally should follow these important rules:

(1) *DO NOT* acknowledge that the union represents a majority of your employees. Once recognition is granted, your company cannot reverse its position and decline recognition. The union is "in" and there can be no election.

(2) *DO NOT* agree to look at any proof of majority support which the union offers, such as authorization cards or membership applications. Examination of cards or applications may be viewed as tacit approval and may preclude the employees and the company from having an election.

(3) *DO NOT* ask to be shown any proof of majority support.

(4) *DO NOT* agree to have a "neutral" party (such as a member of the clergy or a mediator or arbitrator) examine the offered proof of majority status. Once a third party informs you that the union has a majority, you may be precluded from having an election.

(5) *DO NOT* poll your employees to see if they signed authorization cards for the union.

(6) *DO NOT* decline recognition, ask for an election, and then commit unfair labor practices in an effort to destroy the union's strength. Firings and layoffs of known union activists and threats of economic retaliation against supporters of the union may result in the Board setting aside an election and directing the employer to bargain with the union.

WHAT TO DO? The proper response when a union organizer seeks recognition, either by letter or in person, is generally to refer him/her to your superiors who may advise the organizer that: "We must decline to extend recognition to your labor organization unless and until it is certified by the National Labor Relations Board in a manner appropriate for collective bargaining." *SAY NO MORE.* Refuse to accept any documents from the union, such as authorization cards.

5) Petition for Election

If the company refuses to extend recognition voluntarily, the union will probably file a petition for an election with a Regional Office of the NLRB. In fact, many unions file a petition without first making a demand for recognition. The petition will describe the group of employees the union is seeking to represent, such as all office clerical employees, all drivers, all production and maintenance employees or all sales personnel. For the petition to be valid, the union must show the Board that it has the support of at least 30% of the employees in the group   it   wants to represent.

Once a union has petitioned the Board for an election, the employer may consent to the holding of an election. This is recommended when you are sure that the union does not have the support of a majority of your workers and you want to force the issue before the union has a chance to improve its position. If, however, there are contested issues (such as whether the group of employees the union seeks to represent is an appropriate bargaining unit), the Board will hold a hearing to resolve these issues. Usually, the election will be held about six to eight weeks after the petition is filed, although some elections are delayed for longer periods of time.

6) The Election Campaign

In the one- or two-month period before the election, an election "campaign" will take place. Both the company and the union will be trying to convince employees of the wisdom of their respective positions. Once again, the Board has rules governing the conduct of employers and unions during the campaign.

You, as a supervisor, may be expected to support the company's position and you may be asked to be a campaigner for your company. This may mean walking a tightrope between legitimate campaigning and improper conduct.

You may wonder why you must be careful about what you say and do during an election campaign. The law requires that nothing interfere with the employees' free choice in deciding whether they want a union. If the union loses an election, it may file objections to the election with the Board, charging that the employer or a supervisor acted improperly during the campaign or at the time of the election. If the Board finds that the conduct of a supervisor interfered with the employees' freedom in deciding about unionization, it may order a new election. Elections may be set aside where the employer threatens the employees with ominous consequences if they vote the union in, promises employees certain benefits if they vote no, disciplines or discharges union supporters or interrogates employees about their union activities and sentiments.

In cases of very serious violations, the Board can order the employer to bargain with the union, even though the union lost the election. This penalty is imposed when the employer's improper conduct so undermined the union's support that a fair election is deemed impossible. Wholesale firings or elimination of existing benefits are examples of conduct which may result in an order to bargain without a rerun election.

Since the stakes are high, you should be careful to follow the rules in this Chapter and the other instructions that your company and its counsel give you. Remember that often during the campaign it is not necessarily what you say but how you say it that counts. Generally, you are entitled to state your position and explain the position of your company. There are, however, some limitations on what you can say during an election campaign. Your job will not be difficult if you remember that the Board rules are meant to protect employees from interference while still being fair to you and the company.

You *may not* coerce employees or interfere with their right to organize by threatening them with loss of their jobs or a change in their working conditions because of their union sympathies. Nor may you promise them any benefit if they will agree to vote against the union.

Be aware that seemingly innocent statements may later be construed by the Board to be veiled threats. Whether a statement is construed as a "threat" or a "prediction" depends on the context in which the statement is made, including the extent to which the company has control over effectuating the statement, the extent to which the statement is based on a reasonable assessment of the facts, and whether the statement is trivial and made without a background of union animus. For example, predictions that the company might not negotiate with the union, that employees will lose wages or their jobs if the union wins, or that the company will discontinue business for reasons other than economic necessity, many lead the NLRB to set aside the election or order the company to bargain despite a union defeat. Just bear in mind that you have the right to express your opinion of unionization in general and to predict unfavorable consequences which you believe may develop from union representation as long as the predictions are based on reasonable, objective facts, beyond the control of the company, which convey the employer's belief as to demonstrably probable consequences of unionization.

Although the Board in the past has overturned elections on the basis of an employer's misrepresentations during a union campaign, the Board's current policy is that it generally will not probe into the truth or falsity of campaign statements and it will not set an election aside on the basis of misleading statements, including misstatements of fact, misstatements of law, as well as misrepresentations of actions before the Board, such as misstatements that the employer has been the subject of unfair labor charges. This is because the union and the company generally have the opportunity to correct such misstatements. Of course, it is advisable for employers and supervisors to be accurate and tell the truth when discussing union matters, as well as other work-related matters, with employees. Moreover, it is important to ensure that campaign documents are not falsified. Where the union or employer makes a representation in a deceptive manner, such as in the case of forged documents, and employees cannot discern that a misstatement has been made, thereby rendering attempts at correction futile, the Board is likely to set aside the election. Also, the Board in the past has sustained objections to an election where the misstatement is made just prior to the election. If a union misstatement comes to your attention, first discuss it with superiors. Then, with your superiors' approval, point the misstatement out to employees and correct it. It is a good idea to keep records of *all* of your conversations with employees concerning union matters, as this will avoid misquotation later. If an employee has a question which you are not sure how to answer, withhold comment until you have had a chance to discuss it with your superiors. Find out the answer and get back to the employee as soon as you possibly can.

During the election campaign, as always, you must also be careful to treat your employees fairly. The law forbids you from discriminating against employees because of their union beliefs or membership. You are still permitted to discipline employees for poor performance and misconduct, but you must be careful to enforce company rules fairly. *Do not* enforce rules vigorously against union sympathizers and leniently against antiunion employees. You should discipline employees in the same manner as you did before the union drive began. It is critical for you to keep good records of any disciplinary action taken against employees. In this way, you will be able to justify your actions should they be called into question later.

A. What You Can Say and Do:

You generally are free to make many comments about unions and unionization as long as you do not threaten employees or otherwise coerce them. Here are some examples of statements which are typically allowed during election campaigns and will not be considered unfair labor practices. You can tell employees that:

(a) You are opposed to the union and you prefer to deal with employees directly on day-to-day problems, rather than through an outside organization or third party.

(b) You or another member of management are always willing to talk with employees about any matter which they wish to discuss.

(c) No union can obtain more from an employer than it is capable of giving or willing to give in bargaining.

(d) Although the company would be obligated to bargain in good faith with the union if it gets elected, no union can make an employer agree to anything it does not wish to. The duty to bargain with a union does not compel the company to come to an agreement on the union's terms.

(e) Present benefits can be bargained away by the union in exchange for something that it is interested in, such as the check-off of union dues.

(f) There are disadvantages that may result from belonging to a union, such as paying initiation fees, dues, fines, and other assessments.

(g)   If the union tries to force the company to give in to its demands by calling an economic strike, the company can *permanently* replace the economic strikers with new employees.

(h)   If a strike is called by the union, striking employees lose their pay checks but the union rarely loses anything since it does not necessarily pay strike benefits. Even if it pays such benefits, they generally are not very generous. During a strike, union officials still get paid. (Do not convey the impression that a strike is inevitable, however.)

(i)   The union may fine members who work or fail to picket during a strike.

(j)   If the union gets in and labor problems follow, the company *might* lose investors and customers, and that means that everyone in the company may suffer.

(k)   Union or no union, the company will continue to be fair with employees and will try to give them the wages and benefits they deserve.

(l)   No union can guarantee jobs or job security. Collective bargaining agreements almost always state that employees may be fired for just cause.

(m)   The union is not required to take every grievance to arbitration, even if an employee wants his/her grievance arbitrated.

(n)   If the union wins, every employee might be forced to join the union or pay union dues (except in "right-to-work" states).

(o)   Employees are not required to vote for the union in the election just because they signed a union authorization card or application for membership. They are free to vote against the union in the secret ballot election.

(p)   The law guarantees employees the right to resist a union.

You generally may also take any of the following actions during an election campaign:

(1)   Distribute articles containing information about unions in general or the union at your company in particular.

(2)   Enforce plant rules impartially and in accordance with customary practice, irrespective of an employee's membership or activity in the union.

(3)   Lay off, discipline, and discharge for legitimate non-discriminatory reasons, as long as your action follows your normal practice and is done without regard to union membership. You should check with your superior *before* you discipline or discharge an employee.

(4)   Enforce rules requiring that solicitation of union membership or discussion of union affairs be conducted outside of the time during which employees are actually performing job duties. But remember that both union and non-union solicitors must be treated alike.

(5)   Reply to union attacks on company policy and actively campaign in a lawful manner against the union seeking representation.

(6)   Discuss union matters with an employee or small groups of employees, even on company time, at the employees' work station, in the cafeteria, or at any other neutral spot. Be sure not to speak to them in a setting which might be intimidating, such as your office. The Board considers the technique of calling employees into the employer's office individually to urge them to reject the union, in itself, to be conduct calculated to interfere with the employees' free choice.

(7)   If you already have a union, and a rival union is campaigning, state, with supporting reasons, which union the company prefers to deal with. (You must be careful *not* to extend active support to one of the unions, however.)

(8)   Urge all employees to vote in the election. Tell employees that the union will win if it receives the support of a majority of those employees who *actually vote* in the election. This means that not voting may increase the chances of the union winning the election.

(9)   Tell employees that the company would like them to vote against the union.

(10)   Discuss the benefits that employees now enjoy. Remind them that they received these benefits without a union and that they do not need a union now to keep or improve them.

(11)   Tell employees about any experiences you have had with unions.

(12)   Tell employees anything you know about the union or its officers.

(13)   Tell employees about any untrue or misleading statements made by a union organizer or in union handouts. You should give employees the correct facts.

(14)   Tell employees about known racketeering or any other undesirable activities of the union.

(15)   Discuss the negative aspects of the union, its policies, leaders, and record.

(16)   Tell employees about the NLRB's election procedures, the importance of voting, and the secrecy of the ballot.

(17)   Tell employees where their union dues go, such as to pay for the high salaries and expense accounts of union officials.

(18)   Compare employees' wages, benefits, and working conditions with those of workers at other companies, whether unionized or not.

(19)   Tell employees that when they select a bargaining representative, the relationship that existed between them and management will not be the same as it had been before the union's arrival.

B. What You Cannot Say or Do:

As you can see from the following list of prohibited actions, the type of conduct which is forbidden could interfere with employees' freedom to make a decision by intimidating or coercing them to reject the union or "buying" their vote. The Board has ordered rerun elections where supervisors said or did these things. Therefore, you should *NOT:*

(1) Announce that the company will not deal with the union if the union wins the election.

(2) Threaten that the plant will close down or move or that operations will be reduced if the union is elected.

(3) Threaten loss of jobs, reduced pay, or elimination of any privilege or benefit now enjoyed due to the union's election.

(4) Threaten or actually discharge, discipline, or lay off employees because of their activities on behalf of the union.

(5) Threaten, through a third party, any of the above acts of interference or let a third party commit any of them.

(6) Use intimidating or coercive language which may discourage employees from joining or supporting the union.

(7) State that a strike is inevitable if the union wins the election. It is generally lawful to say that a strike *might* be called if the union and the company cannot agree to terms of a contract. Just don't say that a strike *will* be called.

(8) Promise or give employees a pay increase, promotion, benefit, or special favor if they stay out of or vote against the union.

(9) Take any actions that adversely affect an employee's job or rate of pay because of union participation.

(10) Discipline pro-union employees for misconduct while permitting anti-union employees to go unpunished for the same conduct.

(11) Prohibit employees from soliciting for union membership during time when they are not performing job duties, or interfere with employees who distribute union literature in nonworking areas during time in which they are not working.

(12) Discriminate against employees who support the union by assigning them undesirable work because of their union activities, while assigning preferred work to anti-union employees.

(13) Make work assignments for the purpose of causing union sympathizers to quit their jobs.

(14) Deviate from company policy in any way for the purpose of getting rid of a union supporter.

(15) Transfer employees to less desirable positions because of their union affiliation.

(16) Favor anti-union employees over pro-union employees because of their union activities.

(17) Assign work or transfer employees in order to separate pro-union employees from those you believe are not interested in joining the union.

(18) Spy on union meetings, for example, by parking across the street from the meeting place in order to watch employees.

(19) Conduct yourself in any way which would indicate to employees that you are watching them to determine whether they are participating in union activities.

(20) Ask employees whether they or any other employees have attended union meetings.

(21) Ask employees whether they belong to the union or have signed up for the union.

(22) Ask employees for an expression of their thoughts about the union or its officers.

(23) Ask employees how they intend to vote in the election.

(24) Ask job applicants about their union sentiments.

(25) Make anti-union statements during a hiring interview that might show your preference for a non-union employee.

(26) Select employees to be laid off with the intention of weakening the union's strength.

(27) Give financial support or other assistance to a union or to employees for either supporting or opposing the union.

(28) Ask employees about the internal affairs of unions (for example, what happens at meetings). Note that employees may tell you about it of their own accord. It is not an unfair labor practice for you to listen, but do not ask questions to gain such information.

(29) Call employees into your office to discuss union matters or make threatening statements under any circumstances.

(30) Visit the homes of employees for the purpose of urging them to reject the union.

(31) Encourage employees to revoke their union authorization cards.

(32) Distribute forms to use in revoking union authorization cards.

(33) Start or encourage a petition against the union.

(34) Suggest the formation of an employee committee to discuss terms and conditions of employment directly with the company.

(35) Interfere with the right of employees to wear union buttons, hats, or t-shirts. In certain circumstances where the employee has contact with the public and the button, hat, or shirt is conspicuous and conflicts with a uniform, you may by able to limit the wearing of union buttons, but you should check with your superiors and counsel first.

(36) Force employees to wear "vote no" or "no union" buttons. However, you may leave this type of button in a box and allow employees who want to wear one to pick one up, provided that the box is placed where you cannot watch which employees choose buttons.

(37) Reproduce and distribute to eligible voters sample NLRB ballots with the "NO" box checked.

The above list is not all-inclusive, but it does describe some of the types of conduct which are prohibited. In addition to these prohibitions, there is a rule known as the "24 hour rule," which prohibits both the company and the union from making campaign speeches on company time to a group of employees within 24 hours of the election.

If the rule is violated, the Board will set aside an election victory of the side supported by the speaker and order a new election. The rule does not prohibit, within the 24-hour period, the dissemination of election documents or the making of campaign speeches, either on or off company property, if employee attendance is voluntary and on their own time.

All these "don'ts" basically fall into six categories of things you should not do:

(a) Threaten
(b) Promise
(c) Spy
(d) Ask employees how they will vote or how they feel about the union
(e) Discriminate, or
(f) Alter or deface Board literature.

If you remember these six "don'ts," you should have no trouble obeying the law.

C. What the Union Cannot Do:

Just as the union can file objections with the Board about conduct by you and the company during a campaign, the company can file objections to improper union conduct. A union's improper conduct during an election campaign may warrant a rerun election if the union wins and the Board finds that the union violated the law. You should be familiar with what union officials, organizers, and other union agents cannot do so that you can immediately report union misconduct to your superiors.

Specifically, union officials and organizers, and their agents cannot:

(1) Threaten employees who refuse to join or assist the union or who refuse to sign authorization cards.

(2) Waive initiation fees only for those employees who sign authorization cards or otherwise commit themselves to supporting the union. (However, the union *can* promise to waive initiation fees if this applies to *all* voters, and not just to union supporters.)

(3) Promise a monetary reward for each signed authorization card an employee produces or each fellow employee he or she convinces to join a picket line.

(4)   Make promises or give gifts to employees that are contingent on how they vote in the election. Gifts are allowed, however, if used solely to promote attendance at union meetings.

(5)   Distribute fake or forged campaign materials, which are not recognizable as campaign propaganda, so as to confuse voters.

(6)   Distribute sample NLRB ballots with the "YES" box marked.

(7)   Disregard an employer's "no distribution" or "no solicitation" rules.

(8)   Hold meetings on company working time without permission from the company.

(9)   Predict or threaten loss of jobs if the union loses the election.

(10)   Make racial appeals to employees to inflame prejudices.

(11)   Picket the company, for the purpose of gaining recognition, for more than 30 days without filing a petition with the Board.

Note that unions *can* do some things that employers are expressly prohibited from doing. For example, unions generally may poll employees during nonworking hours and may also promise employees substantial benefits if the union wins the election. Why can the union make promises while you and the company cannot? The union organizer is like a salesperson; he/she has no power to grant the benefits promised. As a supervisor, you do have the authority to give employees benefits. Employees know this and, according to the Board, this rule is meant to make sure that employee votes are not "bought" with promises from their employer.

7) Election Day

The NLRB has specific rules governing conduct on the day of the election as well as during the campaign period. At the election site only the Board officials, employee observers (an equal number appointed by both the company and the union) and voters are permitted to be present. During the balloting, *no one* from the company or the union and no employee is allowed to engage in any last minute electioneering among the employees entering the area to vote or standing in line to cast

459

their ballots. A mistake by you at the very end of an election campaign may cause months of hard work and effective campaigning to go down the drain, because the Board may overturn an election that is tainted at the ballot box by last minute electioneering. And, of course, report to your superiors immediately if you observe any union electioneering at the polls.

Once the voting has been completed, an official from the Board will open the ballot box, count the secret ballots in front of representatives from the company, the union, and the employees and inform all present of the election results. Hopefully, if the company opposed the union, with the help of your effective campaigning and adherence to all these guidelines, a majority of the ballots cast will be marked "NO" and the union will have been defeated in its attempt to unionize your company (at least for a period of one year, after which it can start its drive all over again). If, however, a majority of the ballots are marked "YES," then the union is "in" (assuming the count stands up after post-election objections) and the Board will certify it as the exclusive bargaining representative of your employees.

Following an election, any party has the right to file post-election objections to the conduct of the election or the conduct of other parties or of Board agents which allegedly prejudiced the proceedings. Such objections must be filed within seven days after the tally of the ballots has been furnished to the parties. The Board's regional office investigates any objections and may schedule a hearing if it determines that substantial issues are presented. If a party's objections are sustained, the Board will usually set aside the election and direct that a new one be held. In the event of serious misconduct by the company which is inherently destructive of employee free choice, however, the Board may order the company to bargain with the union, even if the union lost the election.

8) "Corporate" Campaigns

In recent years, many unions have abandoned traditional organizing techniques for more creative approaches to increasing union membership. One of these is the "corporate campaign." Corporate campaigns are an attempt to generate outside pressure on employers by appealing to the public. To do so, the union attacks the company's public image in a manner that goes beyond the central labor-management dispute.

The union may scrutinize the company's financial profile, its officers and directors, court records, land and property records, suppliers and customers, and assemble a full picture of the company's vulnerabilities. Then pressure is applied on several fronts through a variety of approaches including consumer boycotts, direct communication with stockholders, and public demonstrations. Embarrassing company executives by using such tactics as picketing their homes or mounting personal attacks is another way of pressuring the target employer. A corporate campaign may also entail the filing of charges with the NLRB, OSHA, EPA or other governmental agencies which regulate the company, or lodging complaints with state and federal legislators and officials. It may also include agitating Wall Street in an effort to reduce company stock prices, or exposing trade secrets and other confidential information of the company. The goal of a corporate campaign is to force the company into a defensive position while the union carries out its organizing campaign.

The National Labor Relations Act offers only limited protection against corporate campaigns, and efforts to obtain such relief may run into First Amendment protection and federal preemption issues. An employer's legal strategies in confronting a corporate campaign are limited but may include, in some instances, claims for tortious interference with business relationships, trespass, or defamation. Public relations can be as important, if not more so, as legal action in responding to a corporate campaign. It may be costly and time-consuming for employers to respond to the union's tactics, but such efforts are often essential. If your company is the target of a corporate campaign, you may be asked to assist in these efforts.

11.02 Bargaining with the Union

Soon after the union is certified or recognized as the bargaining representative of your employees, negotiations for a collective bargaining agreement between the company and the union will begin. The NLRA requires that an employer bargain collectively with a union which represents its employees and try to reach a contract. The Act requires that the

parties bargain in good faith; it does *not* require that the parties reach an agreement or that the company agree to anything it thinks is unreasonable or undesirable.

You may play an important role during the collective bargaining process although you may not be directly involved in the actual negotiations. Because you are the representative of the company in your employees' eyes, your activities and statements may have an impact on them and, indirectly, on the union.

Although the NLRA guarantees your right of free speech, there are some limitations on what you can say during the negotiation process. Remember that your statements generally are attributed to the company, so you must not say anything which might be construed as threatening or coercive or evidence of bad faith bargaining by the company. Comments, even if off-the-cuff, to the effect that the company will never agree to a contract with the union, or that in the event of a strike the company will shut down, may be considered threatening or evidence of bad faith. Another danger in discussing the negotiations with employees is the possibility that you might appear to be bypassing the union and dealing directly with employees.

During negotiations it is also important not to take unilateral action in regard to mandatory subjects of collective bargaining. Thus, you may not, on your own, change wages or other employment conditions about which you are required to bargain with the union, without first giving the union notice of the proposed change and an opportunity to bargain about it. In addition, you may not take any other action designed to undermine the union's position, such as discharging employees for union activity or threatening to close the plant to avoid dealing with the union.

Keeping a few rules in mind will help you to avoid any of these violations of the law.

During negotiations, you generally are allowed to:

(1) Tell employees, factually and truthfully, how the negotiations are progressing.

(2) Spell out the proposals each side has put forth and relate which ones have been accepted and which rejected.

(3) Express the reasonableness of the company's position.

(4) Discuss proposals the union has already rejected.

(5) Urge employees to ratify the latest proposals given to the union, provided that your communications with the employees are not threatening.

Generally, if you remember to relate only the facts and the truth you will be safe. There are still some pitfalls to avoid. You should *not*:

(1) Discuss proposals which have not yet been given to the union.
(2) Undermine the union's negotiations.
(3) Pressure, threaten or coerce employees.
(4) Misrepresent facts to employees.
(5) Comment that the union's negotiators are ineffective.

As you can see, if you use discretion and good judgment, it is not difficult to avoid unfair labor practices. If an employee asks you a question about the negotiations and you do not know the answer, just say "I don't know." Then, talk to your superior or labor relations officer to get the answer.

11.03 Protected Concerted Activity

The NLRA does not protect only employees engaged in union activity. Employees who do not belong to a union and who are not engaged in union-related activities are still protected by the law from reprisals by you or the company if they are engaged in what is called "protected concerted activity." If employee conduct is not protected concerted activity, nothing in the NLRA prevents you from disciplining or discharging the employees for their activity. But if the conduct is protected and concerted, it is a violation of the law for you to discipline or discharge the employees for their conduct.

Concerted activity generally refers to group action by employees in pursuit of a common goal. An individual's activity which furthers only his/her own interests generally is not concerted. The key is that the activity must be aimed at furthering a group interest. Discussions between two employees may be concerted activity if they are preparing for group activity. It is conceivable for *one* employee to be engaged in concerted activity if he/she is trying to enlist the support of fellow employees to present a work-related complaint or if his/her actions would benefit a group of employees, even if the other employees decide they are not interested. For example, an employee trying to get his/her co-workers to protest allegedly unsafe working conditions generally would be engaged in concerted activity. In sum, the essence of concerted activity is either group activity or individual activity designed to encourage or prepare other employees to engage in group action or individual activity where a group of employees designated that individual to act on its behalf.

For an activity to be protected, it must not only be concerted, but it must also be for the purpose of collective bargaining or for other mutual aid or protection. Collective bargaining refers to efforts of employees to authorize a representative to bargain with their employer over working conditions. However, employees may be engaged in protected activity even though no union activity or collective bargaining is contemplated if the employees are seeking to correct a work-related problem or are bringing a work-related grievance. The grievance need not have merit, as long as the employees' concerns are legitimate.

Protected concerted activity may extend to activity of one employee which involves a matter of overall, common concern. A common example is an employee's refusal to submit to an investigatory interview by the employer without union representation present if the interview is one which the employee believes may result in discipline. This is protected concerted activity because of the impact on all employees. In addition, the Board requires that, upon the request of the employee, employers must permit the employee to engage in a consultation with his representative before an interview and the employer must inform the employee of the subject matter of the investigation. The NLRB has vacillated over whether non-union employees have such rights. The Board currently holds that non-union employees do not have such rights, although a non-union employee's *request* for such rights is protected. At least one court of appeals has upheld the Board's approach as reasonable but has stated that the Board could also reasonably hold that non-union employees have such rights. You should check with your superiors or with the company's labor counsel to determine what the company's position on this issue is.

Individual action may be considered protected concerted activity in several circumstances. Pursuant to a Supreme Court decision, an individual complaint is deemed to be made on behalf of a group of employees if the claim can be linked to a collective bargaining agreement. In addition, where an individual's claim has a source in a statute or public regulation, it may be considered protected concerted activity,

(13) Any individual employee action which involves only his/her own interest and not the interest of a group.
(14) Employees' actions seeking to alter or influence the managerial structure, hierarchy, or ownership of the company.
(15) An employee's disclosure of confidential medical or salary information when not disclosed in order to induce group action.

11.04 Strikes, Handbilling and Picketing

Perhaps the most emotionally charged and nerve-racking labor relations situations that you may face are strikes, handbilling and picketing. These are generally regarded as unions' ultimate weapons against employers. Through this mass concerted activity, a union tries to achieve some objective that it could not attain by more moderate means. During strikes, handbilling and picketing, your loyalty to the company will be most severely tested and your services to the company will be most sorely needed. Familiarity with some general principles and practical guidelines will help both you and the company get through these difficult times.

1) Strike Preparation

Your role may begin before a strike ever materializes. The company may be aware, sometime prior to a strike, that a strike is likely. Careful preparation by you and the company can go a long way towards softening the impact of a strike. Your greatest contribution to the company during this pre-strike period will be your ability to schedule and make contingency plans. If possible, all *essential* work and production should be completed before the strike target date. It might also be a good idea to stockpile inventories and production supplies during this period so that you will be able to continue work if your supply lines are interrupted. The company may decide to use supervisors or replacement workers to do the work during the strike. You may be asked to talk with company suppliers so that they can make plans of their own. As the threat of a strike grows more imminent, you may be asked to talk with customers and creditors, so that they too can make proper plans. Be frank in these discussions. If you feel input and output can be maintained, then tell them so. But if you honestly are not certain they can be, let them be aware of this too.

The company will also need to plan its security requirements carefully. If there are not enough security personnel in the facility or if the security staff may refuse to cross a picket line, then additional help should be lined up before the strike begins. You may be involved in deciding what security needs the company may have in the event of a strike. Because acts of violence and sabotage sometimes occur during a strike, it is important to be prepared to handle these situations and to protect yourself and the company's place of business.

As soon as the strike appears likely, the company should contact the local police and alert them to the fact of the strike. Their protection is free and you should take advantage of it, although police should not always be counted on to respond expeditiously to conduct which the company believes may be improper. You should also keep a record, including photographs, of any incidents of violence, threats or sabotage which occur.

2) The Strike
Legal Strikes

While the NLRA guarantees employees the right to strike, not all strikes are legal. The three main types of legal strikes are unfair labor practice strikes, economic strikes, and sympathy strikes. A strike during which employees walk out in protest over alleged unfair labor practices of the employer is called an "unfair labor practice strike." A strike by employees over higher wages or benefits is called an "economic strike." An economic strike may become an unfair labor practice strike, however, if the employer also commits unfair labor practices. Employees who refuse to cross another union's picket line are on a "sympathy strike."

The kind of strike makes a significant difference to employees, especially with respect to their right to reinstatement to their jobs after the strike. Employees on a legal strike cannot be fired for participating in the strike. But to keep the company operating, an employer may hire new employees, either on a temporary or a permanent basis, to replace striking workers. The permanent replacements may keep their new jobs even after the strike ends if it was an economic strike. The strikers are not fired, but they may have their old jobs back only if an opening occurs. The striker remains entitled to an offer of reinstatement whenever a vacancy occurs which he/she is qualified to fill. An employee loses this right to reinstatement if he/she gets a similar job elsewhere, if he/she turns down a company reinstatement offer once, or if the company has valid business reasons for not rehiring him/her. At the end of an unfair labor practice strike, however, the strikers are entitled to their old jobs back even if replacement workers have been doing their jobs during the strike; the replacements hired after an unfair labor practice strike began must be discharged, if necessary, to make room for the returning strikers. Sympathy strikers have the same rights as those with whom they sympathize.

Therefore, if employees refuse to cross a picket line involving an economic strike, they themselves become economic strikers subject to the rules of replacement and reinstatement discussed above.

Strikers are not entitled to reinstatement if they struck for an unlawful purpose or engaged in an economic or sympathy strike in violation of a valid no-strike clause prohibiting such conduct. Rights to reinstatement are also extinguished for strikers who break the law during the strike. If they engage in violence or other serious misconduct while striking, they may lose their reinstatement rights and may be discharged. If you observe any illegal behavior by strikers, you should inform your superiors because these employees may not have a right to a job after the strike. You should also maintain a record of possibly illegal behavior.

Illegal Strikes

Employees only have a right to return to their jobs if they were engaged in a lawful strike. If a strike is unlawful, the employees involved may be discharged and they will have no right of reinstatement. There are many different types of illegal strikes and work stoppages, including:

(1) Sit down strikes by employees on working time.
(2) Employee production slowdowns.
(3) "Hit and run" strikes—short, sporadic and repetitive.
(4) Strikes over union jurisdictional disputes.
(5) Strikes over work assignments.
(6) Wildcat strikes which are in violation of a no-strike clause in the collective bargaining agreement or an arbitration award prohibiting a strike.
(7) Strikes for any illegal purpose.
(8) Otherwise lawful strikes carried out in an unlawful manner.

If a union engages in any of these illegal work actions, an employer may seek help either from the Board or the courts. Because the forum the employer uses will depend on the type of strike or work action and the manner in which it is carried out, it is important for you to observe and make notes of all details concerning the illegal actions, including names, dates and places, so that the company can take the correct legal action against the union or the employees involved.

A union may not restrict an employee's right to resign from the union. Thus, a union rule which prohibits resignations during a strike is invalid, and fines imposed for violations of such a rule are unenforceable. In addition, a union may not discipline its members for refusing to participate in unlawful or unprotected activity.

As you can see, the rules regarding legal and illegal strikes are sometimes complicated. Thus, if you have any doubts about what you should do in a strike situation, you should contact your superiors or the company's counsel.

Picketing

While picketing does not necessarily accompany a strike, it usually does. As with strikes, peaceful picketing by employees, as well as by non-employees, enjoys a certain amount of legal protection. Here, the protection arises out of the right of free speech. But, again, this right is not unlimited. In order to be protected, picketing must be done at the right time, in the right manner and for the right objective. If the picketers violate these constraints, the company may take legal action against them. In the case of an illegal work action, you may be asked to make notes of the following for your employer:

(1) The day and time the picketing starts.

(2) The number of pickets.

(3) The premises being picketed and where in particular the pickets are congregated. Pay close attention to detail here and make notes of all relevant facts, including streets, gates, doors, and exits, and whether the picketers blocked entrances or exits.

(4) Identify the picketers by name, if possible, and try to determine how many are employees.

(5) The conduct of the picketers. Did they engage in any verbal intimidation, or violence, or distribution of literature?

(8) Take special care to protect important facilities, such as fuel, storage, water supply, computers (especially payroll), and power plant.

(9) Remind nonstrikers that they can legally cross picket lines. Have them report to you all instances of name calling, verbal abuse, or violence.

(10) Keep track of all costs due to the strike over and above the normal costs of operation.

(11) Do not talk to the media unless you are given express permission from your superiors. Publicity must be tightly controlled during a strike and the company should have only one spokesperson.

(12) Do not volunteer any information to a customer unless it has to do with a service the company could perform for them. If asked why the strike is taking place, explain the strike as simply as possible. For example, if applicable, you might be authorized by your company to respond: "The strike arose because of unreasonable demands of the union which would require charges to our customers which we feel would be excessive, and our negotiators are trying their best to resolve all issues." If the strike is an industry-wide strike, inform them of this fact also.

Above all, show restraint and exercise good judgment. Do not let your acts turn an economic strike into an unfair labor practice strike. Therefore, *DO NOT:*

(1) Urge employees to return to work with the promise of greater seniority to those who return.

(2) Solicit replaced employees to return as new employees.

(3) State that the company will never forget which employees went out on strike.

(4) Threaten employees to get back to work.

(5) Go over the union's head and try to negotiate with individual employees.

(6) Fire nonstrikers who refuse to take over a striker's job.

Throughout the strike you should try to maintain cordial relations with all employees. Remember that many of the strikers will probably be coming back to work for the company once the strike is over. Therefore, avoid bad feelings and bitterness at all costs. A good rule to remember is to say as little to the strikers as possible. If they ask you how negotiations are going, tell them truthfully where the negotiations stand and explain the company's position in a conciliatory manner, if you know. (If you don't know, do not say anything.)

3) Returning to Normal after a Strike

Once the strike ends and employees return to work they will be looking to you for company reaction to the strike. Your goal during this period is to get things back to normal as quickly as possible. The atmosphere may be somewhat tense for several weeks after the strike. Do not hold a grudge against employees and do not show any favoritism to nonstrikers over strikers. Be cordial and friendly to everybody. Give all employees the benefit of the doubt without being lax. Enforce all company policies and rules consistently and even handedly. Before long, things should be back to normal.

4) Handbilling

Handbilling, like picketing, is used by a union to organize employees, as well as to exert economic pressure upon employers to achieve certain objectives. However, handbilling has traditionally enjoyed greater free speech protection under the First Amendment than have picketing and striking. But the right to handbill is not unlimited, and in order to be lawful under the Act, the handbilling generally must be truthful, distributed in a peaceful manner and unaccompanied by any improper picketing or threats to boycott or urging of a work stoppage. Handbilling that follows or is done in conjunction with unprotected activity will generally be found unlawful. The requirement that the handbilling be truthful does not mean that its contents must be 100% accurate, but there must be no intent to deceive and no substantial departure from fact.

As with other union activity, employees can be prohibited from distributing handbills during working time and in work areas where handbilling would be disruptive to business. With very few narrow exceptions, the union or other nonemployees may not trespass upon private property to handbill or leaflet where an alternative means of access to employees is available. Union access to private property is only allowed where the union's access to employees is substantially burdensome and ineffective; mere logistical difficulties in reaching employees is insufficient.

As a supervisor, you should report any handbilling and observe how the activity is carried out to assist the company in dealing with the handbilling. If possible, obtain a handbill so that a record can be preserved for the company.

11.05 Employee Actions against Unions

After the union has been at your company for some time, an employee or group of employees may come to you and ask: "Is there any way we can get rid of the union? It's just not working out," or "Do we really have to belong to the union? Aren't there any ways around the union shop clause in the contract?" or "Can we revoke our union authorization cards?" Knowing how to respond to these questions is vitally important because the wrong answer may be a violation of the law. To complicate matters further, each of these questions requires a different response.

1) Decertification Petitions
Just as the NLRA gives employees the right to choose a union, it gives employees the right to choose not to have a union. Some time after your employees have voted a union in, they may decide that they no longer want the union. In that event, they may file a decertification petition which, if signed by 30% of the unit employees, will lead to an election over whether the employees still want to be represented by the union. If a majority of the voting employees vote to decertify the union, then the union will be "out" as the bargaining representative of your workers.

A decertification proceeding will be barred under certain circumstances. A valid contract covering the unit employees for up to three years will bar decertification. In such a situation, a decertification petition generally will be timely only if it is filed in the "open period," which is the period 60 to 90 days prior to the expiration date of the contract (or 90 to 120 days in health care facilities), or after a contract expires and before a new one is negotiated. In addition, absent unusual circumstances, *e.g.*, where a union has been dissolved or the number of unit employees has increased substantially, the Board will not direct an election if it has issued a certification covering the same unit in the previous twelve months.

If an employee or group of employees comes to you and asks how they can get rid of their union, you may give them information concerning the availability of decertification procedures and the mechanics of the decertification process, as long as you are acting in response to an employee request and your aid is merely "ministerial."

It is permissible to provide an employee with language to be used in a decertification petition, without more, if the employee requested it. Information about timing may also be offered if it simply reflects the NLRB's procedures.

While providing information is permissible, however, the law places restrictions on management's involvement with decertification petitions. As a supervisor, you are prohibited from suggesting to employees that they file them or from assisting in the filing of them. If a union feels that the company has encouraged employees to file a decertification petition, it may file an unfair labor practice charge (called a "blocking charge"). If a blocking charge is filed, the decertification petition will not be acted upon until the Board determines whether the charge is meritorious. For a decertification petition to be effective, therefore, you must not commit any unfair labor practices which might attract blocking charges.

For this reason, you should avoid any actions which may be considered encouragement of decertification or substantial aid in the preparation of a petition. For example, *DO NOT:*

    (a) Draft or sponsor a decertification petition for employees to sign.

    (b) Provide employees with a pre-printed petition, published by the Board.

    (c) Offer to prepare a decertification petition.

    (d) Encourage employees to sign a decertification petition.

    (e) Allow a decertification petition to be circulated on the company letterhead.

    (f) Promise employees benefits if they sign the petition.

    (g) Threaten reprisals against employees for failing to sign the petition.

(h) Provide employees with an attorney, or promise to pay their legal fees in connection with the petition.

(i) Retaliate against an employee for refusing to sign the petition. (The union, on the other hand, can suspend or expel any member who files a decertification petition.)

(l) Allow the petition to be circulated on company time if there is a valid no solicitation rule in effect.

(m) Ask an employee to deliver the petition to the Board once enough signatures have been gathered.

(n) Let an employee take a company car to deliver the petition to the Board, or reimburse transportation and parking expenses incurred.

(o) Pay an employee for time off to deliver the petition to the Board.

(p) Ask employees if they have signed the petition.

(q) Let someone associated with management, like a relative, a salesperson, or a labor consultant, initiate or assist in the filing of the decertification petition.

(r) Break off negotiations with the union over a new contract if a decertification petition is filed. Do not stop negotiating, no matter how many employees signed the petition, until the company attorney is consulted.

2) Deauthorization Petitions

Many collective bargaining agreements contain a "union security clause" requiring employees to join or remain members of the union. A union security clause can be removed from a collective bargaining agreement by a deauthorization election. The rest of the collective bargaining agreement remains unchanged.

The rules that govern decertification petitions also apply to deauthorization petitions (including the requirement that 30% of the employees must sign the petition before an election will be ordered). Thus, you *can* explain to employees what a deauthorization petition is and how to get an election. You still cannot suggest or assist in the filing of a deauthorization petition. Unlike decertification petitions, however, deauthorization petitions may be filed at any time during the life of the agreement. It is as important to avoid unfair labor practices in the deauthorization context as it is in decertification drives, because the "blocking charge" rule applies here too. In other words, an unfair labor practice charge filed by the union will block a deauthorization election until the NLRB decides if the charge is true.

To win a deauthorization vote, a majority of the employees eligible to vote (not just a majority of those who do vote, as is the case with other elections) must vote to eliminate the union security clause. Therefore you should try to "get out the vote," because an employee who does not vote in effect counts as a "no" vote in the deauthorization effort.

3) Revocation of Union Authorization Cards

Employees sometimes decide that they wish they had not signed a union authorization card. This usually happens before the election actually takes place. The most important point to remember is that you should do nothing to encourage or solicit employees to revoke their authorization cards. It is an unfair labor practice for you to interfere with employees' card signing. Therefore, *DO NOT*:

(a)   Urge employees to withdraw from the union or revoke their union authorization cards.

(b)   Prepare or circulate an authorization card revocation petition or ask employees to sign one which is already drawn up.

(c)   Indirectly ask employees to revoke their cards, such as by asking them how they could be talked out of joining the union.

(d)   Promise employees benefits for revoking their cards.

(e)   Punish an employee for refusing to revoke his authorization card.

(f)   Ask employees to send you copies of letters that they write to the union requesting the return of their cards.

You may inform employees of their right to revoke their cards even when the employees have not solicited this information, as long as you do not attempt to ascertain whether they will do so, and you do not offer assistance or otherwise make the employees feel that they would suffer negative consequences in refraining from revocation. If employees have already decided that they wish to revoke their cards and they simply want your advice about how to accomplish the revocation, you have much more leeway. Then you may advise them that they have the right to ask the union to return their cards, as long as you do not solicit or encourage them to do so. In fact, in an atmosphere free of any unfair labor practices at all, you or the company attorney can draft the letters of revocation if the employees come to you and ask you to, as long as you do not follow up on the letters in any way, such as by asking the employees later who signed the letters and who did not. Be very careful, though, because it is an unfair labor practice if you encourage the employees to revoke their authorization cards.

4) Resignation from the Union

Employees may ask you if there is a way for them to resign from the union. You are free to tell them how to do this. Generally, union constitutions and by-laws provide procedures by which a member can resign. In response to employee questions, you may tell them about such procedures.

The employer can go one step further. You have the right to notify employees, by letter, of the procedures in the union's by-laws. You may even send along a sample resignation letter. But this notification must not be coercive in any way. Neither you nor the company can actively encourage employees to resign from the union.

While you may tell employees how to resign if they ask, there is still a danger of committing unfair labor practices in this area. Under no circumstances can you urge employees to resign from the union. If you do, and a charge is filed, the Board will most likely find that you committed an unfair labor practice. Therefore, do not even jokingly try to persuade employees that the union is no good and that they should resign from it.

11.06 Supervisor's Responsibilities to the Company

The main purpose of the NLRA is to protect the rights of *employees* to organize and join unions. Recognizing that a supervisor's first allegiance must be to the employer and not to a union, the Act specifically states that supervisors are not considered employees within the meaning of the NLRA. Therefore, in contrast to the many protections employees enjoy under the NLRA, supervisors have few rights, but many responsibilities.

1) Pro-Union Activities by Supervisors

As a supervisor you have only a qualified right to belong to a union. The NLRA prohibits you from joining a union unless your employer agrees. Your employer has the right to have you excluded from a bargaining unit of non-supervisory rank-and-file employees.

Supervisors who are not in the unit which the union is seeking to represent are not free to campaign for the union. If you campaign for the union behind your employer's back there is a danger that employees will believe that your pro-union position represents the employer's position or that they face future retaliation if they refuse to support the union. To avoid this, you *cannot* circulate petitions, urge employees to join the union, organize meetings and rallies, distribute union authorization cards, or threaten employees for voting against the union. If you do actively assist the union in these ways and the union wins, the election will be set aside and a new election held.

A rerun election is only one of the consequences of your campaigning for the union without your employer's knowledge. Since supervisors are not employees under the NLRA and therefore have no organizational rights, your employer may terminate or otherwise discipline you for engaging in pro-union activities. It is the company's right to choose its management team and if it feels that your attitude or behavior may help the union or encourage membership in it, you can be fired.

For example, your employer generally can discharge you for:

(1)   Refusing to follow instructions to tell employees why the employer is opposed to the union.

(2)   Failing to campaign as effectively as your employer wished during an organizational campaign.

(3)   Refusing to cooperate with a company attorney preparing for an NLRB proceeding.

2) Activities as a Union Member

If your employer permits you to join a union and the union wins the election, you will find that your activity as a union member is greatly curtailed. You are not permitted to be a shop steward for the union or a member of the union negotiating committee that bargains with the company. You cannot vote in internal union elections choosing who is to represent the union against your employer. This includes elections for members of the bargaining committee, the grievance committee, or for the business representative who will represent the union in its dealings with your company. You are also prohibited from voting in the contract ratification election that follows the negotiation of a contract between the company and the union.

Why are your activities within the union so restricted? The law recognizes that the company deserves your undivided loyalty even if you belong to a union. The rules against your full participation in the union are designed to prevent conflicts of interest and ensure your allegiance to your employer.

The law not only limits what you can do *for* the union; it limits what the union can do *to* you. These limitations offer you protections against union discipline not available to rank-and-file employees. An employer is free to choose which of its supervisors will be on the company negotiating committee and which supervisors will have a role in the settling of grievances. The company may select supervisors to perform these functions who are union members. When this happens, the NLRA limits the right of the union to discipline these supervisors, because the union discipline may interfere with the company's right to choose the members of management it wants to perform these duties. If you are a union member and feel that the union has imposed sanctions and rules upon you which inhibit your effectiveness on the job in any way, report this to your superior so that corrective measures may be taken. The union's right to discipline you for activity during a strike is also somewhat limited. If you cross a union picket line and perform your normal supervisory duties during a strike, the union *cannot* punish you for crossing that line.

11.07 Living with the Union

As you have seen, a union at your company will bring many changes in your relationship with employees. With a third party, the union, interposed between you and your employees, direct dealings between you and your workers are no longer always appropriate. Both you and the employees sometimes have to go to the union, rather than to each other.

With a unionized workforce you have to make an affirmative and conscious effort to avoid infringing on any of the rights guaranteed by the NLRA. Since your acts are considered the acts of your company, the NLRB may find your company liable for an unfair labor practice if you infringe on employee or union rights. With a general understanding of the five major types of unfair labor practices, you will be prepared to avoid conduct which is prohibited, while at the same time contribute to harmony in your workforce.

1) Interference, Restraint, and Coercion

Section 8(a)(1) of the NLRA makes it an unfair labor practice for an employer to interfere with, restrain, or coerce employees in the exercise of their Section 7 rights to participate in union activities and protected concerted activities. Generally, any conduct which has an anti-union motivation behind it is a violation of the law. Even if an act appears to be neutral, it may violate the NLRA if it has a dampening effect on employee unionization efforts. Most of the acts which you were advised against committing during the union organization campaign are violations of this subsection because they interfere with employees' organizational rights. Other violations of this subsection include:

(a) Threats against employees for their unionization efforts.
(b) Espionage and surveillance of union or protected concerted activities.
(c) Blacklisting employees.
(d) Promising benefits to those who resist unionization.
(e) Racial appeals to employees.
(f) Interrogation of employees.
(g) Polling employees to ascertain whether the union represents a majority of employees (unless the employer has substantial objective evidence of loss of union support).
(h) Physical attacks upon employees for union activities.
(i) Withholding benefits from union activists.
(j) Strikebreaking (that is, employing illegal means like physical violence to break up a lawful strike).
(k) Union favoritism (that is, an act, such as premature recognition of a rival union, which favors one union over another).

2) Domination of a Union

Section 8(a)(2) of the Act makes it an unfair labor practice for any employer to dominate or interfere with the formation or the administration of a labor organization or to contribute financial or other support to it. This provision is designed to protect the right of employees to be represented by an organization of their own choosing or none at all, if they prefer. While employers and unions must cooperate with each other to a certain degree in order to ensure stability in the workplace, an employer commits an unfair labor practice if its support or domination of a union is so great that the union is not really representing the rights of the employees as it should. Board remedies for violations of this provision range from simply ordering the employer to cease and desist from its support to the "disestablishment" of the union and allowing the employees to freely select their bargaining representative (in another election if need be). Which remedy the Board adopts depends on the degree of support and domination exerted by the employer.

Because a supervisor active in union affairs raises the potential for a violation of this provision, the Board has set limits on the degree of union activity which it will permit by a supervisor. In deciding whether a supervisor has overstepped permissible bounds, the Board will look into the nature of the supervisor's position, the degree to which the position requires the supervisor to identify with management, the permanence of the position, and its place in the management hierarchy (generally, the lower the supervisor's position, the greater amount of union activity he or she is permitted).

It is usually not one activity alone but a series of acts which together establish excessive support or domination. Examples of questionable activity include:

(1) Supervisors actively soliciting union members.
(2) Activity against any rival union that is attempting to organize the company's workers.
(3) Loaning employees money to pay membership fees.
(4) Linking benefits to membership in the union favored by the employer.

(5) Giving financial aid to the union, paying for its attorneys, or contributing to the cost of union administration.

(6) Giving the union access to company facilities, such as copy machines and office space.

(7) Coercing employees to join the union.

(8) Urging employees to start their own labor organization and assisting them in starting one.

(9) The inclusion of safeguards for the employer in the union constitution and by-laws, such as providing for employer representation at union meetings.

It is also possible to violate Section 8(a)(2) even when a traditional union is not in place. Indeed, any group in which employees participate and which "deals with" the employer concerning grievances, labor disputes, wages, rates of pay, hours of employment or conditions of work has the potential to violate the Act if it is "dominated" by the employer. This has called into question the legality of employee participation groups or committees formed by employers in an effort to improve communication and employee morale. In some cases, committees have been found to "deal with" employers when their members represent employees and make proposals to management concerning working conditions. Domination has been found where the company establishes the committee, funds it, allows meetings on paid company time and controls its agenda.

Although the state of the law in this area is currently in flux, a violation generally will not be found where the purpose of the committee is limited to achieving "quality" or "efficiency," or where it is designed to be a "communication device" to promote generally the interests of quality or efficiency.

Because of the uncertainty in this area, it is advisable for your company to review its existing or planned employee committees with labor counsel to determine if they violate the Act. Generally speaking, it is possible to structure committees in such a way that they do not "deal with" the company and/or are not "dominated" by the company. If they are so structured, employee committees are lawful and can serve a useful purpose.

3) Discrimination to Encourage or Discourage Union Membership

Section 8(a)(3) of the NLRA makes it an unfair labor practice for an employer to encourage or discourage membership in any labor organization by discrimination in hiring, firing or any other term or condition of employment. The basic premise of this extremely important section of the Act is that employees should not be discriminated against in any manner because of their union activities. The term discrimination, as it is used here, refers only to discrimination because of union activities and not discrimination on the basis of race, color, religion, sex, national origin, age, disability or other characteristics protected by other federal, state and local laws, such as Title VII of the 1964 Civil Rights Act and the Americans with Disabilities Act.

Section 8(a)(3) is a "catch-all" provision, written in very broad language, to prohibit virtually every act that might inhibit free unionization. While an employer is entitled to run its business the way it sees fit, it is not allowed to base personnel decisions on anti-union motivations. For example, employees may be fired for cause or for no cause at all under the NLRA, but they may not be fired solely because of their pro-union or protected concerted activities. Employees may be given special benefits and incentives, but these may not be based on the degree of the employees' union participation.

Some common violations of this section are:

(1) Refusing to hire a prospective employee because of his/her pro-union sentiments or history of union membership.
(2) Discharging, demoting, or otherwise disciplining employees because of their union or protected concerted activity.
(3) Transferring or laying off employees in an effort to dissipate the union's strength.
(4) Refusing to reinstate striking employees who are entitled to reinstatement.
(5) Granting special favors or benefits to anti-union employees.
(6) Subjecting union sympathizers to such intolerable working conditions that they quit their jobs.

Since many of the actions prohibited by this section involve personnel decisions which you, as a supervisor, are frequently called upon to make, this section is of special importance to you. If you are thinking of disciplining or discharging an employee, particularly one who is active in the union, *DO NOT* act impetuously. It is a good idea to render discipline progressively and to document carefully each stage of discipline with an explanation of the reasons. If your action might appear to be punishment for union activities, consult your superior first. Violations of this provision can be expensive for your company, which might be required to reinstate the wrongfully discharged employee and give back pay for the period of discharge. It is best to proceed with caution. If you act with care, and discipline only for legitimate nondiscriminatory reasons, such as misconduct or poor performance, the company should be able to defend your action if an 8(a)(3) charge is filed.

4) Discrimination for Filing Charges

Section 8(a)(4) of the NLRA makes it an unfair labor practice for an employer to discharge or discriminate against an employee for filing an unfair labor practice charge or testifying in any Board proceeding. Essentially, this section prohibits the same anti-union acts as the preceding section. It is included for the simple reason that Congress *expressly* wanted to provide protection to employees who help enforce the policies of the NLRA by detecting and reporting their employer's unfair labor practices. Therefore, treat employees who have filed unfair labor practice charges or testified before the Board in a normal, even-handed fashion. *DO NOT* subject them to any treatment which might be viewed as retaliation or punishment for their participation in the enforcement of the NLRA.

5) Refusal to Bargain

Section 8(a)(5) of the Act makes it an unfair labor practice for an employer to refuse to bargain collectively with the duly authorized representative of the employees. This provision is often thought of as the cornerstone of the NLRA since much of the Act is geared toward the negotiation of a collective bargaining agreement and maintenance of stable labor-management relations. However, the NLRA does not require that either the company or the union agree to anything. Instead, it mandates that they bargain in "good faith." Roughly translated, this means that each side should make a sincere and above-board effort to reach an agreement and should not engage in any tactics which would undermine the opposing side.

Generally, high-level company officials and members of the company negotiating committee will be responsible for the actual bargaining with the union. This does not mean that you can ignore the guidelines set forth here, however.

The following are just some of the many possible violations of Section 8(a)(5):

(1) Changing any of the terms and conditions of employment contained in the collective bargaining agreement without giving the union notice and sufficient opportunity to discuss the changes.

(2) Bypassing the union and negotiating directly with employees.

(3) Showing hostility and ill-feeling toward the union during negotiations.

(4) Being extremely unyielding during the bargaining process.

(5) Refusing to give the union reasonable and necessary information concerning the company upon request, including information relating to grievances, so that the union can bargain for or administer a labor contract effectively.

Conclusion

This Chapter was written with one very important goal in mind—to help develop and maintain harmonious and lawful labor relations at your company. The importance of achieving this goal cannot be overemphasized. While it is true that you cannot control many of the external factors that affect the employer-employee relationship, there are significant internal factors over which you do have control. An understanding of the law outlined in this Chapter can help you grasp the extent to which the preservation of employment stability depends on your actions. The days of belligerence are gone. Today, with the growing sophistication of unions, management must be progressive and enlightened, yet firm, in its labor relations. Knowing your rights and knowing the law will help achieve this goal.

One final word of caution. Since the workplace is such a mix of constantly changing factors, you will undoubtedly encounter many situations not specifically covered by this Chapter. Many of the more important aspects of the employer-employee relationship under the NLRA have been covered, but it was impossible to touch on every conceivable situation that you might face. If you are confronted with a problem you are not sure how to handle, talk to your superiors. They can check with their attorneys to find out what to do. By keeping in mind, at all times, a simple rule of thumb, you will be able to handle effectively most emergencies that arise: *always use common sense and good judgment*. By treating your workers *fairly* and by acting with discretion, you will help ensure that the company enjoys successful labor relations.

Chapter 12

The First Amendment and Free Speech

By Turner D. Madden and Whitney Hoffman

12.00 Introduction

The First Amendment is well known and often cited by people wishing to express their viewpoint, wherever and whenever they wish to do so. In fact, the free speech provision of the First Amendment is narrowly restricted based on what is being said, where it is being said and in what manner, commonly known as the time, place and manner restrictions. The most well known example of such a restriction on the First Amendment is preventing a person from yelling "Fire!" in a crowded theater. Restrictions on the First Amendment right to free speech are carefully evaluated, as to prevent a "chilling effect" on the free expression of thoughts or ideas that we hold central to our nation's guarantees of liberty promised in the Declaration of Independence. Thus if any restriction of free expression is to withstand Constitutional muster, it must be a regulation that does not edit the content, thought or idea being expressed, no matter how distasteful or offensive, but merely restricts where, when, and how the expression is occurring.

12.01 Place Restrictions - What is the Public Forum Doctrine?

The Public Forum Doctrine has been set forth by the Supreme Court to guide the public in the use, classification, and availability of public facilities to individuals and what restrictions on such use may be legally imposed.

In *Calash v. City of Bridgeport*[1], the Court of Appeals reviewed the municipal outdoor arena. The court stated that three categories of public property exist:

---

[1] 788 F.2d 80, (2d Cir. 1986).

1. **Traditional Public Forums,** such as "public streets and parks, dedicated to assembly and debate 'by tradition or by governmental fiat'";
2. **Limited Public Forums,** "which the government has as a 'place or channel of communication for use by the public at large ... [or] for the use by certain speakers, or for the discussion of certain subjects'"; and
3. **Non-Public Forums,** which are not considered to be open forums for public communication by design or tradition.[2]

The use of any facility and the right to access must be evaluated according to these classifications. If a facility is a traditional public forum, the Government must show that any content-based exclusions are necessary to serve a compelling state interest and is narrowly drawn to achieve this purpose.[3] Narrow content-neutral time, place and manner restrictions are allowed, as long as adequate alternative channels of communication are available.[4] For limited public forums, the government may restrict access to such facilities, but in those areas in which it remains open, it may only restrict access under the same standards set forth for traditional forums. For non-public forums, the government is allowed to "reserve the forum for its intended purposes, communicative or otherwise" as long as any imposed regulations are not based on disapproval of the speaker's views.[5]

In *Calash,* the City of Bridgeport denied the use of Kennedy Stadium, a large outdoor arena, built with federal grants for use as a service facility, to a for-profit concert promoter, seeking its use for several rock music concerts. After being denied access on two occasions, the concert promoter sued, stating he was denied equal protection under the law and his first amendment rights to free speech had been violated.[6] In the past, the facility had been used largely for football and soccer, but was also used for festivals and a charitable rock concert, sponsored by a local corporation.

---

[2] Id. at 81.
[3] Id. at 82.
[4] Id.
[5] Id.
[6] Id. at 80.

The promoter felt that he was denied access solely because he was seeking a profit from the proposed use of the facility, which does not deny him of first amendment protections.[7]

While musical entertainment is a protected form of speech under the First Amendment,[8] the court ruled that the Stadium in question was a non-public forum, restricted for use by civic, charitable and non-profit organizations alone. Although the stadium did not have written guidelines at the time the suit was filed, it was clear that the Stadium had not been used by for-profit ventures in the past. The court also stated that had the Stadium become a limited public forum by permitting a non-profit concert to be held there in the past, this did not guarantee access to the promoter, as the Stadium could reasonably restrict access to "entities of the same character," in this case, charitable or non-profit events.[9]

Clearly, the crux of the problem in this case dealt with the confusion caused by lack of written guidelines for use of the facility in question. The City had a clear history of limiting access to charitable and civic events, which helped establish its designation as a non-public or limited public forum. Because such limitations were content neutral, the City could deny access to a for-profit concert promoter, since the problem arose not over the type of communication proposed, in this case a rock concert, but based on the commitment of the community to use its "service facility" for activities that would benefit the general public rather than specific individuals seeking a profit.

Likewise, in *National Socialist White People's Party v. Ringers*,[10] a racist political group sought to use a local public school's auditorium for its political meetings. Several applications for the use were denied by the School Board, on various grounds ranging from fear that the property would be abused by the group and disrupt the tranquillity of the community,[11] to fear that the group's racially discriminatory practices would give the impression the State condoned the group's beliefs, amounting to state action in the violation

---

[7] Id.
[8] Id. at 82.
[9] Id. at 84.
[10] 473 F.2d 1010 (4th Cir. 1972).
[11] Id. at 1013.

of civil rights of others.[12] The court found that because the Board had a history of renting the auditorium to a wide variety of public and private groups, the Board had turned the facility into a public forum, dedicated to the exercise of first amendment rights of freedom of speech, association, and assembly.[13]

Because the School Board did not have a history of limiting the access of its facilities in the past, it was not allowed to do so in the future, and had essentially given up it's rights to do so by making its auditorium a public forum for expression of ideas. Clearly, a facility manager must be careful of what activities are allowed, because past conduct will be strongly considered when determinations are made as to whether a facility is a public forum or not.

In *Rupp v. Lindsay*,[14] the director of the George Wallace campaign for the Presidency sought the use of Shea Stadium for a political rally a month prior to the elections. Contract negotiations were entered into, but shortly before an agreement could be signed, the Commissioner of Parks stated he could not enter into the contract because the rally did not "fit into the permitted purposes for which the stadium is maintained."[15] The Administrative Code of the City of New York however, allowed the Commissioner to enter into such contracts for use of the facility for a litany of reasons, including "events of civic, community and general public interest".[16] It was clear to the Supreme Court of New York that partisan political activity, especially in a national campaign, was clearly permissible within the guidelines as "civic, community and general public interest"[17] and the Commissioner's exercise of his discretion was unreasonable.

Facility managers should thus be aware of any local administrative codes or other regulations that may also circumscribe their decision making when contemplating license of their facility to a group.

---

[12] Id.

[13] Id. at 1014.

[14] 293 N.Y.S.2d 812 (1968).

[15] Id. at 814.

[16] Id. at 816.

[17] Id.

In *Lewis v. Colorado Rockies Baseball Club,*[18], publishers of an "alternative" baseball programs and scorecards were harassed and ticketed for trespass while attempting to sell their products on the walkways surrounding Coors Field in Denver. The Rockies, who have a long term contract with a concession service, sought to prohibit the sale or distribution of these materials on the walkways surrounding the stadium, alleging that the walkways in question were not traditional public forums[19] and that their policy prohibiting such a restriction on vendors was justified by its concerns about premise liability, crowd control, safety, pedestrian movement, and maximizing revenue.[20] The Supreme Court of Colorado held that the stadium had been specifically designed to be "fully integrated"[21] into downtown Denver's street grid, and not solely used for access to the stadium, allowing them to function as a "traditional public forum" as defined above. One walkway was directly in front of a gate to the stadium and was physically separated in part from the closest city street by a stairway, and the court found that at least 300 feet of this walkway was also a public forum, due to its general accessibility to the public.[22] The court also determined that the Rockies' restriction was content-neutral, or not related to the content of the message the Publisher's sought to distribute, but was aimed at protecting revenue and maintaining crowd control at the stadium. However, the court held that the economic interests of the Rockies were on equal footing of those of the Publishers, and that the restrictions were broader than necessary to promote the Rockies' interests in crowd control.[23]

This case is similar to that of *Carreras v. City of Anaheim,*[24] in which a religious organization sought to solicit donations and distribute literature outside of Anaheim Stadium and Convention Center.[25]

---

[18]No. 96 SA 381, 1997 Colo. LEXIS 520 (June 30, 1997), 941 P.2d 266 (Colo. 1997).
[19] Id. at *19.
[20] Id. at *25.
[21] Id. at *5, *20.
[22] Id. at *23.
[23] Id. at *27-28, *30.
[24] 768 F.2d 1039 (9th Cir. 1985), more fully described *infra*.
[25] Id.

The sidewalks in question in that case were also held to be a traditional public forum for the exercise of free speech, requiring that the City of Anaheim show that any restrictions placed on such speech were permissible time, place and manner restrictions, and not unduly burdensome, or unfairly restrictive of the first amendment rights of the solicitors. Likewise, in the Rockies' case, the sidewalks, well integrated into downtown Denver, were indistinguishable from any other public street and that any regulation of free speech in those areas was not unconstitutionally restrictive.

What a facility manager should take away from this line of cases is that the classification of the facility as a public forum will depend on the following:

- Whether there has been open access of the facility to groups of all types, or whether the access has been historically restricted;[26]
- Whether the facility's purpose in creation has been, in part, for the free expression of ideas;[27]
- Whether the facility is designed in such a way that permits open public access, or whether such access is restricted; and lastly
- Whether the facility is municipally owned or operated, whether police officers are utilized in enforcement of regulations, or other possible involvement of the state in facility affairs that permit federal constitutional claims to be maintained against the facility.[28]

If the facility wishes to be a limited public forum or a non-public forum, access to the facility must be limited in some way from open public, and the facility will not be able to limit the exercise of free speech in the areas that are clearly accessible to the public at large, such as sidewalks or open parking areas surrounding the facility.

---

[26] See *Calash v. City of Bridgeport,* and *National Socialists White People's Party v. Ringers,* supra.

[27] See *National Socialists White People's Party v. Ringers,* and *Rupp v. Lindsay,* supra.

[28] The concept of state action and the application of 42 U.S.C. § 1983 in a private party bringing an action for the violation of his or her civil rights will not be fully discussed here.

12.02 Restrictions on Free Speech in Facilities: Permissible and Non-Permissible Place and Manner Restrictions in Action

As the tobacco industry is receiving criticism about its billboards and marketing to youth, the question arises as to what kind of signage and expression of First Amendment rights is allowed in public facilities/public forums. As we will see from the line of cases presented, there is a difference depending on the type of speech sought to be regulated, private speech, political speech or commercial speech.

1) Private Speech
In *Aubrey v. City of Cincinnati*,[29] an ordained minister sought to place a banner in Riverfront Stadium during a World Series baseball game carrying a religious message based on the Bible passage John 3:16. Riverfront Stadium was leased by the City of Cincinnati from Hamilton County, Ohio, and in turn sublet to the Cincinnati Reds for use for baseball games. Security personnel at the World Series Game included both private security officers and City of Cincinnati police officers.

The Reds had a policy regarding banners that stated banners were permitted "as long as they were in good taste (as determined by the Reds Management)" and as long as the banners did not interfere with the line of sight of the game participants or obstruct the view of fans in the stands.[30] The minister's sign was of a permissible size, but was confiscated by security personnel because it was felt that it violated the "good taste" regulation. Police officers enforced the Reds policy by explaining to the Minister that his sign would not be allowed because it was not related to baseball.[31] The District Court held that the regulation was unconstitutionally overbroad and vague, leaving it up to the sole discretion of the enforcers of the policy what was in good or bad taste, and in fact, many of the people charged with enforcement of the Reds policy, including City police officers, could not agree on what was in good or bad taste.[32]

---

[29] 815 F.Supp. 1100 (S.D. Ohio 1993)
[30] Id. at 1102.
[31] Id. at 1103.
[32] Id. at 1102, 1106.

Further, the City of Cincinnati itself was implicated by allowing on duty and off duty police officers to enforce the Reds policy that was facially unconstitutional for its ambiguous language and the discretion left to the decision maker without any clear standards on which to base a decision.[33]

Again, we see that the lack of a clear, narrowly drawn policy and standards for banners at the stadium led to this suit. A facility manager must consider the goals of any regulations they wish to impose in their facility, and try to specifically tailor any policies or regulations to reach that goal, setting forth appropriate standards to be used by those enforcing such rules.

Similarly, in *Stewart v. District of Columbia Armory Board*,[34] the Armory Board adopted a regulation regarding banners permissible at RFK Stadium, stating in part that banners must pertain to the event, shall not be commercial, vulgar or derogatory, and shall not exceed 4 x 6 feet in dimension.[35] A patron in attendance of a Redskins football game placed two signs in the stadium, one referring to John 3:3 and another referring to Mark 8:36.[36] Both signs were removed by employees of the Stadium, based on the content regulation, and upon the request of the National Football League. No other signs were removed despite several having content clearly not related to the event. Additionally, the patron had displayed similar signs at prior events at the Stadium, but had never before had any of the banners removed. The court determined that the signs were clearly protected speech, that sufficient evidence was presented that RFK could be considered a public forum, and there was no compelling state interest in prohibiting religious speech in the Stadium.[37] Additionally, the regulation's prohibition of "vulgar" or "derogatory" language and "pertaining to the event" were significantly vague as to offer little guideline in what messages were permissible and what were not.[38]

We see that even when banner regulations are in place, specificity as to what is permitted and what is not, with examples and guidelines are necessary.

---

[33] Id. at 1104.
[34] 789 F. Supp. 402 (U.S. D.C. 1992).
[35] Id.
[36] Id. at 403, 404.
[37] Id. at 404.
[38] Id. at 405.

Vague and imprecise terms such as "bad taste," "vulgar" and the like do not provide security personnel with any real guidance in determining what is allowed and disallowed, and leaves them in a position of using their discretion, which could easily lead to a First Amendment violation problem.

(2) Commercial Speech

In a slightly different vein, in *Hubbard Broadcasting v. Metropolitan Sports Facilities Commission,*[39] a radio and television broadcaster, Hubbard, alleged their first amendment rights to free speech and equal protection were violated when an exclusive right to advertise on the Metrodome's scoreboard was awarded to its competitor. The scoreboard in question was installed in the Metrodome under an agreement whereby the manufacturer had exclusive rights to sell advertising space on the scoreboard for a ten year period, and the Metrodome would not allow any advertising within it that would directly compete the scoreboard advertising.[40] Hubbard claimed that selling advertising space within the Metrodome designated the stadium as a public forum for commercial speech.[41] The court ruled that in fact the Metrodome was not a public forum for commercial speech, and may not be a public forum at all.[42] Further, the exclusive ten year contracts, available on a first come, first served basis, without competing advertising allowed elsewhere in the facility made the advertising contracts more valuable, and that this regulation was also content-neutral.[43] No effort was being made to suppress a particular point of view, but Hubbard's advertising was denied access to the Metrodome because it failed to bid for the advertising space before a contract was given to its competitor.[44]

In this case, advertising signage was at issue, as was "commercial speech." Facility managers must be aware that advertising also enjoys First Amendment protections, and that contracts for exclusive advertising available on an equal footing will be allowed.

---

[39] 797 F.2d 552 (8th Cir. 1986).
[40] Id. at 554.
[41] Id. at 555.
[42] Id.
[43] Id. at 556.
[44] Id.

Further, a manager should also be aware that such a policy is also valid, as long as it is not trying to edit the content of the advertising in question.

In *Hampton International Communications, Inc., v. Las Vegas Convention and Visitors Authority,* [45] the Las Vegas Convention and Visitors Authority (LVCVA) leased the Las Vegas Convention Center to Interface Group-Nevada for its annual COMDEX tradeshow on October 18, 1993. COMDEX received a leasehold interest in the convention center and parking lots. On November 8, 1993 LVCVA leased the Convention Center to Electronic Industries Association for its annual consumer electronics tradeshow (CES). Hampton International publishes various newspapers and commercial tabloids relevant to the computer industry and attempted to distribute the "dailies" on the walkways leading to the Convention Center. Tradeshow promoters prohibited Hampton's conduct since distribution of commercial materials was limited to certain areas and only allowed by organizations that had paid for the exclusive right to distribute their materials on Convention Center grounds. Hampton claimed that it had been deprived of its first amendment rights, and sought both a temporary and permanent injunction allowing it to distribute its materials on the walkways of the convention center during the COMDEX show. Two months later, Hampton filed a similar claim regarding the CES show. The injunction was denied, and Hampton sought a jury trial on the issue of damages. COMDEX and Hampton settled their dispute subsequently, leaving the claims against LVCVA and the claims of state action in infringing Hampton's first amendment rights.

The court held that the LVCVA and its involvement in managing the shows under the lease agreements indeed constituted state action, and that under the public forum doctrine, the convention center walkways were not traditional public forums, but were largely private in nature. The court stated that the government had a substantial interest in keeping the walkways into the convention center clear, and that the government had a legitimate interest in selling exclusive advertising rights and to set up such advertisers within the convention center itself rather than on walkways, and thus granted the LVCVA's motion for summary judgment.

---

[45] 913 F.Supp. 1402 (Nev. 1995).

In *Southlake Property Associates, LTD., v. City of Morrow, Georgia*,[46] Southlake owned unimproved property adjacent to Interstate Highway 75 (I-75) in Morrow, GA and desired to erect four offsite billboards on the property to advertise to motorists driving on I-75. Southlake sought to enjoin the City's sign ordinance as violating the First and Fourteenth Amendments of the Constitution. Southlake had sought certification that the signs complied with the City's sign ordinance and it was denied. The ordinance in question prohibited billboards outright. The Trial Court found that the ordinance did not violate the Constitution, and the Court of Appeals agreed, stating that the City had an interest in maintaining "clean, aesthetically pleasing and safe business thoroughfares" that allowed the City to make reasonable regulations of the time, pace and manner of commercial speech. The ordinance was content neutral as to commercial or non-commercial speech, but as a practice, Morrow had only prohibited commercial speech billboards, not those with non-commercial speech messages (like public service announcements, etc.) The ordinance permitted onsite advertising, but not off-site advertising by billboard, as proposed by Southlake. The Court of Appeals held that non-commercial messages were "on-site" wherever the speaker placed it, but clearly commercial messages were off-site when they were not located at the place of business or commercial activity, and that such regulation was constitutionally appropriate and did not unnecessarily limit commercial speech.

(3) Political Speech

In *Sistrunk v. City of Strongsville*,[47] a woman was prohibited by the Bush-Quayle '92 committee from expressing views opposing the Bush reelection campaign at a rally held on public property. She claimed that the Committee was a state actor when it denied her access to the Strongville Commons during the rally. The Strongville Republic Organization had obtained a permit to use Strongville Commons for a political rally on October 28, 1992, and the permit limited access to the grounds to members of the organization and their invitees.

---

[46] 112 F.3d 1114 (11th Cir. 1997).
[47] 99 F.3d 194 (6th Cir. 1996).

The committee was also permitted to restrict access by category of invitation, and invitations were available at no charge at City Hall, available on a first come, first served basis.[48] The woman alleged that the Commons was a public forum, located at the center of the City, even though the Mayor had the power to regulate use of the Commons by ordinance. Committee members disallowed buttons, signs or the like critical of President Bush, but allowed content neutral or supporting signs, buttons, messages and the like to be displayed. The woman, a high school student, obtained a ticket and tried to attend the rally wearing several buttons, including one supporting Bill Clinton, and was forced to relinquish her Bill Clinton button before being allowed into the rally. The Trial Court held that neither the City nor the Committee violated the woman's free speech rights based on the content of her speech, and the City's involvement was merely passive and diverse public property.

In *International Society for Krishna Consciousness, Inc. v. New Jersey Sports and Exposition Authority,* [49] the Krishna organization sought to distribute leaflets and solicit contributions at the racetrack and stadiums located in the Meadowlands Complex in New Jersey. The New Jersey Sports and Exposition Authority was created by the State of New Jersey to operate the sports complex known as the Meadowlands, which gave long term leases to both the New York Football Giants and the Cosmos Soccer Club, and leases said complex to other events as well. The racetrack located in the complex is also run by the Authority and shares a parking lot with the stadium, with pari-mutuel betting being the major source of revenue from the track.[50] The Authority adopted a policy prohibiting anyone from soliciting money or distributing literature at the complex.[51] While the ban did not apply to concessionaires at the complex, the policy was uniform and non-discriminatory, with all requests for permission to solicit contributions or distribute literature being turned down, regardless of the group. The Authority likewise refused to allow the Krishna group to solicit funds, and the Kirshnas sued, claiming that the Authority's policy was unconstitutional.

---

[48] Id. at 196.
[49] 691 F.2d 155 (3d Cir. 1982).
[50] Id. at 158.
[51] Id.

The Court of Appeals held that the Meadowlands complex, while being operated by the State of New Jersey, was none the less not a public forum, and thus a ban on any form of communication, as long as it was reasonable and content-neutral was permissible.[52] The Meadowlands is a commercial venture by the State of New Jersey and the court noted that the state's obligation to observe the Constitution did not cease while it was operating as a proprietor of the complex.[53] The ban on solicitation was justified by the need to maintain public order, that the Krishnas would be competing with the State for the money of its patrons, and that the patrons of the Meadowlands were a captive audience who would not be able to escape the message put forth by the Krishnas, should they wish to do so.[54]

This case is a good example of how a policy forbidding conduct was upheld due to its reasonableness and its uniform application to individuals and groups regardless of their identity.

In an almost identical case, *Carreras v. City of Anaheim*,[55] the Krishnas sought to distribute literature and seek contributions outside Anaheim Stadium and the walkways of the Anaheim Convention Center. A city ordinance required people soliciting within the city limits to obtain a perm it, and the Krishna organization was denied such a permit.[56] The Krishna organization had an informal agreement that it could solicit at the Convention Center but not the stadium. The Krishna organization chose to sue, alleging the ordinance requiring solicitation permits was unconstitutional.[57] The Court of Appeals ruled that the parking areas of the Stadium and the walkways of the Convention Center were public forums, and such locations must be open to expressive activity unless the activity was incompatible with the intended use of the facility.[58] Since the public was free to come and go as they pleased, the court felt the solicitation was not unduly burdensome, nor did it compete in a meaningful manner with the Stadium.[59]

---

[52] Id. at 162.
[53] Id. at 161.
[54] Id. at 162.
[55] 768 F.2d 1039 (9th Cir. 1985).
[56] Id. at 1041.
[57] Id.
[58] Id. at 1045.
[59] Id. at 1046.

The court also went on to determine that the ordinance was unconstitutional by placing impermissible limits on speech under the California Constitution.[60]

The difference between Anaheim Stadium case and the Meadowlands case is most likely due to the "snugness"[61] of the Meadowlands complex. Soliciting at the stadium was seen as being in direct competition with the betting activity at the racetrack. In the Anaheim case, solicitation did not reasonably interfere with the free flow of traffic and any impact from solicitation on concession sales at the Stadium.[62]

4) Photographic Restrictions and Freedom of the Press

In *D'Amario v. The Providence Civic Center Authority*,[63] a freelance photojournalist sought to take pictures at various rock concerts presented at the Providence Civic Center. The Civic Center leased its facility to Gemini, a promoter of entertainment events, who in turn contracted with various entertainers for their services. Several entertainers specified in their contracts with Gemini that no photographs or recordings of their concerts be allowed, and that such a restriction was non-negotiable. The photojournalist tried on several occasions to take pictures of the concerts where photographs were prohibited. The journalist sued after several unsuccessful attempts to smuggle his photographic equipment into the Center.[64] The journalist alleged that as a member of the press, prohibiting him from taking photographs violated his first amendment right to freedom of the press. The court recognized that while entertainment is a form of protected speech, and the dissemination of photographs is protected, limiting the access of the photographer was allowed, as the "First Amendment does not guarantee the press a constitutional right of special access to information not available to the public generally."[65]

---

[60] Id. at 1048.

[61] *International Society for Krishna Consciousness, Inc. v. New Jersey Sports and Exposition Authority*, 691 F.2d at 158.

[62] *Carreras v. City of Anaheim*, 768 F.2d at 1046.

[63] 639 F.Supp. 1538 (R.I. 1986).

[64] Id. at 1541.

[65] Id. at 1542, citing *Branzburg v. Hayes*, 408 U.S. at 684.

The photographer's First amendment rights to free speech were not implicated here, as his rights to expression were not limited, but his right to engage in a specific conduct was regulated.[66]

5) Content and Performance Regulations

There have been many attempts on the part of facilities to regulate the content of a performance or restrict the use of the facility by controversial performers. Regulations that are "content" oriented will almost always have a First Amendment aspect. The only way to validly limit access for acts deemed to be "inappropriate" for a facility would be based on safety or another basis that seeks only to regulate the time, place or manner of the speech.

(1) Events

In *Marilyn Manson Inc. v. New Jersey Sports & Exposition Authority,* [67] the New Jersey Sports & Exposition Authority (Authority) wished to prevent "OzzFest '97," a concert to be held at Giants Stadium on June 15, 1997, which was to include the heavy metal band Marilyn Manson, due to the fact the Authority found the band objectionable.[68] The court ordered the Authority to appear and show why they should not be enjoined from prohibiting Manson's appearance at the concert. Manson is a popular nationally performing band and has performed publicly without any legal problems or incidents.

The promoters of the event met with Authority officials in January or February of 1997 regarding staging of the concert. The promoters agreed to a provision in the contract allowing the Authority to remove any acts it deemed not within the best interests of the Authority. The Authority sought to have Manson and a group called Pantera removed from the bill, among their other regulations upon use of the stadium.[69] The promoter claimed that Manson was an integral part to the "Ozzfest" tour and the headliners would only appear if Manson appeared. The Authority later then tried to cancel the show and prohibit ticket sales, stating it did not want Manson performing at Giants stadium.

---

[66] Id. at 1541.

[67] No. 97-2229, 1997 U.S. Dist. LEXIS 9607 (May 7, 1997), 971 F.Supp. 875 (D. NJ 1997).

[68] Id. at *2.

[69] Id. at *7.

However, this attempt to cancel the event was after the initial advertising had been published and tickets had been printed. The court ruled that the prohibition was impermissible under the first amendment and issued an injunction allowing the concert to proceed. The court felt that the Authority could not cite legitimate safety concerns involving Manson's performance especially since additional safety personnel were required under the contract, and the guidelines used to identify problems were at best vague.

In *Ginsberg v. City of Miami,*[70] the Miami Marine Stadium had been rented for a reading of poetry by Allen Ginsberg. The Assistant City Manager interrupted the presentation because he felt the poetry was obscene and should not be allowed to continue due to the presence of teenagers in the audience.[71] Such an interruption of the performance was impermissible, largely because a determination of obscenity must be determined by proper judicial authority at an adversary hearing,[72] and not determined by someone in the audience. In restitution, the City of Miami was forced to make the stadium available to Ginsberg at no cost on another date in order to finish his reading.

In a slightly different vein, in *Redgrave v. Boston Symphony Orchestra,*[73] the Boston Symphony (BSO) canceled a contract it had with Vanessa Redgrave to act as narrator in several performances of "Oedipus Rex".[74] The BSO canceled the performances due to the protests of its subscribers and community members. The protest concerns Redgrave's political support of the Palestine Liberation Organization and her views regarding the state of Israel.[75] Redgrave sought both contractual damages and damages based on the alleged violation of her right to free speech both under the federal constitution and the Massachusetts Civil Rights Act.[76] While Redgrave prevailed on her contractually based claims, she did not prevail on her civil rights claims.

---

[70] 307 F.Supp. 675 (S.D. Fla. 1969).

[71] Id. at 676.

[72] Id.

[73] 855 F.2d 888 (1st Cir. 1988).

[74] Id.

[75] Id. at 890, 891.

[76] Id. at 890. The Massachusetts Civil Rights act applies to private citizens as well as the State, therefore a determination of whether state action was involved in this claim was unnecessary.

The Court of Appeals agreed with the Supreme Judicial Court of Massa-chusetts that one must balance private rights of free speech against each other.[77] In this case, the BSO did not deprive Ms. Redgrave of her civil rights, because it did not attempt to curb her free speech as to her political views, but just succumbed to pressure by those who did not agree with her viewpoint. While the Supreme Judicial Court felt that the BSO could be held liable for caving to third party pressure, and could do defend itself by asserting that it was also motivated by concerns of economic loss, physical safety and other business concerns,[78] the Court of Appeals held that the remarks made by the BSO in canceling the performances did not constitute "interference by threats, intimidation or coercion" of Redgrave's free speech rights.[79] The Court of Appeals declined to reach the federal first amendment claims asserted by Redgrave in order to avoid resolution of difficult and novel questions of constitutional law and to avoid further dispute with the state over state law issues.[80]

In *Promotions, Limited v. City of Southeast Charlotte, North Carolina,*[81] a promoter sought to put on the play "HAIR" in the Char-lotte Auditorium, but the Civic Center Authority disapproved of the play despite the fact that the play was successful in other markets. The Au-thority had hosted Broadway shows in the past, the auditorium was available when requested, and the promoter's attorneys assured the Authority that no local obscenity laws would be violated by HAIR's famous six-second nude scene. The Authority was not granted any censoring powers in its charter, but the Authority felt that the play would be against the "family entertainment" image they sought to maintain, regardless of the fact that the play was predicted to play to full or nearly full houses and generate a profit. The promoters sought an injunction to force the Authority to let them use the Auditorium to put on the play as planned, and the court granted the injunction. The court stated "it is much too late in the history of the First Amendment to seriously suggest that public officials managing a public facility may pick and choose the philosophical and ideological content of programs using public audito-

---

[77] *Redgrave,* at 904.

[78] Id. at 902.

[79] Id. at 910, citing the Supreme Judicial Court's plurality opinion, 502 N.E. 2d at 97.

[80] Id. at 912.

[81] 333 F.Supp. 345 (W.D. N.C. 1971).

riums"[82] and issued an injunction allowing the play to be performed as requested.

Many music acts have been subject to accusations that their work is obscene or potentially disrupting to the general peace. Most recently, the Meadowlands sought to prevent the heavy metal band, Marilyn Manson, from performing, alleging security concerns (see case above). Perhaps the most litigated band in recent history was 2 Live Crew, a Florida rap group, famous for their explicit lyrics. The sheriff of Ft. Lauderdale, FL sought a declaration that the group's album "As Nasty As They Want To Be" was obscene. Having been granted this order, the sheriff sought to prohibit local record stores from selling the album, but the court prohibited such a prior restraint.[83] The Federal District Court declared the album obscene, but the decision was reversed by the Court of Appeals, and the Supreme Court denied certiorari.

During this process, a club in Rhode Island was threatened to have its entertainment licenses revoked if they allowed 2 Live Crew to play at their club. In *Atlantic Beach Casino, Inc., d/b/a the Windjammer v. Morenzoni*, [84] the plaintiffs operated a club which featured live bands and had contracted with 2 Live Crew for a performance on October 6, 1990. On June 6, 1990, a federal judge in Florida had declared the group's album obscene under civil standards, and this prompted the town counsel to send a letter to the managers of the Windjammer to appear before the council regarding the scheduled 2 Live Crew performance. At the meeting, members stated their disapproval of the group's lyrics and their contribution to "America's slide into the sewer," concerns about public safety and possible rowdy behavior of fans. The Council voted to refer the obscenity issue to the State Attorney General, but notified the Windjammer that it was considering revoking its liquor and entertainment licenses. A date was set for a show cause hearing on the licensing. The Windjammer filed suit, seeking to enjoin the council from revoking its licenses.

---

[82] Id. at 351, quoting Judge Craven in *United States Serviceman's Fund v. Shands*, 440 F.2d 44 (1971).

[83] See *Skyywalker Records, Inc. v. Nicholas Navarro*, 739 F. Supp. 578 (S.D. Fla.1990), and rev'd 960 F.2d 134 (11ᵗʰ Cir. 1992) and Cert. Denied 113 S.Ct. 659 (1992).

[84] 749 F. Supp. 38 (D. R.I. 1990).

The court clearly found that the licensing statute vested un-bridled discretion in governmental officials, as the ordinance regarding licenses was utterly devoid of standards. The court issued an injunction allowing the concert to go on as scheduled and to prohibit revocation of the Windjammer's licenses. The Town Council's attempt to prevent the concert was found to be a prior restraint on free speech and bore a heavy presumption of unconstitutionality. The Town Council was prohibited from preventing the performance directly, or indirectly by revocation of the entertainment licenses of the club hosting the concert.

6) Speech by Attendees

In *Sparrow et. al. v. Goodman et. al.,*[85] in 1971, several people were denied access and ejected from a rally where Billy Graham and President Nixon appeared together. Most of the individuals were told that their valid tickets were "counterfeit," many were members of anti-Viet Nam war protesters, and many had long hair. The people were forcibly ejected and arrested from the Coliseum and sued the police chief of Charlotte, the Secret Service, and others for violating their constitutional rights. The local police alleged they were merely complying with the requests of the Secret Service by maintaining security for the President. The Secret Service and the Marshall, Mr. Helms, were not very forth-coming with any rationalization for their decisions on who should be ejected. Although it was admitted that if an individual posed a threat to the President, the Secret Service would have taken care of the matter, and in this case it left removal of all seated "offending" patrons to the local authorities who claimed they were acting under the direction of the Secret Service.

The court found that the plaintiffs were manhandled, abused and excluded from the public gathering in a public place for which no restrictions had been placed other than having a ticket. The marshals had excluded the Plaintiffs unjustly and none of those excluded had any history of law breaking or violence or disruption of public proceedings. No one arrested was convicted of any crime. No adequate reason was advanced for having treated the Plaintiffs in that manner. The court found that the Secret Service or other government officials were responsible for such an exclusion, and that dissent with the government was the reason for exclusion. The court also found

---

[85] 361 F.Supp. 566 (W.D. N.C. 1973).

that the Charlotte Police aided in the exclusions. Constitutional rights were violated in wholesale fashion under the First, Fourth and Fifth Amendments (speech and assembly; unlawful arrest, denial of due process and Fourth amendment rights against search and seizure without warrants). The court then held that the case was properly certified as a class action, and that the deplorable actions of the Defendants required that they be enjoined from discriminatorily arresting, detaining or keeping Plaintiffs and others on account of their dress, hairstyle, lifestyle, or exercise of constitutionally protected rights without probable cause, or for any other cause not rationally related to the personal safety of the President. The court ruled that the case would go forward to trial for the damage claims.

12.03 How Can Facilities Best Work Around the Public Forum Doctrine?

1) Classification of the Facility

As we can see from many of the above cases, whether a restriction or policy will be constitutionally valid depends on whether the facility is a public forum, limited public forum, or a non-public forum. Even when the State runs a facility as in *International Society for Krishna Consciousness Inc. v. Murphy,*[86] this does not guarantee that the facility will be considered a public forum. Most facilities will be safely within the limited public forum or non-public forum realm, allowing it more flexibility in setting policies and regulations restricting forms of expression in its boundaries. However, if a facility has been consistently opened up to the public for a wide variety of uses as in *National Socialist White People's Party v. Ringers,*[87] it can be considered to be a traditional public forum, just like a public street or park.

2) Written Guidelines

As noted above, many facilities have policies that are not written or spelled out in any document or manual. Managers, security officers or others can rely on for guidance in dealing with problems that may involve the First Amendment and its free speech provisions.

---

[86] See *Calash v. City of Bridgeport*, supra.
[87] 473 F.2d 1010 (4th Cir. 1972).

The lack of written guidelines can cause confusion in the classification of a facility as a limited public forum or non-public forum, and thus change the test used for determining whether the restriction in question is valid.

Further, written standards can be helpful to those enforcing the policies of the facility, by providing guidance as to what is viewed as permissible behavior, leaving little room for arbitrary enforcement of regulations.[88]

Care must be taken when drawing up any policies or guidelines, making sure they specifically regulate behavior in the way proposed. Vagueness and over-inclusive regulations will not withstand constitutional challenge. Vague phrases like "tasteful" "vulgar" and "derogatory" do not state with specificity what regulation is sought, but a phrase such as "no obscene language or messages not pertaining to the event at which the banner is placed," followed by examples of permissible and impermissible signs may have allowed the City of Cincinnati and the Reds baseball team to prohibit the religious message sign they confiscated in *Aubrey v. City of Cincinnati*[89] in a constitutionally-correct way, as this phrasing, along with examples, leaves little discretion to those enforcing the policy.

Additionally, restrictions on activities such as recording of concerts or productions, or photography are allowed, but their presence in written form either in the contract with the performer or in the facility's handbook or both make it clear that such prohibitions have been clearly addressed.[90]

3) Consistent Application of Established Guidelines
Once guidelines or policies are in place, it becomes imperative that they are applied to everyone in an evenhanded manner. If a rule is promulgated prohibiting solicitation, a facility cannot exclude religious organizations but permit civic or charitable groups to solicit without violating the constitutionally protected freedoms of the prohibited group. Likewise, a facility manager must take care that enforcement of its policies are equally applied, regardless of whom seeks a variance from established guidelines.

---

[88] See *Aubrey v. City of Cincinnati*, supra.
[89] Supra.
[90] See *D'Amario v. The Providence Civic Center Authority*, supra.

If such a variation in application of the policy is allowed, then the variation must become the new established policy, and all similarly situated individuals must be treated in the same manner.

Chapter 13

Related State and Federal Statutes

By Turner D. Madden

13.00   Introduction

The purpose of this chapter is to cover material of interest to facilities and their managers, which do not warrant separate chapters on their own. Topics from the copyright law, to liquor licensing, special events and their regulations, the Freedom of Information Act, are covered in this chapter. I hope that you will find this chapter of interest, covering a broad range of topics that may or may not affect your facility.

13.01   The Federal Copyright Act

1) Trademarks and Copyrights

A copyright is a form of protecting an author's or creator's original work, such as literary, musical, artistic, dramatic or other intellectual works. The protection can be granted to both published and unpublished works and is granted for a specific period of time, before the work is deemed part of the public domain.

The goal of the copyright process is to encourage the development of new ideas, writings and discoveries by initially benefiting the creator and later benefiting the public as a whole. While copyright law has occasionally been modified to reflect changes in technology or philosophy, its essence has remained the same over time. The patent and copyright clause contained in the Constitution empowers Congress to "promote the progress of science and useful arts by securing for limited times to authors and inventors, the exclusive right to their respective writings and discoveries." Significantly, this is the only right mentioned in the body of the Constitution itself, with all other "rights" to be found in the amendments to the Constitution.

Congress passed the first copyright law in 1790, limiting protection to books, charts and maps. This copyright protection granted authors a monopoly on their works for a limited time, after which the works would become public domain. Congress, wishing to avoid "secret" copyrights, imposed a number of technical requirements to anyone wishing to claim a copyright. A "c" within a circle, followed by the author's name and date of publication was required. Additionally, the work had to be registered and renewed, and two copies of the document had to be sent to the government. If any of these requirements were not met, a copyright could not be enforced and the work fell into the public domain. Over time, the formalities have faded away, with Congress eliminating the last mandatory requirement of copyright notice in 1989.

While the formal requirements to copyright one's work have diminished, the rights under the copyright law have expanded. The original term for a copyright was only fourteen years; now it is the author's life plus fifty years, quite a long time indeed. Likewise, for works created by employees during their employment, the term is for seventy-five years from the date of first publication.

Protection under the subject matter provisions of the Act extends to seven areas of work including literary works, from books, articles and scripts to computer programs; musical works, dramatic works, pantomimes and choreographic works, pictorial, graphical or sculptural works; motion pictures, and sound recordings. Protection is excluded for names, titles, short phrases, slogans, familiar symbols or designs, variations in typeface, lettering or coloring, and mere lists of ingredients and contents. Ideas, procedures, methods, systems, processes, concepts, principles, discoveries and devices are also excluded from copyright protection, while a description, explanation or illustration of any of the above could be protected.

The original authorship requirement is also important. Merely compiling information in the public domain does not allow copyright. You cannot copyright the telephone book; it is just an alphabetical list of local citizens and there is no "originality" or creativity involved in its creation. Additionally, musical works, choreographs, speeches, or performances and the like must be notated or recorded in order to qualify for copyright protection.

Without recording or written documentation, no copyright protection can be granted. Once the documentation or "fixation" has taken place, the work is protected; no further registration is required.

However, people still register their works with the copyright office. The registration process is a prerequisite to sue someone for violation of a copyright, and while one can still sue for infringement without having a copyright certificate issued by the copyright office, the copyright office must still be notified of your claim. The copyright certificate serves as prima facie evidence of the validity of the claimed copyright, and, in business, possession of the certificate is necessary to satisfy the buyer of rights, a bank, or the like. Timely registration also allows the owner of the copyright to receive statutory damages and attorney's fees in an infringement case. Damages are granted automatically once an infringement is shown; actual damages do not have to be shown, which often could be expensive or next to impossible to prove. Statutory damages range from $500 to $20,000, and willful infringement could increase the damages to $100,000.

In order to register a copyright, an application, a deposit of the work or identifying material and a check for $20.00 is required. Six forms of registration exist: 1) TX, for text, including computer programs; 2) SE for serials, including magazines, newspapers and journals; 3) PA performing arts covering musical, dramatic or choreographed works, films or other audio-visual work; 4) VA covering visual arts including pictures, graphics and sculpture; 5) SR covering sound recordings, and lastly 6) RE covering renewal of copyright claims under federal law prior to 1978. Once copyrighted, the owner of a work has the exclusive right to reproduce copies of the work, prepare translations or derivatives of the work, distribute copies of the work publicly, perform or display the work publicly, and authorize anyone else to do the same. If any of these rights are violated, one can sue the person who has infringed on the right. In 1976, a section of the copyright law was amended as to allow any of the rights associated with copyright to be owned or transferred separately, meaning book rights, movie rights, magazine rights, foreign rights and the like could all be sold separately, allowing for much greater bargaining power for the creator of the work.

Under the work-for-hire provision, if a work is recreated in the scope of employment, the copyright law treats the employer as the owner of the right, not the author. This provision is to protect employers who are directing and paying for the work created, and allows them to thus benefit from the work so created, it is critical in the record, film and publishing industries.

There are several exceptions to the copyright law, including the fair use provision. Under the fair use provision, a court can consider whether the alleged infringement of a copyright has been used for a commercial or non-profit educational purpose; what the nature of the copyrighted work is; the amount and substantiality of the portion used in relation to the copyrighted work as a whole and the effect of such a use on the potential market for or value of the copyrighted work. For example, if someone borrows one line out of a novel for his or her own publication, the portion used probably is not substantial, nor reduces the market for the copyrighted work. In contrast, if whole chapters were excerpted, the case would be substantially different. Fair use allows copying without permission from nor payment to the owner of the copyright, where the use is reasonable and non-harmful. This allows the use of work without permission or compensation when used for teaching, research, comment, criticism and news reporting. Other exceptions cover use for limited purposes and under compulsory licenses, where the consent of the author is not required, but compensation is made at a fixed rate.

Thus, the overall purpose of the copyright act is to allow the author or creator of a work to reap the benefits of his or her work, for a limited time, and then to allow us all to enjoy and use the work without restriction thereafter. Imagine having to pay a license fee every time "Happy Birthday" was sung, or the "Star Spangled Banner." By limiting the time for a copyright, these works have become public domain and are available for use, for free, by us all.

In *Maryland Stadium Authority v. Becker*,[1] the Stadium Authority (MSA), which operates Camden Yards Baseball Park sued a vendor for the wrongful use of the mark "Camden Yards" on his tee shirts and other articles of clothing.[2]

---

[1] 806 F.Supp. 1236 (D. Md. 1992), aff'd per curiam 36 F.3d 1093 (4th Cir. 1994).

[2] Id. at 1237.

Both parties moved for summary judgment. The Park was constructed between 1989 and 1991, and was officially opened in the spring of 1992. The name "Oriole Park at Camden Yards" was chosen. In 1991, the vendor began selling tee shirts outside Memorial Stadium, the previous home of the Orioles with a message stating "Camden Yards means baseball." He sold shirts on the street, through mail order, sports bars, stores and in local publications. In August of 1991, MSA wrote Becker and demanded that he stop using the name "Camden Yards." Becker did not respond to the letter, and MSA filed suit under the Lanham Act, which allows federal claims for unfair competition by use of a trademark or trade name, even if the mark or name had not been federally registered. To establish infringement of an unregistered mark, a person must establish (1) the adoption and use of the mark and entitlement to enforce it, and that (2) the adoption and use of a junior user of the mark (the vendor) is likely to cause confusion that the goods or services emanate from the senior user.[3] Essentially this is to prevent someone from trading on the good will or reputation of others, for their own profit.

The court held that the name Camden Yards first became associated with the stadium in 1987; the Stadium used "Camden Yards" in all publicity events and references to the new stadium all during the construction process, and when Becker began to use the name, promotional efforts of MSA were already bearing fruit. The court also ruled that confusion was likely and thus granted summary judgment to MSA and permanently enjoined Becker from using the Camden Yards mark.[4]

In *The Sports Authority, Inc. v. Prime Hospitality Corp.*,[5] The Sports Authority (TSA) sued Prime Hospitality under the Lanham Act[6] for Prime's use of the words "sports authority" in the name of its sports-oriented restaurants, advertising and signs as an infringement and diluted value of TSA's registered trademarks.

TSA is a sporting goods and apparels retailer with stores throughout the U.S., and owns a federal trademark and service mark to the words "The Sports Authority," and a service mark for its logo.

---

[3] Id. at 1238.
[4] Id. at 1241, 1242.
[5] 89 F.3d 955 (2d Cir. 1996).
[6] 15 U.S.C. § 1051.

TSA advertises extensively, and had significant exposure in the New York market. Prime owns and operates hotels throughout the U.S. and runs eight sports-related restaurants called the "Sports Authority Food, Spirits and Sports," mainly in the greater New York area. The first restaurant opened in 1991 in Fairfield, New Jersey, and the restaurants are widely advertised in print, radio and signs. In September, 1991, TSA informed Prime it had become aware of it using the name "Sports Authority" and requested it cease and desist in the use of the name, to which Prime responded it did not think its use was an infringement on TSA's trademarks or service marks. Prime conducted a search shortly thereafter, confirming TSA's marks and their registration numbers. Prime filed an application for its mark with the Patent and Trademark office, which initially refused its application, until Prime said "Food, Spirits and Sports" was part of its mark, after which the mark was published by the Trademark office. TSO filed its opposition to Prime's mark.[7] In July 1993, TSA filed suit against Prime, and in November, the trademark office suspended opposition proceedings in light of the suit. In July 1994, the parties both moved for summary judgment, and the district court, applying a balancing test, concluded that the factors did not support TSA's claim of trademark infringement and granted judgment to Prime. TSA appealed, and the Court of Appeals held that TSA's claim to the mark had existed for five years without challenge and was a strong claim to the mark. TSA also provided evidence that Prime used the words "Sports Authority" in advertisement without the trailing words "Food Spirits & Sports," including advertisement on local, sports radio stations, clearly using "Sports Authority" without the trailing words, where TSA also advertised its sporting goods stores, and the use of the words were identical. Prime's employees also answered the telephone only as "sports authority" without the trailing words, and were listed in the phone book as just the "Sports Authority." While the services provided by the businesses are different, they did advertise in the same marketplace, including on the same radio station. In addition, many telephone calls were made to Prime's restaurants, seeking TSA's stores, and vice versa, helping to support an argument of public confusion between the two businesses.

---

[7] 89 F.3d at 959.

While the district court concluded that the confusion, if any, would not affect TSA's business, TSA contended, and the Court of Appeals agreed, that the public could conclude TSA sponsored the restaurants, and TSA had no way of controlling quality or public perception of the restaurants, and thus any crossover opinion as to TSA's businesses.

Prime could not show that it was using the mark in good faith, although it denied any knowledge of TSA's mark until it received the cease and desist letter several months after opening its first restaurant. In fact, Prime had not consulted an attorney before using the name and continued to use just the words "sports authority" after receiving the cease and desist letter, and in fact continued to expand its restaurant business using the name. The Court of Appeals vacated the lower court's summary judgment in favor of Prime and remanded the case for further action consistent with its opinion and analysis.[8]

In *Boston Athletic Association v. Sullivan*,[9] The Boston Athletic Association (BAA) sued sellers of T-shirts for violation of their copyrighted service mark, "Boston Marathon." The BAA yearly sponsors the Boston Marathon, and due to increasing costs to sponsor the race, had sought ways to raise funds to pay for the event. The BAA was issued copyrights to "Boston Marathon" and "BAA Marathon," and entered into exclusive licensing agreements with Image Impact, Inc. to manufacture and distribute items with its logo and copyrighted mark.[10] Sullivan and Beau Tease developed T-shirts with a logo stating "1987 Marathon" and showed three runners, then underneath stated "Hopkinton to Boston," the route of the Marathon. The BAA sued, alleging infringement on its copyright. The court reviewed the design and held that while everyone would know that the race referred to the Boston Marathon, there was no direct infringement on the copyrighted mark, the copyright law could not be so broadly construed as to prohibit the words Boston and Marathon from being used at all, the licensed material was clearly of better quality, and the mark itself did not give rise to any

---

[8] Id. at 965.
[9] No. 87-0802-Y, 1988 U.S. Dist. LEXIS 17953 (D. Mass. March 7, 1988).
[10] Id. at *3, *4.

confusion among members of the public that the products were authorized by the BAA, and thus the T-shirts could be sold by Sullivan and
Beau Tease.[11]

2) Naming Rights and Advertising Contracts

In today's competitive marketplace, we are all looking for new
and creative ways to generate revenues. One of the most innovative ways
to bring in a steady stream of revenue from advertising is to sell the
naming rights of your facility to a company. This is perhaps one of the
best ways to get a company's name or product before the public. Having
the name used in association with a sports arena, stadium or performing
arts center would permit a company's name, product name or service to
be referred to in all press releases, sports media announcements, and even
day-to-day references between individuals. A company's name could be
referred to in every news broadcast, in newspapers, and by word of
mouth whenever your facility is mentioned.

As you know, it is expensive to advertise. The positive exposure
from a naming rights contract can have a substantial and long-term
financial impact for the facility and a long-term strategic impact for the
purchasing company. This is the main reason such companies as America West, ARCO, AT&T Bank One, Blockbuster, Carrier, Coca-Coca,
Continental Airlines, CoreStates Bank, Coors, Delta, Fleet Bank, Her-
shey, Kellogg, MCI, Sony, United and US Airlines have chosen to
purchase naming rights.[12] Some of these facilities are new, state-of-the-
art arenas. Even older, well-known stadiums and performing arts centers
have been renamed with much success. Other companies have also used
this opportunity to purchase luxury boxes at the facility that can then be
used for client entertainment, meetings, conferences, or rewards to
performance oriented employees. Pro Player, a sporting goods
manufacturer, uses the stadium which bears its name in Florida for sales
meetings and shoots all of its commercials there as well. However, the
naming and renaming of facilities has also spawned some litigation, as
we will see below.

---

[11] Id. at *7, *8, *9.

[12] Please note that all of the companies listed herein have registered
trademarks in their products and company names.

In *Pilot Air Freight Corp. v. City of Buffalo*,[13] Pilot purchased "naming rights" for a ball park in Buffalo, NY from the City, where Bison Baseball held its home games. The contract was entered into in 1986 and provided that for a yearly fee, the stadium would be known for a term of twenty years as "Pilot Field" in all advertising, promotion, any sort of media coverage, and by any persons using the stadium, including the Bisons. Pilot was also required to lease a luxury box at the stadium for a fee of $4,300. Pilot sued the city when it was forced to lease the box directly from the Bisons at a rate higher than that provided in its contract with the city and sued the city for violation of the naming rights contract when Bison had referred to the field as "Home of the Bisons" and "Ballpark" rather than as "Pilot Field." Bison claimed it was granted exclusive advertising rights under its contract with the city, generic references were not interferences with the Pilot-City contract, and that it should not have to indemnify city for any damages alleged by Pilot for failure to properly use the name or for leasing the box at a higher rate. The results of this litigation are still pending; however it points out that the separate contractual arrangements between the city, Bison and Pilot without any overriding three-party agreement clearly led to the ongoing disagreement. This issue may have been properly avoided had the city, Bison and Pilot agreed to appropriate rental fees for the luxury box and the use of the name "Pilot Field" rather than having subsequent third party beneficiary disagreements at a later date.

In *Post Newsweek Stations-Connecticut, Inc. v. Traveler's Insurance Company*,[14] the 1981 World Figure Skating Championships were placed at the Skating Club of Hartford by the International Skating Union, a group that controls world-class amateur skating. The ISU had granted exclusive television rights in 1978 to Candid productions, associated with ABC. These rights included exclusivity against television news broadcasts of any length that included video film or videotaped coverage of the championships prior to telecast.

When the Hartford Skating Club learned of its contract to host the championships, it wrote to local news stations, informing them of the ISU's contracts with Candid/ABC.

---

[13] No. 91-CV-308E, 1992 U.S. Dist. LEXIS 12341 (July 28, 1992) and No. 91-CV-0308E(M), 1996 U.S. Dist. LEXIS 2800 (March 8, 1996).
[14] 510 F. Supp. 81 (D. Conn. 1981).

This advisory letter arrived with an indemnity agreement attached, proposing that in consideration for entrance to the Hartford Civic Center Coliseum, a TV station must agree to refrain from broadcasting any footage of the event until ABC had concluded the entire telecast of the event. The TV station was also asked to indemnify the Skating Club and other parties for costs and attorney's fees incurred if the station violated any part of the agreement. [15]

A TV station claimed that the agreement infringed on its First and Fourteenth amendment rights to report newsworthy events. The court reviewed prior cases that had held a station could be liable in tort for broadcasting the entire act of a performer, as it diminished the commercial value of seeing the performance live. The question in this case pivoted around whether the station could have "special access" to the championships. The court held that the ISU could properly contract with parties regarding the distribution of its entertainment product, and that the restrictions it sought to prohibit TV cameras without a signed indemnity agreement, were universally enforced. The court found that the press had no special right of access to the championships with TV cameras not allowed to the general public, but had right of access on the same terms as everyone else, i.e. they could enter with their cameras only if they signed the indemnity agreement.

It was considered whether, because the Civic Center was municipally owned, special access rules applied, and whether or not state action could be implied by the denial of access without indemnity agreements. The court held that the Civic Center functioned as a proprietary rather than governmental institution, seeking to make a profit. Since the State was acting as if it were a private individual in this case, any contractual restrictions would be upheld if they were not arbitrary and capricious. The court held that the restrictions imposed were not arbitrary, nor was censorship at play, and therefore the preliminary injunction and restraining order sought by the TV station were denied.

In *Philip Morris, Incorporated v. Pittsburgh Penguins, Inc.,* [16] Philip Morris sought to enjoin the Penguins and the Civic Arena Corporation from interfering with an advertising contract between Philip Morris and the Penguins, and from interfering with advertising sold or rented to Philip Morris under the contract.

---

[15] Id. at 84.
[16] 589 F.Supp. 912 (W.D. Pa. 1983); aff'd 738 F.2d 424 (3d Cir. 1984).

On June 1, 1971, The Public Auditorium Authority, which operated the Civic Arena in Pittsburgh, entered into a ten year license with the Pittsburgh Penguins allowing hockey games to be played in the arena. The initial license forbade the Penguins from advertising in the arena. In 1975, a new group acquired the Penguins, and continued to license the arena under an assignment of the original agreement. In 1976, the Authority wished to enter into a new ten-year agreement with the Penguins, also prohibiting advertising within the arena. Later in 1976, the Authority entered into a separate advertising agreement with the Penguins, allowing the team to sell advertising within the arena, if the Authority approved the ads. The advertising agreement between the Penguins and the Authority was to expire in 1978.

In 1977, the Penguins entered into a contract with Philip Morris for advertising on the scoreboard for $13,500 per year, for a ten-year period. The advertising began in 1977, and the Penguins and the Authority split the funds received, 25% for the Authority, 75% for the Penguins. In late 1978, the DeBartolo Corporation took control of the Penguins, and in review of the Penguins contracts, felt the contract with Philip Morris was unenforceable, since the Penguins' right to sell advertising in the arena expired in 1978. Nothing was done about the contract, so Philip Morris continued to make payments per the 1977 contract through 1982. When the Civic Arena Corporation, (CAC) also owned by DeBartolo took over management of the Arena, the division of the advertising revenue, including the money received from Philip Morris changed to 40% CAX, 40% Penguins and 20% to the Spirit, the indoor soccer team tenant of the arena.

In early 1983, the need for a new scoreboard was discussed and AS&I outlined a proposal for a new scoreboard, indicating much larger advertising revenues could be generated per year. The Penguins and CAC accepted AS&I's proposal by letter of intent on July 23, 1983. AS&I eventually entered into an agreement with RJ Reynolds tobacco company for advertising on the scoreboard. In June of 1983, representatives from CAC and AS&I met with Philip Morris proposing that Philip Morris pay $100,000 per year for advertising rights in the arena, which Philip Morris rejected, still believing their 1977 contract was in effect. Philip Morris the sought to enjoin the Penguins and CAC from interfering in the existing advertising contract.

The District Court found that the advertising rights granted to the Penguins in 1976 were "unfettered" and although the advertising agreement was only 2 years in duration, nothing in the agreement prohibited the Penguins from selling long-term contracts over that period to potential advertisers. The Authority itself approved of the Philip Morris contract, including the length of the contract, and the Authority and CAC continued to accept Philip Morris' advertising money long after they suspected the contract might be unenforceable. It was only when CAC learned that much greater revenues were available with a new scoreboard that they sought to terminate the Philip Morris agreement. The court further noted that CAC and the Penguins were both owned by DeBartolo, and that CAC and the Penguins both benefited from the contract with Philip Morris. The court held that CAC could not repudiate the contract, especially after benefiting from the contract for two years without complaint. Therefore, CAC and the Penguins were enjoined from removing any of Philip Morris' advertising for the duration of the contract or from interfering with any of the other rights granted to Philip Morris under the 1977 agreement.

3) Music Licensing

The purpose of this section is to provide some general information about the copyright law, an analysis of a music licensing "facility" agreement and alternatives to entering into a music license agreement. This information may not be applicable or useful to facilities that work with music licensing on a daily basis or promote music events.

Many of the events held in public assembly facilities include copyrighted music. The responsibility for obtaining a music license lies with the promoter or organization sponsoring the event. Prior to Nov. 19, 1990, states and their local governments were immune from copyright infringement liability under the Eleventh Amendment of the U.S. Constitution. The U.S. Congress amended the Copyright Act in 1990 with the Copyright Remedy Clarification Act, which specified that states and their local governments may be liable for the infringement of copyrighted music and materials. Public facilities are obligated to obtain a license when they use live or prerecorded music for their own purposes.

The Federal Copyright Act of 1976 provides authors and composers with basic protection against copyright infringement, including substantial monetary damages for copyright infringement ranging from $500 to $20,000 for each infringement.

The American Society of Composers, Authors and Publishers (ASCAP), Broadcast Music, Inc. (BMI) and other organizations have requested that public facilities enter into music license agreements that cover copyright works of music performed or displayed "publicly" in their facilities. These copyright license organizations receive their right to license non-dramatic copyrighted music from the original authors and composers.

a) Blanket Music License Agreements

ASCAP and BMI attempt to minimize copyright infringement and encourage entities to execute blanket license agreements by filing copyright infringement lawsuits. Because of this, some of our industry associations are challenging the ASCAP and BMI blanket license agreements. These license agreements are worded in favor of the copyright owner and provide for substantial penalties for not reporting events or for slow payment. BMI's Standard Facility Agreement has several provisions that should seriously concern facility managers. Section 15 (a) of BMI's agreement provides that the facility must pay a fee according to a schedule for each performance of copyrighted music, whether or not the facility is promoting or co-promoting the attraction or permitting the facility to be used by an outside promoter.

This provision gives BMI the right to receive a fee from both the facility and the promoter for the same performance.

There are other questionable provisions in the BMI agreement. For example, Section 7(a) allows BMI to audit the books and records of the facility; Section 15 requires quarterly schedules and payments. If none are submitted by the facility, payments are due for each performance whether or not BMI holds the license to said music. Furthermore, in reviewing BMI's "Facility Report forms," the primary information requested from BMI seems to be the list of promoters that sponsored activities in the facility.

These license agreements should be reviewed with extreme care.

b) Copyright Infringement

In order to explain how a copyright infringement action is applied in a commercial lease, we must understand the legal concept of vicarious liability. Vicarious liability is where liability is imposed on parties other than the one that performed the wrongful act. *Shapiro, Bernstein & Co. v. H.L. Green, Co.*,[17] is the leading case on vicarious liability for infringement of copyrighted music. In this case, the Federal Court of Appeals for the Second Circuit found the owner of a chain store liable for copyright infringement based on sales of "bootleg" records sold by a concessionaire that operated the record departments in the chain stores. in its decision, the Court reviewed two lines of cases. The first concerned landlords who leased property to tenants who engaged in copyright infringing conduct on the leased premises. The other line of cases concerned so-called "dance hall" cases where a hall's proprietor hires a band, which draws customers and profits by performing copyrighted music without a license.

The Court states that "If the landlord lets his premises without knowledge of the impending infringement by his tenant, exercises no supervision over him, charges a fixed rental and receives no other benefit from the infringement, and contributes in no way to it, it has been held that the landlord is not liable for his tenant's wrongdoing." However, the Court cites the dance hall cases that indicate that where a proprietor has the right and ability to supervise the infringing activity, and an obvious and direct financial interest in exploiting the copyrighted materials, that he will be liable for copyright infringement whether or not the proprietor has actual knowledge of the composition to be played or any control over their selection. The Court then applied these legal principles to the facts in the Shapiro, Bernstein case. The Court found that the chain store owner:

1. Retained the ultimate right of supervision over the conduct of the record concession and its employees; and

2. Reserved a share of the gross receipts from the licensee or subcontractor's sale of records.

The Court applied the concept of vicarious liability and found that the chain store owner was liable for the tenant's unauthorized sales of bootleg records.

---

[17] 316 F.2b 304 (CA2 1963).

The Court noted that landlords that do not have the intention to infringe, or knowledge of the infringement, have the ability to protect themselves against copyright infringement liability by the execution of a hold harmless agreement or indemnity agreement with tenants, or by purchasing insurance to cover the potential liability.

There is another basis for ascribing liability to a facility under the theory of contributory infringement. The test for this was set forth in *Gershwin Publishing Corps. v. Columbia Artists Management, Inc.*[18] The Court stated that a person "... with knowledge of infringing activity, induces, causes, or materially contributes to the infringing conduct of another, may be held liable as a contributory infringer."

c) Alternatives to Music Licensing Agreements

As the Court stated in *Shapiro, Bernstein,* landlords have the ability to protect themselves by inserting a hold harmless clause in their lease agreements. Facility managers should use the control test. Please note that the more control the facility has over the tenant and the gross receipts, the more likely a court will impose vicarious liability for copyright infringement. The following language represents a clause that could be included in your facility rental agreement:

> "The (Promoter or other Party) represents and warrants that all copyrighted music will be performed or produced, with the express permission from the copyright owner. The Promoter or other party represents and warrants that any and all obligations under the copyright license shall be performed or completed by the (Promoter). The (Promoter) agrees to save, hold harmless and indemnify the (facility and its employees) for any and all liability, claims, costs, actions expenses including legal fees and that may arise out of or from a copyright license agreement or copyright infringement lawsuit or both or any representation or warranty made herein."

---

[18] 443 F.2d 1159 (CA2 1971).

Concerning insurance, copyright infringement actions are usually excluded from coverage under general liability insurance policies. A special rider or policy is necessary to insure the risk of copyright infringement.

Depending on the use of the facility, it may be appropriate to enter into a license agreement with ASCAP or BMI. However, if your facility occasionally has performances that include non-dramatic copyright music you must manage the risk of copyright infringement by appropriately structuring your license agreements or by insuring the infringement risk.

13.02 Local Permits and Licenses for Events

In *SEG Sports Corp. v. State Athletic Commission,*[19] SEG again sought to put on its Ultimate Fighting Championship, this time in Niagara Falls, NY on February 7, 1997, one day after the effective date of a statute that required a license be obtained from the New York State Athletic Commission to stage combative sporting events. SEG had held 13 prior Ultimate Fighting events, including one in Buffalo, NY in August of 1995. Ticket sales of over $150,000 had been sold to a live audience for the Niagara Falls event, with plans to broadcast the event by cable. SEG entered into contracts with various individuals including the Niagara Falls Convention and Civic Center, DirecTV, and individual fighters. On January 30, 1997, The Athletic Commission issued temporary rules regulating combative sports, including regulations regarding the size of the ring, wearing of gloves, and rules regarding head butts, choke holds and kicks above the shoulders. SEG sought to enjoin the Commission from enforcing their rules, and allow SEG to use its rules instead.[20] The court found that the new rules imposed did not pose irreparable harm or loss of good will for SEG. The court indicated that the cancellation of the event was measurable in money, but that long range damages to SEG's reputation were speculative and thus, SEG could not show irreparable harm necessary to enjoin the Commission from enforcing their rules.[21]

---

[19] 952 F.Supp. 202 (S.D. NY 1997).
[20] Id. at 204.
[21] Id. at 205.

In *Charlevoix Productions, Inc. v. County of Charlevoix,*[22] the owner of Castle Farms Music Theater where outdoor festivals and performances were held, challenged the constitutionality of a Mass Gathering Ordinance that required certain security, medical, food and drink, plumbing, traffic control and other services be provided for any event attracting above 2,000 persons. The Castle Farms claimed that such regulations were burdensome and restricted First Amendment speech and assembly rights. The court held that the government certainly has a legitimate purpose in trying to control public safety, but that exemptions present in the regulation covering governmental and charitable organizations was an improper classification to be drawn by and did deny the Plaintiff of his equal protection rights and treating him differently than governmental or charitable institutions.[23]

13.03 Registration for a Business Licensee

In *Andree v. Ashland County,*[24] owners of the Idlewild resort attempted to stage an outdoor rock festival, anticipating 2000 to 4000 people to attend.[25] A local sheriff learned that Idlewild had not obtained a permit under a local ordinance requiring detailed provisions be made for large gatherings, covering plumbing, food and drink, medical treatment, security, parking, and telephone service and post a bond.[26] The sheriff had a deputy deliver a copy of the ordinance to Idlewild, who stated they would not comply because "it was not worth the paper it was written on."[27] The sheriff attempted to enjoin the concert but failed, and instead had deputies attend the concert in full dress uniform, equipped with riot batons and weapons to check for violations of the liquor law.[28] Idlewild sued, alleging that the ordinance was unconstitutional, the officers intimidated and harassed the patrons, and thus caused concert attendance to be much lower than anticipated, only 100 to 350 people, causing Idlewild to lose significant amounts on the concert.[29]

---

[22] 1990 U.S. Dist. LEXIS 11020 (Aug. 20, 1990).
[23] Id. at *6, *7.
[24] 818 F.2d 1306 (7th Cir. 1987).
[25] Id. at 1308.
[26] Id.
[27] Id.
[28] Id at 1308, 1309.
[29] Id. at 1310.

The court held that while the ordinance may be unconstitutional, it was not obviously so, being content-neutral and merely regulating time, place and manner restrictions allowed under the Constitution.[30] The unsuccessful attempt to enforce the ordinance did not deprive Idlewild of its First Amendment rights, nor did the patrolling of the concert area violate any Fourth Amendment rights against unlawful search and seizure.[31] Since there was no actual proof of any actions of the police officers to substantiate the claims of harassment, and the mere presence of officers was not a First Amendment violation, the decision of the District Court to dismiss the case was upheld.[32]

In *Great White Whale Advertising, Inc. v. First Festival Productions,* [33] Great White Whale (GWW) provided advertising services to First Production for a rock concert held in Ontario, Canada.[34] Alleging that $78,000 was owed to it by First Festival, GWW obtained an ex-parte order of attachment of funds from ticket sales in possession of Ticketron, without having first commenced an action to recover the sums owed.[35] The funds from ticket sales through Ticketron had already been pledged by First Festival to Vector, a Canadian corporation, as security for a loan of $325,000. Vector moved to vacate GWW's order of attachment, which was denied due to lack of jurisdiction over the corporation that was not licensed to do business in New York. GWW's motion to confirm the attachment after levy by the sheriff had not been acted upon.[36] Vector appealed its motion, and the court held that all transactions Vector made with First Festival were in Canada; that Vector was not "doing business" without a license in New York; and that its motion to vacate could indeed be recognized by the court and should be granted.[37]

---

[30] Id. at 1313- see also Chapter 11 for more detailed explanation of time place and manner restrictions allowed under the First Amendment.
[31] Id. at 1313, 1314.
[32] Id. at 1316.
[33] 438 N.Y.S. 2d 655 (3rd Dept. 1981).
[34] Id. at 656.
[35] Id.
[36] Id.
[37] Id at 657.

This case explains that corporations must be registered to do business in every state in which they intend to transact business. Such a failure to register could potentially deny a corporation access to the courts of the state, and could potentially lead to problems in being unable to legally resolve issues in another state.

13.04 General Overview of State Liquor Licenses

Alcohol regulation varies greatly from state to state and from locality to locality. We are all familiar with the so-called "blue laws" which prohibit the sale of alcohol on Sundays, certain holidays and election day, or regulate where and when alcohol can be sold. Because the laws in each jurisdiction vary greatly, we urge you to become familiar with the alcohol regulations that apply in your locality.

For example, in Pennsylvania, no beer or liquor may be sold by proprietors, lessees, keepers or managers of any theater, circus, museum, or other place of amusement.[38] However, nothing in the statute prevents the grant of a restaurant liquor license. This means a caterer may be able to serve alcohol at a theater, but the theater itself cannot hold a liquor license. Stadiums may only serve "malt or brewed" beverages and thus are prohibited from selling any hard liquor.[39] A secondary service area can extend the liquor license of a stadium to include one additional permanent structure, fitting certain statutory guidelines.[40] Sunday sales are restricted at stadiums and may only occur from 12 noon until 10:00 p.m. Notably, Pennsylvania still has State-owned liquor stores, although it allows the sale of beer from "package" stores.

In New York, non-alcoholic seating accommodations are required in facilities hosting sporting events, consisting of at least 6% of the permanent seating accommodations for the given event, including stadiums, arenas, ballparks, and other athletic fields.[41]

In Florida, a liquor license may be issued to a civic center or sports arena authority and can be transferred to a qualified applicant authorized by contract to provide food service for the facility, but the

---

[38] 47 P.S. 4-463 (1997).
[39] 47 P.S. 4-408.2 (1997).
[40] 47 P.S. 4-406.1 (1997).
[41] NY CLS Al Bev. §106b (1997).

license will remain at all times the exclusive property of the authority.[42] A special license may be issued for performing art centers for consumption on premises only during events offered by the center.[43] Also in Florida, beer and wine are widely available at grocery stores, although hard liquor is relegated to a separate area or store rather than being allowed in any aisle.

In Arizona, the Superintendent of the Department of Liquor Licenses may issue temporary alcohol permits to different concessionaires to serve beer and wine within Arizona Veterans Memorial Coliseum, but no temporary permit may be requested in conjunction with circus performances, non-sport ice shows and musical concerts the state fair board determines are inappropriate for the serving of beer and wine.[44] This does give the state some latitude in refusing to serve alcohol during events it feels has potential for getting rowdy, without any first amendment implications.

In an opinion from the California Attorney General, the Attorney General concluded that businesses that purport to provide free or complimentary alcoholic beverages along with a service, such as bed & breakfasts, limousines, buses, and the like are not exempt from the liquor licensing statutes. The Attorney General opined that because the beverages are only available in conjunction with purchased services, the beverages are actually being paid for, and that to allow such providers to be exempt from obtaining a liquor license would undermine the liquor control laws of the State.

This is of concern to convention centers, performing arts centers or other facilities that might consider offering a wine and cheese reception for its patrons. It may be necessary for facilities in California to obtain a liquor license if they intend to serve alcoholic beverages, even if a fee is not charged for the drink.

In *Pittsburgh Stadium Concessions, Inc., v. Commonwealth of Pennsylvania*, [45] PSC applied for a performing arts facility license, to allow it to serve wine and liquor to patrons throughout the stadium during performing arts events, under the Liquor Code, which

---

[42] Fla. Stat. §561.20 (1997).

[43] Id.

[44] A.R.S. §3-1013 (1997).

[45] 674 A.2d 334 (Pa. Commw. 1996).

allowed the Board to issue licenses to operators of performing arts theaters permanently located at a single site with seating accommodations for at least 1,000 patrons. PSC was responsible for food and drink concessions at the Stadium, and although patrons of performing arts events were seated in private boxes or in the Allegheny Club, a restaurant in the stadium, may be served any sort of alcoholic beverage, patrons in general admissions area were only allowed to purchase and consume beer.[46] The Pennsylvania denied a liquor license application submitted by Pittsburgh Stadium Concessions, Inc. (PSC) for a performing arts facility license. The license would have permitted PSC to serve wine and liquor to patrons of a performing arts event held at three Rivers Stadium. The Court of Common Pleas overruled the Board's denial, and the Liquor Control Board appealed to the Commonwealth Court.

After an evidentiary hearing, the Board refused PSC's application because it was within 200 feet of other establishments licensed by the Board, that PSC did not qualify as an operator of a theater for the performing arts, and had not operated as a theater for the performing arts for at least a year prior to application.[47] PSC appealed to the trial court, where the court held that when the stadium hosted performing arts events, it acted like a theater for the performing arts under the Liquor Code, and that similar facilities in the region had also been granted liquor licenses. The Board appealed, contending that the Stadium did not have a permanent stage, and that it already had a liquor license limited to beer as required by the code for Stadiums and Arenas, while the Stadium contended that a permanent stage was not necessary for the license sought under the code.

The Commonwealth Court concluded that the stadium, used primarily for sporting events, and only used for performing arts events two or three times per year, did not qualify as a performing arts center under the Code. The court contrasted similar facilities in the area to the stadium, stating that they hosted many more performing arts, trade shows and civic events. The court found that the Liquor Control Board's decision was rational and consistent with past decisions.

---

[46] Id. at 335.
[47] Id.

The Board did not act arbitrarily in restricting sale of wine and hard liquor in general admission areas of the facility by allowing it under the stadium's restaurant license and private box areas. Thus, the court reversed the trial court's decision and reinstated the Liquor Control Board's denial of the license to PSC.

13.05 The Freedom of Information Act and Similar State Sunshine Laws

In *Indianapolis Convention & Visitors Association, Inc. v. Indianapolis Newspapers, Inc.,*[48] The Indiana News sought copies of internal expense vouchers from the Indianapolis Convention & Visitors Association, Inc. (ICVA), under the Indiana Access to Public Records Act. The ICVA is a not-for-profit organization that receives funding from advertising income, membership dues, and money from the Capital Improvement Board of Managers of Marion County (CIB), which is based on a percentage of the hotel-motel tax revenues received by the CIB, paid to the ICVA in monthly installments.[49] The trial court found that approximately 60% to 79% of the ICVA expenditures over the past four years had been funded by the CIB money, and that the ICVA was subject to an audit by the state for its use of public funds.[50] The Court of Appeals agreed that the ICVA was a public entity, but was only willing to grant the Indiana News access to receipts for the period the ICVA was made aware by the state that it was subject to state auditing. The Supreme Court of Indiana agreed with the trial court that the News could obtain the vouchers requested from 1984 on, the effective date of the Public Records Act, because the ICVA had been a public agency subject to the Act and had received public funding during that period, whether it was aware it was subject to a state audit or not.[51]

In *Atlantic City Convention Center Authority v. South Jersey Publishing Co., Inc.,*[52] the media sought to copy and publish audiotapes of a public body's executive session, not open to the public, in

---

[48] 577 N.E.2d 208 (Ind. 1991).
[49] Id. at 209, 210.
[50] Id. at 210.
[51] Id. at 215, 216.
[52] 637 A.2d 1261 (NJ 1994).

which certain personnel matters had been discussed.[53] The court held that the media was entitled to access to these records subject to prior removal of confidential or privileged information under the Open Public Meetings Act.[54] The Atlantic City Convention Center Authority operates the Atlantic City convention center, and as an agency of the State, it was subject to the Open Public Meetings Act. At its meetings, the Authority tape-recorded executive sessions in order to aid the secretary with preparation of the minutes of the meeting. The press sought to obtain the audio tapes, not just the written official minutes, in conjunction with the resignation or dismissal of the chief officer of the visitor's bureau and his subsequent rehiring by the Authority as an independent contractor to attract convention business to the non-casino hotels in Atlantic City. When asked for the tapes, the Authority asked permission from the former officer-now independent contractor, who refused. The Authority asked for direction from the Chancery Court, who ruled the executive session minutes should be released, and the press then sought access to the audio tapes, clearly not the official records of the Authority. The New Jersey Supreme Court held that the audio tapes were common-law public records, subject to balanced disclosure, and directed the Chancery Court to review the audio tapes, redact any portions that constituted confidential or privileged information or that would unnecessarily intrude on the deliberative process, and the release the redacted tapes to the press.[55] The balanced disclosure of the executive session tapes was necessary to preserve the privacy and candid nature with which the Authority conducted its business and not unduly deprive the press of its right to know privileges under the law.

In *City of Fort Worth v. Groves,*[56] Tarrant County and Fort Worth entered into an agreement to lease the Tarrant County Convention Center (TCCC). Various bond issues initially financed TCCC, beginning in 1968, but by 1983 began to become a drain on County finances.[57]

---

[53] Id. at 1262.

[54] Id. at 1263.

[55] Id. at 1269.

[56] 746 S.W.2d 907 (Tex. App. 1988).

[57] Id. at 909.

The County entered into an agreement to lease TCCC to the CC, including $2 million in improvements scheduled for the next two years but the County would be responsible for the bond payments. Groves, a county taxpayer, brought suit claiming that the lease agreement had not been properly posted before the County Commissioner's meeting to allow appropriate public access, and the agenda for the meeting was not posted in a place accessible to the public. The court held that the County Commissioners had failed to get an appraisal of TCCC and entered into a lease agreement allowing inadequate rental for the property ($30 for 30 years, amounting to a gift to the City)[58], in violation of its prior bond issues by effectively lending its credit to the City. The court also held that the lease was void, as business done in violation of the Public Records Act.[59]

13.06 Vending Laws

In *Kelly v. Buffalo Bills Football Club,*[60] the Buffalo Bills and Erie County, NY alleged that vendors trespassed and created a nuisance outside an area of Erie County Stadium when selling food and merchandise on game days.[61] The vendors sought declaratory relief to determine the legality of their conducting their business outside the stadium on game day, and to enjoin the County and the Bills from interference with their activities. The County contended that the vending licenses issued by the Town of Orchard Park did not allow them to vend in the county right of way, under the stadium's pedestrian and traffic control, having been leased by the County to the Bills. The Bills had been granted exclusive rights of use and occupancy of the Stadium by the County, which included the area in which the vendors set up their businesses. No evidence showed that the vendors in any way restricted traffic flow, and all had proper permits issued by the Town of Orchard Park, and the County had no additional licensing regulations. A highway-engineering expert testified that safety did require that the area occupied by the vendors on game day could pose a hazard to vehicular traffic.

---

[58] Id. at 911.
[59] Id. at 915.
[60] 655 N.Y.S.2d 275 (1997).
[61] Id.

It was also noted that any physical injuries and property damage that had occurred at the stadium within the last 5 years did not in any way involve any vendor, although alcohol consumption was. The court could not find that the vendors posed a safety hazard nor were a nuisance in conducting their business, and thus the Bills and County were enjoined from interfering with the vendors.

13.07 The Administrative Procedure Act and Related State Procedures

When the U.S. Congress, the states or municipalities enact a new program statute, they typically prefer to legislate a policy in terms of broad standards. They certainly do not prescribe every detail for the agency. The agency is required to issue "rules" that provide the agency staff and primarily the public, with notice of the "rules." There are many reasons for this. In many cases it is just not possible for the legislative body to foresee every little detail that should be addressed in the statute. Furthermore, it is harder to go back and have the legislature amend the original statute then it is to issue "rules." Consequently, agency rules have become an increasingly important part of our system of laws.

The key federal statute, of which many state statutes are modeled after, is the Administrative Procedure Act ("APA")[62] Enacted in 1946, the APA basically guides an agency through the rulemaking process. The APA uses the term "rule" rather than the term "regulation." The term rule is given a very broad definition, it means:

> "Rule means the whole or any part of an agency statement of general or particular applicability and future effect designed to implement, interpret, or prescribe law or policy or describing the organization, procedure, or practice requirements of an agency."

There are two types of rulemaking under the APA. They are commonly referred to as "formal" and "informal" rulemaking. Formal rulemaking under the APA involves a trial-type hearing on the record with a transcript, depositions and witnesses.

---

[62] 5 U.S.C. § 551 - 559

The most common form of rulemaking is informal rulemaking. This is the procedure for a notice and comment period.[63] The first step in the process is the publication of a proposed regulation in the Federal Register. The Federal Register is a daily publication printed and distributed by the United States Government Printing Office. Individual states, cities and municipalities have their own method of communicating the changes in the law. The agency then allows a period of time during which interested parties (the public) may participate in the rulemaking process. The participation is usually by written comment and sometimes by oral testimony at a public hearing. After the notice and comment period the agency considers the public's comments and determines the final content of the rules. The agency is also required to publish a "concise general statement" of the basis and purpose of the rule.[64] The United States Court of Appeals for the District of Columbia Circuit provides us the following summary of the informal rulemaking process:

> " The APA sets out three procedural requirements: notice of the proposed rulemaking, an opportunity for interested persons to comment, and a concise general statement of [the] basis and purpose of the rules ultimately adopted.... As interpreted by recent decisions of this court, these procedural requirements are intended to assist judicial review as well as to provide fair treatment for persons affected by the rule.... To this end there must be an <u>exchange</u> of views, information and criticism between interested persons and the agency.... Consequently, the notice required by the APA, or the information subsequently supplied to the public, must disclose in detail the thinking that has animated the form of a proposed rule and the data upon which that rule is based.... Moreover, a dialogue is a two-way street: the opportunity to comment is meaningless unless

---

[63] 5 U.S.C. § 553.
[64] 5 U.S.C. § 553(c).

the agency responds to significant points raised by the public...." [65]

Prior to 1990, proposed rules were usually drafted by agency staff, based on the agency's own expertise. Nothing prohibited agencies from consulting with interested parties at this stage, but this was rarely conducted by agencies. In 1990, Congress provided the framework for "negotiated rulemaking" by enacting the Negotiated Rulemaking Act of 1990.[66] Under this Act, a committee composed of agency representatives and other interested parties drafts a proposed rule. The negotiated rule-making process is optional, an agency's decision to use or not to use it is not subject to judicial review, and use of the procedure does not entitle the rule to any greater importance that it would normally receive.

Congress has authorized governmental agencies to promulgate rules and regulations under The Administrative Procedure Act to deli-neate the scope of laws passed by Congress. For example, under the Americans with Disabilities Act, Congress has stated that it is illegal to discriminate against those with disabilities in public accommodations. It is largely in the rules and regulations promulgated under the Act that we find out such things as to whom the law applies, what level of impair-ment is required to be considered disabled, the definition of a public accommodation, etc. The rules and regulations also will spell out how to get relief under the Act, whether one can proceed directly to court or whether there are administrative procedures that must first be exhausted before one can go to court, and the like.

Administrative agencies have elements of all three branches of government. They are able to enact rules and regulations which act like laws, a legislative duty; they enforce the rules and regulations, an executive duty; and many agencies have judicial procedures and courts in which to challenge the rules, regulations, and decisions made by that agency in a more informal setting than that of the court room. Agencies are specialized, allowing them to deal with a small area and able to better serve those whom they are regulating than Con-gress as a whole by being more aware of the area of law and by

---

[65] *Home Box Office, Inc. v. FCC*, 567 F.2d at 35-36.
[66] Pub. L. No. 101-648, 104 Stat. 4969 (1990), 5 U.S.C. § 581-590.

being able to respond to problems more rapidly. In addition, States also have their own administrative agencies and like those of the federal government, are in charge of making rules and regulations to expound on and enforce state law.

Once an agency of the government has enacted rules and regulations, they have the force of law and are published in the Code of Federal Regulation (C.F.R.) or in the State's code of regulation. Such regulations will often delineate the procedures to be followed should a problem arise. For example, OSHA is a governmental agency in charge of workplace safety and has promulgated rules and regulations regarding the same. Should OSHA receive a complaint that a workplace is unsafe, or during an inspection discover hazards, they may issue citations and even levy fines against the employer. (Cite Beiro case). The employer may then wish to appeal the citation or fine. What does he do?

The first thing necessary is to see whether the agency has administrative procedures that must be followed. Often, the first step may be as informal as writing a letter to the agency regarding the problem, and requesting reconsideration or a hearing. The agency will then investigate the problem further and either issue a statement or set a hearing. A good example of this is the Internal Revenue Service. If a taxpayer is sent a notice that he owes additional tax, a taxpayer may dispute this by sending a letter and perhaps supporting documents to the IRS, which may then send a letter back revising or affirming its decision, at which time the taxpayer may request a hearing. The procedures required by the particular agency can be found either in the Code of Regulation, either State or Federal, or often by calling the agency and asking about the procedure required.

Once a hearing is set in the matter, an agency will issue a date and time the parties are to appear before them regarding the issue at hand. Sometimes written briefs regarding the issues will be required. Usually there will be several parties at the hearing - representatives from the agency, concerned parties, any witnesses, and an administrative hearing officer, who is a neutral party in charge of taking evidence and attempting to resolve the dispute at hand. Hearing officers are like judges and may issue subpoenas, take in evidence, hear testimony from the parties and witnesses, request additional evidence or briefs, and will make decisions regarding the credibility of evidence and issue a written decision on the case.

Agency files are largely public documents and are open for inspection except for confidential, classified or other documents not open for public inspection. Since agencies are branches of the government, they are subject to "Sunshine" or public records laws and often the hearings will be open to the public.

In the hearing itself, the hearing officer will often open the case with a brief statement about what issues are to be heard, who requested the hearing and why, and identify the parties and witnesses to be heard. The parties will be sworn in, as in a courtroom. Opening statements may be taken from each side, and then the agency's case will be presented, followed by that of the party or parties challenging the agency's actions, followed by closing arguments if appropriate. The formal rules of evidence are not required to be followed at a hearing, but it is important to keep all evidence relevant, concise and from getting repetitive. The hearing officer will make his decision based on the substantial weight of the evidence, meaning that in considering all the evidence and testimony before him, the officer feels that one party's case is stronger than the other, but a showing of "beyond a shadow of doubt" is certainly not necessary. The hearing will then conclude, and the officer will take the matter under consideration. Often he will ask the parties to submit proposed findings of fact and conclusions of law. The hearing officer will review these materials and issue a ruling at a later date, notifying the parties by mail of the decision.

If the hearing officer's decision is disputed, often an appeals process within the agency will exist, to an additional hearing board. The procedure here is like that below, except there is usually a panel of people with expertise in the area that will review the agency's action, the dispute, and the hearing officer's adjudication of the claim. They will often not hear any additional witnesses, but will make their decision "upon the record" and will give deference to the hearing officer who did see and hear the parties and witnesses at the hearing. This emphasizes the importance of submitting all evidence a party wants considered in the case before the hearing officer, since any "forgotten" evidence will most likely be prohibited from submission at a later date. A final adjudication or ruling on the case will then be made. It is only after this administrative procedure is exhausted that one can then proceed to the "normal" courts of law for review of agency actions. Failure to exhaust administrative remedies is often a reason why Courts of Law dismiss appeals of administrative cases.

Courts have some limits on their review of agency decisions. At times, the courts may not review agency decisions by statute. Most frequently this arises when the statute provides a certain period during which a decision by the agency must be appealed, and if that time has expired; the court will refuse to hear any appeals by parties failing to meet the time deadlines imposed.

It should also be noted that because the government delegates its duties to agencies, it also allows them discretion in promulgating and enforcing rules and regulations. If something has been left to agency discretion, this often is not reviewable upon appeal. For example, when an agency has maintained a supervisory role, such as allowing it to review rents charged by private landlords in subsidized housing, or a VA hospital administrator's decision to transfer a physician due to strained personal relations with colleagues, these actions have been held to be within an agency's discretion and will not be judicially reviewed. While these are limited examples, they do show that when an agency is performing a largely managerial function, they are often granted deference and any challenge to such a decision will not be heard.

Also, a party appealing an agency decision must have standing, meaning they have an "injury" or harm caused by the agency decision, and they have a legal interest in the matter at hand. An association can sue on behalf of its members, for example, when the members could have sued on their own, and the interests the association seeks to protect are relevant to the association's purpose and the participation of the individual members is not required.

The courts of law give the agency the benefit of the doubt in appeals, using the "arbitrary and capricious" standard, and only reversing hearing officers decisions if they feel the decision made was against the weight of the evidence and was an unreasonable decision or conclusion drawn by the hearing officer. The courts will compel agency action unlawfully withheld or unreasonably delayed; set aside agency actions found to be an abuse of discretion, contrary to constitutional rights, in excess of the jurisdiction or authority of the agency, or unsupported by substantial evidence upon review of the record.

This basically means that unless the agency was acting in manner exceeding its authority or made a decision against the weight of the evidence, its ruling will be upheld.

Because agencies are so varied, a facility manager could expect to potentially run into any of the following agencies in the course of business: The Internal Revenue Service, National Labor Relations Board, Occupational Safety and Health Administration, Social Security Administration, Worker's Compensation Board, Unemployment Compensation Board, Equal Employment Opportunity Commission, ADA, Environmental Protection Agency, State social welfare agencies or the Veteran's Administration. Many of these agencies will deal with problems encountered by employees, and may necessitate merely filling out forms for the employee regarding injuries, employment status and salary, or the like. Others may involve more substantial disputes or claims against the facility or its operators, at which point legal counsel may become necessary.

Rules have the force and effect of law. Rules, if properly enacted, are binding on all concerned including the issuing agency. The agency cannot waive their application on an ad hoc basis or a situational basis.

In *Kozala v. National Association of Stock Car Auto Racing, Inc.,*[67] Stevens, driving Kozala's car, trailed in second place most of the race. On the 95th lap, Stevens passed the leader (Evans). However, before the lap was completed, the yellow caution flag was displayed, requiring the cars to hold their positions. While the cars were running under the yellow flag, the track official ordered Stevens to pull back behind the previous leader, Evans. Immediately thereafter, the green flag was displayed, Stevens came in second, and Evans won the race. Stevens claimed the cars should not have been realigned during the yellow flag.

NASCAR referred the matter to their competition director, who ruled Evans was the winner, because Evans obeyed the realignment directed by the track official, crossed the finish line first, and could not be penalized a lap or by a time penalty after the race was completed. Koszela sought reconsideration of the decision and the director informed them of their right to appeal the decision to NASCAR headquarters.

---

[67] 646F2d 749 (2nd Cir. 1981).

At a hearing, an official testified that Stevens had not fully passed Evans and pulled ahead when the yellow flag came out, leading to the realignment of the cars. Koszela sought review by the NASCAR commissioner, but that post was vacant. Then in Stafford Springs, a few months later, Stevens again drove for Koszela in a 200-lap race. Stevens led for most of the race and took the checkered flag, with second place to a driver named Cleary. The public address system announced that Stevens won the race, and he was awarded the trophy. Cleary complained to a scorer about the results, arguing he had not received credit for a lap completed while making a pit stop. The Chief scorer ruled that Cleary had actually completed the 200 laps before Stevens, and declared Cleary the official winner. Immediately thereafter, Koszela delivered a written protest and a protest fee to the Chief Steward at Stafford. The Steward upheld the scorer's decision, but referred the matter to the NASCAR competition director, who in turn referred the matter to the Chief Timer and scorer, who in review also declared Cleary the winner. Koszela again appealed to the Commission, who affirmed the scorer's ruling. Koszela and Stevens then brought this action, alleging that NASCAR breached its membership contract by failing to adhere to its own rules, and alleging that the rulings as to both races were arbitrary and erroneous. They also alleged that the absence of a national commissioner had thwarted their right to an appeal. NASCAR sought summary judgment, arguing the court should not interfere with the internal workings of the private association.[68] The District Court had found that the law of voluntary associations did not apply to NASCAR, and judicial restraint was not justified when NASCAR had a "stranglehold" on the field and did not afford its members any rights of control or governance. While this did not allow the court to roam at will through NASCAR's rulebook or proceedings, the court found that the decisions in both races were final and unreviewable under NASCAR rules and that the Plaintiffs had received all the due process to which they were entitled. The Plaintiffs again appealed, and the Court of Appeals held that the membership contract with NASCAR did not contemplate the second-guessing of the jurisdiction of track officials, the Plaintiffs had exhausted all their available remedies, and NASCAR had satisfied its contractual obligations.

---

[68] Id. at 753.

Even in absence of a national commissioner, the disputes in question were not actually protests, but arguments as to race procedure, and thus the Plaintiffs were not entitled to an appeal to the racing commissioner, so the vacancy had no effect on the outcome of either case.

13.08 IRS Withholding Rules Concerning Payments to Foreign Entertainers

Recently, the Internal Revenue Service ("IRS") sent out 253 notice letters to arenas and stadiums, with over 8,000 seats, informing them of their "responsibility and potential liability" as a tax withholding agent for payments to foreign entertainers performing in their venues. The letters state that "Payments to foreign entertainer(s) who participate in events held in the United States are payments subject to Internal Revenue Code (IRC) §1441 (Withholding of Tax on Nonresident Aliens) and the corresponding Income Tax Regulations." According to the IRS, the purpose of these letters is to make sure as venue managers we raise the question of "Who is responsible for withholding the tax?" Is it the promoter, an agent, a U.S. corporation or does the foreign entertainer have a Central Withholding Agreement ("CWA") in place with the IRS? The ultimate purpose of the letters is of course to make sure the US receives the collection of the tax. Withholding taxes especially "at the source" plays an important role in collection when the tax payer is a foreign person or entity, because one country will generally not assist another country in the collection of a tax.[69] The IRS places the legal burden of collecting the tax on a U.S. company or person that deals with the foreign entertainers or foreign athletes.

What determines if a facility is a withholding agent?
Under §1441, a withholding agent is any U.S. or foreign person (including a corporation or other entity) that has control, receipt, custody, disposal or payment of any item of income of a foreign person subject to withholding. Consequently, §1441 is extremely broad and could include anyone that collects the proceeds or funds from the concert or event. For example, if the venue has control of

---

[69] See Mr. Harvey P. Dale, Withholding Tax on Payments to Foreign Persons, 36 Tax L. Rev. 49, 52 (1980).

the box office receipts for the event, the IRS may consider the venue a withholding agent. Therefore, until we have further discussions with the IRS, and come up with some clear and concise guidance on the with-holding obligations, venues should seek written assurances from the promoter or the agent that the taxes are being withheld by them. Fur-thermore, the IRS states in the letter that "Venues may have an erroneous belief that they are not a withholding agent if the contract that they have entered into is not with the foreign entertainer but rather, with a promoter or agent. If the personal services of a foreign entertainer are contracted for, the withholding rules under IRC 1441 apply.....If a withholding agent fails to withhold the proper amount of taxes, the withholding agent is liable for payment of such taxes, interest and penalties. Even if the foreign entertainer pays the tax, the withholding agent is liable for interest and penalties under IRC 1463." If the tax is not withheld by the promoter or agent, because of the fixed assets (the building), the IRS currently considers assembly facilities to be a good alternative withholding agent if it has control or custody of the funds from which the payment will be made to the entertainer. The IRS has enforced "at the source" withhold-ing obligations for over 65 years.[70]

If the facts determine your facility is a withholding agent, how much should you withhold? If the determination of the source of the income or the amount subject to tax depends on facts that are not known at the time of payment after the event, the promoter, the agent or facility that has control or custody receipts must withhold an amount sufficient to ensure that at least 30% of the amount subsequently determined to be subject to withholding is withheld. In no case, however, should anyone withhold more than 30% of the total amount paid for services.

What are Central Withholding Agreements? According to the IRS, foreign entertainers and athletes who are making a tour of the United States may wish to enter into a "Central Withholding Agreement" with the IRS. The CWA is signed by a withholding agent, the foreign entertainer and a representative from the IRS.

---

[70] See Tonopah & T.R. Co. v. Commissioner of the IRS, 112 F.2nd 970 (9th Cir. 1940) which discusses who held control of the withholding payments to nonresident aliens.

The IRS indicates that such agreements generally reduce the amount of taxes withheld on the U.S. source gross receipts of the foreign athlete or entertainer.[71] A request for a central withholding agreement should be created at least 90 days before the agreement is to take effect. For additional information on obtaining a CWA, contact the IRS at CWA.Program@irs.gov .

<u>What can the facility do to protect itself from liability under the IRS Code?</u> Until the IRS develops clear and concise guidance on the withholding obligations for public assembly facilities, if you have foreign entertainers performing in your facility you may want ask the promoter and agent in writing who is the withholding agent under §1441 of the Internal Revenue Code. If they do not have a CWA in place with the IRS and you do not regularly deal with the promoter or agent you may want to request a bond to cover the tax as part of your facility lease agreement or if you in fact control the box office receipts, withhold the appropriate amount as indicated by your accounting personnel. You may also refer to IRS Publication 515, Withholding of Tax on Nonresident Aliens and Foreign Entities and the IRS website http://www.irs.gov/businesses/small/international/article/0,,id=129240,00.html.

---

[71] See Rev. Proc. 89-47, 1989-2 C.B. 598

Chapter 14

Construction Disputes

By Richard Smith, Jonathan D. Shaffer and Claire E. Kresse[*]

14.01   Contracting Process

1) Risk Allocation

There are inherent risks involved with the performance of any contract. It is important, therefore, for an owner or manager to take steps to allocate potential risk and prevent loss or delay through the careful selection of contract type and particular contract /clauses. Additionally, the chances for a successful project will increase if the owner is willing to clearly identify and allocate risk fairly between itself and the general contractor. Failing to carefully consider the types of risk that may be encountered can lead to drastic increases in the total project cost due to unforeseen contingencies and dispute resolution. An owner who is aware and has considered predictable risks can draft a contract which results in diminished project costs and healthier business relationships for all parties involved.

There are various methods for allocating risk on major construction projects. They run from one extreme where the owner places all of the risk on the contractor, to standard form contracts which provide the owner little to no legal protection. The modern method for allocating risk, however, is characterized by a clear sharing of the risks by the owner and contractor. It is well accepted by the construction industry that the most cost effective contract is one that assigns each element of risk to the party that is best equipped to manage and minimize that risk. This is based on the principle that the risk should be placed with the party that is best able to evaluate, control, bear the cost, and benefit from the assumption of risk.

---

[*] Richard Smith, Jonathan D. Shaffer and Claire E. Kresse are with the law firm of Smith, Pachter, McWhorter & D'Ambrosio, P.L.C., at 8000 Towers Crescent Drive, Suite 800, Vienna, VA 22182.

If risk allocation is approached in this manner, public assembly facilities ("facilities" or "facility") are more likely to receive a completed project that meets their needs and expectations, which is completed on time and at a fair price. Contractors are able to provide lower bid prices because the contract identifies particular risks that the facility is willing to assume, and thus the contractor does not have to include a contingency for that risk. The risks that a facility manager should evaluate in the early planning stages of any project can be grouped into three categories: (1) requirements for project start-up and resource risks; (2) performance risks; and (3) risks presented by external factors.

Examples of resource and project start-up risks that facility procurement personnel should preplan for are (a) funding, e.g., inclusion of a termination for convenience clause in case the facility runs out of money and sufficient contingency funds to cover the costs of changes that are inevitable; (b) permits, licenses, utilities and zoning—the facility must identify in the solicitation all requirements for construction of the project, but the contractor should share some responsibility; and (c) ensuring that all requirements for site access are met. Another resource risk to be considered is the adequacy of the labor force. However, the contractor, rather than the facility, is best able to assess the availability of labor in the area, by trade, and its impact on project materials and schedule.

Risks related to performance of the project must also be properly allocated. When the facility is funding the design, it bears a substantial portion of the risk associated with the sufficiency of the project plans and specifications. A facility can protect against this risk by providing adequate funding for the design effort, selecting a qualified design professional, performing constructibility reviews and including formulas and procedures for the reimbursement of changes to the contract (changes clause). If the facility will provide any material or equipment, and any of those items are late or defective, then the facility should be responsible. The opposite is true for any contractor provided material and equipment. Subsurface conditions present another risk that is for the most part assignable to the facility as the one who owns the project site and has the best opportunity in time and access to perform evaluations of the site. The risk can be mitigated by the facility's efforts to conduct an adequate subsurface investigation ahead of time.

This includes obtaining and providing geotechnical information to identify the composition of subsurface materials and the existence and location of subsurface obstacles. Currently, under most contracts, some of the risk associated with subsurface conditions is now being shared between the facility owners and contractors with the use of differing site condition clauses. These clauses are discussed in detail in section 14.03 of this chapter.

Performance related risks that are in most cases allocated to the contractor include: the underestimation of costs, although the sufficiency of the plans can create facility risk; the means and method of construction; and productivity of the labor force, and site safety. However, changes and acceleration may also cause some facility risk. These risks can be allocated to the contractor by using standard, clear contract language. A facility should also recognize the risk of delay in presenting, addressing and solving problems. These risks should be properly allocated between the party who has the ability to solve the problem and the party who has the ability to give notice of the problem. The risk of delay in presenting problems is shared by the contractor following and the facility enforcing the contract's notice requirements. Upon notice, the facility procurement official(s) receiving notice has an obligation to address and solve problems promptly. This is done by delegating decision-making authority.

There are external factors that also must be considered by the facility in risk allocation, such as (a) bad weather or acts of God; (b) unforeseeable escalation in costs; and (c) acts by the government in its sovereign capacity. All of these risks should be shared by the facility and contractor on the basis that they are not foreseeable or controllable. However, to prevent the contractor from increasing its bid contingency to mitigate the risk of acts by the government in its sovereign capacity, the facility should include a suspension of work clause which allows for a reasonable period of free suspension and makes costs (not profits) compensable.

Adverse weather and acts of God, otherwise referred to as force major events, cannot be anticipated or controlled by either party, therefore the risk could be mitigated by a time extension clause in the contract which could allow the contractor time, without pay, for the period affected. Finally, on long term contracts, there is the risk of an escalation in costs.

This risk can be allocated by including in the contract, a formula for the facility owner to pay any escalation that may occur. A facility that considers and implements the fair risk allocation measures described above will go a long way toward reducing its total project costs by reducing the need for contractors to have contingencies in their bids or proposals.

The contracting arrangement that the facility selects will determine the relationships and responsibilities between the parties. In addition to risk, the facility must consider various other factors in selecting the contract type. Among other things, the facility should determine whether it has the ability in-house to take on the management and oversight responsibilities for the design and construction of the project and the schedule for project completion. Additionally, the facility must evaluate the relationship that it wants to have with design, construction and other project personnel, and what relationship it wants these groups to have with each other.

2) Construction Management Contracting

Construction management is defined by the American Institute of Architects ("AIA") as: Management services provided to an Owner of a Project during the Design Phase, Construction Phase or both by a person or entity possessing requisite training and experience. Such management services may include advice on the time and cost consequences of design and construction decisions, scheduling, cost control, coordination of contract negotiations and awards, timely purchasing of critical materials and long-lead items, and coordination of construction activities.[1]

The construction management approach is centered around the owner's hiring of a construction manager ("CM") to provide overall leadership for the project team. The role and responsibilities of the CM will vary from project to project because the construction management approach varies depending on the project's contractual arrangement. However, regardless of the contract method used, the CM is someone who (1) should have a great deal of experience and knowledge about all

---

[1] AIA, THE ARCHITECT'S HANDBOOK OF PROFESSIONAL PRACTICE , Vol. 3 Glossary, at 8 (1994).

aspects of construction and (2) should act as the owner's agent and represent the owner's interests from an early point in planning the project.

The CM can be an architect/engineer, a general contractor, a construction management company or an individual with his own consulting firm. The AIA publishes a standard Construction Management Contract which describes some of the CM's responsibilities during the design phase of a project, including: monitoring the design to ensure it meets a facility's requirements, cost estimating and evaluating, scheduling, reviewing bids and advising the owner on the acceptability of bids. The AIA standard CM contract provides that during the construction phase the CM will, *inter alia*, jointly administer the contract with the architect, coordinate the work of all contractors, monitor costs and maintain records. In some cases, the CM will remain the agent of the facility during construction of the project. When the CM remains an agent of the facility, they are typically referred to as "agency-CM's" or "CMs-for-fee" since they perform their management responsibilities for a fee. Here, the CM coordinates and oversees the work of the subcontractors, but the subcontractors have contracts directly with the facility and the CM does not have any liability for successful completion of the project.

In a different version of the construction management approach, the CM will act as a general contractor—"CM/GC" or "CM-at-risk". When the design phase is near complete the CM/GC will submit a fixed price or a guaranteed maximum price and contract directly with the specialty subcontractors. Thus, the CM/GC, in essence, assumes the same, legal, financial and contractual position as if it were a general contractor. Obviously, this approach is more attractive to owners who do not want to take on the risk associated with having multiple trade contractors, and wants the assurance of a total maximum project price. However, with the CM/GM approach the owner is giving up a major proponent of its interests that it had in the agency-CM approach.

a. Selection of a Construction Manager

Once a facility has decided to use the construction management approach, the task of choosing a CM may begin. The process will depend on the form of construction management being used, i.e., an agency-CM, or a CM/GC. If the facility is using an agency-CM, it should use a selection process similar to that used when hiring a design professional. If the facility manager is looking for a CM/GM then the process should match that used for selecting a general contractor. The timing of selecting a CM should be considered. Some believe that the CM should be the first member of the project team retained, while others believe the architect/engineer should be the first retained. Public facility owners may be subject to legal constraints on the selection of a CM. In addition, the facility should consider the method for obtaining and evaluating proposals—whether competition will be free and open, or from a pre-selected short list of CM firms.

The general sequence of events that facility procurement officials should follow in selecting a CM is: (1) identify the specific services to be provided by the CM through all phases of the project; (2) create requests for statements of qualifications (the facility should provide the weight that different qualification factors will be given during the evaluation of proposals) and identify how CMs are to be solicited; (3) after receipt of statements of qualifications, generate a short list of qualified candidates; (4) request project proposals from the CMs on the facility's short list—usually broken down into technical and cost proposals; (5) evaluate the proposals received and conduct interviews—at a minimum proposals should be evaluated for (a) how well they reflect the CM's understanding of the facility's needs, (b) their staffing experience, (c) familiarity with the locale and project and (d) the management approach being proposed by the CM; and, (6) negotiation and award of the contract.

3) Design-Build Contracting

The design-build approach to construction contracting is sometimes referred to as "turnkey" contracting. In this arrangement, the facility enters into a contract with a single entity that will be responsible for both design and construction of the project. Design-build was traditionally not an option for public assembly facilities due to legal constraints, but now, many statutory changes allow such facilities to use the design-build process. In some instances, the contractor already has a finished design that it has even used before. However, in many cases, the contractor provides the design by hiring an architect/engineer ("Architect/ Engineer") or uses its own design professionals.

When the contractor provides a new design for the project, although it bases the design on specifications provided by the facility, the contractor assumes liability for any design defects or deficiencies unless this liability is specifically waived or limited by the contract.[2] In fact, some courts have treated these arrangements as a contract for the sale of goods rather than for services, and thus the contractor is subject to liability on a warranty theory.[3]

Although design-build contracts can be priced on a cost-plus/cost reimbursable, or lump-sum/fixed price basis, often, the facility will require a fixed price contract to further limit its risk. Therefore, the fixed price design-build contractor must be able to perform within its bid price that it offered under competitive processes. In addition, because a facility in design-build contracting only has to deal with one entity, this arrangement is much more conducive to fast-tracking a project, (*see* discussion of "fast-tracking" in section 14.01(5), below). Based on these facts, using the design-build approach tends to be well suited for facility construction contracts.[4]

Nevertheless, there is risk for a facility in design-build contracting. Under this approach the facility is relying entirely on one entity for design and performance requirements and timely, on budget completion. Also, when the design and construction elements are performed separately, there are inherent checks-and-balances built into the process. In design-build contracting by one entity, however, that benefit is lost unless a facility's representative is hired to tightly monitor progress.

4) Cost-Reimbursement Contracting

Cost-reimbursement contracting removes virtually all financial risk from the contractor. The facility contracts for performance of the project work on the basis that all costs will be reimbursed plus a fixed or incentive based fee. A pure cost-reimbursement arrangement should only

---

[2] *Mobile Hous. Env'ts v. Barton & Barton*, 432 F. Supp. 1343, 1346 (D. Colo. 1977); *C&L Construction Co. v. The United States*, 6 Cl. Ct. 791, 794 (1984).

[3] *See, e.g., The Mead Corp. v. McNally-Pittsburgh Manufacturing Corp.*, 654 F.2d 1197, 1199 (6th Cir. 1981) (citing *Omaha Pollution Control Corp. v. Carver-Greenfield Corp.*, 413 F. Supp. 1069 (D. Neb. 1976).

[4] *See, e.g., Aiken County v. BSP Division of Envirotech Corp.*, 866 F.2d 661 (4th Cir. 1989).

be considered by a facility in cases of extreme urgency or if construction conditions are highly uncertain since there is little to no incentive for the contractor to control costs. If this type of contract is used, a cost reimbursement arrangement with preset limits and a clear statement of allowable costs must be determined to assist in controlling costs.

On occasion, a facility and contractor will agree to use a variation of cost-reimbursement contracting, "force account" contracting. Under this method, the facility agrees to pay the contractor the costs of construction, if the contractor performs the work with its own personnel and keeps detailed records of its costs for performance. However, this method is primarily used for added or changed work which cannot be forward priced or a dispute exists as to the proper costs to be paid.

5) Other Contracting Types
a. Traditional Contracting

In the traditional approach to construction, contracting the owner has a limited role. The design is first performed by the architect/engineer and then, after design is complete and after a selection process, the general contractor begins construction. The architect/engineer is hired directly by the facility owner and is responsible for the plans and specifications. The architect usually does not guarantee that the plans and specifications provided are perfect, but rather that they are prepared within the standard of care for design professionals in the area. The architect usually remains involved during construction to assist the general contractor in interpreting the specifications, evaluating changes and reviewing the contractor's work.

A general contractor is typically selected on the basis of the lowest price, or a "best value" analysis. The contractor is responsible for the "means, methods and sequence" of its work and agrees to complete the work within a specified schedule and for a firm price. If there are changes to the contractor's scope of work, the contractor is to be paid under the changes clause of the contract for the additional costs incurred. The traditional approach to contracting allocates a large portion of the risk to the contractor. Despite the benefits to the contracting facility, there are also aspects that are not so favorable. For example, the facility is placed in the middle of any architect/contractor disputes, and therefore, leadership and team building will be very difficult. Moreover, the architect does not guarantee that its design is perfect, yet the facility warrants the sufficiency of the design to the contractor. Accordingly, under the *Spearin* doctrine (*see* discussion, *infra*, section 14.03), adopted by a large majority of the states, the contractor is entitled to be paid for changes precipitated by errors in the design. Further, the traditional method—requiring completion of the design before the bid stage can be initiated—may not be the most time efficient approach to large construction projects.

b. Multiple Prime Contracting

Rather than having a general contractor hire and be responsible for multiple specialized trade subcontractors, under the multiple prime approach, the facility contracts directly with the trade contractors. This allows the facility to avoid paying the general contractor a fee for being a broker who does not actually perform significant portions of the work, but has the responsibility to coordinate the work. In *Broadway Maintenance Corp. v. Rutgers, the State University,* two prime contractors sued Rutgers for damages caused by delays in the construction of a medical school for the University.[5] Rutgers used a multi-prime arrangement and the contracts with the various prime contractors provided that: (a) time was of the essence; (b) each contractor must perform in accordance with the schedule and under the supervision of the general contractor; and (c) that each contractor was liable for all costs and expenses incurred by other contractors due to any unnecessary delays.[6] The Supreme Court of New Jersey held that the University was not liable for the delays in construction where it had delegated responsibility for supervision of work to the general contractor, even though the University had the power to terminate the contract, withhold funds, and had representatives involved in the negotiations with contractors and reviewing contractors' performance.[7]

---

[5] 90 N.J. 253, 447 A.2d 906 (1982).
[6] *Id.*
[7] *Id.*

The multiple prime approach may work well with fast-track projects. A fast-track project means that the design and construction work are coordinated so that portions of each can take place simultaneously, rather than deferring bidding on construction until design is complete. Absent significant changes and schedule disruptions, fast-tracking can result in significant cost savings. Note that by statute certain public facilities may be required to use the multiple prime approach, however, they cannot start bidding on construction until design is complete.[8]

14.02   Changes and Claims

A changes clause is essential to any construction contract for the protection of both the facility and the contractor. A standard changes clause will allow a facility to make changes to the work within the general scope of the contract at any time during or shortly after performance of the contract, but provides that the contractor will be reimbursed for any increase in costs or time associated with the change given an "equitable adjustment."[9].

---

[8] *See, e.g.*, N. C. Gen. Stat. § 143-128 (1989); N.Y. State Fin. Law § 135 (1994).

[9] Once it has been established that the contractor was required to perform work constituting a material change, the contractor is entitled to an equitable adjustment in the cost of, and/or time required for that work. Under a standard changes clause the contractor is entitled to the reasonable costs incurred for performing the changed work, plus profit. *Bruce Construction Corp. v. U.S.*, 324 F.2d 516 (Ct. Cl. 1963). However, if the contractor has placed a contingency amount in its bid, the contractor may only recover costs incurred in excess of the contingency amount under the contract's differing site conditions clause. *Construction Aggregates Corp.*, ENGBCA No. 2442, December 31, 1980, 81-1 BCA ¶ 14,855. If the changed work has increased the contractor's costs of performing work in other areas of the contract, these costs may also be recovered. *See, e.g., Kenny Construction Co. v. Metropolitan Sanitary Dist.*, 309 N.E.2d 221 (Ill. 1974).

In addition, the clause will usually include: (1) the procedure which a contractor must follow when submitting a claim for increased costs resulting from changes to the work not formally identified as changes (a "constructive change"); and (2) a requirement to continue work in accordance with the facility's directive while the claim is being processed.

In some cases, it will be necessary for the facility to draft a customized changes clause. However, the facility should use a clause based on the federal changes clause, which allows owners to make changes to (a) drawings, designs, or specifications, (b) the method or place of delivery, (c) the method and manner of performance, (d) availability of government furnished facilities, equipment, materials, or sites, and (e) acceleration of the time of performance of the work.[10] In the alternative, the facility can use the AIA's standard changes clause, which provides in part:

7.1.1   Changes in the Work may be accomplished after execution of the Contract, and without invalidating the Contract, by Change Order, Construction Change Directive or order for a minor change in the Work, subject to the limitations stated in this Article 7 and elsewhere in the Contract Documents.

7.1.2   A Change Order shall be based upon agreement among the Owner, Contractor and Architect; a Construction Change Directive requires agreement by the Owner and Architect and may or may not be agreed to by the Contractor; an order for a minor change in the Work may be issued by the Architect alone.[11]

It is better for the facility to use one, or some combination, of these clauses because of the vast body of precedent interpreting these clauses. This section outlines several potential issues that may arise with regard to the changes clause.

---

[10] *See* FAR § 52.243-4.
[11] AIA Doc. A201, art. 7 (1997).

1) Facility Directed Changes

A facility has broad rights under the contract's changes clause to order changes to the contractor's work. However, its power is usually limited to ordering changes within the general scope of the contract. Consequently, the extent of the facility's power to order changes will be determined by the types of changes described in the clause, and how they are defined.[12] The language used in the AIA standard form broadly describes the types of changes covered by the clause as "additions, deletions and other revisions."[13] Thus, there is little restriction on the facility's right to order changes. The federal changes clause provides that specifications (including drawings and designs), are changes covered by the clause. Depending on whether specifications, drawings and designs are construed liberally or narrowly, the facility's power to order changes will be expanded or limited.

Substantial changes in the quantity of major items or materials and the deletion of items or work to be furnished under the contract that are so significant that they alter the original bargain between the parties have generally been found to be beyond the scope of the contract and unauthorized by the changes clause. Public facilities ability to direct changes may also be limited by state or local competitive bidding statutes which prohibit the facility from ordering changes for additional work when that work would normally be obtained through competitive bidding. For example, in *Albert Elia Building Co. v. Urban Development Corp.*,[14] the Urban Development Corp. ("Development Corp.") awarded a competitive contract to build a convention center. During performance of the contract the Development Corp. issued a change order for the construction of a tunnel to link the convention center with an adjacent building. The cost of the building the tunnel exceeded the limit for changes awardable without competitive bidding and therefore the court found the tunnel to be a separate project beyond the scope of the original contract. A specific dollar amount should be stated in the contract to indicate that a change is subject to competitive bidding limitations.

---

[12] *See* § FAR 52.243-4(a)(1)-(4).
[13] AIA Doc. A201, art. 7.3.1 (1997).
[14] 54 A.D.2d 337, 388 N.Y.S. 2d 462 (App.Div. 1976).

Traditionally, changes to the schedule completion date by the owner have not been considered authorized by the changes clause. However, if changes to the specifications are authorized under the clause and the contract schedule is interpreted as being part of the specifications, or if changes to the schedule are specifically listed in the clause, then the facility may have sufficient authority to change the contract schedule.

In *Foster Wheeler Enviresponse Inc. v. Franklin County Convention Facilities Authority,*[15] the Convention Facilities Authority (CFA) hired Lawhon and Associates ("Lawhon") to perform hazardous materials consulting services at the construction site of the Franklin County Convention Center in 1990. During the early phases of construction, an excavator tore a hole in a large wooden box buried beneath the surface, and coal tar waste, creosote, was released from the box into a sewer trench. Lab analysis indicated enough benzene was present in the material to declare it hazardous waste. Upon advice of Lawhon and concurrence with the Ohio EPA, the CFA elected a remediation plan involving removal of clean and contaminated soil, transporting the material to a hazardous waste landfill, and backfilling the area with clean fill. The removal of the waste was opened up to public bidding, and Enviresponse was the low bidder at $165,000.

The CFA and Enviresponse contract provided in part that the scope of work was to change only upon written notice by CFA, with cost adjustments to be made for additions or omissions to the scope of work as bid. Because the bid involved a unit cost, alterations were not to be considered a waiver of any conditions of the contract. On October 15, 1991, Enviresponse began excavation of the soil and waste, but began to encounter odors and saturated soil sooner than anticipated in the contract. Enviresponse's manager then contacted CFA, informing them that more waste was present at the site than originally contemplated in the contract. CFA told the manager to contact Lawhon, and "take direction from them" as to how to proceed.[16]

---

[15] 678 N.E.2d 519, 78 Ohio St. 3d 353 (Ohio 1997).
[16] *Id.*

When CFA checked on the status of the project they found that an additional 1,400 yards of material above the original estimate of 140 yards had been removed and taken to a landfill for disposal, increasing the cost of disposal to $371,000, with an additional 800 yards still to be removed at a cost of $212,000. Lawhon then directed Enviresponse that no additional material, other than that specified in the contract, was to be removed without prior authorization from them, but Enviresponse continued to excavate and transport material to the landfill, until October 31, when Lawhon told them to stop.[17]

Prior to Lawhon's October 31 stop order, Enviresponse continued its excavation and transportation work because Lawhon's on-site manager kept signing hazardous waste manifests and shipping loads, giving Enviresponse the impression Lawhon had approved the excavation of the additional material. Ultimately, a total of 3,546 yards of material was removed at a per unit cost of $939,690. Upon CFA's refusal to compensate Enviresponse for the additional work, Enviresponse sued CFA for breach of contract and Lawhon on the basis that it had negligently misrepresented the amount of material to be removed and the need for written authorizations.[18]

CFA and Lawhon moved for summary judgment which the trial court granted. On appeal, the court reversed the judgment as to CFA but upheld the judgment as to Lawhon, stating that Enviresponse could not show that it had suffered a loss based on the representations of Lawhon. The parties appealed. The Supreme Court of Ohio stated, based on the contract between CFA and Enviresponse, that interpretation as to whether written authorization was necessary for any removal above the original 140 yards under the contract, required an individualized analysis.[19] As a basic rule of contracts, it is presumed that the intent of the parties resides in the language they chose to employ in the agreement, and that common words would be given their ordinary meaning unless some other meaning was clearly meant from the face or overall content of the agreement. Technical words are given their technical meaning unless a different intention is clearly expressed.

---

[17] *Id.*
[18] *Id.*
[19] *Id.*

Additionally, writings are read as a whole, with the intent of the parts to be gathered from consideration of the whole.

Under the contract, the parties agreed that any changes in the scope of the work were to occur in writing, with written authorization for these changes to come from CFA. The main issue became whether the "scope of work" meant the removal of all the contaminated soil and waste, or only the initial amount of material to be removed, namely 140 yards. The Court of Appeals had opined that the scope of work had not changed when additional material was removed, so no written authorization was required, but the Supreme Court disagreed. The Court stated that the increased amount of material was an alteration in the original bid, requiring prior written authorization before Enviresponse was to proceed. The Court explained that to interpret the contract, as Enviresponse urged, as a prenegotiated waiver of the requirement for written authorization would allow one part of the contract to negate another, and this is why the document had to be read as a whole. The entire reason for requiring written authorization was to protect the convention center owner from exorbitant and unjust claims for additional work. Enviresponse further argued that CFA knew of the changes and increased amount of material being removed, and asserted no objection, but the Court stated that mere knowledge and acquiescence was not enough for recovery, and judgment for CFA was entered. The Court agreed with the Court of Appeals that Enviresponse did not have a contract with Lawhon and relied on its manager's signing of the manifests at its peril. Therefore, summary judgment was granted to Lawhon.[20]

This case is an excellent example of how contractors can proceed with their work without authority, and how requiring written change orders protected the owner from additional costs close to one million dollars. It is vital that facility managers know the terms of any such contracts and that any changes in the scope of work to be accomplished be required in writing to protect both the facility and the contractor in case of future disagreement. It is good practice for changes clauses to require change orders to be made in writing because some courts will deny a claim for a price adjustment based on the lack of a written change order.

---

[20] *Id.*

However, the federal changes clause, FAR § 52.243-4, is liberal in not requiring written orders and many courts will not prevent a contractor from recovering an equitable adjustment if the facility induces a contractor to perform additional work through a verbal or constructive change order. Usually, the court will hold that the public or private owner has waived the requirement that an order be in writing when they issue a verbal order.[21]

Most changes clauses include language assigning the contractor a duty to proceed upon receipt of a change order. This duty is strictly enforced in federal contract cases, but less so in state, local and private contracts. In *Dick Corp. v. State Pub. School Building Authority*, the court held that the contractor did not have to proceed where the contract required change orders to be in writing and the agency owner would not issue a written order.[22] Similarly, in *R. G. Pope Construction Co. v. Guard Rail of Roanoke, Inc.*, where the owner did not make the site available to the contractor until seven months after the scheduled completion date, and costs had increased substantially, the court held that the contractor was under no duty to proceed. "A contractor may be justified in not proceeding with performance when (a) the changed condition causes a substantial increase in the contractor's costs; (b) the contractor can not continue funding the work without an immediate increase in the contract price; and (c) the owner refuses to negotiate such an adjustment."[23]

The AIA standard changes clause[24] contains language which allows for unilateral change orders, where the price is not determined prior to the performance of the changed work, or bilateral change orders, pre-priced change orders.

---

[21] *See Owens v. City of Bartlett*, 528 P.2d 1235 (Kan. 1974); *D. K. Meyer Corp. v. Bevco, Inc.*, 292 N.W.2d 773 (Neb. 1980) (owner found to have waived the requirement for a written order where it issued oral orders for change).

[22]

[23] *Metropolitan Sewerage Comm'n v. R. W. Construction, Inc.*, 241 N.W.2d 371, 383, 72 Wis. 2d 365 (Wis. 1976).

[24] *See* note , *supra.*

It will usually benefit the facility to negotiate the price of the change order work before the work is executed. If time allows, the facility may request that the contractor analyze a proposed change order and submit a written proposal before the change order is issued. The changes clause should address which party will be responsible for the costs associated with preparation of the proposal. Nevertheless, it is also important for the facility to have the flexibility to issue unilateral change orders when time does not allow for pre-pricing. The facility can attempt to limit a subsequent price adjustment by the contractor by adding language that the price of the change is "not to exceed" a stated amount. But, the facility should be careful to review the returned change order for any modification to its language or reservation of rights by the contractor.

Minor changes are defined by the AIA as those that do not cause a change in price or require a time extension. Standard construction contracts usually allow an architect to make unilateral minor changes.[25]

2) Contractor Changes

Contractor suggested changes are generally considered outside the scope of the contract work and therefore treated as change order proposals. A contractor may suggest more time and cost efficient changes to the work once it becomes involved with the planning and construction of the project, but, the facility must carefully review any contractor proposed change since it will be responsible for reimbursing the contractor the price and profit associated with any approved change.

Since less expensive methods of performance may lead to a reduction in the contractor's profit there is little incentive for the contractor to propose such changes. However, the concept of value engineering works to ease this problem by offering the contractor a share of the cost savings. The standard federal value engineering clause for construction contracts is found at FAR § 52.248-3. In federal contracting, the value-engineering clause has been held to apply to all contractor proposed

---

[25] *See, e.g.*, AIA Doc. A201, art. 7.4 (General Conditions) (1997).

changes, whether the change is minor or a correction of an error in the specifications.[26]

3) Types of Contractor Claims

When a contractor incurs costs above those originally anticipated it will most likely request reimbursement for its cost overruns from the facility. The changes clause frequently comes into play in private contracting where the contract includes the procedure for contractors to follow in asserting such claims. For claims involving a contract's changes clause, there are three initial questions to be addressed: "has the [facility] ordered more work, was the [facility] at fault in causing the contractor to incur additional costs, and were the procedures of the contract followed in submitting the claim."[27]

a) Constructive Changes

Most contractor claims result from facility initiated change orders, express or implied, to the contractor for additions, deletions, or alterations to the contractor's original scope of work. The facility's power to order these changes is derived from the contract's changes clause. The changes clause requires change orders to be in writing, however, a constructive change occurs when the owner verbally, or by implication, alters the contractor's work without issuing a written change order. An affirmative act, a course of conduct, or a failure to act can support a constructive change claim.[28]

As in the case of a written change order, a contractor is entitled to an equitable adjustment[29] under the changes clause for constructive changes to the work that result in delay or increased costs. The elements of proving a constructive change are generally: (a) extra work beyond the scope of the contract; (b) action by the facility requiring the contractor to

---

[26] *See The Cardan Company, Inc.*, ASBCA No. 25765, February 4, 1982, 82-1 BCA ¶ 15,628, at 77,199.
[27] Ralph C. Nash, CONSTRUCTION CONTRACTING, Ch. 6, "Changes and Claims," at 532 (1991).
[28] *See, e.g., Brown Construction Company*, ASBCA No. 22648, March 8, 1979, 79-1 BCA ¶ 13,745.
[29] *See* note , *supra* for brief discussion of "equitable adjustments."

perform work not included in the original contract; and (c) notice given by the contractor to the facility within a "reasonable period of time" of learning of the constructive change.[30] The formula typically used when pricing an equitable adjustment is the cost of the changed scope of work minus the cost of the original scope of work -- not the contractor's bid price of the original scope of work.

The discussion that follows of claims involving, defective specifications, contract interpretation and an owner's failure to disclose vital information, etc., are all examples of constructive changes.

b) Defective Specifications

Private, state and local construction contracts typically call for disputes over the interpretation of specifications to be resolved by the architect or engineer that prepared the specifications.[31] However, private, state and local construction cases, with few exceptions, will recognize a facility's liability for defective specifications.[32] The owner is deemed by law to impliedly warrant that the plans and specifications are accurate, and suitable for their intended use.[33] The facility's liability is based on the owner's initial responsibility to provide reasonably accurate information—the *Spearin* doctrine.[34]

Therefore, if a contractor incurs increased costs because of defective specifications, then the contractor can file a claim that correcting or dealing with the erroneous specifications was a breach of the facility's implied warranty that its specifications were fit for their intended purpose and imposed a constructive change to the

---

[30] *Jo-Bar Mfg. Corp. v. United States*, 535 F.2d 62, 210 Ct. Cl. 149 (Ct. Cl. 1976).

[31] *See* AIA Doc. A201, art. 4.2.11 (1997).

[32] *Mooney's, Inc. v. South Dakota Dept. of Transp.*, 482 N.W.2d 43 (S.D. 1992) (South Dakota has not adopted the *Spearin* implied warranty doctrine).

[33] *City of Seattle v. Dyad Constr., Inc.*, 565 P.2d 423 (Wash. Ct. App. 1977); *McGovney & McKee, Inc. v. City of Berea*, 448 F. Supp. 1049, 1056 (E.D. Ky. 1978) *aff'd*, 627 F.2d 1091 (6th Cir. 1980) *Kelley v. Bank Bldg. & Equipment Corp. of America*, 453 F.2d 774 (10th Cir. 1972); *Nelse Mortensen & Co. v. Group Health Coop.*, 566 P.2d 560 (Wash. Ct. App. 1978), *aff'd*, 586 P.2d 469 (Wash. 1978).

[34] *United States v. Spearin*, 248 U.S. 132, 39 S.Ct. 59, 63 L.Ed 166 (1918).

scope of work. When the contractor maintains that performance is impossible or impractical based on the owner provided specifications, some courts have allowed the contractor to recover on a constructive change theory under the changes clause. Impracticability of performance has been defined as "conditions, that although literally *possible*, are commercially wasteful and impractical due to the great unanticipated expense, difficulty, and length of time required to finish the job."[35]

Where courts have allowed for recovery based on an owner's breach of its implied warranty, damages include the costs incurred by the contractor for idleness resulting from the defective specifications. "The defendant [owner] cannot, by errors in the specifications, cause delay in the [contractor's] completion of the work and then compensate [the contractor] merely by extending its performance time and by payment of any added direct cost occasioned by changes to correct those errors."[36]

Some courts have held that the contractor waived its right to rely on the facility's specifications if it should have known about the defect(s).[37] Courts have also distinguished design specifications from performance specifications and found no basis for contractor recovery based on alleged defects in performance specifications.[38] Yet, other courts have rejected such a distinction and held that "[c]ontracts are viewed in their entirety and given the meaning imputed to a 'reasonably intelligent contractor' acquainted with the involved circumstances."[39]

---

[35] The George Washington University Law School Government Contracts Program, "Contract Claims" Fall, 1997, at 11.
[36] *Laburnum Constr. Corp. v. United States*, 325 F.2d 451, 163 Ct. Cl. 339 (1963).
[37] *Bromley Contracting Co. v. United States*, 14 Cl. Ct. 69 (1987), *aff'd without opinion*, 861 F.2d 729 (Fed. Cir. 1988); *Lott Constructors, Inc. v. Jackson Township Bd. of Educ.*, 1992 U.S. Dist. LEXIS 12891 (D.N.J. Aug. 12, 1992); see also *Fidelity & Deposit Co. v. City of Sheboygan Falls*, 713 F.2d 1261, 1271 (7th Cir. 1983) (language to the effect that by an express assumption of the risk, the contractor may be liable).
[38] Design specifications set forth the specific details of the work. Performance specifications state only the required outcome of the contract. Most specifications are mixed design and performance specifications which must be carefully analyzed to determine the cause of the problem.
[39] *Zinger Construction Co. v. United States*, 807 F.2d 979 (Fed. Cir. 1986).

Facilities can attempt to limit or avoid liability for defective plans and specifications by getting the contractor to expressly (1) warrant the performance of the work (2) assume responsibility for the design, or (3) include a disclaimer in the contract. Such attempts have had mixed results. For example, in *Atlantic National Bank of Jacksonville v. Modular Age, Inc.*, the court held that the owner's implied warranty of the plans and specifications could not be avoided by delegating the responsibility for design to the general contractor by an express guaranty that was found in the standard AIA contract documents that were used.[40] Similarly, in *U.S. v. Spearin*, the United States Supreme Court rejected a disclaimer for the contractor to check the plans.[41]

Oftentimes a facility will look to the party who authored the plans and specifications, its architect or engineer, for reimbursement of the loss it sustains due to defects in the plans and/or specifications. It is important for the facility to be familiar with the applicable state law so that it may determine the ability of the contractor to recover directly from the architect. The best way for a facility to protect itself is to be aware of the potential liability for defective design and specifications and take steps to assure that the plans and specifications are prepared in a professional environment with open communication between all project participants.

The following case notes describe contractor efforts to recover extra costs based on defective specifications:

In *Arkansas Rice Growers Coop. Assn. v. Alchemy Industries, Inc.*, Alchemy & Pitt, Inc. contracted to provide "the necessary engineering plant layout and equipment design and the onsite engineering supervision and start-up engineering services" for the construction of a hull-burning plant capable of achieving certain performance criteria; the court held that by furnishing plans and specifications Alchemy & Pitt, Inc. warranted their sufficiency for the purpose in view.[42]

---

[40] 363 So.2d 1152 (Fla. Ct. App. 1978); *Fidelity & Deposit Co. v. City of Sheboygan Falls*, 713 F.2d 1261, 1271 (7th Cir. 1983); *City of Orlando v. H.L. Coble Construction Co.*, 282 So.2d 25 (Fla. Ct. App. 1973); *Lewis v. Anchorage Asphalt Paving Co.*, 535 P.2d 1188 (Alaska 1975); *Mooney's, Inc. v. South Dakota Dept. of Transp.*, 482 N.W.2d 43 9S.D. 1992).

[41] *See* note , *supra*.

[42] 797 F.2d 565 (8th Cir. 1986).

In *Blue Bell, Inc. v. Cassidy*, a contractor was held not responsible to an owner (in the absence of an express warranty) for damages due to the partial collapse of a building which was caused by either the defective design of footings, bad soil conditions or both. The contractor followed the designs provided by the owner and his architect and had not warranted design or performance of the footings or soils under the AIA standard for agreement.[43]

c) Interpretation of Contracts

The principles of contract interpretation will determine which party's reading of the contract requirements will prevail in the event of a dispute. A facility should review the applicable state law for interpretation of contracts; however, some general standards that courts and state or local governing bodies may apply include the following. The plain meaning of the contract prevails over the subjective intent of the parties.[44] Contract terms are defined according to their common usage or in the case of technical terms according to their normal technical meaning as used in the particular trade in question. Contract interpretations which conflict with other parts of the contract or render other terms meaningless will not be enforced.[45]

Where the contract language is ambiguous, interpretations prior to the dispute, interpretations implicit in current performance of the work and the prior course of dealings between the two parties, can offer insight into what the parties thought the contract required before the filing of a claim and the initiation of a dispute.[46]

If the contract language proves ambiguous or reasonably susceptible of the interpretation given it by the contractor and the contractor relied on its interpretation when bidding, then the courts and state or local governing authority will likely enforce the contractor's interpretation

---

[43] 200 F. Supp. 443 (N.D. Miss. 1961).
[44] *George Hyman Contr. Co. v. United States*, 832 F.2d 574 (Fed. Cir. 1987).
[45] *Hol-Gar Manufacturing v. United States*, 169 Ct. Cl. 384, 351 F.2d 972 (1965).
[46] *Romala Corp. v. United States*, 20 Cl. Ct. 435 (1990), aff'd 927 F.2d 1219 (Fed. Cir. 1991).

against the facility under the *contra proferentum* rule which states that contractual ambiguities are construed against the drafter of the contract—which is usually the owner. Application of this rule is generally a last resort used only after all other efforts fail to resolve a contractual ambiguity.

If the contract contains an obvious ambiguity the contractor, and not the facility, has an affirmative duty to ask the facility for clarification of the terms. Failure to seek clarification prevents the contractor from bringing a claim later for damages incurred due to a misrepresentation of the contract language.

d) Facility's Failure to Disclose

The facility's failure to disclose information important to the contractor's work, or providing misleading information, often results in extra work for which courts and boards have allowed recovery based on constructive change or breach of contract theories. In federal public contract cases where there are costs resulting from both government nondisclosure and contractor fault, some boards have apportioned the costs.[47] However, others have found government nondisclosure to be the more serious fault and held the government fully liable.[48] Moreover, in the case of latent defects or conditions, the government has been held responsible on the basis that contractors have the right to rely on an owner's specifications where a reasonable pre-bid inspection would not have uncovered the defect(s).[49]

Although a facility's duty to disclose information will depend on the contract type and the data involved, ***the facility generally has a duty to communicate all known information essential to the contractor's performance.*** The contract should include provisions dealing with the facility's responsibility to provide information. Information that the facility will typically be obligated to provide includes:

---

[47] *Pacific Western Construction, Inc.*, DOTCAB No. 1084, September 20, 1982, 82-2 BCA ¶ 16,045.
[48] *Commercial Mechanical Contractors, Inc.*, ASBCA No. 25695, August 9, 1983 83-2 BCA ¶ 16,768; *Record Electric, Inc.*, ASBCA No. 26385, April 30, 1982, 82-1 BCA ¶ 15,784.
[49] *Mike McAdams Roofing Co., Inc.*, ASBCA No. 27339, May 7, 1985, 85-2 BCA ¶ 18,113.

1) Reasonable evidence of its financial arrangements, before execution of the contract, or at the request of the contractor;
2) Surveys or studies describing the physical characteristics, legal limitations and utility locations for the site, and a legal description of the site;
3) Approvals, easements, assessments and charges required for construction, use or occupancy of existing facilities;
4) Mechanics' lien information;
5) Consultant services that are reasonable, required and requested by the architect, in addition to geotechnical engineers' services; and
6) Drawings and specifications, free of charge.[50]

Whether a facility's informational duties are specified in the contract or not, the contract's scope of work provision can also be determinative of such responsibilities. Duties to supply available information may be implied to the facility based on tasks not included in the contractor's scope of work. For example, if, under the contract, the facility has assumed the duties to select the site and determine the subsoil conditions, he cannot reasonably assert that the architect or general contractor was negligent with regard to these tasks.[51] The differing site conditions clause in most public and private construction contracts will obligate a facility to compensate the contractor when the conditions encountered differ materially from those described in the contract. These clauses will be discussed in greater detail later.

e) Hindrance and Delay
All parties to a construction contract have an implied duty of good faith and fair dealing.[52] A facility should consult the applicable state law to determine whether it also has an implied contractual obligation to cooperate and not to hinder or obstruct the contractor in performing its work.

---

[50] *See, e.g.*, AIA Doc. A201, ¶¶ 2.1.2, 2.2 and 3.2 (1997); and AIA Doc. B141 (1997 ed.), Article 4, Owner's Responsibilities.
[51] *Housing Authority of City of Carolton v. Ayrs*, 88 S.E.2d 368, 371 (Ga. 1955).
[52] RESTATEMENT (SECOND) OF CONTRACTS § 205 (1979); *see also*, 17A AM. JUR. 2d *Contracts* § 256 (1991).

If so, a contractor may file a claim for a constructive change resulting from interference, failure to cooperate, delay and/or disruption by the facility.[53] In federal government contracts these claims are pursued on breach of contract and constructive change theories. The government's conduct is measured for reasonableness under the circumstances and whether the government had notice of any problems and did not act to correct them. Further, notice is required in almost all construction contract changes clauses, public or private.[54] In federal construction cases courts have not strictly interpreted the notice requirements in the federal changes clause. Rather, they have enforced notice requirements based on fairness. The General Services Administration Board of Contract Appeals, in *Powers Regulator Company*, stated that the federal notice provision would not be enforced when:

1) Written notice is in fact given the contracting officer;
2) The contracting officer has actual or imputed knowledge of the facts giving rise to the claim;
3) Notice to the contracting officer would have been useless;
4) The contracting officer frustrated the giving of notice; and
5) The contracting officer considered the claim on the merits.[55]

State courts, on the other hand, have been stricter in their enforcement of notice requirements—enforcing the contract notice requirements even where government employees had actual

---

[53] *See e.g., M. De Mateo Constr.. Co. v. Maine Turnpike Authority*, 184 F. Supp. 907 (S. D. Me. 1960); *City of Seattle v. Dyad Constr.., Inc.*, 565 P.2d 423 (Wash. Ct. App. 1977).

[54] *See e.g.*, FAR 52.243-4, ¶¶ (b), (d) and (e) (1998); AIA Doc. A 201, ¶¶ 4.3.1 and 4.3.2 (1997)(written notice of claims is required within 21 days of the occurrence of the event giving rise to the claim or when the contractor first recognizes the condition giving rise to the claim, whichever is later).

[55] GSBCA Nos. 4668, 4778 and 4838, April 30, 1980, 80-2 BCA ¶ 14,463, at 71,320.

knowedge of the circumstances that were the basis for the contractor's claim.[56]

f) Scheduling Problems/Acceleration

"Acceleration occurs when there is an attempt to complete performance earlier than would have been required if the contract schedule had been properly adjusted to reflect excusable delays."[57] Acceleration may happen via a direct order from the facility or constructively through demand by the facility that the contractor complete performance by a date that has not been extended to compensate for excusable delays.

The elements of acceleration under federal contract law are:

- Excusable delay;
- The government's actual or constructive knowledge of the delay at the time the acceleration is ordered;
- Notice by the contractor to the government of such delay;
- Some action, direct or constructive, by the government which could reasonably be construed as an order to accelerate; and
- Additional costs incurred as a result of, or related to the acceleration.[58]

The success of an acceleration claim depends heavily on the facts and circumstances of each case. In *Norair Engineering Corp. v. United States*, the Court of Claims found that the denial of a contractor's request for time extensions and government pressure to complete the work on schedule were effectively an order to perform according to the original schedule, and thus, an acceleration order.[59]

The contractor may have a right to finish early, but this varies depending upon state law. In federal contracting, this right was

---

[56] *State Highway Dept. v. Hewitt Contracting Co.*, 149 S.E.2d 499 (Ga. Ct. App. 1966).

[57] The George Washington University Law School Government Contracts Program, "Contract Claims" Fall, 1997, p. 18.

[58] *Id.*, at 19 (citing *Associated Industrial Contracting, Inc.*, ENG BCA No. 5370, 88-2 BCA ¶ 20,708; *Fermont Div. Dynamics Corp. of America*, ASBCA No. 25806, 75-1 BCA ¶ 11, 139 (1975), *aff'd*, 216 Ct. Cl. 448 (1978); *see also* Richard F. Smith, "Scheduling and Proof of Claims," CONSTRUCTION BRIEFINGS, NO. 82-6 (1982).

[59] 229 Ct. Cl. 160, 666 F.2d 546 (1981)

recognized in *Interstate General Government Contractors, Inc. v. West.*[60] In that case, the Federal Circuit held that a contractor was entitled to recover extended overhead for a period of delay where it "shows from the outset of the contract it: (a) intended to complete the contract early; (b) had the capability to do so; [and,] (c) actually would have completed early, but for the government's actions." *Id.*

g) Cumulative Impact

There are an increasing number of claims by contractors against owners for "impact costs." Impact costs are additional costs caused to unchanged work by unexpected conditions or added work directed by the facility. Federal courts and boards have recognized the validity of a separate claim for the cumulative impact of excessive change orders and delay even though the contractor may already have been compensated for performing the changed work under the contract's changes clause. In *Shintech, Inc. v. Group Constructors, Inc.,* the contractor sought, *inter alia,* cumulative impact costs for upsets to its schedule caused by excessive change orders by the owner.[61] The contractor had already received compensation for the changes under the change orders and the owner alleged that by accepting such compensation, the contractor had been fully paid for the changes and had thus waived its right to recover for the delay. *Id.* The court rejected this argument and found that the contractor was entitled to cumulative impact costs because the changes and extra work clauses of the contract did not include impact costs resulting from the changes.[62] Another Texas court recognized a contractor's right to recover impact costs for several hundred changes even though the owner had already paid the contractor over $2 million for the changes in *City of Houston v. R. F. Ball Construction Company, Inc..*[63] In this case, the court said that owner's payment was for the "direct" costs of the changes and did not cover the "indirect" or "impact" costs occasioned by the "delay, disruption, and general hindrance of efficient work which inevitably resulted from the changes."[64] The court, however, concluded that the contract's "no damage for delay" clause barred the contractor's

---

[60] 12 F.3d 1053 (Fed. Cir. 1993).
[61] 688 S. W.2d 144 (Tex. App. - Houston 1985).
[62] *Id.*
[63] 570 S.W.2d 75 (Tex. Civ. App. - Houston 1978).
[64] *Id.*, at 76.

recovery of delay damages.[65] Some courts base the contractor's right to recover the reasonable value of the work it performed in excess of the original contract amount (impact costs) on a *quantum meruit* basis.[66]

4. Notice

As mentioned above, public and private construction contracts typically set a time in which the contractor will have to give the facility written notice of its intent to seek recovery of costs for changes or delays due to change to the contract work or face forfeiture of its claim.[67] However, depending on the forum, late notice or lack of notice may not preclude a contractor's claim. Typically, federal courts and boards will only defeat a claim for relief because of lack of notice if the government shows that it was prejudiced by the defect in notice.[68] If a facility has sufficient knowledge to substitute for formal notice, it may be characterized as a waiver of the notice requirement.[69]

If the contract work is delayed or interrupted by conduct of the government or its agent, the standard federal clause states that: A claim . . . . shall not be allowed (1) for any costs incurred more than 20 days before the Contractor shall have notified the Contracting Officer in writing of the act or failure to act involved, and (2) unless the claim, in an amount stated, is asserted in writing as soon as practicable after the termination of the delay or interruption, but not later than the day of final payment under the contract.[70]

---

[65] *Id.*

[66] *Peterson v. Container Corp. of America*, 172 Cal. App. 3d 628, *modified*, 173 Cal. App. 3d 348B (1985) (citations omitted).

[67] *See* FAR §§ 52.243-1, 2, 3, and 4 (1998); AIA Doc. A201, art. 9.7.1 (1997).

[68] *See e.g.*, *Michael, Inc.*, ASBCA No. 39,653, 92-1 BCA ¶ 24,412 (1991); *Chimera Corp.*, ASBCA No. 18690, 76-1 BCA ¶ 11,901 (1976).

[69] *J.D. Abrams*, ENG BCA No. 4332, 89-1 BCA ¶ 21,379 (1988); *West Land Builders*, VABCA No. 1663, 83-1 BCA ¶ 16,235 (1983).

[70] FAR § 52.242-17(b) (1998).

Boards have interpreted this provision, or similar versions, as requiring that the contractor provide the government owner with reasonable identification of the claimed action causing delay.[71]

14.03   Differing Site Conditions Clauses

In *U.S. v. Spearin,*[72] the Supreme Court stated that when "one agrees to do, for a fixed sum, a thing possible to be performed, he will not be excused or become entitled to additional compensation, because unforeseen difficulties are encountered." Therefore, in the absence of a special risk-shifting clause (*e.g.,* a differing site conditions or changed conditions clause), a contractor will be responsible for any additional costs resulting from unforeseen difficulties. Courts, however, have granted relief to contractors in the absence of a differing site conditions clause, based on: (1) commercial impracticability—where a differing site condition caused material changes in the cost and method of performance and these changes were not contemplated by the parties at the time the contract awarded;[73] and, (2) mutual mistake—where parties assume a fact, necessary for performance based on the design documents, that turns out to be nonexistent.[74]

Because of the risk of large contingencies to the contractor and the facility's potential obligation to compensate the contractor for legitimate changed conditions, most public and private construction contracts attempt to allocate the risk between the parties. In rare or unique instances it may be necessary for the facility to draft a project specific suspension of work clause.

---

[71] *Lane-Verdugo*, ASBCA Nos. 16327, 73-2 BCA ¶ 10, 271, at 48,514 (citing *Hoel-Steffen Construction Co. v. United States*, 197 Ct. Cl. 561, 456 F.2d 760 (1972)); *see also Cameo Bronze, Inc.*, GSBCA No. 3656, 73-2 BCA ¶ 10,135.

[72] *See note , supra.*

[73] *Xplo Corp.*, DOTCAB No. 1289, 86-3 BCA ¶ 19,125.

[74] *Gevyn Constr. Corp. v. U.S.*, 357 F.Supp. 18 (S.D.N.Y. 1972) (the parties mistakenly believed that a drain tap into the State's storm sewer was feasible); *but see Picard Constr. Co. v. Board of Comm'rs*, 109 So. 816 (La. 1926).

Because of the ast precedent that exists, however, the standard federal or AIA clauses that are available should be used as models.[75]

The AIA standard differing site conditions clause generally places financial responsibility for these conditions on the facility. The AIA standard differing site conditions clause provides that a contractor must give notice within 21 days; and the architect will then investigate whether the concealed physical conditions are substantially different from those usually found to exist and generally recognized as inherent in construction activities provided for under the contract. The architect will then recommend either an equitable adjustment for the contractor or that no change exists. If the facility or contractor wish to dispute the architect's decision, any objection must be made within 21 days after notice of the decision and the dispute will be referred to the architect for further proceedings.[76]

---

[75] FAR § 52.236-2 (1998); AIA Doc. A201, ¶. 4.3.4 (1997). The AIA clause is substantially the same as the federal clause. The federal clause states:

FAR § 52.236-2 Differing Site Conditions.

(a) The Contractor shall promptly, and before the conditions are disturbed, give a written notice to the Contracting Officer of (1) subsurface or latent physical conditions at the site which differ materially from those indicated in this contract, or (2) unknown physical conditions at the site, of an unusual nature, which differ materially from those ordinarily encountered and generally recognized as inhering in work of the character provided for in the contract. (b) The Contracting Officer shall investigate the site conditions promptly after receiving the notice. If the conditions do materially so differ and cause an increase or decrease in the Contractor's cost of, or the time required for, performing any part of the work under this contract, whether or not changed as a result of the conditions, an equitable adjustment shall be made under this clause and the contract modified in writing accordingly. (c) No request by the Contractor for an equitable adjustment to the contract under this clause shall be allowed, unless the Contractor has given the written notice required; *provided*, that the time prescribed in (a) above for giving written notice may be extended by the Contracting Officer. (d) No request by the Contractor for an equitable adjustment to the contract for differing site conditions shall be allowed if made after final payment under this contract.

[76] AIA Doc. A201, art. 4.3.4 (1997).

A facility may include disclaimers intended to relieve itself of liability for additional work necessitated by unforeseen conditions. However, the enforceability of disclaimers is greatly affected by the jurisdiction and facts of the case. The facility, however, may be able to support the enforcement of its disclaimer by obtaining soils information, but not any representations concerning it, or by not making it part of the contract documents. Typically, principles of equity and fairness will govern the enforceability of such disclaimers.

1. Site Investigation

Site inspection clauses which place responsibility on the contractor to investigate the worksite generally do not overcome the requirements of a differing site conditions clause.[77] Therefore, a differing site conditions clause may directly obligate the facility to provide an equitable adjustment. If the contractor establishes a right to compensation for the differing or changed condition, the facility may be responsible for: (1) the direct costs of performing the changed work; (2) delay costs of idle labor and equipment, or inefficient operations; (3) increased overhead costs; and (4) other impact costs. Consequently, it is important for the facility to take all reasonable steps to gather and disclose any relevant information concerning the project and the conditions under which it must be performed which the contractor could not otherwise obtain.

2. Geotechnical Basis of Design

One of the initial steps in a construction project is the soils engineering evaluation of the site. The facility typically provides the soil boring information to the contractor in the form of a site geology report. The goal or purpose of the report is to provide a reasonably

---

[77] *Stuyvesant Dredging Co. v. United States*, 834 F.2d 1576 (Fed. Cir. 1987).

accurate picture of the soil and the relevant geotechnical features of the site. Where the facility is responsible for providing the contractor with the soils report, some courts have imposed an implied warranty of the sufficiency of the soil report on the owner.[78] Another court, however, concluded differently and held that in the absence of a changed conditions clause and where a soils disclaimer shifted the risk to the contractor, the contractor assumed the risk of unforeseen conditions. And thus, there was no implied warranty of the sufficiency of soil to support the building.[79]

3. Disclosure of Relevant Documents

As discussed above,[80] the facility's duty to provide information will vary with the type of contract and its terms. With regard to site related information, contractors are entitled to rely upon information provided by the facility, such as soil and geological reports. Therefore, if a facility intentionally conceals information which is material or significant to the contractor's performance, the concealment or non-disclosure is actionable on the theory of negligent or fraudulent misrepresentation. To recover for misrepresentation, a contractor must establish that (a) he was not reasonably able to discover true facts and (b) that the misrepresentation was material.[81]

---

[78] *Berkel & Co. Contractors v. Providence Hosp.*, 454 So.2d 496, 503 (Ala. 1964); *Metropolitan Sewerage Comm'n v. R.W. Constr., Inc.*, 241 N.W. 2d 371, 378 (1976) (it is well settled that contractors are entitled to rely on soil borings; when the conditions encountered vary significantly from those described in the soil report, the owner supplying the information may be responsible for additional costs incurred); *Brown Bros. v. Metropolitan Gov't*, 877 S.W.2d 745 (Tenn. Ct. App. 1993).

[79] *Eastern Tunneling Corp. v. Southgate Sanitation Dist.*, 487 F. Supp. 109, 113 (D. Colo. 1979); *see also Green Constr. Co. v. Kansas Power & Light Co.*, 1 F.3d 1005 (10th Cir.1993).

[80] *See* § 14.02(3)(iv) of this chapter, *supra.*

[81] *Eastern Tunneling Corp. v. Southgate Sanitation Dist.*, 487 F. Supp. 109, 113 (D. Colo. 1979); *Anderson v. Golden*, 569 F. Supp 122, 143 (S.D. Ga. 1982) (citing *Robert E. McKee, Inc. v. City of Atlanta*, 414 F. Supp. 959-60 (N.D. Ga. 1976).

14.04   Suspension of Work Clauses

If a contract is delayed, the terms of the contract determine whether the contractor may recover time and costs associated with the delay. Standard "suspension of work" clauses define those situations in which a contractor may or may not recover the costs incurred by delay. In general, the contractor is responsible for the costs of delay which it caused or which are within its control, and the facility will be responsible for delays which it caused, are under its control, or for which it has agreed to compensate the contractor. The federal suspension of work clause is, again, a good model to use when the contracting circumstances allow because of the precedent that exists.[82] Under the federal clause, the government may order the suspension, delay, or interruption of all or any part of the contract work. But, if the work is suspended, delayed or

---

[82] FAR § 52.242-14 Suspension of Work (1998): (a) The Contracting Officer may order the Contractor, in writing, to suspend, delay, or interrupt all or any part of the work of this contract for the period of time that the Contracting Officer determines appropriate for the convenience of the Government. (b) If the performance of all or any part of the work is, for an unreasonable period of time, suspended, delayed, or interrupted (1) by an act of the Contracting Officer in the administration of this contract, or (2) by the Contracting Officer's failure to act within the time specified in this contract (or within a reasonable time if not specified), an adjustment shall be made for any increase in the cost of performance of this contract (excluding profit) necessarily caused by the unreasonable suspension, delay, or interruption, and the contract modified in writing accordingly. However, no adjustment shall be made under this clause for any suspension, delay, or interruption to the extent that performance would have been so suspended, delayed, or interrupted by any other cause, including the fault or negligence of the Contractor, or for which an equitable adjustment is provided for or excluded under any other term or condition of this contract. (c) A claim under this clause shall not be allowed (1) for any costs incurred more than 20 days before the Contractor shall have notified the Contracting Officer in writing of the act or failure to act involved (but this requirement shall not apply as to a claim resulting from a suspension order), and (2) unless the claim, in an amount stated, is asserted in writing as soon as practicable after the termination of the suspension, delay, or interruption, but not later than the date of final payment under the contract.

interrupted "for an unreasonable period of time" because of an action or omission by the government, the contractor is entitled to compensation unless such compensation is otherwise precluded under the contract.[83] The federal clause covers both ordered and constructive suspensions—when the work is stopped or delayed without an express order by the contracting officer—but the government is still responsible for the suspension of work. Compensable delay can also occur because of the facility's delay in providing funding, inspecting the work, issuing change orders, approvals, or a notice to proceed, in making the site available to the contractor, or by interfering with the contractor's work.

14.05   Liquidated Damages Clauses

Liquidated damages clauses are regularly included in construction contracts. Since the loss that a facility sustains as a result of late completion of a construction project is usually difficult to determine, the purpose of including a liquidated damages clause is to provide a formula for estimating and measuring this loss. Both the FAR and the ABA's Model Procurement Code and Recommended Regulations provide model liquidated damages clauses.[84] A liquidated damages provision for recovery in the event of late completion will generally be enforced if: (1) it is providing compensation for the reasonable losses sustained and is

---

[83] *Id.*

[84] FAR § 52.211-12 (1998); MPC Recommended Regulation R5-401.10 (1997). The federal clause states: FAR § 52.211-12 Liquidated Damages—Construction (a) If the Contractor fails to complete the work within the time specified in the contract, or any extension, the Contractor shall pay to the Government as liquidated damages, the sum of .... [Contracting Officer insert amount] for each day of delay. (b) If the Government terminates the Contractor's right to proceed, the resulting damage will consist of liquidated damages until such reasonable time as may be required for final completion of the work together with any increased costs occasioned the Government in completing the work. (c) If the Government does not terminate the Contractor's right to proceed, the resulting damage will consist of liquidated damages until the work is completed or accepted.

not a penalty for the contractor's breach; (2) the parties intended the clause to be a genuine liquidated damages provision; (3) the loss resulting from late completion is uncertain or difficult to determine accurately; and (4) the amount stipulated to in the liquidated damages provision is a reasonable forecast of the loss that will result from late completion. Whether a particular liquidated damages provision is enforceable is determined on the particular facts of each case. Therefore, a facility should consult the applicable state law when formulating such a clause.

In general, however, in order to recover liquidated damages a facility must show that:

- The contract was not completed by the contract completion date with all adjustments by the terms of the contract;
- Liquidated damages are due under the contract; and
- The period of assessing the liquidated damages was proper.

Some federal courts have allowed the government or owner to recover liquidated damages even if the owner has not suffered any actual damages as a result of the delayed completion.[85] Others have precluded recovery of liquidated damages in the absence of a reasonable forecast of probable damages in the event of a breach and actual damages.[86] However, actual damages do not have to be monetary to support a claim for liquidated damages, i.e., having to re-procure a contract creates a loss sufficient to warrant liquidated damages. Further, liquidated damages will not be assessed after the date on which the contract work is substantially complete.[87]

---

[85] *See, e.g., Central Ohio Building Co.*, PSBCA No. 2742, 1991 WL 187546 (August 30, 1991); *David Nassif Assoc. v. United States*, 226 Ct. Cl. 372, 644 F.2d 4 (Ct. Cl. 1981).
[86] *See, e.g., Great Western Utility Corp.*, ENGBCA No. 4934, April 5, 1985, 85-2 BCA ¶ 18,022.
[87] *Lindwall Construction Co.*, ASBCA No. 23148, April 18, 1979, 79-1 BCA ¶ 13,822; *Dillon Construction, Inc.*, ENGBCA No. PCC-36, October 23, 1981, 81-2 BCA ¶ 15,416.

14.06   No Damages for Delay Clauses

Construction contracts containing "no damage for delay" clauses expressly preclude a price adjustment for delay resulting from the action or inaction of the other party. Although no damage for delay clauses are generally valid and enforceable, it is important for a facility to consult applicable state law to determine if, and to what extent, a particular jurisdiction enforces these clauses. Facilities should be aware that some courts have held that no damage for delay clauses are to be strictly construed because of their harsh effects. For example, in *John E. Green Plumbing & Heating Co. v. Turner Constr. Co.*, the relevant clause prohibited the recovery of damages if the contractor was delayed in the "'commencement, prosecution, or completion of the project.'"[88] The court held that the clause must be strictly construed, and thus, it only barred recovery of delay damages and not other kinds of damages, such as damages for hindering work on the project, which the contractor was complaining about.[89] Most cases treat broadly stated no damage for delay clauses as extending to every kind of delay. But, there are several judicially created exceptions: In general terms, a contractor may recover for unreasonable delays in the construction process notwithstanding the presence of 'no damage' clauses, if the delay: (1) was of a kind not contemplated by the parties, (2) amounted to an abandonment of the contract, (3) was caused by bad faith, or (4) was caused by active interference.[90]

14.07   Inspection, Acceptance and Warranties

If defects are found the provisions of the contract that describes the: contract work; standards and procedures for inspection and quality assurance; conditions for acceptance of the work;and rights and obligations of the parties, allow a facility to monitor the contractor's progress and compliance with these provisions and to demand corrective measures when the contract requirements are not met. To assure that the

---

[88] 742 F.2d 965, 966 (6th Cir. 1984).

[89] *John E. Green*, 742 F.2d 965, *supra*.

[90] *Peter Kiewit Sons' Co. v. Iowa S. Utils. Co.*, 355 F. Supp. 376 (Iowa 1973); *see also, United States Steel Corp. v. Missouri Pac. R.R. Co.*, 668 F.2d 435 (8th Cir. 1982).

facility receives what it contracted for, proper inspection is critical. Standard inspection clauses in federal, state and private construction contracts place the burden of inspection and quality control on the contractor and/or the architect or engineer.[91] However, as the facility's rights will be limited after final acceptance of the contract work, careful oversight of the quality of the work by the facility during construction and before acceptance is essential.

Under most government and private construction contracts the contractor will warrant to the facility that the work is of good quality and meets the requirements of the contract. And thus, work that does not meet the requirements of the contract is defective and may be rejected by the facility. But, the rejection of work that is in substantial compliance with the contract requirements is not permitted.[92] In the case where the work is defective, construction contracts often include a provision providing that the contractor will correct the work, or, if the contractor fails to correct the defect, the facility may make the repairs itself and deduct from the contractor's payments the cost of repairing the defects in performance.[93] Note, however, that the facility must give the contractor prompt notice[94] and an opportunity to correct any defects.[95]

---

[91] *See, e.g.*, FAR § 52.246-12 (Inspection of Construction) (1998); AIA Doc A201, ¶¶ 3.3, 4.2.2, 4.2.3, 4.2.6, 4.2.7, 4.2.9 and 9.10.

[92] *Downes Swimming Pool, Inc. v. North Shore Nat'l Bank*, 464 N.E.2d 761 (Ill. App. Ct. 1984).

[93] *See, e.g.*, FAR § 52.246-12 (1998). Paragraphs (f) and (g) state: (f) The Contractor shall, without charge, replace or correct work found by the Government not to conform to contract requirements, unless in the public interest the Government consents to accept the work with an appropriate adjustment in contract price. The Contractor shall promptly segregate and remove rejected material from the premises. (g) If the Contractor does not promptly replace or correct rejected work, the Government may (1) by contract or otherwise, replace or correct the work and charge the cost to the Contractor or (2) terminate for default the Contractor's right to proceed.

[94] *Phoenix-Georgetown, Inc. v. Charles H. Tompkins Co.*, 477 A.2d 215, n. 22 (D.C. 1984).

[95] *Burras v. Canal Constr. & Design Co.*, 470 N.E.2d 1362 (Ind. Ct. App. 1984).

It is important for a facility to understand what circumstances trigger final acceptance because it limits the facility's rights relating to patent defects, shifts the risk-of-loss of the work from the contractor to the facility, and may start the running of warranties. In private construction contracts, what constitutes "final acceptance" is a question of fact, and therefore, the law may differ between jurisdictions. Accordingly, the facility should refer to the applicable state's law when drafting contract language which will specify the exact event marking final completion of work and acceptance.

Federal and private construction contracts often include a "use and possession clause" to define the facility's or Government's right to occupy and use the completed, or partially completed work, without inducing final acceptance of work under the contract.[96] It is important, however, that use and possession of the contract work has been held to constitute acceptance when it is accompanied by conduct clearly indicating acceptance.[97]

It is well established that where defects in the contract work are patent—readily discoverable—final inspection and acceptance of the work discharges any right to damages for the defects. Yet, government and private construction contracts also provide that acceptance will not be final with regard to "latent defects, fraud, gross mistakes amounting to fraud, or the Government's rights under any warranty or guarantee."[98] The last exception, allows government and private contracts to include specified and implied warranties that give the owner remedies for defects discovered after acceptance. Examples of such warranties include express warranties: a one-year obligation to correct defective or non-conforming work; and that materials and equipment furnished under the contract are of good quality and new unless otherwise provided for in the contract and implied warranties of fitness, workmanlike quality and habitability; and, that the work will be sufficient for a particular purpose or result. These warranty clauses will be interpreted narrowly and the party asserting a breach of the warranty has the burden of proof.

---

[96] *See, e.g.,* FAR § 52.236-11; ABA MPC Recommended Regulations §9.9 (1997). MPC § 9.9.3 states: Unless otherwise agreed upon, partial occupancy or use of a portion or portions of the Work shall not constitute acceptance of Work not complying with the requirements of the Contract Documents.

[97] *See, e.g., Aubrey v. Helton,* 159 So. 2d 837 (Ala. 1964).

[98] FAR § 52.246-12(i) (1998).

In addition, a contractor is often required, under a one-year warranty in the contract provisions, to correct any latent defects discovered during that period. But, that obligation is not exclusive and does not limit a facility's right to sue for damages resulting from such latent defects.[99] In *Herley Industries, Inc.*, the Armed Services Board of Contract Appeals defined latent defects as "defects at the time of final acceptance which were hidden from knowledge as well as sight and could not be discovered by the exercise of reasonable care. . . . [D]efects which can be discovered readily by an ordinary examination or test are not latent and a failure to make the examination or test does not make them so . . . ."[100] Moreover, in federal construction cases, courts have held that if the Government had reason to know of the defect, then it is not latent.[101] To avoid final acceptance based on one of the exceptions listed above, i.e., latent defect, the facility has to prove (1) that the defect existed at the time of acceptance, (2) that acceptance was revoked within a reasonable time after the facility discovered, or should have discovered the defect, (3) that the condition falls within the exception on which it relies, and (4) the failure was caused by the defect.

14.08   Termination Clauses

Once performance of the contract has begun, a construction contract may be terminated on the basis of (1) material breach by the other party, or (2) the party's power to terminate as defined by the terms of the contract. Termination resulting from the violation of an act, for which the contract provides termination as a remedy, is generally referred to as "default termination." A facility manager drafting a construction contract may choose to include termination rights only for itself, however, many standard industry contracts allow both the facility and contractor to terminate the contract based on a failure by the other party that

---

[99] *First National Bank v. Cann*, 503 F. Supp. 419 (N.D. Ohio 1980), *aff'd*, 669 F.2d 415 (6th Cir. 1982).
[100] ASBCA No. 13727, May 14, 1971, 71-1 BCA ¶ 8888, at 41,309.
[101] *U.S. v. Lembke Constr. Co.*, 786 F.2d 1386 (9th Cir. 1986).

is enumerated in the contract termination clause(s).[102] Good examples of a typical termination by the owner provision are found at FAR § 52.249-10 and AIA Doc. A201, art. 14 (1997). Termination by the facility will require the facility to: give the contractor written notice, obtain certification from the architect that sufficient cause exists to justify termination and act in good faith—be able to show that sufficient facts exist to justify terminating the contract. Circumstances that justify default termination by the facility in private construction cases include: (1) failure of timely performance or delay, (2) contractor failure to make prompt payment for labor, material, and subcontracts,[103] (3) substantial breach of a provision of the contract documents, and (4) a statement by the contractor that it cannot or will not perform. Some courts have found that the owner waived its right to terminate the contractor for default when it allowed the contractor to continue its performance and did not take steps to terminate within a reasonable time after having knowledge of the grounds for termination.[104]

Construction contracts should also include a provision allowing the facility to terminate a contractor for convenience—without cause. A termination for convenience clause gives a facility the exclusive right to unilaterally terminate the contractor for virtually any reason. In exchange for the facility's extensive rights to terminate the contract for convenience, the facility agrees to reimburse the contractor for the work it has performed and preparations it has made for work that has been cut short.

FAR § 52.249-2 provides a good model for drafting a private construction contract termination for convenience clause. The federal clause, however, should be distinguished because it does not require the government to give advance notice of its plans to terminate for convenience. Moreover, even if the termination for convenience clause is omitted, the government still has the right to terminate on that basis. To

---

[102] *See, e.g.,* AIA Doc A201, art. 14 (Termination By The Contractor) (1997).
[103] Some courts have required the owner to have suffered some loss in order to justify a default termination, *see U.S. ex rel. Pickard v. Southern Constr. Co.,* 293 F.2d 493 (6th Cir. 1961), *rev'd in part on other grounds,* 371 U.S. 57 (1962), other have not, *see, e.g., Fabrizio v. Fabrizio,* 48 A.2d 375 (Conn. 1946).
[104] *E.V. Cox Constr. Co. v. Brookline Assocs.,* 604 P.2d 867 (Okla. 1979); *Plymouth Village Fire Dist. v. New Amsterdam Casualty Co.,* 130 F. Supp. 798, 801 (D.N.H. 1955). *But see, Fields Eng'r & Equip. Inc. v. Cargill, Inc.,* 651 F.2d 589 (8th Cir. 1981).

the contrary, private contracts usually require notice, inclusion of the specific clause, *and* good faith.[105]

14.09   Payment Issues

1) Right to Withhold Payment

If specific problems arise with the contractor's performance of the contract, the facility may withhold amounts necessary to cover defective work by the contractor from payments due. Federal construction contract cases have established that the public facility owner has an implied right to withhold payment for the cost of correcting defective work.[106] But, it is good practice to enumerate the right to withhold money from payments due by express contract language. In any case, the amount withheld must be a reasonable estimation of the amount that will be due to the facility as a result of the contractor's defective performance.

FAR § 52.232-5(e), of the federal payments clause for payments under fixed-price construction contracts, states:... [I]f satisfactory progress has not been made, the Contracting Officer may retain a maximum of 10 percent of the amount of the payment until satisfactory progress is achieved.

When the work is substantially complete, the Contracting Officer may retain from previously withheld funds and future progress payments that amount the Contracting Officer considers adequate for protection of the Government and shall release to the Contractor all the remaining withheld funds. . . .

Similarly, private construction contracts allow facilities to withhold payments under the following circumstances:

- Defective work not remedied (contractor must be given the opportunity to correct and the defect must not be minor);[107]

---

[105] *EDO Corp. v. Beech Aircraft Corp.*, 911 F.2d 1447, 1452-53 (10th Cir. 1990).

[106] *Building Maintenance Specialist, Inc.*, ENGBCA No. 4115, June 23, 1983, 83-2 BCA ¶ 16,629.

[107] *Austin Paving v. Cimarron Constr.*, 511 S.W.2d 417 (Tex. Ct. App. 1974).

- When a third party claim has been filed, or there is reasonable evidence that one will be filed;[108]

- Contractor's failure to make proper payments for labor, materials, equipment, or to subcontractors;[109]

- The contract work cannot be completed for the unpaid balance of the contract sum;[110]

- The remaining work will not be completed on time, and the unpaid balance will not cover damages resulting from the delay;[111] or,

- Continual failure to perform the work in conformance with the contract requirements.

2) Penalties for Delayed Payment

In private contracting, if the facility has no legal right under the contract to withhold payment, the failure to pay is a breach of contract.[112] Penalties the facility may face when payment is improperly delayed or withheld include: (1) having to pay interest on the amount withheld, (2) the contractor stopping performance, and/or (3) injunctive relief for the contractor. A contractor's right to recover interest on payments wrongfully withheld by a State, local government or private facility, the period for which such interest can be recovered, and the rate of recovery, will vary from state to state. Therefore, it is important for facility procurement

---

[108] *Montgomery v. Karavas*, 114 P.2d 776 (N.M. 1941).

[109] *Willard, Inc. v. Powertherm Corp.*, 444 A.2d 93 (Pa. 1982).

[110] *Devlin v. Milwaukie Covenant Church*, 525 P.2d 998 (Or. 1974); *Montgomery v. Karavas*, 114 P.2d 776 (N.M. 1941).

[111] *See Wagoner v. Turpin Park Irrigation Co.*, 489 P.2d 630 (Wyo. 1971), however, a facility can waive the right to withhold payment by continuing to make payments after it is apparent that the contract work will not be completed on time, or when the owner acts unreasonably with regard to repeated requests for time extensions and change orders. *See, e.g., J.R. Graham & Son, Inc. v. Randolph County Bd. of Educ.*, 212 S.E.2d 542 (N.C. Ct. App. 1975).

[112] In federal government contracts, the contractor is usually entitled to interest on late payment under the Prompt Payment Act or the Contract Disputes Act. *See* note 103, *infra*.

personnel to review the applicable state law in this area. Generally, a contractor can recover interest on any delayed payments whether the facility's breach is material or immaterial. The AIA standard contract states that delayed payments "shall bear interest."[113] And, the ABA MPC recommends that the recovery of interest be mandatory in cases where it is determined that payment is wrongfully withheld from the date the claim arose through the date of decision or judgment, whichever is later.[114] If a particular interest rate is not specified in the contract, the applicable state law will usually provide a fixed rate.[115]

Under federal construction contracts, as stated above, an interest penalty for late payment is imposed by contract or by statute.[116] However, the Prompt Payment clause in FAR § 52.232-27(a)(4)(iv) also states that "interest penalties are not required on payment delays due to disagreement between the Government and Contractor over the payment amount or other issues involving contract compliance . . . ." Facility managers should review the federal clause on Prompt Payment for help in drafting contract language that addresses the facility's obligations in the case of delayed payments.

Another possible penalty that a facility which fails to properly make payments may face is the refusal to continue performance. The federal Disputes clause, however, states:

(I) The Contractor shall proceed diligently with performance of this contract, pending final resolution of any request for relief, claim, appeal, or action arising under the contract . . . . Consequently, it is well established that the government may default terminate a contractor who stops work in violation of the duty to proceed.[117] Yet, courts have allowed federal contractors to stop work when nonpayment constitutes a *material* breach of the contract. Whether the nonpayment constitutes a material breach depends on the amount of money involved, the period of time and

---

[113] AIA Doc. A201, ¶ 13.6.1 (1997).

[114] MPC § R9-103.06 (1997).

[115] *See, e.g.*, D.C. Code § 28-3302 (6%); Cal. Civ. Code § 926.17 (15%).

[116] *See* FAR § 52.232-27 (1998); 31 U.S.C. § 3901 *et seq.* (the Prompt Payment Act); 41 U.S.C. § 611 (the Contract Disputes Act).

[117] *Stoeckert v. U.S.*, 391 F.2d 639 (Ct. Cl. 1968).

the number of payments that were not made and the procedures for payment set forth in the contract.[118]

Similarly, in the state, local government or private construction contract setting, if the contract does not require the contractor to continue performance despite nonpayment or other disputes, the right to stop work will depend on whether the failure to make proper payment constitutes a material breach. Whether the breach is material or not depends on such factors as: (a) the course of dealing between the parties,[119] (b) whether the facility's nonpayment prevents the contractor from continuing performance[120] and (c) the facts of each particular case. Since the question of whether a facility's failure to properly pay the contractor is a material breach is typically a question of fact for the jury, injunctive relief is not usually a penalty imposed on owners in the context of a non-federal construction contract.

14.10 Payment and Performance Bonds

Payment and performance bonds guarantee the contractor's ability to pay any persons furnishing material and labor for contract work and the performance of the contractor, respectively. Prime contractors working on federal construction contracts exceeding $25,000 are required, by statute and regulation,[121] (unless the requirement is waived pursuant to FAR § 28.102-1(a) (1998), to post payment and performance bonds. The applicable state law should be consulted because most states have statutory payment and performance bond requirements similar to the Miller Act.

Performance bonds will work principally for the protection of the facility in the event that the contractor is unable to complete performance of the contract work, by naming a surety who will be

---

[118] *See General Dynamics Corp.*, DOTCAB No. 1232, 83-1 BCA ¶ 16,386; *TEM Assocs., Inc.*, DOTCAB No. 2024, 89-1 BCA ¶ 21,266; *Consumers Oil Co.*, ASBCA No. 24172, 86-1 BCA ¶ 18,647. *See also Southeastern Airways Corp. v. U.S.*, 673 F.2d 368 (Ct. Cl. 1982); *Monarch Enterprises*, VABCA No. 2239, 86-3 BCA ¶ 19,281.
[119] *Texas Bank & Trust v. Campbell Bros.*, 569 S.W.2d 35 (Tex. Ct. App. 1978).
[120] *Voight v. Nanz*, 213 N.W.2d 749 (Wis. 1974).
[121] *See* 40 U.S.C. § 270a (The Miller Act); and FAR § 28.102 (1998).

responsible for fulfilling the contractor's performance. In the event a contractor or subcontractor becomes insolvent, payment bonds provide security to: (1) subcontractors and/or materialmen—by guaranteeing payment for any work performed or materials furnished; and (2) facility owners—by relieving them of complaints and delays that may result from the contractor's inability to pay. Therefore, it is in the facility's best interest to include in the contract, a provision setting forth the contractor's obligations to obtain payment and performance bonds. The clauses used in federal contracts are found at FAR § 52.228-15 (1998), for contracts exceeding $100,000 and § FAR 52.228-13 for those greater than $25,000, but not exceeding $100,000. The following is an example of a provision that may be used in a negotiated private facility/contractor contract:

PAYMENT AND PERFORMANCE BONDS

(a) If and when required before or during performance of the Contract, Contractor shall obtain, at the expense of Owner, a Bond or Bonds for the amount and in the form specified by Owner. The Bond(s) shall be delivered to Engineers within ten (10) days after award of the Contract or subsequent notice of a requirement for Payment and Performance Bond or Bonds during performance of the Contract.

(b) Such Bond or Bonds shall be executed in a form acceptable to Owner, and by a Corporation acceptable to Owner, licensed and authorized to issue Payment and Performance Bonds in the State of   , and on the U.S. treasury Department list of acceptable sureties. The bond shall be accompanied by a certified copy of the Power of Attorney authorizing the Attorney-in-Fact of the corporate Surety to execute and deliver the bond on behalf of the Surety, together with a currently executed certificate of an authorized officer of the Surety stating that the Power of Attorney is in full force and effect.

14.11   Liability of Architects and Engineers

Standard facility-architect and facility-engineer contracts establish the professional standard of care as the measure of the architect's and engineer's performance under the contract. The following is an example of such a provision:

1.2.3.2   The Architect's services shall be performed as expeditiously as is consistent with professional skill and care and the orderly progress of the Project.[122] The facility could also attempt to raise the standard of care in such an agreement.

A facility's agreement with the architect and/or the engineer defines the architect or engineer's responsibility for providing services under the contract. Therefore, when drafting such agreements, facilities should be careful of architects or engineers attempting to limit their responsibilities under the contract, such as, on-site observations or inspections, approval of payments to contractors, or providing construction cost estimates.

An architect or engineer may be liable to the facility in contract, tort, or both. But, perhaps the most significant liability issue to consider is the growing number of jurisdictions that refuse to apply the "economic loss rule" as a bar to the recovery of damages sustained by third parties (i.e., contractors, subcontractors, and materialmen), due to the architect or engineer's negligence. The economic loss rule generally precludes these third parties from recovering economic loss damages—usually contract damages—from parties with whom they have no contract. In other words, a contractor may not recover economic losses from the architect or engineer whose contract is with the facility. Conversely, the rule may also preclude facilities from recovering economic loss damages from subcontractors, design professionals and materialmen that are not in privity of contract with the facility. As stated above, however, many jurisdictions have rejected the economic loss rule and allowed contractors to recover for negligence by the architect or engineer.[123] But, it is not

---

[122] AIA Document B141 Article 1.2.3 (Standard Form of Agreement Between Owner and Architect with Standard Form of Architect's Services) (1997 ed.).
[123] *See, e.g., Berkel & Co. Contractors, Inc. v. Providence Hosp.*, 454 So.2d 496 (Ala. 1984); *Mattingly v. Sheldon Jackson College*, 743 P.2d 356 (Alaska 1987); *Wolther v. Schaarschmidt*, 738 P.2d 25 (Colo. App.

always clear when the economic loss rule will be rejected or applied, thus the applicable state law should be carefully review.

14.12 Alternative Dispute Resolution

Resolving construction disputes through litigation is expensive, time consuming, adversarial and risky. In addition to direct costs, (i.e., legal fees and expenses), a company may incur costs in the form of lost time for its personnel and lost profits on other work. There are no controls on the amount or scope of award and the adversarial nature of litigation may foreclose future business opportunities with the opposing party. Alternative dispute resolution, ("ADR"), allows parties to control costs, preserve customer relations, avoid publicity, participate in formulating the decision and to reduce time and much of the risk associated with traditional litigation. Nearly 93% the United States District Courts have established formal ADR procedures, at least 16 states have created state dispute resolution offices (i.e., Alabama, California, Florida, Minnesota and New York) and in early 1996, President Clinton signed an Executive Order calling for all government agencies involved in civil litigation to use ADR. Nevertheless, there are trade-offs to consider. For example, proposing ADR may be seen by the opposing side as an admission of weaknesses in your case. However, a facility manager initiating ADR can emphasize that it is proposed as a cost savings measure for both parties. Also, if a contractor expects to recover 100 cents on the dollar for its claim or a facility believes that it will totally defeat the opposing party's claim, ADR is not the appropriate venue. The following are several questions a manager should ask before agreeing to alternative means of dispute resolution:

- Do the parties want to be bound by the decision?
- Are there fundamental difference on factual issues?
- Are there significant legal issues separating the parties?
- Is there animosity between the parties?
- Are costs a major concern?

1986); *Guardian Const. Co. v. Tetra Tech Richardson, Inc.*, 583 A.2d 1378 (Del. Super. 1990); *National Sand, Inc. v. Nagel Const., Inc.*, 451 N.W. 2d 618 (Mich. App.), *cert. denied*, 456 N.W.2d 390 (Mich. 1990); and, *Gilliland v. Elmwood Properties*, 391 S.E.2d 577 (S.C. 1990).

1) Mediation

Mediation is a flexible process that involves a meeting between the disputing parties, their representatives and a neutral mediator designed to assist the parties in reaching a mutually acceptable resolution. A recent study of 449 cases from four major ADR providers found that 78% of the cases that went to mediation settled, the costs and time of mediation were less than arbitration and the respondents' reported greater satisfaction with mediation than arbitration.

There are two common approaches to mediation—facilitative and evaluative. In facilitative mediation the mediator will not offer opinions on any legal or factual disputes, but merely try to force the parties to understand and evaluate for themselves the opposing party's positions. The mediator, in evaluative mediation, will bluntly evaluate the strengths and weaknesses of both parties' cases, including direct representations as to the chances for success on particular issues in court, in an effort to bring the parties' expectations closer together.

Evaluative mediation is virtually essential in construction disputes because there are usually so many complicated issues that the mediator must "weed-out" the certain winners and losers in order t o move the process forward. Most clients and attorneys seek evaluative mediation.

Under the new AIA standard construction contract, (document A201), mediation is now mandatory. Article 4.5 of A201 makes mediation a condition precedent to arbitration and litigation and requires a written Request for Mediation be filed with the opposing party and the American Arbitration Association ("AAA") (unless the parties agree not to use the AAA). However, claims related to aesthetic effect are not subject to mediation (AIA document A201, Article 4.5.1) or arbitration (Article 4.6.1) as a condition precedent to litigation.[124] An outline of steps to follow in the mediation process is provided below. Agreeing to me-

---

[124] Note, under AIA Document A201-1997, a demand for arbitration must be filed within 30 days of the Architect's decision, regardless of the status of mediation. Therefore, it is good practice to file a demand for arbitration and mediation simultaneously. The arbitration will automatically be stayed for 60 days, pending the outcome of mediation, unless the parties agree to a longer period. *See generally*, AIA Document A201-1997 § 4.4.6 (1997).

diate is the first step in the mediation process. Parties should agree to split the mediator's fee and any filing fees. The mediation should occur at the place of the project or some other neutral location agreed upon by the parties. Choosing a mediator is perhaps the most important decision in the process. Credibility and selecting an evaluative mediator are critical. In terms of conducting the mediation, preparation dollars will be well spent. Written materials that will be submitted to the mediator should be focused, yet with a high level of detail, and persuasive without attacking. The oral presentation should be factual, simple and credible. During the negotiation phase, keep in mind that resolution is the objective and avoid an adversarial approach. Finally, creativity in crafting a multi-dimensional settlement can often be the key to a successful mediation. For example, providing the contractor with the opportunity for future business under a right of first refusal or structuring a pay out over time, with service.

STEPS IN THE MEDIATION PROCESS

A. **Agreeing to Mediate** - Identify the Parties' Needs and Objectives
   1. Review Surrounding Circumstances
   2. Identify Potential Benefits to Each Party
   3. Define Objectives

B. **Negotiating the Mediation Agreement** -- The Mediation Agreement must reflect the needs and objectives of the parties and clearly establish the guidelines for the mediation. It should be the product of a series of agreements by the parties, which will build momentum towards creating agreement on the ultimate issue. Also, the Mediation Agreement should be executed by the highest level person available to demonstrate commitment to the mediation process.

C. **Selecting the Mediator** -- Potentially the most important element of the mediation process. The parties must be trust the judgment and impartiality of the mediator. This selection should be the result of detailed research, including personal interviews and contacting references.

D. **Conducting the Mediation**

1) *Submission of Written Materials* -- Generally the materials include a joint statement of facts and a position paper from each party.

2) *Oral Presentation* -- Keep it simple! Focus more on your merits than the opposing party's faults.

3) *Negotiation Sessions* -- Usually accomplished through "break-out" sessions, where the mediator will meet with each party individually. Small groups are preferable (i.e., the decision maker, a principal and the party's attorney). There should be a defined plan of what information you want to release to the mediator and in what fashion. Creativity is encouraged and candor in assessing risks is essential.

4) *Closing the Settlement* -- Once an agreement is reached, it should be memorialized immediately in a written memorandum of understanding.

2) **Arbitration**

Arbitration is an alternative means of dispute resolution, available under private, public and federal construction contracts,[125] in which the parties make adversarial presentations to a neutral panel of experts who render a binding decision, enforceable in court. Arbitration can be less expensive and time consuming than litigation and still provide a final disposition of the dispute. Parties will usually decide whether to submit disputes to arbitration when drafting the contract, but parties can agree to arbitrate a dispute after it has arisen even if the contract is silent on arbitration. Arbitration differs from litigation in that arbitrators are less constrained by case law and procedural and evidentiary rules than judges. Arbitrators may fashion particular rules and solutions for each dispute. The binding nature of the decision is unique to arbitration versus reviewable court decisions and mediation which is purely advisory.

Some of the advantages of arbitration described above, however, must be weighed against the down sides. For example, in a relatively simple dispute that can be resolved in a few days, arbitration

---

[125] *See* Jonathan D. Shaffer, Carl T. Hahn, and William A. Focht, *Challenges & Pitfalls in Drafting "Arbitration" Clauses*, CONSTRUCTION BRIEFINGS, SECOND SERIES, March 1997, at 2-3.

presents an inexpensive and expeditious alternative to courtroom litigation. But, in a large complex construction dispute, arbitration can create expenses and risks that will surprise and frustrate both parties. In arbitration the parties must pay an administration fee to the arbitration organization, compensate the individual arbitrators, and contend with difficulties generated by the lack of procedural and evidentiary rules. In arbitration discovery rules are only voluntary and therefore a party may not know the opposing sides witnesses, documents, or theories and defenses until the arbitration proceeding is underway. In addition, while arbitration proceedings typically begin sooner than a court trial, due to scheduling, arbitrations are often conducted piecemeal over a prolonged period of time.

Consequently, arbitration becomes inefficient and costs are affected due to increased travel and preparation time. The standard form "Arbitration" clauses that are recommended by various organizations may provide a good starting point, but they are based on the presumption that all disputes will be submitted to arbitration. AIA Document A201-1997 § 4.6 (Arbitration) states:

4.6.1   Any Claim arising out of or related to the Contract, except Claims relating to aesthetic effect and except those waived as provided for in Subparagraphs 4.3.10, 9.10.4 and 9.10.5, shall after decision by the Architect or 30 days after submission of the Claim to the Architect, be subject to arbitration. Prior ro arbitration, the parties shall endeavor to resolve disputes by mediation in accordance with the provisions of Paragraph 4.5.

In order to maintain control over the dispute resolution process, the facility manager may want to customize a standard form clause to reflect your intentions.[126] For example, you can specify the number of arbitrators and any special qualifications the arbitrators must have. The location of the arbitration and a choice-of-law provision, such as: "In rendering the award, the arbitrator shall determine the rights and obligations of the parties according to the substantive and procedural laws of [State]," can also be included.[127] In addition, consider including a statement acknowledging that the agreement pertains

---

[126] For a comprehensive discussion of typical arbitration clauses, arbitration procedural rules and the remedies available to the arbitrator *see id.*, at 4-10. However, note that important changes were made to the 1997 edition of AIA Document A201.

[127] *Id.*, at 4.

to a transaction involving interstate commerce and a second statement "that the Federal Arbitration Act ("FAA") shall govern the interpretation, enforcement, and proceedings under the 'Arbitration' clause."[128]

---

[128] *Id.*, at 5.

Table of Cases

599

Public Assembly Facility Law

Brown Bros. v. Metropolitan Gov't, 877 S.W.2d 745 (Tenn. Ct. App. 1993)., p. 578
Bruce Construction Corp. v. U.S., 324 F.2d 516 (Ct. Cl. 1963)., p.556
Burns v. Mayor and City Council of Rockville, 525 A.2d 255 (Ct. Spec. App. Md. 1987)., p. 8
Burras v. Canal Constr. & Design Co., 470 N.E.2d 1362 (Ind. Ct. App. 1984)., p. 583
Calash v. City of Bridgeport, 788 F.2d 80, (2d Cir. 1986)., p. 489, 490, 494, 508
Carreras v. City of Anaheim, 768 F.2d 1039 (9th Cir. 1985)., p. 493, 501, 502
Carroll v. Otis Elevator Company, 896 F.2d 210 (7th Cir. 1990)., p. 253
Caruso v. Blockbuster-Sony Music Entertainment Centre, No. 95-3400 (JEI), 1997 U.S. Dist.
     LEXIS 9401 (NJ June 25, 1997)., p. 86, 87, 88, 96
Charlevoix Productions, Inc. v. County of Charlevoix, No. L89-50054 CA, 1990 U.S. Dist.
     LEXIS 11020 (W.D. Mich. Aug. 20, 1990)., p. 527
Charles Breseler, Co., ASBCA No. 22669, 78-2 BCA ¶ 13,483., p. 116
Chelton v. Tallahassee-Leon County Civic Center Authority, 525 So.2d 972
     (Fla. Ct. App. 1988)., p. 235
City of Orlando v. H.L. Coble Construction Co., 282 So.2d 25 (Fla. Ct. App. 1973)., p. 567
C&L Construction Co. v. The United States, 6 Cl. Ct. 791, 794 (1984)., p. 553
Clarkson et. al. v. Coughlin 898 F. Supp 1019 (S.D. N.Y. 1995)., p. 77
Clemons v. The Big Ten Conference, No. 96 C 0124, 1997 U.S. Dist. LEXIS 1939
     (N.D. Ill. Feb. 24, 1997)., p. 383
Cleveland, City of v. Carney Aud. et. al., 174 N.E. 2d 254 (Ohio 1961)., p. 13
Coalition of Montanans Concerned with Disabilities, Inc., v. Gallatin Airport Authority, 957 F.
     Supp. 1166 (1997)., p. 66
Commonwealth v. Santangelo, 520 N.E.2d 1340 (1988)., p. 322
Coniglio v. Highwood Services, Inc., et. al., 1973 Trade Cas. (CCH) p. 74, 795
     (W.D. NY 1973)., p.327
Connecticut v. Leary, 587 A.2d 85 (Conn. 1991)., p. 321
Connecticut Performing Arts Foundation v. Brown, 47 B.R. 911 (Bankr. D. Conn. 1985)., p. 30
Cook County Bar Auxiliary et. al. v. Hyatt Corporation, No. 83 C 6384, 1986 U.S. Dist. LEXIS
     27639 (March 26, 1986)., p. 221
Cortez et. al. v. National Basketball Association, et. al., 960 F. Supp. 113
     (W.D. Tex. 1997)., p. 55
Creel v. Washington Parish Fair Association et. al., 597 So.2d 487 (La. Ct. App.
     1st Cir. 1992)., p. 262
Crouch v. National Association for Stock Car Auto Racing, Inc., 845 F.2d 397
     (2d Cir. 1988)., p. 37
D'Amario v. The Providence Civic Center Authority, 639 F.Supp. 1538
     (R.I. 1986)., p. 502, 509
David Nassif Assoc. v. United States, 226 Ct. Cl. 372, 644 F.2d 4 (Ct. Cl. 1981)., p. 581
DeFulio v. Spectraguard, Inc. No.6199, 1995 Phila. Cty. Rptr. LEXIS 40 (June 23, 1995)., p. 277
Denver Center for the Performing Arts v. Briggs, 696 P.2d 299 (Colo. 1985)., p. 11
Devlin v. Milwaukie Covenant Church, 525 P.2d 998 (Or. 1974)., p. 588
Diamond v. Springfield Metropolitan Exposition Authority, 44 F.3d 599 (7th Cir. 1995)., p. 7
Dick Corp v. State Public School Building Authority., p. 562
Dictiomatic, Inc. v. U.S. Fid. & Guar. Co. (S.D.Fla. 1997) 958 F.Supp.594, 602., p. 227
D. K. Meyer Corp. v. Bevco, Inc., 292 N.W.2d 773 (Neb. 1980)., p. 552
Donovan v. A.A. Beiro Construction Co., Inc. 746 F.2d 894 (D.C. 1984)., p. 244
Dowis v. Continental Elevator Company, Inc, 486 N.W.2d 916 (Neb. 192)., p. 252
Downes Swimming Pool, Inc. v. North Shore Nat'l Bank, 464 N.E.2d 761 (Ill. App.
     Ct. 1984)., p. 583
Driskill v. Dallas Cowboys Football Club, Inc., 1973 Trade Cas. (CCH) p. 74, 544
     (N.D. Texas 1973)., p. 327
Dunbar v. Latting et. al., 621 N.E. 2d 232 (Ill. 3d Dist. 1993)., p. 263
Eastern Tunneling Corp. v. Southgate Sanitation Dist., 487 F. Supp. 109, 113
     (D. Colo. 1979)., p. 578

Appendices

EDO Corp. v. Beech Aircraft Corp., 911 F.2d 1447, 1452-53 (10th Cir. 1990)., p. 587

Ellit v. USA Hockey, 922 F. Supp. 217 (E.D. Mo. 1996)., p. 52

Emery v. Caravan of Dreams, Inc., 879 F. Supp. 640 (N.D. Tex. 1995)., p. 53

Engel Stadium Corporation v. Chattanooga, [no number in original] 1993 Tenn. App. LEXIS 398 (June 2, 1993)., p. 146

E.V. Cox Constr. Co. v. Brookline Assocs., 604 P.2d 867 (Okla. 1979)., p. 586

Evans v. Valley Forge Convention Center, No. 95-658, 1996 U.S. Dist. LEXIS 12091 (E.D. Pa. Aug. 15, 1996)., p. 158

Event Producers, Inc., v. Tyser & Co., 854 F.Supp. 35 (D. P.R. 1993)., p. 222

Fabrizio v. Fabrizio, 48 A.2d 375 (Conn. 1946)., p. 586

Fairbanks, City of v. Fairbanks Convention Center and Visitors Bureau, 818 P.2d 1153 (Alaska 1991)., p. 42,

Federal Sign v. Texas Southern University, No. 94-1317, 1997 Tex. LEXIS 58 (June 20, 1997)., p. 10, 42

Feldt v. Marriott Corporation, 322 A.2d 913 (App. D. C. 1974)., p. 257

Fiedler v. American Multi-Cinema Inc., 871 F. Supp. 35 (US DC 1994)., p. 83

Fields Eng'r & Equip. Inc. v. Cargill, Inc., 651 F.2d 589 (8th Cir. 1981)., p. 586

Fidelity & Deposit Co. v. City of Sheboygan Falls, 713 F.2d 1261, 1271 (7th Cir. 1983)., p. 566, 567

Filmore v. Convention Center & Visitor's Bureau, No. 61269, 1992 Ohio App. LEXIS 5493 (October 29, 1992)., p. 236

First National Bank v. Cann, 503 F. Supp. 419 (N.D. Ohio 1980), aff'd, 669 F.2d 415 (6th Cir. 1982)., p. 585

First National Bank Association v. Federal Deposit Insurance Corporation 79 F 3d 362 (3rd Cir 1996)., p. 58

Flip Side Productions Inc., v. Jam Productions, Ltd., et. al., 843 F.2d 1024 (7th Cir. 1988)., p. 302

Flores v. Villerose, Inc., No. 96-2549, 1996 U.S. Dist. LEXIS 11171 (July 29, 1996)., p. 106

Florida Panthers Hockey Club, Ltd., v. Miami Sports and Exhibition Authority, et. al., 939 F. Supp. 855 (S.D. Fla. 1996)., p. 194

Foster Wheeler Enviresponse Inc. v. Franklin County Convention Facilities Authority, 678 N.E.2d 519 (Ohio 1997)., p. 559

Fort Worth, City of v. Groves, 746 S.W. 2d 907 (Tex. App. 1988)., p. 533

Fox v. Dees, 362 S.E.2d 699 (Va. 1987)., p. 180

Freeman v. County of Fresno, 126 Cal. App. 3d 459 (1981)., p. 15

Friendship Medical Center, Ltd. v. Space Rentals, 62 F.R.D. 106 (N.D. Ill. 1974)., p. 171

Gallagher v. Constable, 49 F.3d 1442 (10th Cir. 1995)., p. 275

George Hyman Contr. Co. v. United States, 832 F.2d 574 (Fed. Cir. 1987)., p. 568

Gershwin Publishing Corps. v. Columbia Artists Management,Inc 443 F.2d 1159 (CA2 1971)., p. 525

Gevyn Constr. Corp. v. U.S., 357 F.Supp. 18 (S.D.N.Y. 1972)., p. 575

Gibson v. Shelby County Fair Association, 65 N.W. 2d 433 (Iowa 1954)., p. 242

Gilliland v. Elmwood Properties, 391 S.E.2d 577 (S.C. 1990)., p. 593

Ginsberg v. City of Miami, 307 F. Supp. 675 (S.D. Fla. 1969)., p. 504

Golden West Baseball Company v. City of Anaheim, 25 Cal. App. 4th 11 (1994)., p. 179

Great White Whale Advertising, Inc. v. First Festival Productions, 438 N.Y.S. 2d 655 (3rd Dept. 1981)., p. 528

Green Constr. Co. v. Kansas Power & Light Co., 1 F.3d 1005 (10th Cir.1993)., p. 578

Green, John E. Plumbing & Heating Co. v. Turner Construction Company, 742 F.2d 965, 966 (6th Cir. 1984)., p. 582

Guardian Const. Co. v. Tetra Tech Richardson, Inc., 583 A.2d 1378 (Del. Super. 1990)., p. 592

Gunther v. Charlotte Baseball, Inc., 854 F.Supp. 424 (D.S.C. 1994)., p. 238

Half-A-Car II, Inc. v. Interstate Hotels Corporation, No. 93-5834, 1994 U.S. Dist. LEXIS (Oct. 25, 1994)., p. 184

Appendices

Kahn et. al. v. Brown, 259 A.2d 61 (Md. Ct. App. 1969)., p. 207

Katz v. U.S. 389 U.S. 347 (1967)., p. 272

Katzenbach v. McClung, 379 U.S. 294 (1964)., p. 50

Kearney Convention Center v. Anderson-Divan Cottrell Insurance Inc. et. al, 370 N. W.2d 86 (Neb. 1985)., p. 230

Kelley v. BankBldg. & Equipment Corp. of America, 453 F.2d 774 (10th Cir. 1972)., p. 565

Kelly v. Buffalo Bills Football Club et. al., 655 N.Y.S.2d 275 (1997)., p. 534

Kennedy Theater Ticket Service v. Ticketron, Inc., 342 F.Supp. 922 (E.D. PA. 1972)., p. 334

Kenny Construction Co. v. Metropolitan Sanitary Dist., 309 N.E.2d 221 (Ill. 1974)., p. 556

Kinney v. Yerus, 812 F. Supp. 547 (E.D. Pa. 1993) aff'd 3rd Cir. 1993, cert. Denied sub. nom. v. Kinney, 511 U.S. 1033 (1994)., p. 110

Kleinknecht v. Gettysburg College, 989 F.2d 1360 (3rd Cir. 1993)., p. 265

Klinger v. Pocono International Raceway, inc., 433 A.2d 1357 (Pa. Super. 1980)., p. 165

Koszela v. NASCAR, 646 F.2d 749 (2d. Cir. 1981)., p. 39, 541

Kully v. Goldman, 305 N.W. 2d 800 (Neb. 1981)., p. 327

Kurland v. United Pac. Ins. Co., 59 Cal. Rptr. 258 (Cal. Ct. App. 1971)., p. 130

Laburnum Constr. Corp. v. United States, 325 F.2d 451, 163 Ct. Cl.339 (1963)., p. 566

Lafayette, City of v. Louisana Power & Light Co. 435 US 389, 98 S.Ct. 1123 (1978)., p. 299

LaFrenz v. Lake County Fair Board, 360 N.E.2d 605 (Ind. App. 1977)., p. 260

Laing v. Minnesota Vikings Football Club, Inc., 1973 Trade Cas. (CCH) p. 74, 601 (D. Minn. 1973)., p. 327

Latino v. Kaiser, 58 F.3d 310 (7th Cir. 1995)., p. 316

Lewis v. Anchorage Asphalt Paving Co., 535 P.2d 1188 (Alaska 1975)., p. 567

Leventhal v. Philadelphia, No. 1849, 16 Phila. 605, 1987 Phila. Cty. Rptr. LEXIS 56 (Dec. 15, 1987)., p. 19

Lewis v. Colorado Rockies Baseball Club, No. 96SA381, 1997 Colo. LEXIS 520 (Colo. June 30, 1997)., p. 493

Londono v. Washington Metropolitan Area Transit Authority, 247 U.S. App. D.C. 79, 766 F.2d 569 (D.C. Cir. 1985)., p. 254

Loska v. Superior Court of Los Angeles County, 188 Cal. App. 3d 569 (1986)., p. 316

Lott Constructors, Inc. v. Jackson Township Bd. of Educ., 1992 U.S. Dist. LEXIS 12891 (D.N.J. Aug. 12, 1992)., p. 566

Lowe v. California League of Professional Baseball, 56 Cal. App. 4th 112, 1997 Cal. App. LEXIS 532 (July 1, 1997)., p. 240

MCM Partners, Inc., v. Andrews-Bartlett Exposition Services, et. al., 62 F.3d 967 (7th Cir. 1995)., p. 307

MacLean v. First Northwest Industries of America, Inc., 600 P.2d 1027 (Wash. Ct. App. 1979)., p. 336

Maldanado v. Louisiana Superdome Commission, 687 So.2d 1087 (La. Ct. App.1997)., p. 236

Marilyn Manson Inc. v. New Jersey Sports & Exposition Authority, No. 97-2229, 1997 U.S. Dist. LEXIS 9607 (D. N.J. May 7, 1997)., p. 503

Maro v. Potash et. al, 531 A.2d 407 (NJ Super. 1987)., p. 225

Martin, Casey v PGA Tour, Inc. N. 097 – 6309 TC, 1998 U.S. Dist LEXIS 1503., p. 97, 105

Maryland Stadium Authority v. Becker, 806 A.2d 1236 (D. Md. 1992)., p. 514

Mattingly v. Sheldon Jackson College, 743 P.2d 356 (Alaska 1987)., p. 592

James McHugh Constr. Co., ENGBCA No. 4600, March 12, 1982, 82-1 BCA ¶15, 682., p. 130

McGovney & McKee, Inc. v. City of Berea, 448 F. Supp. 1049, 1056 (E.D. Ky. 1978) aff'd, 627 F.2d 1091 (6th Cir. 1980)., p. 565

McKenna v. Insurance Company of North America, 11 Phila. 617 (Phila. CT. of Common Pleas 1984)., p. 250

McLaughlin, Joan v. Home Indemnity Insurance Co., 361 So.2d 1227 (1978)., p. 233

603

The Mead Corp. v. McNally-Pittsburgh Manufacturing Corp., 654 F.2d 1197, 1199 (6th Cir. 1981)., p. 553

Metropolitan Sewerage Comm'n v. R. W. Construction, Inc., 241 N.W.2d 371, 383, 72 Wis. 2d 365 (Wis. 1976)., p. 562, 578

Metropolitan Sports Facilities Commission v. General Mills, Inc., 460 N.W. 2d 625 (Minn. App. 1990)., p. 20

Metropolitan Tickets, Inc. v. City of St. Louis, 849 S.W.2d 52 (Mo. Ct. App. 1993)., p. 32

M. De Mateo Constr.. Co. v. Maine Turnpike Authority, 184 F. Supp. 907 (S. D. Me. 1960)., p. 570

Miami, City of v. Joseph Robbie et. al., 454 So. 2d 606 (Fla. App. 1984)., p. 152

Mile High Enterprises Inc., v. Dee, 558 P.2d 568 (Co. 1977)., p. 6

Mine Safety Appliances Co., B-233052, 89-1 CPD ¶ 12., p. 124

Mobile Hous. Env'ts v. Barton & Barton, 432 F. Supp. 1343, 1346 (D. Colo. 1977)., p. 553

Monitor Plastics Co., ASBCA 14447, August 3, 1972, 72-2 BCA ¶., p. 127

Montgomery v. Karavas, 114 P.2d 776 (N.M. 1941)., p. 588

Montgomery, City of v. JYD International, Inc., 534 So.2d 592 (Ala. 1988)., p. 154

Montgomery Elevator Company v. Building Engineering Services Co., Inc., 730 F.2d 377 (5th Cir. 1984)., p. 215, 255

Mooney's, Inc. v. South Dakota Dept. of Transp., 482 N.W.2d 43 (S.D.1992) ., p. 565, 567

Naiman v. New York University, No. 95 Civ. 6469 (LMM) 1997 U.S. Dist. LEXIS 6616 (S.D. N.Y. May 13, 1997)., p. 77

Nakamoto v. Fasi, 635 P.2d 946 (Haw. 1981)., p. 273

Nassau, County of v. Spectacor Management Group, et al, No. 33533/97, 1997 N.Y. Misc. LEXIS 677 (Dec. 9, 1997)., p. 181

National Collegiate Athletic Association v. Commissioner, 914 F.2d 1417 (10th Cir. 1990)., p. 26

National Sand, Inc. v. Nagel Const., Inc., 451 N.W. 2d 618 (Mich. App.)., p. 593

National Socialist White People's Party v. Ringers, 473 F.2d 1010 (4th Cir. 1972)., p.491, 494, 508

Nelse Mortensen & Co. v. Group Health Coop., 566 P.2d 560 (Wash. Ct. App. 1978), aff'd, 586 P.2d 469 (Wash. 1978)., p. 565

Norair Engineering Corp. v. United States, 229 Ct. Cl. 160, 666 F.2d 546 (1981)., p. 572

Oakland Stadium v. Underwriter's at Lloyd's, London, 313 P.2d 602 (Cal. Ct. App. 1957)., p. 219

Ohio v. Cleveland, No. 42235, Ct. of Appeals, Ohio (Slip Opinion). June 2, 1980., p. 179

Ohio, State of v. Kuehne, No. C-910454, C-910455, 1992 Ohio App. LEXIS 2128 (1st Dist. April 22, 1992)., p. 279

Omaha Pollution ControlCorp. v. Carver-Greenfield Corp., 413 F. Supp. 1069 (D. Neb. 1976)., p. 553

Owens v. City of Bartlett, 528 P.2d 1235 (Kan. 1974)., p. 562

Paralyzed Veterans of America v. DC Arena LP, No. 97-7005, 1997 US App. LEXIS 16148 (D.C. July 1, 1997)., p. 85

Parker v. Brown, 317 US 341, 63 S.Ct. 307 (1943)., p. 299

Peat Marwick Main & Co., v. New York City Department of Finance, 546 N.Y.S. 851 (1st Dept. 1989)., p. 331

People v. Shepherd, 74 Cal. App. 3d 334 (1977)., p. 317

People of the State of New York v. Johnson, 278 N.Y.S.2d 80 (1967)., p. 317

People of the State of New York v. U.S.T.A National Tennis Center, Inc., 544 N.Y.S.2d 458 (N.Y. Crim. Ct. 1989)., p. 241

Peter Kiewit Sons' Co. v. Iowa S. Utils. Co., 355 F. Supp. 376 (Iowa 1973)., p. 582

Peterson v. City of San Diego, 134 Cal. App. 3d 31 (4th Dist. 1982)., p. 18

Peterson v. Container Corp. of America, 172 Cal. App. 3d 628, modified, 173 Cal. App. 3d 348B (1985) (citations omitted)., p. 574

Pfeiffer v. New England Patriots Football Club, Inc., 1973 Trade Cas. (CCH) p. 74, 267 (D. Mass. 1972)., p. 327

Philip Morris, Incorporated v. Pittsburgh Penguins, Inc., 589 F. Supp. 912 (W.D. Pa. 1983)., p. 520

Appendices

Phoenix, City of v. Phoenix Civic Auditorium & Convention Center Association, Inc. 408 P. 2d 818 (Ariz 1965)., p. 41

Phoenix-Georgetown, Inc. v. Charles H. Tompkins Co., 477 A.2d 215, n. 22 (D.C. 1984)., p. 583

Picard Constr. Co. v. Board of Comm'rs, 109 So. 816 (La. 1926)., p. 575

Pier 30 Associates v. School District of Philadelphia, 493 A.2d 126 (Pa. Commw. 1985)., p. 16

Pilot Air Freight Corp. v. City of Buffalo, No. 91-CV-308E, 1992 U.S. Dist. LEXIS 12341 (W.D. N.Y. July 28, 1992) and 91-CV-0308E(M), 1996 U.S. Dist. LEXIS 2800 (W.D. N.Y. March 8, 1996)., p. 519

Pittsburgh Stadium Concessions, Inc. v. Commonwealth of Pennsylvania, 674 A.2d 334 (Pa. Commw. 1996)., p. 530

Plumstead Theater Society, Inc. v. Commissioner, 74 T.C. 97 (1980) aff'd per curiam, 675 F.2d 244 (9th Cir. 1982)., p. 28

Plymouth Village Fire Dist. v. New Amsterdam Casualty Co., 130 F. Supp. 798, 801 (D.N.H. 1955)., p. 586

Poe v. Hillsborough County, No. 90-223 1997 Fla. LEXIS 686 (Fla. May 22, 1997)., p. 17

Polozo v. Garlock, 343 So.2d 1000 (La. 1977)., p. 153.

Post Newsweek Stations-Connecticut, Inc. v. Traveler's Insurance Company, 510 F.Supp. 81 (D. Conn, 1981)., p. 519

Promotions Limited v. City of Southeast Charlotte, N.C., 33 F. Supp. 345 (W.D. N.C. 1971)., p. 505

Ptasnik v. Johnston, 234 N.W.2d 548 (Mich. Ct. App. 1975)., p. 281

Rainbow Travel Service, Inc. v. Hilton Hotels Corporation, 896 F.2d 1233 (10th Cir. 1990)., p. 177

Ramirez v. Texas, No. 05-95-00688-CR, 1997 Tex. App. LEXIS 23 (Tex. Ct. App. Jan. 23, 1997)., p. 278

Redgrave v. Boston Symphony Orchestra, 855 F.2d 888 (1st Cir. 1988)., p. 504, 505

Reed v. Cleveland Browns, No. 95-L-194, 1996 Ohio App. LEXIS 5797 (Dec. 20, 1996)., p. 326

R.G. Pope Construction Co. v. Guard Rail of Roanoke, Inc., 241 N.W.2d 371, 383, 72 Wis. 2d 365 (Wis. 1976)., p. 562

Richman et. al. v. The Chicago Bears Football Club, Inc., 468 N.E.2d 487 (Ill. Ct. App. 1984)., p. 328

Rider v. City of San Diego, No. D026652, 1996 Cal. App. LEXIS 1208 (Dec. 27, 1996)., p. 19

Robert E. McKee, Inc. v. City of Atlanta, 414 F. Supp. 959-60 (N.D. Ga. 1976)., p. 578

Romala Corp. v. United States, 20 Cl. Ct. 435 (1990), aff'd 927 F.2d 1219 (Fed. Cir. 1991)., p. 568

Rosenberger v. Central Louisiana District Livestock Show Inc., et. al., 312 So.2d 300 (La. 1975)., p. 261

Rothman v. Emory University, 828 F.Supp. 537 (N.D. Ill. 1993)., p. 101

Roundabout Theatre Co. v. Continental Casualty Co., 751 N.Y.S.2d 4, 5 (App. Div. 2002)., p.229

Rowley v. Mayor and City Council of Baltimore, 484 A.2d 306 (Ct.Spec. App. Md. 1984)., p. 282

Rupp v. Lindsay, 293 N.Y.S.2d 812 (1968)., p. 492, 494

Russo v. the Range, Inc., 395 N.E.2d 10 (Ill. App. 1979)., p. 263

San Jose, City of v. Carlson, No. H014572, 1997 Cal. App. LEXIS 772 (Sept. 25, 1997)., p. 14

Schneckloth v. Bustamonte, 412 U.S .218 (1973)., p. 272

Schonfeld v. City of Carlsbad 978 F. Supp. 1329 (S.D. Cal. 1997)., p. 109, 110

City of Seattle v. Dyad Constr., Inc., 565 P.2d 423 (Wash. Ct. AppCity of Seattle v. Dyad 1977)., p. 565, 570

SEG Sports Corp. v. State Athletic Commission, 952 F. Supp. 202 (S.D. N.Y. 1997)., p. 526

Seko Air Freight Inc. v. Transworld Systems, Inc. 22 F.3d 774 (7th Cir. 1994)., p. 326

Semophore Entertainment Group Sports Corp. v. Gonzalez, 919 F. Supp. 543 (D.C. P.R. 1996)., p. 259

Shapiro, Bernstein & Co. v. H.L. Green, Co 316 F.2b 304 (CA2 1963)., p. 524, 525

Appendices

Voight v. Nanz, 213 N.W.2d 749 (Wis. 1974)., p. 590

Vogel v. Saenger Theatres, Inc. 22 So.2d 189 (La 1945)., p. 45

Vons Companies v. Seabest Foods, Inc. et al 14 Cal 4th 434 (Cal 1996)., p. 257

Wagoner v. Turpin Park Irrigation Co., 489 P.2d 630 (Wyo. 1971)., p. 588

Wagner v. Wagner, 821 S.W.2d 819 (Ky. Ct. App. 1992)., p. 329

Warner Bros. Pictures, Inc. v. James Bumgarner 197 Cal. App. 2d 331 (1961)., p. 150

Washington National Arena Limited Partnership v. Comptroller of Treasury, 519 A.2d 1277 (Md. Ct. App. 1987)., p. 334

White v. Milner Hotels, Inc., 518 P.2d 631 (Ore. 1974)., p. 251

Willard, Inc. v. Powertherm Corp., 444 A.2d 93 (Pa. 1982)., p. 588

Williams v. 312 Walnut Limited Partnership, No. C-960368, 1996 Ohio App. LEXIS 5887 (Ohio Ct. App. Dec. 31, 1996)., p. 237

Williams v. Aer Lingus Irish Airlines, et. al., 655 F. Supp. 425 (S.D. NY 1987)., p. 253

Wilson v. Proctors Theater & Arts Center of Schenectady, Inc., 223 A.D. 2d 826 (N.Y. App. Div. 3rd Dept. 1996)., p. 244

Wolther v. Schaarschmidt, 738 P.2d 25 (Colo. App. 1986)., p. 592

World Championship Wrestling, Inc. v. City of Macon, 493 S.E. 2d 629 (Ga App. 1997)., p. 219

W.R. Winkler v. Appalachian Amusement Company, 79 S.E. 2d 185 (N.C. 1953)., p. 155

Wyatt v. Otis Elevator Company 921 F.2d 1224 (11th Cir 1991)., p. 249

Zinger Construction Co. v. United States, 807 F.2d 979 (Fed. Cir. 1986)., p. 566

Zurich American Insurance Co. v. ABM Industries, Inc. No. 04-0445-cv (Fed. 2nd Cir. Feb. 9, 2005)., p. 227

Table of Facilities

Appendices

Glossary of Terms

ADA: Americans with Disabilities Act. Enacted in 1990, it states that all places of public accommodation must be accessible to those with physical and other disabilities. Provisions in the law also attempt to do away with discrimination in employment for those with physical challenges.

Court of Appeals: In the United States, the court systems in the states and the federal courts parallel each other in structure. There is a trial court level, the local court or federal district court, at which lawsuits are initially filed. If one is unhappy with the results of the trial court's decision, then one can appeal to the regional Court of Appeals, who will reconsider the trial court's decision, looking for errors. In the federal system, this would be the Circuit Court of Appeals, and it would be a similar Court of Appeals at the state level. If a party is still unhappy with the result, they can appeal to the next level of court, the Supreme Court for the state or for the U.S., if it is a federal court decision. State Supreme Court decisions can also be appealed to the Federal Supreme Court. The U.S. Supreme Court has great latitude in deciding which cases it wishes to hear, and grants hearings through a writ of certiorari. In order to access the federal courts, there must be a minimum dollar amount in controversy of at least $50,000 and there must be diversity of citizenship, meaning the parties on each side of the lawsuit must be citizens of different states.

Defendant: The person against whom a lawsuit is filed; the person or people who defend themselves against the accusations made in a lawsuit.

Injunction: a court order prohibiting someone from doing an act, or forcing them to undo a harm. In order for a court to issue an injunction, the prohibition sought must be the only adequate and just compensation or remedy, in other words; money damages would be inappropriate to "fix" the potential or actual harm. Injunctions can be preliminary, temporary, provisional, or even permanent in nature.

Injunctive relief: When a party seeks an injunction to prohibit someone from acting, they are seeking injunctive relief from the harm or potential harm. A good example is that a court might issue an injunction forcing a facility to rent space to a controversial speaker or performer (See Ginsberg v. Miami) despite the facility's reluctance to do so based on their objection to the content of the proposed performance.

License Agreement: Please note that many of the agreements between facilities and their users are referred to as "license" agreements instead of "license" agreements. The reason for this is that under the law of real property in most states, the licensee has more rights to the land or licensed space than a licenser under a license. Under a license, the licensee (the user) does not have any real property rights to the space. For example, under a license agreement, the applicable state law may provide that the licensee has limited holdover rights that would prevent your next user from moving into the facility. Under a license agreement, the real property laws of the jurisdiction would not be applicable to a licensee.

Motions: an application made to a court requesting that the court take action. For example, if a party moves for a new trial, they are in effect asking the court to disregard the first trial and allow them to try the case again, as if for the very first time.

Naming Rights: When a facility is constructed, the name of the facility can be an asset for which companies or individuals may pay large sums of money for the right to have the facility named after them or their product. These agreements may have a limited life, such as 10 to 20 years, after which the facility could be renamed and this asset could be "resold" to another.

Plaintiff: The person who brings or initiates a lawsuit; in other words, the person bringing a complaint about another to a court of law.

Rule under the Administrative Procedure Act: an agency statement of general or particular applicability designed to implement, interpret or prescribe law or policy, or describing the organization, procedure or practice requirements of an agency, such as fixing of rates or prices, valuation of goods, costs, accounting procedures, or the like. This is in effect the making of a regulation under the specific agency's control.

Sovereign Immunity: a legal doctrine which prevents the government from being sued without its consent. Through state and federal laws, usually called Tort Immunity Laws, the government is immune from liability for the wrongs committed by its officers and agents unless that immunity is specifically waived by statute.

Summary Judgment: when a plaintiff or defendant in a law suit says there is no factual dispute between the parties, and based on the facts presented, the only possible result would be to grant a judgment in the moving party's favor, in essence saying they win the lawsuit before going to trial. If a defendant moves for summary judgment, they are in effect asking the Court to dismiss the claims against them, and that given the facts as presented by the Plaintiff, the Plaintiff cannot show an injury for which the Defendant is responsible.

Tax Exempt Organization: Corporations, any community chest, fund or foundation organized exclusively for religious, charitable, scientific, literary or educational purposes. No part of the net earnings of the corporation can go to benefit a private shareholder or individual and the group or corporation cannot attempt to influence legislation or support a candidate for political office. Under the Internal Revenue Code, charitable organizations are exempt from having to pay federal income tax if it meets the requirements above. In most states, hospitals, churches, religious organizations, volunteer groups and the like can qualify to be tax exempt organizations.

LaVergne, TN USA
21 January 2011

213338LV00003B/1/P